MAY IT PLEASE THE COURT

MAY IT PLEASE THE COURT

THE MOST SIGNIFICANT ORAL
ARGUMENTS MADE BEFORE THE
SUPREME COURT SINCE 1955

*Edited by Peter Irons and
Stephanie Guitton*

THE NEW PRESS

NEW YORK
LONDON

Requests for permission to reproduce selections from this book
should be mailed to: Permissions Department, The New Press,
38 Greene Street, New York, NY 10013.

Published in the United States by The New Press, New York, 2007
Distributed by W. W. Norton & Company, Inc., New York

Published in conjunction with the Earl Warren Bill of Rights Project
and the Northwest Public Affairs Network

ISBN 978-1-59558-090-0 (pbk)
CIP data available

The New Press was established in 1990 as a not-for-profit alternative to the large, commercial publishing houses currently dominating the book publishing industry. The New Press operates in the public interest rather than for private gain, and is committed to publishing, in innovative ways, works of educational, cultural, and community value that are often deemed insufficiently profitable.

www.thenewpress.com

Printed in the United States of America

2 4 6 8 10 9 7 5 3 1

THIS BOOK IS DEDICATED TO

JUSTICE WILLIAM J. BRENNAN, JR.,
AND
JUSTICE THURGOOD MARSHALL

WITH GRATITUDE AND

ADMIRATION FOR HELPING TO PRESERVE

OUR CONSTITUTION

AS A LIVING DOCUMENT THAT PROTECTS

THE RIGHTS AND DIGNITY

OF EVERY AMERICAN

PREFACE

"MAY IT PLEASE THE COURT." This short phrase has long served as the opening of oral arguments before the United States Supreme Court. When a lawyer stands at the Court's podium and begins an argument with these traditional words, every person in the chamber shares a feeling of excitement. The Supreme Court hears arguments in just a tiny fraction of the cases submitted to the justices each year for review. Each raises important and unresolved questions of law, issues that affect not only the parties but the entire nation. Many of these cases involve provisions of the Bill of Rights, the basic charter of liberties for all Americans. Lawyers on both sides know that oral argument in the Supreme Court offers the final chance to speak for their client and respond to questions from the justices.

Several million people each year visit Washington, D.C., and many thousands tour the White House and the Capitol. But few have the chance to sit in the Supreme Court chamber and witness an entire oral argument. Most tourists are given just three minutes before they are shuttled out and a new group shuttled in. In cases that attract headlines, seats for the public are scarce and waiting lines are long. And the Court sits in open session less than two hundred hours each year. Television cameras and radio microphones are still banned from the chamber, and only a few hundred people—at most—can actually witness oral arguments. Protected by a marble wall from public access, the Supreme Court has long been the least understood of the three branches of our federal government.

This book and set of audio cassettes, *May It Please the Court*, move inside the marble wall and offer every American a front-row seat for the arguments in historic Bill of Rights cases. We can thank Chief Justice Earl Warren for this opportunity. Beginning in 1955, Warren approved the tape recording of all arguments through microphones on the lawyers' podium and the justices' bench. Since that time, arguments in more than five thousand cases have been recorded, and the tapes deposited in the National Archives. Outside of law professors, who may purchase copies of tapes for classroom use, few people even know of this unique educational resource. The tapes are not advertised, and obtaining copies is costly and time-consuming.

The background of this project is instructive. It stems from a book, *The Courage of Their Convictions*, written in 1988 by Peter Irons, professor of political science at the University of California, San Diego (UCSD). This book is based on interviews with sixteen ordinary Americans who initiated Bill of Rights cases that reached the Supreme Court between 1940 and 1986. The cases begin with Lillian Gobitis, who was expelled from junior high school for refusing as a Jehovah's Witness to salute the American flag; they end with Michael Hardwick, a gay man who challenged a Georgia law that punished acts of sodomy with twenty years in prison. The cases in between deal with such issues as racial covenants in housing, loyalty oaths for teachers, and prayers in public schools.

Professor Irons was surprised and delighted by the positive response to his book. Students and teachers wrote letters and called from high schools and colleges across the country. Students said they enjoyed the first-person stories and asked for information to follow up the cases for papers and presentations. Teachers said their textbooks were boring and bland and asked for additional materials that could bring the Bill of Rights to life. Irons was the founding director in 1983 of the UCSD Law and Society Program, sponsored by Earl Warren College, which was named to honor this great Californian. He proposed the Earl Warren Bill of Rights Project in 1990 as a means to produce innovative curricular materials in this field, and was appointed director by the Law and Society faculty.

Professor Irons selected twenty-three Bill of Rights cases and copied the tapes at the National Archives. He picked cases in five important fields: governmental powers, the First Amendment, criminal law, equal protection, and privacy rights. Some are famous cases that most Americans recognize: the *Watergate Tapes* case, the *Pentagon Papers* case, *Miranda v. Arizona*, *Regents v. Bakke*, *Roe v. Wade*. Others are less known but still important: the "black armband" case, the "stop and frisk" case, and the "swimming pool" case. Regardless of fame, each case raises an important Bill of Rights issue, and each features an exciting oral argument on both sides. He also produced an introductory tape that shows how cases reach the Supreme Court and how lawyers prepare for oral argument.

Professor Irons was fortunate in recruiting Stephanie Guitton as associate director of this project. She holds a law degree from the University of Poitiers in France and is currently a Ph.D. candidate in the Boalt Hall School of Law at the University of California, Berkeley. They worked closely in editing the original tapes from the National Archives; Professor Irons wrote the narration for the *May It Please the Court* series, and Ms. Guitton edited the Supreme Court opinions for this book and compiled the case bibliographies.

The authors consider it essential to place these oral arguments in the context of American history. More than 150 years ago, a young French aristocrat, Alexis de Tocqueville, visited a young nation and wrote a perceptive book about his travels, *Democracy in America*. "Scarcely any political question arises in the United States," he noted in 1835, "that is not resolved, sooner or later, into a judicial question." Robert H. Jackson, who served as Attorney General and who joined the Supreme Court in 1941, wrote that "constitutional lawsuits are the stuff of power politics in America." These observations, made a hundred years apart, remain true as the Court enters its third century.

This country has changed dramatically since the Constitution was ratified in 1789, but many of the issues that divided Americans of that time still come before the Supreme Court in different form. The United States has grown from thirteen to fifty states, which now reach beyond our continent, and our population has increased fortyfold in two centuries. But the justices still face disputes over the balance of federal power and states' rights. The institution of slavery, accepted by the Constitution's framers, led to a fratricidal Civil War that claimed more than 600,000 lives on both sides. Arguments over the legal status of African-Americans have shifted from citizenship to civil rights, but every Supreme Court term brings new questions of race and ethnicity. As the nation moved from an agrarian to industrial economy, disputes between farmers and railroads were replaced with strikes by air traffic controllers. But the Court still hears arguments about business regulation and labor disputes. Each of these issues, whether social or economic in origin, becomes a "political question" by the time it reaches the Court for decision.

Americans no longer argue about ferry monopolies on the Hudson River or the rates of grain elevators in Chicago. The Supreme Court decided these issues in the nineteenth century. Early in the twentieth century, the Court settled disputes over maximum hours for bakers in New York and minimum wages for women in Oregon. Within the decades after World War II, the justices have spoken clearly against school segregation and for the principle of "one person, one vote" in state and federal elections. They have given criminal defendants the right to remain silent and allowed states to carry out sentences of death. They have granted women a privacy right to abortion and denied a similar right to homosexuals. Each of these issues—historical and contemporary—has divided Americans, and each has divided the Supreme Court.

The Court has already begun its third century of deciding hard cases. Americans live in an increasingly fractured society, and the justices face issues that divide us along the "fault lines" of race, class, gender, religion, and culture. These questions have no easy answers, and lawyers can make compelling arguments on both sides. But if we listen closely to the arguments in the *May It Please the Court* series, we may find a guide to future decisions. And we should remember that, however the Court decides, we are the ultimate judges. We make the laws with our votes, and we can even amend the Constitution, a process that is difficult and lengthy by design. During the next century, Americans will continue to argue over controversial issues. And lawyers will continue to stand at the Supreme Court podium and begin with these words: "May it please the Court."

ACKNOWLEDGMENTS

"MAY IT PLEASE THE COURT" is a project that could not have been completed without the support of many groups and individuals. The greatest incentive, and the most important help, came from the Deer Creek Foundation of St. Louis, Missouri. Mary Stake Hawker, who administers the fund, solicited the original proposal for this project and responded with enthusiasm to our initial outline. She also helped to secure additional funding to complete the project and deserves great credit from every person who hears the tape series.

At an early stage, the project received a seed-money grant from the American Civil Liberties Union Foundation. Colleen O'Connor, Loren Siegel, Ira Glasser, and Nadine Strossen of the ACLU have all been supportive and deserve thanks.

"May It Please the Court" is a joint production of the Earl Warren Bill of Rights Project of the University of California, San Diego, and the Northwest Public Affairs Network of Seattle, Washington. Professor Peter Irons served as executive director and Stephanie Guitton as associate director of the "May It Please the Court" project. Nell Lake and Monica Spain produced the tape series, and David Messerschmidt was the executive producer. Jim Bachman was the chief engineer. Additional production support was provided by the Jack Straw Foundation in Seattle.

Hamilton Loeb of La Jolla, California, deserves special thanks for raising funds to complete this project. He devoted many hours to "selling" the Bill of Rights to friends and business associates. His generosity and commitment have been essential and are greatly appreciated. Ham Loeb's sister, Alice Bendheim, who served with Peter Irons on the ACLU national board, deserves a hug for suggesting her brother as a supporter.

Loren Siegel, who directs the ACLU's Public Education department, suggested to Peter Irons that he broach this project to André Schiffrin, director of the New Press. André responded with great enthusiasm, and Diane Wachtell, the associate director, has guided this unique project to completion.

The authors would like to acknowledge the support of several other people along the way, before and during their work on this project. Peter Irons wants to thank Priscilla Long and Harry Hirsch, and Stephanie Guitton is thankful to her parents, Marcel and Michel Guitton. The authors also thank Donald Sullivan, Annmarie Levins, and Sarah Weddington, who contributed interviews for the introductory cassette. Our final thanks go to Justices William Brennan and Thurgood Marshall, to whom this book is dedicated. Their devotion to the Bill of Rights has inspired many Americans—lawyers and ordinary citizens—to work in many ways to ensure that our Constitution remains a living, breathing document.

CONTENTS

"The Supreme Court: A Thrilling Place to Be"

Chief Justice Earl Warren: Number 155, Clarence Earl Gideon, petitioner, versus H. G. Cochran, director, Division of Corrections.

Narrator: You just heard Chief Justice Warren, calling for oral argument in the case of Clarence Gideon. In this landmark case, the Court granted all criminal defendants the right to a lawyer at their trials. The justices decided many important cases during Warren's years as Chief Justice, from 1954 to 1969. They outlawed racial segregation in public schools. Their "one person, one vote" ruling ended rural domination of state and federal elections. They ruled against prayer in the public schools and for the right of privacy in access to birth control.

These were controversial decisions, and the Warren Court had both critics and defenders. Controversy continued under Chief Justices Warren Burger and William Rehnquist. Decisions on affirmative action, school busing, and abortion provoked not only debate but demonstrations, even violence. Americans have strong feelings about these issues and many others. We argue in classrooms, living rooms, and street corners. These arguments often turn into lawsuits, and some wind up in the Supreme Court in Washington, D.C.

Chief Justice Warren made it possible for us to sit in the Court's chamber and listen to debates about the Constitution. All Supreme Court arguments have been tape recorded since 1955. The Warren Project staff selected twenty-three important cases under the Bill of Rights. We pared these tapes down to the basics, with arguments by lawyers on both sides and probing questions from the justices. We call this series *May It Please the Court*, the traditional opening of oral arguments.

Three lawyers will introduce us to these arguments. They will explain how lawsuits begin, how they reach the Supreme Court, how the arguments proceed, and how the justices decide cases. Donald Sullivan will begin. He's a lawyer in Cheyenne, Wyoming. In 1985, he filed suit for Joshua DeShaney and his mother, Melody. Their suit claimed that officials in Winnebago County, Wisconsin, failed to protect Joshua against beatings by his father. Joshua was four years old when he suffered permanent brain damage; he's now confined to an institution for the "profoundly retarded." Sullivan describes his first meeting with Melody DeShaney.

Sullivan: When she came to me, she knew that Joshua had been profoundly abused; she knew that he had suffered massive and permanent brain damage, and by that time she had learned that the people who were supposed to be child protection workers in Winnebago County had done a very, very poor job. She did not know at that point what we eventually found out in terms of how really, really awful it was. But she knew there had been some major failures on their part and she wanted to know what we could do legally to get the funds to help Joshua.

Narrator: Sarah Weddington talks about a case that became famous: *Roe versus Wade*. But she was just out of law school in Texas when the case began in 1970. Weddington helped pregnant women find doctors who would perform abortions, which were illegal in Texas. Her first client was "Jane Roe," who agreed to challenge the state law. She and another young lawyer, Linda Coffee, filed a class action lawsuit on behalf of all pregnant women who desired abortions in Texas.

Weddington: We never saw this suit as being about Jane Roe. We saw it as being about the issue, we saw it as being for all women, those who were or might become pregnant in the future. "Jane Roe" was important and symbolic, because she was the one real person who was in fact pregnant at that time.

Narrator: The first step in a civil lawsuit is drafting a complaint, which the plaintiffs file against the defendants. Don Sullivan tells us what this means.

Sullivan: When you're writing the complaint, your job is, first of all, to make sure that you include all the necessary elements, basic things such as, who's bringing this case, who's the case being brought against, if there's a statute involved, as there was in this case, what the identification of that statute is, what the location and what the date of the circumstances were, what the basic actions of the defendant were that you feel entitle you to sue that person or that group of persons and bring them to court and ask for money.

Narrator: Sarah Weddington and Linda Coffee filed a complaint for "Jane Roe" in federal court.

Weddington: We went through and drafted a complaint that included some facts about her, that she was an unmarried pregnant woman, she did not want to go through the pregnancy, a variety of other things. We included the grounds that we were alleging, as part of the Constitution, and we included the relief that we were seeking.

Narrator: Defendants are entitled to answer the legal complaints of plaintiffs.

Sullivan: Typically they will come in and assert a variety of different and often contradictory things. And under our law it's permissible to do that. They will come in and file an answer that says, it didn't happen, we didn't do it, somebody else did it, you weren't hurt, you're not hurt as bad as you say you were, and besides, we weren't there. It's kind of like the situation where somebody says, I'm suing you because your dog bit me, and the guy will come in and defend and say, my dog didn't bite you, besides, my dog is real friendly and never bites anybody, and defense number three, I don't have a dog.

Narrator: Sullivan describes the answer to his complaint.

Sullivan: The state's position came down simply to this: Look, maybe we stood by and watched, maybe we knew that this was going on, but we didn't actually physically hit him, so you can't sue us.

Narrator: In Jane Roe's case, federal judges ruled that the Texas anti-abortion law violated the constitution. But they refused to block its enforcement. Both sides appealed from this split decision. Sarah Weddington knew the Supreme Court had several abortion cases on its docket.

Weddington: We appealed it to the U.S. Supreme Court, really not knowing if they would take it or not, or whether they would take some other case and then just hold ours and wait to see what happened. They did in fact take two cases. One was ours, the Texas case, and the second was a Georgia case, called *Doe versus Bolton*.

Narrator: In Don Sullivan's case, federal judges ruled that Joshua DeShaney had no legal grounds to recover damages for his injuries. Sullivan was confident of Supreme Court review.

Sullivan: We knew right from the outset that ultimately this call was likely to end up in the Supreme Court and, if we were going to protect not only Joshua but other kids in the same kind of situation, it would require a Supreme Court decision.

Narrator: Professor Annmarie Levins teaches at the University of Washington law school. She served as a Supreme Court law clerk to Justice Lewis Powell. She explains how cases reach the Supreme Court.

Levins: Most cases come in on what is known as a petition for certiorari. Those are cases where there's been a decision by a court of appeals—either a federal court of appeals or a highest state court. And in those cases the petitioner is trying to get Supreme Court review, trying to get the Supreme Court to overrule a decision below. Those are discretionary cases, and that is by far the bulk of the cases that come to the Supreme Court. There's another category of cases where there is jurisdiction in the Supreme Court automatically, because a state law, for example, has been held unconstitutional. That's probably the second most important category of cases.

Narrator: Sarah Weddington explains how lawyers draft a petition for certiorari.

Weddington: You have to tell the Court about the history of the case, how it was filed, where it was heard, what the lower courts did. You have to explain the constitutional basis on which you are saying this law is unconstitutional. You have to describe the plaintiffs. You have to then make an argument about why this law is unconstitutional.

Narrator: The Supreme Court receives almost five thousand petitions for certiorari every year. The justices grant full review and argument in about 150 cases, only three percent of the total. Professor Levins explains the criteria.

Levins: With cert petitions, the most important thing is whether there is some big principle involved, something that's going to be of lasting significance. The vast majority of the cases that come to the Supreme Court are extremely important to the litigants, but beyond that particular case they probably don't have a lot of significance. So they can't right every wrong, they can't correct every legal error that they see in the lower courts. But they can pick the ones where there's something that just can't stay that way without having implications beyond the particular case. So what the Court tries to do is find those cases where they can make a principled decision that will have broad impact.

Narrator: When the Court accepts a case for review, the lawyers on both sides submit written briefs on the legal issues. Sarah Weddington remembers the form she received from the Supreme Court clerk.

Weddington: They tell you exactly how big the page can be, how many words can be on it, whether it has to be space-and-a-half in terms of how it's typeset, where to put the footnotes. There are very stringent requirements for how they want it printed.

Narrator: Don Sullivan explains how he writes a brief.

Sullivan: What you do is you narrow, and you refine, and you buff, and you hone, and you sharpen, and you focus, and you go back and you re-research, then you step back and you critique all of what you've worked on, and just continue to make it as narrowly focused and as sharp and as cogent as you possibly can.

Narrator: The Supreme Court allows groups that are not parties to a case to file *amicus curiae* briefs. The Latin words mean "friend of the court." Sarah Weddington explains.

Weddington: It goes back to a tradition that parties that are not officially part of a lawsuit but that have something they want to say about the issue or feel they would also be affected by what the Supreme Court decides, they can also file *amicus curiae* briefs with the Supreme Court. For example, our brief would mention the medical aspects of illegal and legal abortion. And then other groups, that were in fact medical groups, filed a brief that was nothing but about the medical aspects.

The attorney general of Texas filed a brief in opposition, and a number of groups also filed briefs supporting his brief and as *amicus curiae* there. So there was a stack of briefs sitting on the Supreme Court justices' desk on that bench when they got ready to hear this case.

Narrator: Once the briefs are filed, lawyers prepare for oral argument.

Sullivan: Basically you sit down and reread everything you've ever written in your life that has anything to do with the case, and then you start practicing and trying to hone your arguments, and find just the right expression to hopefully make your point as clearly as you humanly can manage to do that. You have some practice sessions with—you get a bunch of other lawyers and have them ask you tough questions; sort of trying to get you ready for whatever questions may come along from the Court.

Narrator: Sarah Weddington spent months preparing for her argument.

Weddington: The more important part of getting ready were doing what I call moot courts, and those are where other people—lawyers, law professors, law students, people just interested in the issue—go through a series of occasions where they play like they are the Supreme Court. They ask you questions; you answer them as best you can, and then those people help perfect your answers. They might say, "Well, your answer was okay, but we think it would be better or stronger if you did it a little bit differently"; or they might say, "That answer's good, but you want to be sure that you get in a certain angle for the Supreme Court, and if they don't give you a question that raises that, be sure you get that in, and here's a way you might do it."

Narrator: On the day set for argument, lawyers walk up the steps of the Supreme Court. This impressive building stands across from the nation's capitol.

Weddington: When you approach the Supreme Court, of course you see those levels of marble steps, reaching up to the entrance. And when you go up them and stand at the entrance to the Supreme Court building, there are a number of columns that seem to just reach into the sky.

Narrator: Sarah Weddington is a minister's daughter. The Court's chamber re-minded her of church.

Weddington: The chamber holds about 350 people, so it is not a really large room, and in fact the way it's done, it has a very intimate feeling. When you come in at the back, there are very heavy red velvet curtains. And just as you go through those curtains, there are three sections of what look like church pews.

Narrator: The chamber has a "three-minute" section for tourists who shuffle in and out during the arguments. Another section is reserved for people who wait in line to sit through an entire session. And lawyers who belong to the Supreme Court bar sit before a gold railing, the "bar" that separates them from the laymen. Professor Levins describes the scene.

Levins: Usually the Court is very full of spectators. Oftentimes they are people who are very interested in a particular case, making up probably half of the audience; the other half are tourists, just there to see the Supreme Court in action.

The Supreme Court courtroom is really a thrilling place to be. If you're there when the Marshal comes and hammers down the gavel and calls the Court to order, it's really very exciting. The justices come out, behind this big curtain and take their seat in a very orderly and formal fashion. The Chief Justice will call the calendar and then call the first case.

Narrator: The Marshal of the United States Supreme Court.

Marshal: The Honorable, the Chief Justice and the Associate Justices of the Supreme Court of the United States. Oyez, oyez, oyez. All persons having business before the Honorable, the Supreme Court of the United States, are admonished to draw near and give their attention, for the Court is now sitting. God save the United States and this Honorable Court.

Narrator: Lawyers sit at large tables, below the justices' raised bench. Between the tables is the lawyers' podium. The Court normally gives each side thirty minutes for argument. We'll listen to Sarah Weddington's opening argument for "Jane Roe." Chief Justice Burger called the case.

Burger: We'll hear arguments in Number 18, *Roe* against *Wade*. Mrs. Weddington, you may proceed whenever you're ready.

Weddington: Mr. Chief Justice, and may it please the court.

I think it's without question that pregnancy to a woman can completely disrupt her life. It disrupts her body, it disrupts her education, it disrupts her employment, and it often disrupts her entire family life. And we feel that, because of the impact on the woman, this certainly, inasfar as there are any rights which are fundamental, is a matter which is of such fundamental and basic concern to the woman involved that she should be allowed to make the choice as to whether to continue or to terminate her pregnancy.

Narrator: Sarah Weddington recalls her feelings when she left the podium.

Weddington: It was a variety of feelings. It was part that great anxiety. It was partly a feeling of real responsibility, a burden of responsibility, because I knew for years and years I would be the only person who would ever be able to present that issue to the Supreme Court and argue on behalf of all women.

Narrator: Don Sullivan was prepared for questions.

Sullivan: You already know going in that the Court normally will give you maybe thirty seconds or something like that to kind of start out with the general introduction to your argument. But that's all they're going to give you. From that point on, it's all question and answer. It's all give and take on a very intense, intellectual-legal basis.

Narrator: Sullivan had this exchange with Chief Justice Rehnquist.

Sullivan: The Court additionally has recognized, I believe, that a child—indeed, any of us—has a constitutionally protected right to physical integrity, to bodily protection. What I'm suggesting . . .

Rehnquist: A right against the state.

Sullivan: And a right that arises out of the Constitution to remain alive, yes, sir.

Rehnquist: Well, but it's protected only against the state. It's not protected against private individuals.

Sullivan: Well, I think that's part of what the Court's going to have to address in this case.

Narrator: Sullivan recalls his feelings.

Sullivan: I can tell you honestly that I was probably as intellectually stimulated as I can remember ever being in my life. Both the—I'll call them "friendly" questions and the "less friendly" questions from the whole range of justices were very fine questions. It was very clear that the entire Court was well prepared; they knew the facts of the case, they knew the legal arguments on both sides, they knew the strengths and weaknesses of the competing legal arguments, and it's a real joy to fight in that kind of a finely prepared arena.

Narrator: After each week's arguments, the justices meet in the court's conference room. Professor Levins.

Levins: The conferences are held on the Fridays after argument, and the justices will go to those conferences with memos that their clerks have prepared, their own notes on what they thought of the argument or the briefs, and they'll go prepared to discuss and debate and ultimately take a position.

At the end, when all the votes have been cast, at least tentatively, the Chief Justice, if he is in the majority, will assign someone to write the opinion. If he's not in the majority, the seniormost justice who is, assigns the opinion. And that's really a critical part of the process, because obviously whoever gets to write the opinion gets to put his or her stamp on the case.

Narrator: Every justice has a different practice in writing opinions. Some rely heavily on the drafts of their law clerks; others write virtually every word themselves.

Levins: In Justice Powell's chambers, he would have dictated a very long memo with his own thoughts on the case, prior to the oral argument. He would first get a bench memo from a clerk, read that, and dictate his own thoughts, based on having read all the briefs too. So when you were assigned an opinion to sit down and write, you had a very good idea of what he thought, as well as what you thought, and would draft the opinion accordingly.

Narrator: Sarah Weddington won her case in 1973. The Court struck down the Texas abortion law and gave women the right of reproductive choice. Twenty years later, she looks back at her oral argument.

Weddington: It was a fantastic experience, one that I can just sit and think about, and it all floods back: the emotions, the scene, the questions, all of the accompanying emotions. It is also something that, if anybody had said to me then, you will still be talking about this in twenty years, I would never have believed it. Because I thought, once the Supreme Court ruled, it was seven to two, it was a clear, short, easy-to-ready opinion. I thought, that's done, now we can move on to other issues. And the current-day situation certainly just says how wrong I was about that.

Narrator: Don Sullivan lost his case in 1989. Chief Justice Rehnquist wrote the ruling that states have no obligation to protect abused children like Joshua DeShaney. Sullivan still has strong feelings.

Sullivan: One of the purposes of bringing this case for Joshua in the first place was to get him enough money so that he could get the kind of very elaborate rehabilitation therapy that would at least give him a little bit of a more enhanced kind of life. And he's deprived now even of that.

I feel kind of like the lawyer who lost the case of *Plessy versus Ferguson*, way back in the 1890s, where the Supreme Court said "separate but equal" is okay. The lawyer that handled that case, I'm sure, was disappointed, as am I, but that lawyer was right, and either he or somebody else kept fighting until the war was won. And I think, when you talk about abused children in our country, I think it's so important that we have to go on fighting until we do win that war.

Narrator: Whether the issue is abortion or abused children, or other questions under the Bill of Rights, the Supreme Court will continue to hear arguments in controversial cases. Even if we can't visit the Court to sit and listen, we can all make our voices heard, and speak up as citizens who treasure our Constitution.

MAY IT PLEASE THE COURT

PART ONE:

"Secure the Blessings of Liberty"

AMERICANS TAKE PRIDE in their system of government. We still turn out for parades on the Fourth of July, place flags on soldiers' graves on Veterans Day, and sing the National Anthem at ball games. Millions of visitors come to the nation's capital every year and tour the White House, the Capitol building, and the Supreme Court chamber. Many foreign visitors to the United States remark about the visible and vocal patriotism that Americans display. This sense of national pride is a source of strength in a vast and diverse country.

But there is another side to outward displays of patriotism. More and more people have become disillusioned with government, with politics and politicians. Barely half of the eligible voters cast ballots for president and Congress. Within the past generation, one president has been assassinated and another has resigned in disgrace. Members of Congress have been sent to prison for taking bribes, and even federal judges have been impeached and convicted for selling their judicial integrity. Episodes like Watergate, Abscam, and the Iran-contra scandal have convinced many people that the abuse of power is widespread in American government.

The Constitution reflects our ambivalent feelings about strong government and weak officials. More than two centuries ago, the framers set forth lofty goals in the preamble: they established a charter of government to "establish justice, insure domestic tranquility, provide for the common defence, promote the general welfare, and secure the blessings of liberty" for future generations of Americans. To achieve these goals, the framers invested great powers in government ·

3

officials. Members of Congress have many powers, including the authority to impose taxes, borrow money, regulate commerce, and declare war. They have an additional power "to make all laws which shall be necessary and proper" to execute their enumerated powers. The Constitution also provides that "the executive power shall be vested in a President," who has a separate power as commander-in-chief of the armed forces. The Constitution requires the president to "take care that the laws be faithfully executed." And the Constitution provides that "the judicial power of the United States shall be vested in one Supreme Court," with power to decide all cases "arising under this Constitution." State and local officials are equally subject to the Constitution as "the supreme law of the land."

These awesome grants of power to officials in all branches and levels of government are checked only by the limitations of the Bill of Rights. Officials are required to obey the Constitution's commands to treat every person with fairness and equality. These commands are stated in the Fifth and Fourteenth amendments, which guarantee "due process of law" and "the equal protection of the laws." But these are merely words on a piece of paper. They are not self-enforcing provisions. A powerful federal official, Assistant Secretary of War John J. McCloy, once dismissed the Constitution as "just a scrap of paper." His attitude was shocking, but his statement was actually true. The Constitution only has meaning and strength if officials can be forced to obey its commands. And only the courts have the ultimate power of enforcement.

The Supreme Court has two major duties under the Constitution: deciding conflicts between officials in different branches of government and deciding cases in which individuals challenge the powers of officials. The Court has faced thousands of difficult cases in the past two centuries. One of the hardest cases came early in the Court's history, in the aftermath of a bitter presidential election in 1800. This case, *Marbury v. Madison*, involved challenges to the powers of all three branches of the federal government. The facts are confusing, but the basic question was political. Did Congress have the power to tell the Court how to decide cases that involved the executive branch? Chief Justice John Marshall answered with strong words: "It is emphatically the province and duty of the judicial department to say what the law is." Marshall reminded Congress that "the Constitution is superior to any ordinary act of the legislature."

The Court has also used the supremacy clause to strike down presidential acts that stretched the Constitution. During the Civil War, Abraham Lincoln suspended the right of habeas corpus and imposed martial law in areas where federal courts were open and operating. A military tribunal in Indiana sentenced Lambdin Milligan to death for allegedly plotting a prison break of Confederate soldiers. The Supreme Court ruled (after President Lincoln's assassination) that Lincoln had no power to impose military law when federal courts were open. The Court's opinion was prophetic: "Wicked men, ambitious of power, with hatred of liberty and contempt of law, may fill the place once occupied by Washington and Lincoln." The nation might not always have "wise and humane rulers, sincerely attached to the principles of the Constitution."

The Court has made it clear over the past two centuries that *every* government official, from president down to police officer, must obey the Constitution. But many of the cases that have challenged official power have raised hard questions. Lawyers on both sides in these cases have argued over issues of authority and accountability. Can the courts order members of state legislatures to redraw district boundaries and possibly end their political careers? Do the rules of criminal evidence apply to the president of the United States? And do county social workers have a legal duty to protect children against violent parents?

Each of these questions, and the arguments before the Supreme Court in these cases, puts the Constitution to its hardest test. How can we balance the legitimate powers of government officials and the rights of the people to "due process" and "equal protection of the laws"? The answer lies in a "scrap of paper" that is interpreted and enforced by a small group of judges. We should remember the words of Justice Oliver Wendell Holmes, who noted a century ago that "the life of the law has not been logic; it has been experience." Holmes also reminded us that "the prejudices which judges share with their fellow-men" have had a great influence "in determining the rules by which men should be governed." The Constitution remains supreme, but the law changes as judges and their prejudices change.

Baker v. Carr

369 U.S. 186 (1962)

The citizen's most prized possession in a representative democracy is the right to vote. But that right is devalued if some voters cast more ballots than others. Population disparities between rural and urban legislative districts often gave cows more votes than people. However, the Supreme Court ruled in 1946 that legislative apportionment was a "political question" and thus beyond the Court's jurisdiction. As millions of Americans moved from farms to cities in postwar years, debate over this issue grew more heated. The Tennessee legislature's refusal to reapportion districts since 1901—in violation of the state constitution —prompted Charles Baker and other urban voters to sue Tennessee's Secretary of State, Joe Carr, in 1959. Reversing its earlier ruling, the Court held in 1962 that lower courts could decide apportionment cases, opening the door for the "one person–one vote" standard the Court soon adopted.

TRANSCRIPT OF EDITED AND NARRATED ARGUMENTS IN
Baker v. *Carr*, 369 U.S. 186 (1962)

Counsel for petitioner: Charles Rhyne, Washington, D.C.
Counsel for respondent: Jack Wilson, Knoxville, Tennessee
Counsel for the United States as amicus curiae: Solicitor General Archibald
Cox; Washington, D.C.

Chief Justice Earl Warren: Number 6, Charles W. Baker et al., appellants,
versus Joe C. Carr et al.

Narrator: We're in the chamber of the United States Supreme Court in Washington, D.C. It's October 9th, 1961. Chief Justice Earl Warren has called a case that could redraw the American political map. The issue is state legislative reapportionment. The legal question is whether federal courts can force states to give urban and rural voters equal strength at the ballot box. The stakes are high: who will control fifty state governments?

Today's case comes from Tennessee. Charles Baker and ten other voters in the state's largest cities sued Secretary of State Joe Carr and other officials. The urban voters claim the state legislature is stacked in favor of rural voters. Tennessee's constitution requires a reapportionment every ten years, on the basis of equal population. The last time the lines were redrawn was 1901. Since then, lawmakers have refused to make any changes. The mayor of Nashville explained the result: "The state is being ruled," he said, "by the hog lot and the cow pasture."

Complaints of rural domination are not limited to Tennessee. Other states have even worse problems. Vermont has a voting disparity of six hundred-to-one between its smallest and largest districts. In California, four million Los Angeles County residents have the same voting strength as fourteen thousand in the Sierra Nevada mountains. The political problem is obvious: rural lawmakers refuse to vote themselves out of office. So they simply ignore reapportionment laws.

But taking the issue to court raises legal problems. Back in 1946, in a case called *Colegrove versus Green,* Illinois voters challenged a population disparity of eight-to-one in congressional districts. The Supreme Court dismissed the case. Justice Felix Frankfurter cited principles of federalism and separation of powers. The federal government should not tell states how to draw legislative boundaries. And courts, Frankfurter wrote, cannot tell lawmakers how to answer "political questions."

Fifteen years later, Tennessee voters are asking the Supreme Court to change its mind. They rely on the Constitution's Fourteenth Amendment, which says states must give every person the "equal protection of the laws." They also use the Civil Rights Act passed by Congress in 1957. This law protects voters against discrimination. A lower federal court found a "clear violation" of Tennessee law but dismissed the case because of the *Colegrove* decision. Charles Rhyne, a former president of the American Bar Association, argues for the Tennessee voters. Chief Justice Warren welcomes him.

Warren: Mr. Rhyne?

Rhyne: Mr. Chief Justice, and may it please the Court.

This is a voting rights case. It's brought here on appeal by eleven Tennessee voters who seek federal court protection to end flagrant discrimination against their right to vote. These eleven Tennessee voters live in five of the largest cities of Tennessee. They are the intended and actual victims of a statutory scheme which devalues, reduces, their right to vote to about one-twentieth of the value of the vote given to certain rural residents. Since the right to vote is the greatest civil right, the most fundamental civil right under our system of government, this system under this statute of Tennessee is as shocking as it is purposeful and successful.

These appellants bring their case here under the Fourteenth Amendment and the Civil Rights Act. Now, the district court, in passing on their complaint, said that it entirely agreed that their rights were violated and that the evil was a serious one which should be corrected without delay. But the court found that it either did not have the power or should not exercise it under the precedents to which it referred.

Narrator: Rhyne attacked the Tennessee law that blocked any further change in legislative districts.

Rhyne: The way in which these voting rights of the plaintiffs have been effectively denied—so effectively, we say, as to be effectively destroyed—is by a so-called reapportionment statute adopted in 1901. Now, the ultimate thrust of that statute today is that one-third of the qualified voters living in the rural areas of the state of Tennessee elect two-thirds of the state legislature. Now, that 1901 statute not only violates this requirement of equality in voting which I have just referred to in the Tennessee constitution, not only violates the requirement of equality in the Fourteenth Amendment of the Constitution of the United States of America, but it flies directly in the teeth of and openly and flagrantly violates another provision of the Tennessee constitution which is designed to, by periodic ten-year reapportionment of the state legislature, to guarantee this equality of which the Tennessee constitution speaks.

The Fourteenth Amendment strikes down discriminations whether they are sophisticated or simple-minded; and we think that, whether you cloak it under the terms of reapportionment or any other cloak, no matter how ingeniously or geniously contrived, that this is a discrimination which is clear from the facts in the complaint, and under those facts these voters have a constitutional right that is invaded and have standing to maintain this suit. Because a man's right to vote is personal to him. It's not shared with anyone. And when these people have their right to vote invaded, diluted, rendered worthless or practically so by this 1901 act, it's a personal wrong to them to have their vote so affected.

Narrator: A justice pressed the issue.

Court: Do you claim that the Fourteenth Amendment requires that each person's vote in the state be given equal weight?

Rhyne: Reasonable equality, reasonable equality.

Court: As a matter of . . .

Rhyne: Not mathematical equality.

Court: Not mathematical equality?

Rhyne: But reasonable equality. I think that that is the thrust of the equal protection of the laws requirement of the Fourteenth Amendment.

Narrator: Justice Frankfurter argued in the *Colegrove* decision that apportionment was a political issue. He and Rhyne debated the question.

Rhyne: To refer these people to a political process which is no remedy at all—if you're going to refer them to any remedy, it must have a reasonable chance of being effective. But to refer these people back to the political process really is a mockery of justice, because until voting rights are enforceable in the federal courts and you have equal—or reasonable—equality, the ballot box is no remedy for the kind of situation that exists here.

Frankfurter: Will you or the Solicitor General tell us what the remedy is to be here, other than to declare this unconstitutional?

Rhyne: Number one, there is a clear violation of a constitutional right. Number two, there is no reasonable basis for the voting discrimination which is laid out in this complaint, and the defendants offer no justification for it, and they cannot offer it on these facts.

And, as I have just said, there is no other remedy. We're at the end of the road. If this is a judicial no-man's land, these people, the two-thirds of the voters of Tennessee, are consigned to be second-class citizens for the rest of their life, because these defendants exalt their position into an untouchable absolute.

Narrator: Solicitor General Archibald Cox argued for the federal government as a "friend of the court." The Tennessee constitution set limits of thirty-three senators and ninety-nine representatives. Cox suggested raising these numbers to give urban voters equal weight. Justices Frankfurter and Potter Stewart were skeptical.

Cox: This would give you a somewhat larger legislature than Tennessee has today and somewhat larger than the constitutional limit fixed in Tennessee. But one would then come up against this question: Tennessee is plainly violating its own constitution today in a number of instances. I would think that the one fixing a ceiling on the numbers was far less important than the requirement of the Fourteenth Amendment and of the Tennessee constitution.

Frankfurter: And you'd have the federal court violate a state constitution in order to correct some violation of another provision of the state constitution?

Cox: I suggest this as one possibility. I can suggest another . . .

Stewart: That's very consistent. You've already told us that whatever the state constitution provides is fundamentally, fundamentally irrelevant to your argument.

Cox: Well, I would think it's fundamentally irrelevant to the argument that the present system violates the Fourteenth Amendment.

Narrator: Cox posed the problem in national terms.

Cox: This is obviously a very important case, one which will affect our representative institutions for a long time, so far as anyone can judge. The issue is not confined to Tennessee. If affects a number of states all over the country. Plainly, it's also a very important question for this Court in terms of this Court's place in our tripartite governmental system. Probably the most difficult questions are those that involve a determination of the proper limits of the judicial function. We fully recognize that there are wrongs which can be righted only by the people or by the legislature. This Court doesn't carry the whole burden of government, and for it to rush in to try and right political wrongs, instead of leaving them to the other branches, the political branches, of the government, could impair its usefulness in our constitutional system.

But I suggest to you that judicial inaction through excessive caution or through a fancied impotence, in the face of crying necessity and very serious wrongs, may also do damage to our constitutional system, may also do them, indeed, greater damage, including the judicial branch.

Narrator: Chief Justice Warren welcomed Assistant Attorney General Jack Wilson. Wilson claimed the Tennessee officials had no responsibility for legislative decisions.

Wilson: The issue is with the legislature of Tennessee. What does that mean, then? It means that this is an issue not with these appellees before the Court. It's an issue with the sovereign state of Tennessee, one of the fifty states. Well, you got 'em here, got 'em here; what are you going to do about it? We're doing this, may it please the Court: we are interposing the plea of sovereignty on behalf of the sovereign state of Tennessee; that it has not, in its constitution, by statute, or otherwise, given its consent to be sued in the federal district court on a reapportionment matter.

Now, may it please the Court, we come to another great constitutional principle, and that is the principle of separation of powers, and that is mentioned only incidentally by the appellants. I wonder why. Did they think it not applicable, or did they wish not to bring it into the open? It may be decisive of this case.

Narrator: Wilson denounced the suggestion that federal judges should order the Tennessee legislature to redraw district lines.

Wilson: Now, at this point, may it please the Court, may I pause just a moment to respond to one of the appellants' insistencies here, that one type of relief in this case might be for this Court to remand the case to the federal district court and in substance do nothing. What does that mean? It means that the appellants would have a three-judge district court sitting here, eyeing 132 members of the Tennessee General Assembly, each saying, "Which will make the first move?"

Is that the way this government of ours operates? Not under the separation of powers. I suggest that we never reach that point. Well, what is that? That's coercion. And some of the newspapers of Tennessee in their editorials have said, "Yes, it's coercion and that's what we want. That's what we must have." Ah. Is it true? Is it so? If this Court will take one defendant, a misdemeanor case, a felony case, and set aside the conviction because of a confession obtained by coercion, would this Court lend its sympathy to coercing a state legislative body where the rights of three-and-a-half million people were involved? I suggest not. I suggest not.

Narrator: Justice Hugo Black, who dissented in the *Colegrove* case, repeated a question he asked fifteen years earlier.

Black: Let's assume that the legislature had provided squarely in its law that the votes of people living in rural communities as here set out—defining geographical areas as rural communities—shall be counted in each election ten times, while they are counted once in the cities. Would you say that would be a denial of equal protection?

Wilson: No sir, I would not.

Black: You would not. You would say that would be a rational classification?

Wilson: I would never reach the question of whether it was rational, may it please the Court. I would say that the apportionment and distribution of legislative representatives within a state is a state matter.

Black: But let's assume that you were overruled on that. Let's just assume that. And it were held to be a justiciable matter, and the act were written in the form that I've stated. Would you say that that could be supported as a rational classification to distinguish between the voters in the rural community and in the city?

Wilson: It might not, may it please the Court. It might not.

Narrator: Black pressed again.

Black: My question was intended to state very specifically that the county you're talking about, we'll say, and six other counties, rural counties, shall have their votes counted in all elections so as to have each vote overcome five votes cast in Shelby County, Tennessee. That would be a very clear standard. It was challenged, then, on the basis that it denied equal protection of the law— it was not a reasonable classification under that amendment. What would you say?

Wilson: Well, may it please the Court, I would say that I wouldn't like it and that morally it might be wrong. I would say there is not a legal or constitutional question there.

Black: Assuming that we get to the merits of the controversy as to whether giving the votes in certain localities, geographical localities, more value in all the elections than the votes in certain other localities—the rural community over the city—would that be a denial of equal protection of the law, if they were given the value of six to one?

Wilson: My answer, may it please the Court, is that it would not be a denial of due process.

Narrator: Chief Justice Warren's final question went to the heart of the case.

Warren: Mr. Wilson, is there any remedy in the courts of Tennessee for these people—if they are, as they say now, at the end of the road—if we don't take this case?

Wilson: I would say, may it please the Court, that on the present status of the case law in Tennessee and of the views held as to the constitutional law in Tennessee, that this right, alleged right, is not enforceable in *any* of the courts of Tennessee to *any* degree whatsoever. And I would be less than truthful to Your Honor if I did not so state.

Narrator: On March 26th, 1962, the Tennessee voters won their case. By a six-to-two vote—one justice did not participate—the Supreme Court ruled that federal judges could decide reapportionment cases. Justice William Brennan wrote for the majority. He answered Justice Frankfurter's claim in the *Colegrove* case that federal courts should avoid the "political thicket" of reapportionment. Brennan said the principle of federalism did not allow states to violate the federal Constitution. The right to an equal vote, he said, "is within the reach of federal protection under the Fourteenth Amendment." The justices sent the case back to the lower court for trial and decision.

Justice Frankfurter complained in dissent of the "massive repudiation" of his *Colegrove* opinion. "There is not under our Constitution," he said, "a judicial remedy for every political mischief, for every undesirable exercise of legislative power." Frankfurter suggested that rural voters might have interests that outweigh those of city dwellers.

Baker versus *Carr* began the process of drawing new political maps in every state. Two years later, in 1964, the Court ruled that the standard of "one person, one vote" must apply in state and federal elections. Chief Justice Warren stated the rule in *Reynolds* versus *Sims*: "Legislators represent people," he said, "not trees or acres. A citizen, a qualified voter, is no more nor less so because he lives in the city or on the farm."

Rural opponents of reapportionment waged a fierce war against the Supreme Court decisions. They proposed constitutional amendments and laws to keep federal courts from ruling on reapportionment cases. They came close to victory but finally failed. Since the 1960s, courts have allowed only minor deviations from the "one person–one vote" standard for all election districts.

Chief Justice Warren called *Baker* versus *Carr* "the most important case of my tenure on the Court." He even placed it above the school integration case of *Brown* versus *Board of Education*. Warren recognized that democracy depends on equal voting rights. That idea has swept across the globe, from America to South Africa and the former Soviet Union. It is truly, as Warren knew, an idea whose time has come.

EDITED SUPREME COURT OPINIONS
Baker v. *Carr*.

MR. JUSTICE BRENNAN delivered the opinion of the Court.

This civil action was brought . . . to redress the alleged deprivation of federal constitutional rights. The complaint, alleging that by means of a 1901 statute of Tennessee apportioning the members of the General Assembly among the State's ninety-five counties, "these plaintiffs and others similarly situated, are denied the equal protection of the laws accorded them by the Fourteenth Amendment to the Constitution of the United States by virtue of the debasement of their votes," was dismissed by a three-judge court . . . in the Middle District of Tennessee. The court held that it lacked jurisdiction of the subject matter and also that no claim was stated upon which relief could be granted. . . . We hold that the dismissal was error, and remand the cause to the District Court for trial and further proceedings consistent with this opinion.

The General Assembly of Tennessee consists of the Senate with thirty-three members and the House of Representatives with ninety-nine members. . . .

. . . Tennessee's standard for allocating legislative representation among her counties is the total number of qualified voters resident in the respective counties, subject only to minor qualifications. Decennial reapportionment in compliance with the constitutional scheme was effected by the General Assembly each decade from 1871 to 1901. . . . In 1901 the General Assembly . . . passed the Apportionment Act here in controversy. In the more than sixty years since that action, all proposals in both Houses of the General Assembly for reapportionment have failed to pass. Between 1901 and 1961, Tennessee has experienced substantial growth and redistribution of her population.

. . . It is . . . alleged that "because of the population changes since 1900, and the failure of the Legislature to reapportion itself since 1901," the 1901 statute became "unconstitutional and obsolete." Appellants also argue that, because of the composition of the legislature effected by the 1901 Apportionment Act, redress in the form of a state constitutional amendment to change the entire mechanism for reapportioning, or any other change short of that, is difficult or impossible. The complaint concludes that "these plaintiffs and others similarly situated, are denied the equal protection of the laws accorded them by the Fourteenth Amendment to the Constitution of the United States by virtue of the debasement of their votes." They seek a declaration that the 1901 statute is unconstitutional and an injunction restraining the appellees from acting to conduct any further elections under it. They also pray that unless and until the General Assembly enacts a valid reapportionment, the District Court should either decree a reapportionment by mathematical application of the Tennessee constitutional formulae to the most recent Federal Census figures, or direct the appellees to conduct legislative elections, primary and general, at large. . . .

In holding that the subject matter of this suit was not justiciable, the District Court relied on *Colegrove* v. *Green, supra,* and subsequent *per curiam* cases. The court stated: "From a review of these decisions there can be no doubt that the federal rule . . . is that the federal courts . . . will not intervene in cases of this type to compel legislative reapportionment." 170 F. Supp., at 826. We understand the District Court to have read the cited cases as compelling the conclusion that since the appellants sought to have a legislative apportionment held unconstitutional, their suit presented a "political question" and was therefore nonjusticiable. We hold that this challenge to an apportionment presents no nonjusticiable "political question." The cited cases do not hold the contrary.

Of course the mere fact that the suit seeks protection of a political right does not mean it presents a political question. . . . Appellants' claim that they are being denied equal protection is justiciable, and if "discrimination is sufficiently shown, the right to relief under the equal protection clause is not diminished by the fact that the discrimination relates to political rights." *Snowden* v. *Hughes* . . .

. . . The nonjusticiability of a political question is primarily a function of the separation of powers. . . . Deciding whether a matter has in any measure been committed by the Constitution to another branch of government, or whether the action of that branch exceeds whatever authority has been committed, is itself a delicate exercise in constitutional interpretation, and is a responsibility of this Court as ultimate interpreter of the Constitution. . . .

We come, finally, to the ultimate inquiry whether our precedents as to what constitutes a nonjusticiable "political question" bring the case before us under the umbrella of that doctrine. A natural beginning is to note whether any of the common characteristics which we have been able to identify and label descriptively are present. We find none: The question here is the consistency of state action with the Federal Constitution. We have no question decided, or to be decided, by a political branch of government coequal with this Court. Nor do we risk embarrassment of our government abroad, or grave disturbance at home if we take issue with Tennessee as to the constitutionality of her action here challenged. Nor need the appellants, in order to succeed in this action, ask the Court to enter upon policy determinations for which judicially manageable standards are lacking. Judicial standards under the Equal Protection Clause are well developed and familiar, and it has been open to courts since the enactment of the Fourteenth Amendment to determine, if on the particular facts they must, that a discrimination reflects *no* policy, but simply arbitrary and capricious action . . .

We conclude then that the nonjusticiability of claims resting on the Guaranty Clause which arises from their embodiment of questions that were thought "political," can have no bearing upon the justiciability of the equal protection claim presented in this case. Finally, we emphasize that it is the involvement in Guaranty Clause claims of the elements thought to define "political questions," and no other feature, which could render them nonjusticiable. Specifically, we have said that such claims are not held nonjusticiable because they touch matters of state governmental organization. . . .

We conclude that the complaint's allegations of a denial of equal protection present a justiciable constitutional cause of action upon which appellants are entitled to a trial and a decision. The right asserted is within the reach of judicial protection under the Fourteenth Amendment.

The judgment of the District Court is reversed and the cause is remanded for further proceedings consistent with this opinion.

Reversed and remanded.

MR. JUSTICE CLARK, concurring.

One emerging from the rash of opinions with their accompanying clashing of views may well find himself suffering a mental blindness. The Court holds that the appellants have alleged a cause of action. However, it refuses to award relief here—although the facts are undisputed—and fails to give the District Court any guidance whatever. . . . I believe it can be shown that . . . a patent violation of the Equal Protection Clause of the United States Constitution has been shown, and that an appropriate remedy may be formulated. . . .

The controlling facts cannot be disputed. It appears from the record that thity-seven percent of the voters of Tennessee elect twenty of the thirty-three

Senators while forty percent of the voters elect sixty-three of the ninety members of the House. . . .

It is true that the apportionment policy incorporated in Tennessee's Constitution, i. e., state-wide numerical equality of representation with certain minor qualifications, is a rational one. . . . However, the root of the trouble is not in Tennessee's Constitution, for admittedly its policy has not been followed. The discrimination lies in the action of Tennessee's Assembly in allocating legislative seats to counties or districts created by it. Try as one may, Tennessee's apportionment just cannot be made to fit the pattern cut by its Constitution. This was the finding of the District Court . . . the apportionment picture in Tennessee is a topsy-turvical of gigantic proportions. This is not to say that some of the disparity cannot be explained, but when the entire table is examined—comparing the voting strength of counties of like population as well as contrasting that of the smaller with the larger counties—it leaves but one conclusion, namely that Tennessee's apportionment is a crazy quilt without rational basis. At the risk of being accused of picking out a few of the horribles I shall allude to a series of examples. . . .

As is admitted, there is a wide disparity of voting strength between the large and small counties. Some samples are: Moore County has a total representation of two with a population (2,340) of only one-eleventh of Rutherford County (25,316) with the same representation; Decatur County (5,563) has the same representation as Carter (23,303) though the latter has four times the population; . . . But it is said that in this illustration all of the under-represented counties contain municipalities of over ten thousand population and they therefore should be included under the "urban" classification, rationalizing this disparity as an attempt to effect a rural-urban political balance. But in so doing one is caught up in the backlash of his own bull whip, for many counties have municipalities with a population exceeding ten thousand, yet the same invidious discrimination is present. . . . This could not be an effort to attain political balance between rural and urban populations. Since discrimination is present among counties of like population, the plan is neither consistent nor rational. It discriminates horizontally creating gross disparities between rural areas themselves as well as between urban areas themselves, still maintaining the wide vertical disparity already pointed out between rural and urban. . . .

As John Rutledge (later Chief Justice) said 175 years ago in the course of the Constitutional Convention, a chief function of the Court is to secure the national rights. Its decision today supports the proposition for which our forebears fought and many died, namely, that to be fully comfortable to the principle of right, the form of government must be representative. That is the keystone upon which our government was founded and lacking which no republic can survive. It is well for this Court to practice self-restraint and discipline in constitutional adjudication, but never in its history have those principles received sanction where the national rights of so many have been so clearly infringed for so long a time. National respect for the courts is more enhanced through the forthright enforcement of those rights rather than by rendering them nugatory through the interposition of subterfuges. In my view the ultimate decision today is in the greatest tradition of this Court.

MR. JUSTICE FRANKFURTER, whom MR. JUSTICE HARLAN joins, dissenting.

The Court today reverses a uniform course of decision established by a dozen cases, including one by which the very claim now sustained was unanimously rejected only five years ago. The impressive body of rulings thus cast aside reflected the equally uniform course of our political history regarding the relationship between population and legislative representation—a wholly different matter from denial of the franchise to individuals because of race, color, religion or sex. Such a massive repudiation of the experience of our whole past in asserting destructively novel judicial power demands a detailed analysis of the role of this Court in our constitutional scheme. Disregard of inherent limits in the effective exercise of the Court's "judicial Power" not only presages the futility of judicial intervention in the essentially political conflict of forces by which the relation between population and representation has time out of mind been and now is determined. It may well impair the Court's position as the ultimate organ of "the supreme Law of the Land" in that vast range of legal problems, often strongly entangled in popular feeling, on which this Court must pronounce. The Court's authority—possessed of neither the purse nor the sword—ultimately rests on sustained public confidence in its moral sanction. Such feeling must be nourished by the Court's complete detachment, in fact and in appearance, from political entanglements and by abstention from injecting itself into the clash of political forces in political settlements. . . .

. . . In effect, today's decision empowers the courts of the country to devise what should constitute the proper composition of the legislatures of the fifty States. If state courts should for one reason or another find themselves unable to discharge this task, the duty of doing so is put on the federal courts or on this Court, if State views do not satisfy this Court's notion of what is proper districting. . . .

What, then, is this question of legislative apportionment? Appellants invoke the right to vote and to have their votes counted. But they are permitted to vote and their votes are counted. They go to the polls, they cast their ballots, they send their representatives to the state councils. Their complaint is simply that the representatives are not sufficiently numerous or powerful—in short, that Tennessee has adopted a basis of representation with which they are dissatisfied. Talk of "debasement" or "dilution" is circular talk. One cannot speak of "debasement" or "dilution" of the value of a vote until there is first defined a standard of reference as to what a vote should be worth. What is actually asked of the Court in this case is to choose among competing bases of representation—ultimately, really, among competing theories of political philosophy—in order to establish an appropriate frame of government for the State of Tennessee and thereby for all the States of the Union. . . .

. . . What Tennessee illustrates is an old and still widespread method of representation—representation by local geographical division, only in part respective of population—in preference to others, others, forsooth, more appealing. Appellants contest this choice and seek to make this Court the arbiter of the disagreement. They would make the Equal Protection Clause the charter of adjudication, asserting that the equality which it guarantees comports, if not the assurance of equal weight to every voter's vote, at least the basic conception that representation ought to be proportionate to population, a standard by reference to which the reasonableness of apportionment plans may be judged.

To find such a political conception legally enforceable in the broad and unspecific guarantee of equal protection is to rewrite the Constitution. . . .

The notion that representation proportioned to the geographic spread of population is so universally accepted as a necessary element of equality between man and man that it must be taken to be the standard of a political equality preserved by the Fourteenth Amendment—that it is, in appellants' words "the basic principle of representative government"—is, to put it bluntly, not true. However desirable and however desired by some among the great political thinkers and framers of our government, it has never been generally practiced, today or in the past. It was not the English system, it was not the colonial system, it was not the system chosen for the national government by the Constitution, it was not the system exclusively or even predominantly practiced by the States at the time of adoption of the Fourteenth Amendment, it is not predominantly practiced by the States today. Unless judges, the judges of this Court, are to make their private views of political wisdom the measure of the Constitution—views which in all honesty cannot but give the appearance, if not reflect the reality, of involvement with the business of partisan politics so inescapably a part of apportionment controversies—the Fourteenth Amendment, "itself a historical product," . . . provides no guide for judicial oversight of the representation problem. . . .

Although the District Court had jurisdiction in the very restricted sense of power to determine whether it could adjudicate the claim, the case is of that class of political controversy which, by the nature of its subject, is unfit for federal judicial action. The judgment of the District Court, in dismissing the complaint for failure to state a claim on which relief can be granted, should therefore be affirmed.

BIBLIOGRAPHY

ATLESON, JAMES B. "The Aftermath of *Baker* v. *Carr*—An Adventure in Judicial Experimentation." *California Law Review* 51 (1963): 535.

BAKER, GORDON E. *The Reapportionment Revolution*. Random House, 1966.

"Court Reversal on Cities' Rights." *Senior Scholastic*. April 11, 1962, p. 20.

DIRKSEN, EVERETT M. "The Supreme Court Is Defying the People." *Saturday Evening Post*. September 12, 1964, p. 10.

EMERSON, THOMAS E. "Malapportionment and Judicial Power." *Yale Law Journal* 72, (1962–63): 64.

HANSON, ROYCE. *The Political Thicket*. Prentice-Hall, 1966.

United States v. Nixon

418 U.S. 683 (1974)

The Watergate scandal did more than drive a president from office in disgrace. It also produced a dramatic courtroom confrontation that threatened to tear apart the American political system. After the criminal indictments in March 1974 of President Richard Nixon's top White House aides, the Watergate special prosecutor secured a subpoena for tape recordings that allegedly showed an Oval Office "cover-up" that included payoffs, document destruction, and perjury. The president claimed that "executive privilege" shielded the tapes from disclosure either to the courts or to Congress, which had begun impeachment proceedings. In July 1974, a unanimous Supreme Court held that the president's "generalized assertion of privilege must yield to the demonstrated, specific need for evidence in a pending criminal trial." Two weeks later, Nixon left the White House in a helicopter, the first president to resign.

EDITED AND NARRATED TRANSCRIPT OF ORAL ARGUMENT IN
United States v. *Nixon*, 418 U.S. 683 (1974).

Counsel for petitioner: Leon Jaworski and Philip Lacovara, Watergate Special
Prosecutors; Washington, D.C.
Counsel for respondent: James St. Clair, Boston, Massachusetts

Narrator: It's July 8th, 1974. Chief Justice Warren Burger has called a case that
raises the profound issues of constitutional law. Spectators lined up two days
ago, hoping to witness the arguments in what we now call the "Watergate tapes
case." But its proper name—the *United States of America* versus *Richard Nixon,
President of the United States*—illustrates the complexity of the issues before the
Court.

In the early morning of June 17th, 1972, a security guard discovered five
men in the Watergate building in Washington, D.C. They were caught placing
telephone taps in offices of the Democratic National Committee. Police and
FBI agents soon linked the men to Nixon's campaign office. The Watergate
burglars were tried and convicted before federal judge John Sirica. Before sentencing, one defendant told the judge that other defendants had been pressured
to lie to cover up in court White House involvement in the Watergate break-in.

Watergate soon exploded into a national scandal. Congress forced the
Nixon administration to appoint a special prosecutor, Archibald Cox. A federal
grand jury indicted seven of the president's top aides and campaign officials for
conspiracy to obstruct justice. Nixon himself was named as an "unindicted coconspirator."

Revelations that Nixon taped his Oval Office meetings prompted Cox to
obtain a subpoena for some of the Watergate tapes. Nixon fired him for this act,
igniting a political firestorm that led Congress to begin impeachment proceedings against the president. The next special prosecutor, Leon Jaworski, obtained
another subpoena for the tapes. Nixon's refusal to honor that subpoena is the
issue before the Court.

The justices today will hear two arguments on presidential powers under
the Constitution. One views the president as an ordinary citizen, obligated like
every other citizen to provide evidence in criminal cases. The other gives the
president the power to withhold records from the courts and Congress. This is
the claim of "executive privilege." Past decisions give the justices very little
guidance in deciding this case.

The Court's junior member—William Rehnquist—is missing this morning. A former aide to Watergate defendant John Mitchell, he has stepped aside
in the case. Leon Jaworski, a prominent Texas lawyer and former president of
the American Bar Association, takes the podium first.

Jaworski: When boiled down, this case really presents one fundamental issue: Who is to be the arbiter of what the Constitution says? Basically this is not a novel question, although the factual situation involved is, of course, unprecedented.

In refusing to produce the evidence sought by a subpoena *duces tecum* in the criminal trial of seven defendants, among them former chief aides and devotees, the president invokes the provisions of the Constitution. His counsel's brief is replete with references to the Constitution as justifying his position. And in his public statements, as we all know, the president has embraced the Constitution as offering him support for his refusal to supply the subpoenaed tapes.

Now the president may be right in how he reads the Constitution. But he may also be wrong. And if he is wrong, who is there to tell him so? And if there is no one, then the president of course is free to pursue his course of erroneous interpretations. What then becomes of our constitutional form of government? So when counsel for the president in his brief states that this case goes to the heart of our basic constitutional system, we agree. Because in our view, this nation's constitutional form of government is in serious jeopardy if the president, any president, is to say that the Constitution means what *he* says it does, and that there is no one, not even the Supreme Court, to tell him otherwise.

Narrator: Justice Potter Stewart broke in.

Stewart: As a matter of law, he's asking, he's making that argument to a court, so that, as a matter of constitutional law, he is correct.

Jaworski: So that, of course, this Court could then not pass upon the constitutional question of how he interprets the Constitution, *if* his position were correct.

Stewart: As a matter of law, if his position is correct, then he is the sole judge, and he's asking this Court to agree with that proposition as a matter of constitutional law.

Jaworski: But what I'm saying is, if he *is* the sole judge, and if he's to be considered the sole judge, and he is in error in his interpretation, then he goes on being in error in his interpretation.

Stewart: Well, then this Court will tell him so. That's what this case is about, isn't it?

Jaworski: Well, that's what I think the case is about, yes, sir.

Narrator: Chief Justice Burger turned the question around.

Burger: He's submitting himself to the judicial process in the same sense that you are, is that no so, Mr. Jaworski? (Jaworski: Well, I can't see that . . .) You take one position and he takes another.

Jaworski: Well, Mr. Chief Justice, in my view, frankly, it is a position where he says, "The Constitution says this, and nobody is going to tell me what the Constitution says," because, up to this point, up to this point he says that he, and he alone, is the proper one to interpret the Constitution.

Narrator: Jaworski reminded the Court of reaction to the firing of Archibald Cox.

Jaworski: Now, the president himself, as we point out in our brief, in announcing the appointment of a new independent prosecutor, stated that, to the nation, that he had no greater interest than to see that the new special prosecutor has the cooperation from the executive branch, and the independence that he needs to bring about that conclusion of the Watergate investigation.

Of course, this independence that was given to the special prosecutor actually was but an echo of public demand, and if I may be permitted to say so, it was the only basis on which, after what had occurred and a predecessor had been discharged, it was the only basis on which the special prosecutor could have felt that he could come in and serve and undertake to perform these functions.

Narrator: Jaworski's view of executive privilege puzzled Justice Stewart.

Jaworski: Now, I want to make it clear that the president at no point, of course, delegated to the special prosecutor the exclusive right to pass on the question of executive privilege or any other privilege—attorney-client privilege, or any other testimonial privilege. What we are merely saying is that we have the clear right to test it in this Court, and this is on what we stand.

Stewart: Are you now arguing that there is no such thing as executive privilege? (Jaworski: No, sir.) I didn't think so.

Jaworski: No, sir. But I said it had no basis for it in the Constitution.

Stewart: You think, if anything, it's a common law privilege, is that your point?

Jaworski: Yes, sir, and that it has been judicially recognized, and appropriately so, in a number of cases, as we see it. We do not think that it is an appropriate one in this case. But we certainly do not, for a moment, feel that it has any constitutional base.

Narrator: Jaworski summed up his argument.

Jaworski: The issue of executive privilege, I should point out here, is a very narrow one, and I think it's important that we bear this in mind. It doesn't involve very large or broad privilege rights. What it really narrows down to is a somewhat simple but very important issue in the administration of criminal justice. And that is whether the president, in a pending prosecution, can withhold material evidence from the court, merely on his assertion that the evidence involves confidential communications. And this is what it really gets down to.

We're not suggesting for a moment here that the matter of executive privilege should not be looked into. This is not . . . it deserves to be tested; it *should* be tested; and we urge that it be tested. But the ultimate decision is not one of saying that it is absolute, it rests on the Constitution, it doesn't entitle anyone, and doesn't authorize anyone, doesn't even authorize this Court to look into it. Because if the courts are the ultimate interpreters of the Constitution and can restrain Congress to operate within constitutional bounds, they certainly shouldn't be empowered any less to measure presidential claims of constitutional powers.

Narrator: President Nixon is represented by James St. Clair, an experienced trial lawyer and partner in a prestigious Boston firm.

Chief Justice Burger: Mr. St. Clair.

St. Clair: Mr. Chief Justice, and members of the Court.

My learned brother has approached this case, I think, in a traditional point of view, namely, this is an attempt by a special prosecutor to obtain what he thinks is desirable evidence in a criminal prosecution that he has the responsibility for. Not once, however, have I heard him mention what I think is really involved, at least in significant part, and that is the co-pendency of impeachment proceedings before the House of Representatives, and the realistic fusion that has taken place with respect to these two proceedings, and the promise of continued fusion, as I understand my brother's position.

Now, my brother says in his brief that this material he *now* seeks of course will be available to the House committee and will be used to determine whether or not the president should be impeached. So this fusion is going to continue. And under the Constitution as we view it, only the legislature has the right to conduct impeachment proceedings. The courts have been, from the history involved and from the language of the provisions, excluded from that function. And yet the special prosecutor is drawing this Court into those proceedings, inevitably and inexorably.

No one could stand here and argue with any candor that the decision of this Court would have no impact whatsoever on the pending inquiry before the House of Representatives concerning the impeachment of the president.

Narrator: Justice Thurgood Marshall pressed St. Clair on the Watergate tapes.

Marshall: What, in any of these tapes, is involved in the impeachment proceedings?

St. Clair: Well, if Your Honor please, the House of Representatives has subpoenaed these and more tapes.

Marshall: Well, I don't know what's in the tapes. I assume you do.

St. Clair: No, I don't.

Marshall: You don't know either. Well, how do you know that they're subject to executive privilege?

St. Clair: Well, I *do* know that there's a preliminary showing that they are conversations between the President and his close aides.

Marshall: Regardless of what it is?

St. Clair: Regardless of what it is. It may involve a number of subjects.

Narrator: Chief Justice Burger broke in.

Burger: Does not the special prosecutor claim that the subject matter is the same?

St. Clair: He claims that, but he has no way of showing it. In fact, he says it's only probable, or likely. He has no way of showing that they in fact involve the subject of Watergate.

Narrator: St. Clair's defense of presidential power did not impress Justice Marshall.

St. Clair: I say the president should decide as a political matter what should be made available to the House (Marshall: Oh?) and that the Court ought not to be drawn into that decision.

Marshall: So that the House can get them, the president can get them, and the only people I know who can't get them is the courts.

St. Clair: What *is* before this Court is a prosecutor's demand for evidence. And I direct my remarks for a moment to that problem. He says that, in effect, we have no right to be here, that we have delegated the who, the when, and with what issues to him. We *have* delegated the who and the when, and pursuant to that he has indicted a number of people, and he has indicted them at such time as he thought appropriate. But even *he* contends that we did not delegate to him what presidential conversations would be used as evidence. That was reserved, and he concedes that that is the fact. And that's what's at issue here, not when and who is to be indicted, but what presidential communications are going to be used as evidence.

Narrator: Justice Marshall demanded to know if the President would obey the Supreme Court.

Marshall: You're still leaving it up to this Court to decide it?

St. Clair: Well, yes, in a sense.

Marshall: Well, in *what* sense?

St. Clair: In the sense that this court has an obligation to determine the law. All right? The president also has an obligation to carry out his constitutional functions.

Marshall: You are submitting it to this Court for us to decide whether or not executive privilege is available in this case?

St. Clair: Well, the problem with the question is even more limited than that. Is the executive privilege, which my brother concedes, absolute or is it only conditional?

Marshall: I said "in this case." Can you make it any narrower than that?

St. Clair: No, sir.

Marshall: Well, do you agree that that's what's before this Court, and you're submitting it to *this* Court for decision?

St. Clair: This is being submitted to this court for its guidance and judgment with respect to the law. The president, on the other hand, has his obligations under the Constitution.

Marshall: Are you submitting it to this Court for this Court's *decision?*

St. Clair: As to what the law is, yes.

Narrator: Chief Justice Burger.

Burger: If it were not so, you would not be here?

St. Clair: I would not be here. Now, my brother says I have no right to even challenge *his* right to be here. And I'd like to deal with that for a moment. This is, as we point out in our brief, essentially an executive department matter. Whatever may have been the arrangements between the branches of the executive matter*sic*with respect to evidentiary matters—and in fact there were *no* arrangements regarding evidentiary matters—it is not the function of the court to direct or rule what evidence will be presented to it by the executive in the executive's duty of prosecuting.

Narrator: Justice Potter Stewart was skeptical.

Stewart: Your argument would be a—*is* a very good one as a matter of political science, and would be a very fine one as a matter of constitutional and probably statutory law, except hasn't your client dealt himself out of that argument by what's been done in the creation of the special prosecutor?

St. Clair: Perhaps with respect to everything except the president did not delegate to the special prosecutor the right to tell him whether or not his confidential communications should be made available as evidence.

Narrator: St. Clair again provoked Justice Marshall.

St. Clair: This Court has no jurisdiction to resolve a dispute as to whether or not they *shculd* be given up, because that would involve this Court in the prosecution of the case.

Marshall: Can this Court decide what's necessary for trial of a criminal case?

St. Clair: It can, sir, with respect to third parties, but it should not involve itself with the executive function of prosecuting the case.

Marshall: My only question was, that this is a subpoena *duces tecum* that was issued by a judge. Right?

St. Clair: Yes, sir.

Marshall: Slightly judicial.

St. Clair: Entirely judicial.

Marshall: And that's what's before us?

St. Clair: And that we moved to quash.

Marshall: But that's what's before us?

St. Clair: The denial of our motion to quash is one of the issues before us, that's right.

Marshall: The *only* thing before us is whether or not the subpoena should issue.

St. Clair: Well, the question is, is it a proper issue of a subpoena. (Marshall: That's right.) Judges make mistakes, as do lawyers, and maybe even presidents, for all I know. But the point I want to make with you, sir, is that this is an executive function, an executive decision, one not delegated . . .

Marshall: The executive function, as I understand your discussion, as to whether he should voluntarily turn them over to the special prosecutor. We are past that stage. We are now at the stage where the prosecutor has asked the court to assist him, and the court has assisted him. Does that not take it a step beyond pure political, or executive?

St. Clair: We submit that the court improperly assisted him, that the court has no right to determine what the executive will offer in evidence.

Narrator: St. Clair insisted on a strong president.

St. Clair: If anything, a decision in this case against the president would tend to diminish the democratic process. This president was elected on the theory that he would have all the powers, duties, and responsibilities of any other president. This president ought not to have any *less* powers than any other president ought to have. The framers envisioned a strong, active president, even in the course of impeachment proceedings. They did not want this country to be led by someone who didn't have those full powers, even if he were then under impeachment. And indeed this president continues to function as president, as he should, even though there are impeachment inquiries underway.

Narrator: Leon Jaworski turned over his rebuttal time to Philip Lacovara, counsel to the special prosecutor and former deputy solicitor general.

Lacovara: The notion that because there is concurrently underway an impeachment inquiry before the House of Representatives, that somehow makes this a nonjusticiable, political question, is, we think, a remarkable notion, which is not supported by sound constitutional law or by any of the decisions of this Court.

   This is a criminal proceeding, a federal criminal case against six defendants. A subpoena has been issued to obtain evidence for use at the trial which is scheduled to begin on September 9th. The Court cannot escape the fact that this is a trial of tremendous national importance. But a trial that was brought to a head without regard to the impeachment inquiry. This is an independent, separate, constitutional process that is underway. And a traditional, ordinary, prosaic remedy, a subpoena, has been utilized to obtain evidence for that trial.

Narrator: James St. Clair had the last word for President Nixon.

St. Clair: As I said earlier, the president is not above the law, nor does he contend that he is. But he does contend that as president the law can be applied to him in only one way, and that's by impeachment, not by naming as a coconspirator in a grand jury indictment, not by indictment, or in any other way. Therefore, in this case, I urge that this Court take such action as is appropriate and overrule Judge Sirica's decision and order that this case be dismissed.

Narrator: Chief Justice Burger.

Burger: Thank you, Mr. St. Clair, thank you, Mr. Jaworski, Mr. Lacovara. The case is submitted.

Narrator: The next day the eight justices met in their conference room. They agreed with St. Clair that the Constitution gave presidents some power of executive privilege. But they also agreed with Jaworski that this power was limited, not absolute, and must defer to judicial power. Their decision was unanimous—President Nixon must turn over the Watergate tapes to Judge Sirica.

Chief Justice Burger wrote the Court's opinion, which he read to another packed audience two weeks later. He rejected St. Clair's argument that the Constitution provides "an absolute privilege of confidentiality for all Presidential communications." Such a claim, he said, conflicts with the "constitutional duty of the Judicial branch to do justice in criminal prosecutions." Even the president must comply with the judicial "demand for every man's evidence."

The Court had decided. But would the president obey? Nixon exploded and threatened defiance of the Court's order. But it was too late. Three days later, the House Judiciary Committee voted to impeach the president for obstruction of justice. James St. Clair finally listened to Watergate tapes and discovered the "smoking gun," Nixon's personal Watergate cover-up order. His impeachment became a certainty.

On August 8, 1974, Richard Nixon dictated an eleven-word letter: "I hereby resign the Office of President of the United States." The next day, he left the White House for the last time.

Presidents before and after Richard Nixon have made sweeping claims of executive privilege. The Supreme Court's opinion in the Watergate case did not close the door on such claims. How the justices would resolve another showdown between judges and presidents is a question without an answer. Hopefully, the Court would help the country avoid another national nightmare.

EDITED SUPREME COURT OPINION
United States v. Nixon

MR. CHIEF JUSTICE BURGER delivered the opinion of the Court.

This litigation presents for review the denial of a motion, filed in the District Court on behalf of the President of the United States, . . . to quash a third-party subpoena *duces tecum* issued by the United States District Court for the District of Columbia, pursuant to Fed. Rule Crim. Proc. 17 (c). The subpoena directed the President to produce certain tape recordings and documents relating to his conversations with aides and advisers. The court rejected the President's claims of absolute executive privilege, of lack of jurisdiction, and of failure to satisfy the requirements of Rule 17 (c). The President appealed to the Court of Appeals. We granted both the United States' petition for certiorari before judgment (No. 73-1766), and also the President's cross-petition for certiorari before judgment (No. 73-1834), because of the public importance of the issues presented and the need for their prompt resolution.

. . . Having determined that the requirements of Rule 17 (c) were satisfied, we turn to the claim that the subpoena should be quashed because it demands "confidential conversations between a President and his close advisors that it would be inconsistent with the public interest to produce." App. 48a. The first contention is a broad claim that the separation of powers doctrine precludes judicial review of a President's claim of privilege. The second contention is that if he does not prevail on the claim of absolute privilege, the court should hold as a matter of constitutional law that the privilege prevails over the subpoena *duces tecum*.

In the performance of assigned constitutional duties each branch of the Government must initially interpret the Constitution, and the interpretation of its powers by any branch is due great respect from the others. . . .

. . . Notwithstanding the deference each branch must accord the others, the "judicial Power of the United States" vested in the federal courts by Art. III. § 1, of the Constitution can no more be shared with the Executive Branch than the Chief Executive, for example, can share with the Judiciary the veto power, or the Congress share with the Judiciary the power to override a Presidential veto. Any other conclusion would be contrary to the basic concept of separation of powers and the checks and balances that flow from the scheme of a tripartite government. . . .

We therefore reaffirm that it is the province and duty of this Court "to say what the law is" with respect to the claim of privilege presented in this case. . . .

In support of his claim of absolute privilege, the President's counsel urges two grounds, one of which is common to all governments and one of which is peculiar to our system of separation of powers. The first ground is the valid need for protection of communications between high Government officials and those who advise and assist them in the performance of their manifold duties; the importance of this confidentiality is too plain to require further discussion. . . .

. . . Whatever the nature of the privilege of confidentiality of Presidential communications in the exercise of Art. II powers, the privilege can be said to derive from the supremacy of each branch within its own assigned area of constitutional duties. Certain powers and privileges flow from the nature of enumerated powers; the protection of the confidentiality of Presidential communications has similar constitutional underpinnings.

The second ground asserted by the President's counsel in support of the claim of absolute privilege rests on the doctrine of separation of powers. Here it is argued that the independence of the Executive Branch within its own sphere . . . insulates a President from a judicial subpoena in an ongoing criminal prosecution, and thereby protects confidential Presidential communications.

However, neither the doctrine of separation of powers, nor the need for confidentiality of high-level communications, without more, can sustain an absolute, unqualified Presidential privilege of immunity from judicial process under all circumstances. The President's need for complete candor and objectivity from advisers calls for great deference from the courts. However, when the privilege depends solely on the broad, undifferentiated claim of public interest in the confidentiality of such conversations, a confrontation with other values arises. Absent a claim of need to protect military, diplomatic, or sensitive national security secrets, we find it difficult to accept the argument that even the very important interest in confidentiality of Presidential communications is significantly diminished by production of such material for *in camera* inspection with all the protection that a district court will be obliged to provide. . . .

Since we conclude that the legitimate needs of the judicial process may outweigh Presidential privilege, it is necessary to resolve those competing interests in a manner that preserves the essential functions of each branch. The right and indeed the duty to resolve that question does not free the Judiciary from according high respect to the representations made on behalf of the President. . . .

The expectation of a President to the confidentiality of his conversations and correspondence, like the claim of confidentiality of judicial deliberations, for example, has all the values to which we accord deference for the privacy of all citizens and, added to those values, is the necessity for protection of the public interest in candid, objective, and even blunt or harsh opinions in Presidential decision-making. A President and those who assist him must be free to explore alternatives in the process of shaping policies and making decisions and to do so in a way many would be unwilling to express except privately. These are the considerations justifying a presumptive privilege for Presidential communications. The privilege is fundamental to the operation of Government and inextricably rooted in the separation of powers under the Constitution. . . .

But this presumptive privilege must be considered in light of our historic commitment to the rule of law. This is nowhere more profoundly manifest than in our view that "the twofold aim [of criminal justice] is that guilt shall not escape or innocence suffer." *Berger* v. *United States*, 295 U. S., at 88. We have elected to employ an adversary system of criminal justice in which the parties contest all issues before a court of law. The need to develop all relevant facts in the adversary system is both fundamental and comprehensive. The ends of criminal justice would be defeated if judgments were to be founded on a partial or speculative presentation of the facts. The very integrity of the judicial system and public confidence in the system depend on full disclosure of all the facts, within the framework of the rules of evidence. To ensure that justice is done, it is imperative to the function of courts that compulsory process be available for the production of evidence needed either by the prosecution or by the defense.

Only recently the Court restated the ancient proposition of law, albeit in the context of a grand jury inquiry rather than a trial,

> "that 'the public . . . has a right to every man's evidence,' except for those persons protected by a constitutional, common-law, or statutory privilege, *United States* v. *Bryan*, 339 U. S. [323, 331 (1950)]; . . .

The right to the production of all evidence at a criminal trial similarly has constitutional dimensions. The Sixth Amendment explicitly confers upon every defendant in a criminal trial the right "to be confronted with the witnesses against him" and "to have compulsory process for obtaining witnesses in his favor." Moreover, the Fifth Amendment also guarantees that no person shall be deprived of liberty without due process of law. It is the manifest duty of the courts to vindicate those guarantees, and to accomplish that it is essential that all relevant and admissible evidence be produced.

. . . [T]he allowance of the privilege to withhold evidence that is demonstrably relevant in a criminal trial would cut deeply into the guarantee of due process of law and gravely impair the basic function of the courts. A President's acknowledged need for confidentiality in the communications of his office is general in nature, whereas the constitutional need for production of relevant evidence in a criminal proceeding is specific and central to the fair adjudication of a particular criminal case in the administration of justice. Without access to specific facts a criminal prosecution may be totally frustrated. The President's broad interest in confidentiality of communications will not be vitiated by disclosure of a limited number of conversations preliminarily shown to have some bearing on the pending criminal cases.

We conclude that when the ground for asserting privilege as to subpoenaed materials sought for use in a criminal trial is based only on the generalized interest in confidentiality, it cannot prevail over the fundamental demands of due process of law in the fair administration of criminal justice. The generalized assertion of privilege must yield to the demonstrated, specific need for evidence in a pending criminal trial. . . .

BIBLIOGRAPHY

DORSEN, NORMAN, AND JOHN H. F. SHATTUCK. "Executive Privilege, The Congress and The Courts." *Ohio State Law Journal* 35 (1974): 1.

DOYLE, JAMES. *Not Above the Law*. Morrow, 1977.

KUTLER, STANLEY I. *The Wars of Watergate*, Knopf, 1990.

SCHWARTZ, BERNARD. "Bad Presidents Make Hard Law: Richard M. Nixon in the Supreme Court." *Rutgers University School of Law Journal* 31 (1978–79): 22.

"The Nixon Crisis and the Constitution." *Senior Scholastic*, September 26, 1974, p. 8.

WOODWARD, BOB, AND SCOTT ARMSTRONG. *The Brethren*. Avon, 1979.

WOODWARD, BOB, AND CARL BERNSTEIN. *The Final Days*. Avon, 1976.

DeShaney v. Winnebago County Department of Social Services

489 U.S. 189 (1989)

At the age of four, Joshua DeShaney suffered a fate perhaps worse than death. Soon after Joshua's birth in 1979, his parents divorced and his father, Randy, was awarded custody in Winnebago County, Wisconsin. Beginning in 1982, county social workers received complaints that Randy was beating his son. He denied the accusations, and the county caseworker did not pursue the case. Even after Joshua was treated three times for "suspicious injuries," the caseworker "recorded these incidents in her files, but she did nothing more." In March 1984, Randy DeShaney beat Joshua again, inflicting "brain damage so severe" that the little boy will always be profoundly retarded. Joshua's mother sued the county, claiming that the caseworker's negligence deprived him of the "liberty" to lead a normal life. But the Supreme Court ruled that the county "had no constitutional duty to protect Joshua against his father's violence."

TRANSCRIPT OF EDITED AND NARRATED ARGUMENTS IN
DeShaney v. *Winnebago County Department of Social Services,*
489 U.S. 189 (1989)

Counsel for petitioner: Donald Sullivan, Laramie, Wyoming
Counsel for respondent: Mark Mingo, Milwaukee, Wisconsin
Counsel for the United States as amicus curiae: Deputy Solicitor General Donald Ayer, Washington, D.C.

Chief Justice Rehnquist: We'll hear argument now in No. 87–154, Joshua DeShaney versus Winnebago County Department of Social Services.

Narrator: It's November 2d, 1988. Chief Justice William Rehnquist has called a case that raises difficult constitutional questions. But the fundamental question goes beyond the law: Am I my brother's keeper?

Today's argument began with a broken marriage. It ended in tragedy. In between, a little boy's life was destroyed. Here's what happened to Joshua De-Shaney. He was born in Wyoming in 1979. Just after Joshua's first birthday, his parents divorced. His father, Randy DeShaney, was given custody and moved to Winnebago County, Wisconsin. In January 1982, police reported a case of suspected case of child abuse to the county Department of Social Services. A caseworker talked with the father, who denied hurting Joshua. He said his son was "accident prone." The caseworker didn't see Joshua and closed the file.

A year later, Joshua was in the emergency room with multiple injuries. The Social Services Department briefly took custody but returned Joshua to his father after three days. The caseworker suspected child abuse but she didn't ask for court supervision. Joshua returned to the emergency room several times. Doctors filed child abuse reports, but they weren't followed up. One caseworker saw cigarette burns on Joshua's face. Randy DeShaney said he scraped his chin on the sidewalk.

In March 1984, DeShaney told the caseworker Joshua had fainted for no reason. "I don't know why," she wrote, "but I did not ask to see Joshua." The next day, the little boy made his last trip to the emergency room. He was in a coma, with bruises all over his body. Surgeons opened his skull and found massive pools of blood. Half of Joshua's brain was dead. He is permanently paralyzed and profoundly retarded. He'll spend the rest of his life in custodial care.

Who is responsible for this tragedy? Randy DeShaney spent two years in prison for child abuse. But Joshua's mother also blamed the caseworkers. Melody DeShaney felt they had a duty to protect her son from his father and failed. She filed a lawsuit in Joshua's name, charging the Social Services Department with "extreme misconduct." Her case rested on the Constitution's Fourteenth Amendment, which provides that no state shall deprive any person of life or liberty without due process of law. Congress has allowed damages against state officials who deprive anyone of rights "secured by the Constitution."

Lower courts dismissed Joshua's lawsuit. They ruled the caseworkers had not violated state law. And the federal Constitution does not impose any legal duty to protect children from their parents. Donald Sullivan, a lawyer from Wyoming, argues the appeal from these rulings. He took a narrow path through legal obstacles.

Sullivan: Mr. Chief Justice, and may it please the Court.

We are here contending today not for a broad constitutional mandate to the states to do all good things to all people, nor do we contend for a broad constitutional duty to prevent all harm or all sadness, nor do we contend for a broad constitutional duty to protect all children in all cases.

We do suggest that there is one, and only one, exquisitely narrow circumstance where there is an affirmative duty. I would suggest that there are two primary elements to the one and only one circumstance for which we argue.

The first is the existence of a child-parent relationship. The other is what I term "enmeshment," intricate intimacy, enmeshment of the agents of the state in a particular circumstance which would have three characteristics: the first, an extreme danger to a particular individual child; the second, abundant actual knowledge on the part of the agents of the state; and the third, an actual undertaking by the state to protect the child.

Narrator: Chief Justice Rehnquist was not sure Sullivan had narrowed his argument enough.

Rehnquist: You derive all this from the language of the due process clause?

Sullivan: Indeed, your honor. We think it arises from that and from the nature of the relationship and from the way the Court has accorded the relationship. If I may explain, it is my view—it is our view that the protector of the child, the raiser of the child, the person with the right and the power and the authority and the duty to educate the child, teach the child, provide medical care, all those parental things, including setting bedtime, is the parent and not the state.

The other side of that coin is that there is one, and only one, circumstance where, when the family unit—and I don't care whether it's a married family or a stepparent or whatever—but when the child is at home and the door is closed to the world, the people with whom that child is locked in, his natural and his inherent protectors, from those individuals alone—whether it's a father, a stepmother, a live-in girlfriend, or what have you—from those protectors alone he has no protection.

What I'm saying is this. Take the situation where the child is locked behind the door with his protector and the protector becomes the predator, and a proceeding is brought at the extreme end of the child protection spectrum to terminate the parental rights. The Court has already said that the Constitution governs that relationship. The Court has already recognized that in the relationship between the adult and the child—that the Constitution prevails and it prevails both substantively and procedurally.

Narrator: More questions from Rehnquist backed Sullivan into a corner.

Sullivan: The Court additionally has recognized, I believe, that a child—indeed, any of us—has a constitutionally protected right to physical integrity, to bodily protection. What I'm suggesting . . .

Rehnquist: A right against the state.

Sullivan: And a right that arises out of the Constitution to remain alive, yes, sir.

Rehnquist: Well, but it's protected only against the state. It's not protected against private individuals.

Sullivan: Well, I think that's part of what the Court's going to have to address in this case.

Rehnquist: Well, why don't we start with the language of the Fourteenth Amendment, which says that a state shall not—what does it say—deprive any person of life, liberty, or property without due process of law. Certainly we've held in many cases that the state may not deprive someone of life, but we've never held that that provision protects, in the constitutional sense, a private attack on another person.

Sullivan: I agree with that, Mr. Chief Justice. And I would further agree that, in the context in which prior to today that question has been addressed by the Court, I agree that that's the correct holding. For example, if you were to hold otherwise, then the police department would have an obligation to prevent the mugging and a whole host of things that are simply unworkable and are not to be found in the Constitution.

Narrator: Justice Sandra O'Connor followed up. Sullivan came out of his corner.

O'Connor: If your theory were to be accepted, it seems to me it would have a real deterrent effect on state child abuse programs. Why would a state want to undertake a child abuse program at all if they face liability if they guess wrong? I can't—I think you're asking the Court to take a step that is perhaps quite unwarranted and quite dangerous.

Sullivan: If the circumstance were as you phrased it, Justice O'Connor, I would agree. But what I'm saying is this. In the whole range of state action dealing with children, all conduct that is—let's assume that we can recognize some standard. All conduct that is proper, obviously, is not actionable. All conduct that is negligent is not actionable. And it's never been in contest that, if we had the circumstance where the police officer or the child protection worker or someone else were inflicting a beating—you know, that's not the kind of case we're talking about. And the next topic, obviously, that we have to address is the question of whether it's gross negligence, deliberate indifference, or what have you.

Narrator: Sullivan went on the offensive.

Sullivan: There are black-and-white absolute mandates in the state statute that say, when you receive a report from a doctor or from a nurse or from an outside social worker or from a police agency suggestive of child abuse, you *shall* investigate. It doesn't go into you-got-to-do-it-this-way-or-that-way, but you got to make a real investigation. You got to do it in a timely manner.

On the first occasion in January of 1982 that the police reported suspected child abuse, they made an investigation which was cursory, but I can't fault them at that point. They complied with the statute. In January of 1983, they had a doctor report from a hospital saying, "I am finding an abused child here." They take custody of the child. Three days later they send the child back to the abusive home.

You know, I lose track of how many different doctor reports of abuse there were and how many different nurse abusive reports there were—reports of abuse there were—and how many direct observations on separate occasions by the caseworker. But I suggest to you that after two years, approximately, of this, when the caseworker goes to the home and sees cigarette burns on the face of the child, I suggest that's knowledge.

Narrator: Justice Harry Blackmun expressed sympathy.

Blackmun: Mr. Sullivan, let me put it another way. This child was severely injured.

Sullivan: Yes, sir.

Blackmun: And the state placed him in a position of extreme danger, did it not?

Sullivan: Eventually they did, yes, sir. Not to rehash, but because I think it's so important, this caseworker—the evidence in the record before the Court demonstrates that she told witnesses, and I think I'm quoting accurately—"I always knew the phone would ring some day and Joshua would be dead."

Narrator: Chief Justice Rehnquist restated his question.

Rehnquist: I don't see how you turn that around and say, from these limitations on the state, we also derive a duty on the state.

Sullivan: Well, what I'm saying is that we recognize that the Constitution has a legitimate place in the relationship between the parent and the child. If it does, I suggest that it should fairly apply both ways. It doesn't make sense to me that the Constitution applies between the parent and the child only for the benefit of the parent. And I think that's the result.

Narrator: The Chief Justice welcomes Mark Mingo, who argues for Winnebago County.

Rehnquist: Mr. Mingo, we'll hear now from you.

Mingo: Thank you, Mr. Chief Justice; may it please the Court.
    We believe this case involves an attempt by the petitioners to transform the private wrongdoing of a natural father into state action for purposes of invoking the Fourteenth Amendment. The primary issue presented is whether a county's failure to prevent the infliction of harm by a third party upon a person at liberty constitutes a due process violation of the Fourteenth Amendment.
    We believe that there was no state deprivation of a constitutionally protected right for three main reasons. First, the Fourteenth Amendment's concept of liberty does not include a right to basic protective services from the state. Secondly, there is no state action in a constitutional sense which caused a deprivation in this case. Third, we believe that the actions of the social worker did not evince the state of mind necessary to invoke the Fourteenth Amendment.

The Fourteenth Amendment has been viewed by this Court as imposing no constitutional duty upon the states to provide substantive services to its citizens. The Court also has held that, if the state chooses to provide some form of protective services, the Fourteenth Amendment does not tell the state how far they must go in providing those services.

Narrator: Justice O'Connor turned her earlier question around.

O'Connor: Mr. Mingo, if this child had been in foster care, placed by the state or the county, would there be potential liability?

Mingo: Justice O'Connor, in that instance, we believe there may well be potential liability because in that case we have, at least arguably, state action in the sense that the state took a child out of his natural surroundings, arguably put him in state-controlled surroundings, and thereby increased the risk of harm to that child.

Narrator: Mingo faced questions from Justice Antonin Scalia.

Scalia: So what you're saying is that what makes a difference is whether you're just returning him to the status he was in before you took over the temporary custody. Is that the difference?

Mingo: I believe that the important factor to be looked at is whether or not the state action can fairly be said to have increased the risk of harm to that child. If the answer to that threshold question is yes, then I believe we have state action in a constitutional sense.

Scalia: Increased it from what? From what it was before the state took custody or from what it was when the state *had* custody?

Mingo: From what it was before the state interjected and took custody.

White: Well, you were just returning it to the person who had the legal right to custody.

Mingo: The parents certainly have a constitutionally protected right which must be observed by the social worker.

Narrator: Justice Harry Blackmun put his feelings into two words.

Justice Blackmun: Poor Joshua.

Narrator: Mingo defended the county employees.

Mingo: All of the professionals in this case—the pediatrician, the child psychologist, the police officer who investigated the case—they all believed that abuse could not be substantiated. Every one of the professionals involved concurred, and the record is absolutely clear in that regard. They all concurred that there was no evidence to substantiate a claim for child **abuse**.

White: I take it you don't agree with your colleague on the other side that the social worker was disregarding her duty under state law?

Mingo: We certainly do not agree with that position, and we believe the record is quite clear. The only duty she had under state law was to investigate when she received a report of abuse. The only report of abuse which the department ever received in this case was the initial report of suspected abuse. Immediately following that report, there was an investigation. The child was placed in the hospital for three days and then, since there was no filing of a petition at the end of three days, the child was automatically returned to the home. After that first incident, there was absolutely no further reports of abuse.

Narrator: Chief Justice Rehnquist returned to his favorite theme.

Rehnquist: Mr. Mingo, I wonder if you wouldn't be better advised to use the term "constitutional duty" rather than state action. There's no doubt that the social worker was a state actor. She was a public employee doing this, and her acts were those of the state. Your point really is that she was not under a constitutional duty to do certain things that your opponent says she was under a duty to do.

Mingo: Yes, Your Honor, you're quite correct. State action can be quite misleading, and when I use the term "state action," I'm trying to use it in a constitutional sense, which necessarily implies a deprivation of a constitutionally protected right.

Kennedy: And under your theory, I take it, if two policemen see a rape and watch it just for their own amusement, no violation of the Constitution?

Mingo: We would concede that there is no constitutional violation in that particular case.

Kennedy: You're arguing it as well as conceding it. (*laughter*)

Mingo: That's correct.

Narrator: Mingo concluded.

Mingo: In this case it is undisputed by both sides that there was no direct deprivation or direct infliction of harm upon the petitioners nor was the petitioner in the custody of the state at the time of the alleged wrongdoing.

Again, we wish to emphasize that the problem with this special relationship or "enmeshment" theory is that it fails to distinguish between privately inflicted harm and state action. On the other hand, we believe that the Court's adherence to the traditional state action or constitutional deprivation requirement provides a bright line standard which would separate actions of private wrongdoing from actions which can fairly or truly be attributed to the states.

Narrator: Donald Ayer, a deputy solicitor general, argues as "friend of the court" for the federal government.

Ayer: I want to address the due process—the deprivation of due process analysis briefly, if I could. But before I do, I'd like to say a few words about the relationship between federal and state government and the role of the federal Constitution, because I think it is reasonably clear that the area of child protection is not one that is crying out for federal constitutional oversight.

First of all, it is not an area where there is any sort of history of hostility between the state and the interests that we're talking about trying to protect. Quite the contrary. There being no constitutional right to this protection in the first place, it's clear, I think, that the state programs that have been set up have all been set up as a matter of state and local government initiative, born of exactly the same sentiments and concerns that everyone feels toward children who are exposed to the kinds of abuse and hazards that we're sadly reviewing in this case.

Second of all, I think there's no reason to think that federal oversight, federal constitutional oversight is going to add very much to the handling of these sensitive and difficult problems. There is, I think, little reason to think that federal courts have any special expertise in the reviewing of what is at least in some sense a balance between interests of parents, respect for the interests of parents in controlling their children, as opposed to the priority of intervening when you need to and must in order to protect the child.

White: Protection is never one of the things that the Constitution would require the state to furnish?

Ayer: I don't think it is. I don't think that the state is obligated to provide a particular service, as desirable as that may be and as concerned as most everyone probably is that that not go on. The idea that that is somehow going to help the resolution of these problems seems to be misguided, and I think there is a good reason to fear that it may well just primarily discourage the involvement of local agencies for fear that they're going to be facing an unmanageable and very expensive situation.

Narrator: The Court decided the case on February 22d, 1989. Joshua could not know or understand, but he lost his case. Chief Justice Rehnquist wrote for the majority. Even judges, he said, "are moved by natural sympathy . . . to find a way for Joshua and his mother to receive adequate compensation for the grievous harm inflicted upon them." But the Fourteenth Amendment did not give Joshua any claim against state officials. The due process clause, Rehnquist wrote, confers "no affirmative right to governmental aid, even where such aid may be necessary to secure life" or protection against bodily harm.

Rehnquist did not defend the caseworkers. They "stood by and did nothing," he said, "when suspicious circumstances dictated a more active role" in protecting Joshua. But "the harm was inflicted not by the state of Wisconsin, but by Joshua's father." States only have a duty of protection for persons in custody—like prisoners or children in foster homes. Joshua had been in the county's custody for three days. But caseworkers returned him to Randy DeShaney, Rehnquist said, "in no worse position" than before his beating. "Under these circumstances," he wrote, "the state had no constitutional duty to protect Joshua against his father's violence."

Three justices dissented. Justice William Brennan read the record differently than Rehnquist. Reports from police, neighbors, doctors, gave the caseworkers, he said, "ever more certain knowledge that Joshua was in grave danger." Their failure to protect Joshua made him a prisoner, Brennan said, "within the walls of Randy DeShaney's violent home." They should not escape liability, he added, only because "they were not the ones who dealt the blows that destroyed Joshua's life."

Justice Harry Blackmun repeated his words at the argument. "Poor Joshua!" he said. He accused the majority of "sterile, formalistic reasoning" that could have justified the nineteenth-century fugitive slave laws. Blackmun said the Fourteenth Amendment can be read narrowly or broadly. "I would adopt a 'sympathetic' reading," he said, "one which comports with dictates of fundamental justice and recognizes that compassion need not be exiled from the province of judging."

Child abuse is a serious problem. More than two million cases of abuse and neglect are reported every year. Caseworkers have tough jobs, and they make hard decisions. When they make mistakes, children can suffer, even die. But who should pay for these mistakes? In Joshua's case, the justices drew a line on the government's side. But there is no bright line that can decide every case. Judges must still balance the Constitution with human compassion. It's not an easy job.

EDITED SUPREME COURT OPINIONS
DeShaney v. Winnebago Cty. Soc. Servs. Dept.

CHIEF JUSTICE REHNQUIST delivered the opinion of the Court.

Petitioner is a boy who was beaten and permanently injured by his father, with whom he lived. Respondents are social workers and other local officials who received complaints that petitioner was being abused by his father and had reason to believe that this was the case, but nonetheless did not act to remove petitioner from his father's custody. Petitioner sued respondents claiming that their failure to act deprived him of his liberty in violation of the Due Process Clause of the Fourteenth Amendment to the United States Constitution. We hold that it did not.

The facts of this case are undeniably tragic. Petitioner Joshua DeShaney was born in 1979. In 1980, a Wyoming court granted his parents a divorce and awarded custody of Joshua to his father, Randy DeShaney. The father shortly thereafter moved to Neenah, a city located in Winnebago County, Wisconsin, taking the infant Joshua with him. There he entered into a second marriage, which also ended in divorce.

The Winnebago County authorities first learned that Joshua DeShaney might be a victim of child abuse in January 1982, when his father's second wife complained to the police, at the time of their divorce, that he had previously "hit the boy causing marks andwasa prime case for child abuse." App. 152–153. The Winnebago County Department of Social Services (DSS) interviewed the father, but he denied the accusations, and DSS did not pursue them further. In January 1983, Joshua was admitted to a local hospital with multiple bruises and abrasions. The examining physician suspected child abuse and notified DSS, which imme- diately obtained an order from a Wisconsin juvenile court placing Joshua in the temporary custody of the hospital. Three days later, the county convened an ad hoc "Child Protection Team"—consisting of a pediatrician, a psychologist, a police detective, the county's lawyer, several DSS caseworkers, and various hospi- tal personnel—to consider Joshua's situation. At this meeting, the Team decided that there was insufficient evidence of child abuse to retain Joshua in the custody of the court. The Team did, however, decide to recommend several measures to protect Joshua, including enrolling him in a preschool program, providing his father with certain counselling services, and encouraging his father's girlfriend to move out of the home. Randy DeShaney entered into a voluntary agreement with DSS in which he promised to cooperate with them in accomplishing these goals.

Based on the recommendation of the Child Protection Team, the juvenile court dismissed the child protection case and returned Joshua to the custody of his father. A month later, emergency room personnel called the DSS caseworker handling Joshua's case to report that he had once again been treated for suspicious injuries. The caseworker concluded that there was no basis for action. For the next six months, the caseworker made monthly visits to the DeShaney home, during which she observed a number of suspicious injuries on Joshua's head; she also noticed that he had not been enrolled in school, and that the girlfriend had not moved out. The caseworker dutifully recorded these incidents in her files, along with her continuing suspicions that someone in the DeShaney household was physically abusing Joshua, but she did nothing more. In November 1983, the emergency room notified DSS that Joshua had been treated once again for injuries that they believed to be caused by child abuse. On the caseworker's next two visits to the DeShaney home, she was told that Joshua was too ill to see her. Still DSS took no action.

In March 1984, Randy DeShaney beat four-year-old Joshua so severely that he fell into a life-threatening coma. Emergency brain surgery revealed a series of hemorrhages caused by traumatic injuries to the head inflicted over a long period of time. Joshua did not die, but he suffered brain damage so severe that he is expected to spend the rest of his life confined to an institution for the profoundly retarded. Randy DeShaney was subsequently tried and convicted of child abuse. . . .

Because of the inconsistent approaches taken by the lower courts in determining when, if ever, the failure of a state or local governmental entity or its agents to provide an individual with adequate protective services constitutes a violation of the individual's due process rights, . . . and the importance of the issue to the administration of state and local governments, we granted certiorari . . .

The Due Process Clause of the Fourteenth Amendment provides that "[n]o State shall . . . deprive any person of life, liberty, or property, without due process of law." Petitioners contend that the State deprived Joshua of his liberty . . . by failing to provide him with adequate protection against his father's violence . . .

But nothing in the language of the Due Process Clause itself requires the State to protect the life, liberty, and property of its citizens against invasion by private actors. The Clause is phrased as a limitation on the State's power to act, not as a guarantee of certain minimal levels of safety and security. It forbids the State itself to deprive individuals of life, liberty, or property without "due process of law," but its language cannot fairly be extended to impose an affirmative obligation on the State to ensure that those interests do not come to harm through other means. Nor does history support such an expansive reading of the constitutional text. . . . Its purpose was to protect the people from the State, not to ensure that the State protected them from each other. The Framers were content to leave the extent of governmental obligation in the latter area to the democratic political processes.

Consistent with these principles, our cases have recognized that the Due Process Clauses generally confer no affirmative right to governmental aid, even where such aid may be necessary to secure life, liberty, or property interests of which the government itself may not deprive the individual. . . . If the Due Process Clause does not require the State to provide its citizens with particular protective services, it follows that the State cannot be held liable under the Clause for injuries that could have been averted had it chosen to provide them. As a general matter, then, we conclude that a State's failure to protect an individual against private violence simply does not constitute a violation of the Due Process Clause.

Petitioners contend, however, that even if the Due Process Clause imposes no affirmative obligation on the State to provide the general public with adequate protective services, such a duty may arise out of certain "special relationships" created or assumed by the State with respect to particular individuals. Brief for Petitioners 13–18. Petitioners argue that such a "special relationship" existed here because the State knew that Joshua faced a special danger of abuse at his father's hands, and specifically proclaimed, by word and by deed, its intention to protect him against that danger. Id., at 18–20. Having actually undertaken to protect Joshua from this danger—which petitioners concede the State played no part in creating—the State acquired an affirmative "duty," enforceable through the Due Process Clause, to do so in a reasonably competent fashion. Its failure to discharge that duty, so the argument goes, was an abuse of governmental power that so "shocks the conscience," Rochin v. California, 342 U.S. 165, 172, 72 S.Ct. 205, 209, 96 L.Ed. 183 (1952), as to constitute a substantive due process violation. . . .

But these cases afford petitioners no help. Taken together, they stand only for the proposition that when the State takes a person into its custody and holds him there against his will, the Constitution imposes upon it a corresponding duty to assume some responsibility for his safety and general well-being. . . . The rationale for this principle is simple enough: when the State by the affirmative exercise of its power so restrains an individual's liberty that it renders him unable to care for himself, and at the same time fails to provide for his basic human needs—e.g., food, clothing, shelter, medical care, and reasonable safety—it transgresses the substantive limits on state action set by the Eighth Amendment and the Due Process Clause. . . . The affirmative duty to protect arises not from the State's knowledge of the individual's predicament or from its expressions of intent to help him, but from the limitation which it has imposed on his freedom to act on his own behalf . . .

Petitioners concede that the harms Joshua suffered did not occur while he was in the State's custody, but while he was in the custody of his natural father, who was in no sense a state actor. While the State may have been aware of the dangers that Joshua faced in the free world, it played no part in their creation, nor did it do anything to render him any more vulnerable to them. That the State once took temporary custody of Joshua does not alter the analysis, for when it returned him to his father's custody, it placed him in no worse position than that in which he would have been had it not acted at all; the State does not become the permanent guarantor of an individual's safety by having once offered him shelter. Under these circumstances, the State had no constitutional duty to protect Joshua. . . .

Judges and lawyers, like other humans, are moved by natural sympathy in a case like this to find a way for Joshua and his mother to receive adequate compensation for the grievous harm inflicted upon them. But before yielding to that impulse, it is well to remember once again that the harm was inflicted not by the State of Wisconsin, but by Joshua's father. The most that can be said of the state functionaries in this case is that they stood by and did nothing when suspicious circumstances dictated a more active role for them. In defense of them it must also be said that had they moved too soon to take custody of the son away from the father, they would likely have been met with charges of improperly intruding into the parent-child relationship, charges based on the same Due Process Clause that forms the basis for the present charge of failure to provide adequate protection.

The people of Wisconsin may well prefer a system of liability which would place upon the State and its officials the responsibility for failure to act in situations such as the present one. They may create such a system, if they do not have it already, by changing the tort law of the State in accordance with the regular lawmaking process. But they should not have it thrust upon them by this Court's expansion of the Due Process Clause of the Fourteenth Amendment.

Affirmed.

JUSTICE BRENNAN with whom JUSTICE MARSHALL and JUSTICE BLACKMUN join, dissenting.

"The most that can be said of the state functionaries in this case," the Court today concludes, "is that they stood by and did nothing when suspicious circumstances dictated a more active role for them." . . . Because I believe that this description of respondents' conduct tells only part of the story and that, accordingly, the Constitution itself "dictated a more active role" for respondents in the circumstances presented here, I cannot agree that respondents had no constitutional duty to help Joshua DeShaney. . . .

The Court's baseline is the absence of positive rights in the Constitution and a concomitant suspicion of any claim that seems to depend on such rights. From this perspective, the DeShaneys' claim is first and foremost about inaction (the failure, here, of respondents to take steps to protect Joshua), and only tangentially about action (the establishment of a state program specifically designed to help children like Joshua). And from this perspective, holding these Wisconsin officials liable—where the only difference between this case and one involving a general claim to protective services is Wisconsin's establishment and operation of a program to protect children—would seem to punish an effort that we should seek to promote.

I would begin from the opposite direction. I would focus first on the action that Wisconsin *has* taken with respect to Joshua and children like him, rather than on the actions that the State failed to take . . .

Wisconsin has established a child-welfare system specifically designed to help children like Joshua. Wisconsin law places upon the local departments of social services such as respondent (DSS or Department) a duty to investigate reported instances of child abuse . . . While other governmental bodies and private persons are largely responsible for the reporting of possible cases of child abuse, . . . Wisconsin law channels all such reports to the local departments of social services for evaluation and, if necessary, further action. . . . Even when it is the sheriff's office or police department that receives a report of suspected child abuse, that report is referred to local social services departments for action, . . . the only exception to this occurs when the reporter fears for the child's *immediate* safety. . . . In this way, Wisconsin law invites—indeed, directs—citizens and other governmental entities to depend on local departments of social services such as respondent to protect children from abuse.

The specific facts before us bear out this view of Wisconsin's system of protecting children. Each time someone voiced a suspicion that Joshua was being abused, that information was relayed to the Department for investigation and possible action. When Randy DeShaney's second wife told the police that he had " 'hit the boy causing marks and [was] a prime case for child abuse,' " the police referred her complaint to DSS. . . . When, on three separate occasions, emergency room personnel noticed suspicious injuries on Joshua's body, they went to DSS with this information. . . . When neighbors informed the police that they had seen or heard Joshua's father or his father's lover beating or otherwise abusing Joshua, the police brought these reports to the attention of DSS. . . . And when respondent Kemmeter, through these reports and through her own observations in the course of nearly 20 visits to the DeShaney home, . . . compiled growing evidence that Joshua was being abused, that information stayed within the Department—chronicled by the social worker in detail that seems almost eerie in light of her failure to act upon it. (As to the extent of the social worker's involvement in, and knowledge of, Joshua's predicament, her reaction to the news of Joshua's last and most devastating injuries is illuminating: "I just knew the phone would ring some day and Joshua would be dead.' ")

Even more telling than these examples is the Department's control over the decision whether to take steps to protect a particular child from suspected abuse. While many different people contributed information and advice to this decision, it was up to the people at DSS to make the ultimate decision (subject to the approval of the local government's corporation counsel) whether to disturb the family's current arrangements. . . . When Joshua first appeared at a local hospital with injuries signaling physical abuse, for example, it was DSS that made the decision to take him into temporary custody for the purpose of studying his situation—and it was DSS, acting in conjunction with the corporation counsel, that returned him to his father. . . . Unfortunately for Joshua DeShaney, the buck effectively stopped with the Department . . .

Because of the posture of this case, we do not know why respondents did not take steps to protect Joshua; the Court, however, tells us that their reason is irrelevant so long as their inaction was not the product of invidious discrimination. Presumably, then, if respondents decided not to help Joshua because his name began with a "J," or because he was born in the spring, or because they did not care enough about him even to formulate an intent to discriminate against him based on an arbitrary reason, respondents would not be liable to the DeShaneys because they were not the ones who dealt the blows that destroyed Joshua's life.

I do not suggest that such irrationality was at work in this case; I emphasize only that we do not know whether or not it was. I would allow Joshua and his mother the opportunity to show that respondents' failure to help him arose, not out of the sound exercise of professional judgment that we recognized . . . as sufficient to preclude liability, . . . but from the kind of arbitrariness that we have in the past condemned. . . .

As the Court today reminds us, "the Due Process Clause of the Fourteenth Amendment was intended to prevent government 'from abusing its power, or employing it as an instrument of oppression.' " . . . My disagreement with the Court arises from its failure to see that inaction can be every bit as abusive of power as action, that oppression can result when a State undertakes a vital duty and then ignores it. Today's opinion construes the Due Process Clause to permit a State to displace private sources of protection and then, at the critical moment, to shrug its shoulders and turn away from the harm that it has promised to try to prevent. Because I cannot agree that our Constitution is indifferent to such indifference, I respectfully dissent.

JUSTICE BLACKMUN, dissenting.

Today, the Court purports to be the dispassionate oracle of the law, unmoved by "natural sympathy." . . . But, in this pretense, the Court itself retreats into a sterile formalism which prevents it from recognizing either the facts of the case before it or the legal norms that should apply to those facts. As JUSTICE BRENNAN demonstrates, the facts here involve not mere passivity, but active state intervention in the life of Joshua DeShaney—intervention that triggered a fundamental duty to aid the boy once the State learned of the severe danger to which he was exposed.

The Court fails to recognize this duty because it attempts to draw a sharp and rigid line between action and inaction. But such formalistic reasoning has no place in the interpretation of the broad and stirring Clauses of the Fourteenth Amendment. Indeed, I submit that these Clauses were designed, at least in part, to undo the formalistic legal reasoning that infected antebellum jurisprudence . . .

Like the antebellum judges who denied relief to fugitive slaves, . . . the Court today claims that its decision, however harsh, is compelled by existing legal doctrine. On the contrary, the question presented by this case is an open one, and our Fourteenth Amendment precedents may be read more broadly or narrowly depending upon how one chooses to read them. Faced with the choice, I would adopt a "sympathetic" reading, one which comports with dictates of fundamental justice and recognizes that compassion need not be exiled from the province of judging. . . .

Poor Joshua! Victim of repeated attacks by an irresponsible, bullying, cowardly, and intemperate father, and abandoned by respondents who placed him in a dangerous predicament and who knew or learned what was going on, and yet did essentially nothing except . . . "dutifully recorded these incidents in [their] files." It is a sad commentary upon American life, and constitutional principles —so full of late of patriotic fervor and proud proclamations about "liberty and justice for all,"—that this child, Joshua DeShaney, now is assigned to live out the remainder of his life profoundly retarded. . . . Joshua and his mother, as petitioners here, deserve—but now are denied by this Court—the opportunity to have the facts of their case considered in the light of constitutional protection . . .

BIBLIOGRAPHY

BJORKLUND, DENNIS A. "Crossing DeShaney . . ." *Iowa Law Review* 75, no. 3 (March 1990): 791.

BOURNE, RICHARD, AND ELI H. NEWBERGER. *Critical Perspectives on Child Abuse.* Lexington, 1979.

PEGELOW, MILDRED D. *Family Violence.* Praeger, 1984.

TOMLINSON, JOHN D. "Constitutional Law—Due Process Clause . . ." *University of Detroit Law Review* 67, no. 1, (Fall, 1989): 635.

WINCHENBACH, LINDA. "Snake Pits and Slippery Slopes: DeShaney Revisited." *American Bar Association Journal* 75 (September, 1989): 62.

ZIRKEL, PERRY A. "Poor Joshua." *Phi Delata Kappan* 70 (June 1989): 828.

PART TWO:

"Congress Shall Make No Law"

AMERICANS ARE A diverse and often disputatious people. They belong to many religions and to none; they speak their minds on every issue that invites argument; they publish thousands of newspapers, magazines, and leaflets; and they march and picket for a multitude of causes that span the political spectrum. Every American city or town has its zealots and dissenters, who often press their views on other citizens in ways that some find annoying or disruptive. Many people resent doorbell ringers, street-corner orators, gossip tabloids, and placard wavers. But we generally tolerate those who set up shop in the "marketplace of ideas" that keeps us informed and fuels our debates on public issues.

But tolerance has its limits. Some ideas and opinions are offensive to many people, and their expression is considered harmful to society. The limits of free expression raise tough questions. Can school officials ask ministers and rabbis to offer prayers at graduations? Should cities be allowed to ban the sale of films and videos that "degrade" women? Should newspapers be required to sell advertising space to those who call the Nazi Holocaust a myth? Can racial bigots be punished for burning crosses on the lawns of African-Americans?

These are not easy questions to answer. And none of them was asked of the men who framed the Bill of Rights. But the framers had bitter memories of efforts by their British rulers to coerce religious belief, to punish "seditious" speech and writings, and to prohibit gatherings of citizens who objected to colonial rule. Led by James Madison of Virginia, they drafted a set of amendments that began with a powerful limitation on the national legislature: "Congress shall make no law respecting an establishment of religion, or prohibiting the free exercise thereof; or abridging the freedom of speech, or of the press; or the right of the people peaceably to assemble, and to petition the government for a redress of grievances."

The First Amendment is not only first in order but also in power. It protects those rights of the people that are paramount in importance. The framers knew from experience that rights of free expression meant nothing if they were not protected from governmental restriction. But it took the Supreme Court more than a century after ratification of the First Amendment to define its limitations. The first case that raised a free speech claim under the First Amendment was sparked by opposition to World War One. Congress moved to punish antiwar agitation with a Sedition Act that provided criminal penalties for speech and writing that "interfered" with military recruiting. Charles Schenck, a Socialist party organizer, circulated a leaflet urging young men to exercise "your right to assert your opposition to the draft." Upholding Schenck's five-year prison term, the Supreme Court rejected his First Amendment claim of free speech. Justice Olive Wendell Holmes announced the "clear and present danger" test of prohibited speech. Schenck's leaflet encouraged draft resistance, Holmes wrote, and thus failed the Court's test. Holmes added a famous line to his opinion: "The most stringent protection of free speech would not protect a man in falsely shouting fire in a theater and causing a panic."

During the years after World War One, those who shouted "fire" the loudest were Communists, who supported the Russian Revolution and advocated a second American Revolution. Many states enacted laws to punish Communists. Benjamin Gitlow was convicted of violating New York's "criminal anarchy" law. Ruling on his appeal, the Supreme Court confronted an 1833 decision that the Bill of Rights applied only to the federal government and did not limit "the government of the individual states" in the field of free expression. But the Court held that the Fourteenth Amendment guarantee of "liberty" for all citizens protected freedom of speech and press "from impairment by the States." Despite this ruling, the Court upheld Gitlow's conviction: "A single revolutionary spark may kindle a fire that . . . may burst into a sweeping and destructive conflagration."

Can words alone—whether spoken or written—really set minds afire and threaten a social conflagration? Many people think so, and many laws have tried to extinguish speech that inflames emotions. The Supreme Court has agreed that certain kinds of speech are so harmful to society that they do not deserve constitutional protection. "These include the lewd and obscene, the profane, the libelous, and the insulting or 'fighting' words." However they are expressed, the Court said in 1942, such words "are no essential part of any exposition of ideas." The concept that some forms of expression are not protected by the First Amendment has provoked hundreds of Supreme Court cases over the past five decades.

Few of these cases have been easy to decide, because they raise the most fundamental questions of the limits of free expression in a free society.

The most difficult question the Supreme Court faces in First Amendment cases is whether the citizen or the state bears the burden of persuasion. The answer to this question will most often decide the outcome. Over the years, the Court has vacillated between two tests. One stresses "the preferred place given in our scheme to the . . . indispensable democratic freedoms secured by the First Amendment." Under this "preferred position" test, government officials must prove a "compelling" reason for laws that restrict free expression. Governments usually fail this stringent test. The alternate test is much easier to pass. This "involves a balancing by the courts of the competing interests at stake" in the case. The "balancing" test places the government's heavy thumb on the scales of justice. Laws judged by this test rarely fail to pass.

The Supreme Court has shifted over the years between the "preferred position" and "balancing" tests in First Amendment cases. In more than a thousand cases decided between 1942 and 1993, the Court has generally upheld the rights of individuals against governmental restrictions. But the justices have consistently applied another test to challenged laws. The "time, place, and manner" test allows reasonable restrictions on free expression to protect the public. Under this test, people can voice their opinions in streets and parks, but not in residential neighborhoods at 3 A.M. They can picket abortion clinics, but they cannot block access to patients. They can use loudspeakers, but not above reasonable decibel levels. Applying this test has not been easy, but the Court has generally allowed protest that takes place in a "public forum" and that does not disrupt the peace and quiet of residential areas.

The cases argued in this section involve every provision of the First Amendment. The first clause of that amendment prohibits any "establishment" of religion. Does that clause ban prayers in public schools? Over thirty years, from 1962 to 1992, the Supreme Court held consistently that official prayers—even those designated as "nonsectarian"—violate the Constitution. The Court has also dealt with laws that place theories of "evolution" and "creationism" against each other. Again, the Court has been consistent in ruling against state restrictions. The First Amendment also protects the "free exercise" of religion. Can minorities like the Amish escape laws that require public school attendance past the eighth grade? The Court's ruling in religion cases have generally maintained the "wall of separation" between church and state and protected the rights of religious minorities.

The "freedom of speech" clause of the First Amendment has provoked the most difficult cases in the Court's history. Words can be potent weapons in the battle of ideas, and "symbolic speech" can be more powerful than words alone. Does the First Amendment protect students who wear black armbands to class as a protest against the Vietnam War? Can the free speech clause be stretched to cover those who burn the American flag as a political statement? Equally hard questions are raised in free press cases. Most Americans oppose government censorship, and the First Amendment was designed to prevent any "prior restraint" on the press. In 1931 the Supreme Court carved an exception to prevent the "publication of the sailing dates of transports or the number and location of troops" during wartime. Does the "troop ship" exception allow the government to ban the publication of classified documents in an official history of the Vietnam War?

The last clause of the First Amendment guarantees "the right of the people peaceably to assemble, and to petition the government for a redress of grievances." Does this clause protect a civil rights organizer who leads a chanting, singing crowd to a courthouse and demands the release of jailed "sit-in" protesters? The Supreme Court has added up all the First Amendment clauses and found an additional freedom, the right of association. Does that right extend to members of the Communist Party, charged during the heyday of Senator Joe McCarthy with advocating the violent overthrow of the government?

All these tough questions were argued before the Supreme Court, with skilled advocates on both sides. The Court's opinions in these cases have sparked controversy—particularly those banning school prayer and protecting flag burners—but they have protected all Americans from what Justice Louis Brandeis called "the occasional tyrannies of governing majorities." For it is a principle of democratic government that today's majority will often become tomorrow's minority and need the protection of the First Amendment to worship, speak, publish, and assemble. The framers recognized the need to place these essential rights, as Justice Robert Jackson wrote in 1943, "beyond the reach of majorities." Our First Amendment rights, he added, "may not be submitted to vote; they depend on the outcome of no elections." Over the past half-century, the Supreme Court has given the First Amendment its place of primacy in the Bill of Rights.

Abington School District v. Schempp

374 U.S. 203 (1963)

The Pennsylvania legislature voted in 1959 that "ten verses from the Holy Bible shall be read" every day in each public school. Students could be excused on a written request from their parents. In Abington Senior High School near Philadelphia, Bible reading was followed by recitation of the Lord's Prayer. Roger and Donna Schempp were students at Abington and belonged to the Unitarian church, whose members reject the Christian Trinity. They sued the school district, claiming that Bible reading violated the establishment clause of the First Amendment. Trial testimony showed that New Testament passages offended Jewish and other non-Christian students. The Supreme Court ruled in 1963 that schools could not favor Christianity over other religions: "In the relationship between man and religion," Justice Tom Clark wrote, "the state is firmly committed to a position of neutrality."

TRANSCRIPT OF EDITED AND NARRATED ARGUMENTS IN
Abington School District v. *Schempp*, 374 U.S. 203 (1963)

Counsel for petitioners: Philip Ward, Philadelphia, Pennsylvania
Counsel for respondents: Henry Sawyer, Philadelphia, Pennsylvania

Chief Justice Earl Warren: Number 142, School District of Abington Township, Pennsylvania, et al., appellants, versus Edward Lewis Schempp, et al.

Narrator: It's February 27th, 1963. Chief Justice Earl Warren has called a case that challenges Bible reading and the Lord's Prayer in public schools. The issue is emotional and divisive. Polls show most Americans support classroom prayer. They feel it fosters morality and good behavior. Others argue that prayer should be personal and private. The New Testament and Lord's Prayer are Christian. Reading and reciting them could offend Jews and other non-Christians.

Today's argument goes to the beginning of the Bill of Rights, the first clause of the First Amendment. "Congress shall make no law respecting an establishment of religion." The Supreme Court applies this provision to all governments, federal, state, and local. The First Amendment is written in sweeping terms. "No law," Justice Hugo Black often said, "means no law." But what *is* an establishment of religion? America was settled by people who opposed the established church of England and religious orthodoxy. But most of the colonies set up established religions. They punished dissenters like Quakers, Baptists, and Catholics with fines, banishment, even death.

The establishment clause erected, the Supreme Court said, a "wall of separation" between church and state. Does that wall keep out any reference to God or public devotion? Our currency reads, "In God We Trust." The Pledge of Allegiance refers to "one nation, under God." Chaplains open sessions of Congress with prayer. And the Court has agreed that "we are a religious people whose institutions presuppose a Supreme Being."

But the Court has resisted efforts to bring the Bible and prayer into public schools. All children must attend school. But not all are Christian or even religious. In 1962 the Supreme Court ruled that New York teachers could not recite an official prayer in their classes. The establishment clause, Justice Black wrote, "put an end to governmental control of religion and of prayer." But the case did not end debate—often in loud voices—over school prayer.

Today's argument continues that debate, with quieter voices. The case began in a suburb of Philadelphia, Pennsylvania. Roger and Donna Schempp are students at Abington Senior High School. They belong to the Unitarian church, whose members reject the Christian Trinity. Pennsylvania law requires daily Bible reading in all schools. Roger and Donna challenged that law. They won in a lower court and the state appealed. Chief Justice Warren welcomes the state's lawyer, Philip Ward.

Warren: Mr. Ward.

Ward: May it please the Court. This case is here on an appeal from the decision of a three-judge district court that held Pennsylvania's Bible-reading statute to be an unconstitutional establishment of religion. We shall argue that the religious liberties of the Schempps, who are the appellees, the plaintiffs in this case, are not infringed; that this case doesn't concern the establishment of religion within the meaning of the Constitution; and that there is no requirement that Pennsylvania must give up an ancient custom simply because it involves the use of the Bible.

We also believe that this case is different from any of the cases, the church-state cases this Court has heretofore considered. We think we have a novel factual situation here. We think the question presented to this Court for the first time is, What does the Constitution require us to do with an old tradition that has undoubted secular value? It's noncompulsory, but yet, it in some ways reflects the religious origin of the country.

Narrator: Ward described what happens in Abington schools.

Ward: At Abington, this is the way it works: between 8:15 and 8:30 on every school day, all the children are in their home rooms, advisory sections. There's a public address system in each of their rooms. At 8:15 the morning exercise starts. First they have what's called an introduction, a "fact for the day." They pull something out of the World Almanac to gain the attention of the children —Mt. Everest is 29,000 feet high—something like that to get them thinking. This is followed by ten verses of the Bible, read without comment. The ten verses of the Bible is followed by the Lord's Prayer, which in turn is followed by the flag salute, which in turn is followed by the school announcements for the day—"The botany class will meet in room A instead of room B." Then you have a conclusion, at which they announce the children who read the preceding announcements. These announcements, this reading, the fact for the day, the Bible, the prayer, are done by the children of the, the students of the television and radio workshop, which is a regular course of the English department at Abington. There are about thirty students in this course, and it's voluntary.

Narrator: Ward defended the Bible as a source of common morality.

Ward: How do we use the Bible in the schools? We say, and the statute says, to bring lessons in morality to the children. The Schempps say, no, you can't be doing this. How can you teach anything, how can you bring lessons in morality to the children, how is it a proper way to teach if you only use one source, we only use one book? If you don't allow any comment to be made on what is being read? If you don't select particular passages that are unusually good? They say, this can't be teaching morality. They say, you're not teaching morality. What in fact you're doing, they say, is you are teaching some kind of a public school creed that doesn't have religion, that's cut adrift from theology.

Gentlemen, that is precisely what we're doing. We're teaching morality without religion, cut adrift from theology. And that is proper for the people of Pennsylvania. We can bring to our children lessons of morality in their school days, as long as we're not bringing religion, not bringing theology. The people of Pennsylvania have wanted to do this, they have since the beginning wanted to bring these lessons in morality to the children. So what do they do? They pick a common source of morality, the Bible.

Narrator: Chief Justice Warren had a question.

Warren: Mr. Ward, may I ask you this, please? Suppose we accept your argument, that this ceremony is moral instruction and is not in any sense religious. And suppose the state next says: following these ceremonies each morning, there shall be one hour of instruction in morals, and during that hour of instruction, nothing shall be done except to read the Bible to the students, and all must attend except those whose parents object to it. Do you think that would be acceptable also?

Ward: I think, as the case before us now, ten verses is acceptable. I think I agree with you, Chief Justice, it could become so bad that you couldn't, reasonable men couldn't say, they are teaching morality. They would have to say, they are doing nothing but using the Bible to indoctrinate those children with religion.

Warren: Well, would an hour of instruction in morals be unconstitutional if a few moments of instruction would not be?

Ward: I think that would be a question of fact. I would think an hour, taken out of the school day, for morality—as Mr. Justice Brennan said, morality is a very important thing to teach. I don't know.

Warren: It is, it is, very important.

Ward: I don't know. I know if the people of Pennsylvania think that's a good way to teach morality, I think the problem would be for the Court to determine.

Narrator: Ward concluded his argument.

Ward: You can sum up our particular problem as this: Can you use, can you keep a tradition which has secular values? It does teach morality. It is noncompulsory; the child doesn't have to be there. But the only problem is, it involves part of the religious tradition of this country. It deals with a document that is of obvious religious origin and to many people an obviously religious book. Must the government rip out that document, that tradition, simply because it involves a religious book? Must the government, any time any tradition, in any way, reflects the fact that we are a religious people—must they rip out any tradition even, even if that tradition nobody has to abide by? The tradition isn't trying to teach anybody anything. The tradition isn't requiring a person to believe or disbelieve. The tradition has secular value; it has a purpose, like the Sunday closing. It has a purpose, to teach morality to the children.

Narrator: Chief Justice Warren welcomed the Schempp's lawyer, Henry Sawyer.

Warren: Mr. Sawyer.

Sawyer: Mr. Chief Justice, and may it please the Court.
    You cannot separate the moral leaven from the religious leaven in the Bible. I think the two go absolutely together. And it teaches—they say it doesn't proselytize—it *teaches*, the book teaches from the opening chapter of Genesis to the last chapter of Revelations. It teaches; it teaches the way the world was created, and it teaches in a sectarian sense from the opening. From the very opening it says, And lo, the Spirit was upon the waters. And in the King James Version, and I'm sure the Douay Version, that word is capitalized. It means the Holy Ghost. This is the beginning of a teaching of the concept of Trinity. It teaches.
    The New Testament is a teaching message. When Jesus said, "Others have said unto you, an eye for an eye and a tooth for a tooth, but I say unto you, thou shall resist not evil. If one smites thee upon one cheek," and so on. This is teaching. And it was highly controversial teaching then, and I submit to your honors, it's highly controversial teaching now. Men do not agree about these things.

Narrator: The First Amendment also protects the "free exercise" of religion. Sawyer's answer to claims that this clause allows school prayer drew questions from Justice Potter Stewart.

Sawyer: The question is, Is it a constitutional right under the free exercise clause to have the state conduct the prayer, or to pray, in other words, under the aegis of the state? And I think clearly not. Even if the overwhelming majority so feel, I think it probably has nothing to do with the question of majorities.

Stewart: Well, let's assume, let's assume there was no statute here, but that they had a student government in this Abington Township high school, which is fairly typical of many public high schools, and the students voted overwhelmingly that they wanted to begin their day by having one of their number— perhaps on a rotating basis—read ten verses from the Bible, whichever Bible the particular student, the reader chose that morning, to begin the school day. And this was attacked under the Constitution, and there was evidence from all of these people who voted that "our religious beliefs tell us we want to do this, in the free exercise of our religion." What kind of case would you have then?

Sawyer: May I ask a question just on the facts? Is this a case . . .

Stewart: I make up the facts as I go along. *(laughter)*

Sawyer: Yes, sir. Do the school authorities say, well then, certainly you can use the PA system and we'll get the children together?

Stewart: Well, yes, the children *are* together, they are together.

Sawyer: What would they be doing otherwise? In other words, I'll answer it this way. If, pursuant to that, the school authorities say, yes, you may use the PA system, we'll have the children doing not something else at the time in the classrooms, then I'd say that it's an establishment nonetheless.

Stewart: Isn't it a gross interference with the free exercise of their religion, of those, in my imaginary case, those ninety-eight percent of the student body who say, our religious beliefs tell us that this is what we want to do?

Sawyer: They have a right to do it, Your Honor, but they haven't got a right to get the state to help them.

Narrator: Dr. Solomon Grayzel, a Jewish scholar, told the lower court that parts of the New Testament were "offensive to Jewish tradition." Verses about Jesus as Messiah could be "psychologically harmful" to Jewish and other non-Christian students. Sawyer stressed this testimony.

Sawyer: The New Testament, the concept of Christ, a man who historically lived, as being the Son of God, is, as Dr. Grayzel testified, to Judaism a blasphemy. This was in fact Christ's crime. It is a blasphemy. You can't gloss this over by saying there's some minor differences. He pointed out that there's ridicule of the Jewish hierarchy throughout the New Testament. He pointed out, and think of it, gentlemen, the scene of the trial of Jesus before Pilate, where the multitude cries not for Barrabas but for Jesus, and Pilate washes his hands. And the version exculpates the Romans for the death of Christ. And then the Jews say, and they're so described, they say, his blood be upon us and our children. And Dr. Grayzel said that sentence has been responsible for more anti-Semitism than any single sentence in history, and I can't doubt it.

Narrator: Sawyer returned to the establishment clause.

Sawyer: Well, we say that there is an establishment. In addition to that, it's clear as crystal and just ingenuous to say that this doesn't prefer one religion over another. And how fine you chop it is another thing. But certainly at the grossest, and at the broadest, and in any sense of the word it prefers Christian religions over non-Christian religions. I think it goes further than that. And that you cannot do, and that the statute does. It is a religious exercise, it seems to me; it was intended to be a religious exercise. I think it's ingenuous to suggest that the legislature had anything else in mind but that. I don't think that you can use the word morality to encompass all that is purveyed to the minds of children by this book. There will be many, many things read, out of the King James Version, which will exclusively—if you can separate them, gentlemen—but it will exclusively concern religious concepts and ideas, without any distinguishable moral truth.

Narrator: Sawyer faced a final question.

Court: Mr. Sawyer, what do you say to Mr. Ward's argument that, well, even if it is religion, it's religious tradition?

Sawyer: I think tradition is not to be scoffed at. But let me say this very candidly. I think it is the final arrogance to talk constantly about "our religious tradition" in this country and equate it with this Bible. Sure, religious tradition. *Whose*

religious tradition? It isn't any part of the religious tradition of a substantial
number of Americans, of a great many, a great many things, and really some of
the salient features of the King James Version, or the Douay Version, for that
matter. And it's just to me a little bit easy and I say arrogant to keep talking
about "our religious tradition." It suggests that the public schools, at least of
Pennsylvania, are a kind of Protestant institution to which others are cordially
invited. And I think to some extent they have been, in our state.

But we have here, in the schools of Pennsylvania, the conducting, mandated by statute, day after day, as an exercise, the reading of the sacred book of
Christianity.

Narrator: On June 17th, 1963, the Supreme Court ruled in favor of Roger and
Donna Schempp. Public schools could not use the Bible and prayer for classroom devotion. Justice Tom Clark wrote the Court's opinion. "The place of
religion in our society," he said, "is an exalted one." But religion's proper place,
Clark added, is in "the home, the church, and . . . the individual heart and
mind." He restated the Court's earlier rulings: "In the relationship between man
and religion, the State is firmly committed to a position of neutrality."

Clark denied that Bible reading simply aided in teaching morality. He
noted "the pervading religious character" of the classroom ceremony and its
official endorsement of Christian belief. Clark emphasized that "the Bible is
worthy of study for its literary and historic qualities" in classes that do not involve
"religious exercises."

Only Justice Potter Stewart dissented. He focused on the First Amendment's "free exercise" clause. Stewart answered Justice Clark. "If schools are to
be truly neutral in the matter of religion," he wrote, they must accommodate
parents who "desire to have their children's school day open with the reading of
passages from the Bible."

Outside the Court, many Americans joined Stewart's dissent. "We are a
Christian nation, under God," one Congressman said. "These decisions do not
help us to be on God's side." Polls showed nearly seventy percent of the public
approved of school prayer. Reverend Billy Graham agreed. "I don't believe that
a small minority should rule the majority of the people." But other religious
leaders supported the Court. "The decision is a good one, deeply rooted in the
spirit of the First Amendment," wrote the editors of a Protestant journal. A
Catholic journal praised the Court for protecting students against "religious
values which they do not accept." And almost all Jewish leaders praised the
decision.

The Supreme Court decides constitutional questions. But it cannot decide
political controversies. The Court has reaffirmed its school prayer decisions
many times since 1963. And yet, many teachers continue to lead students in

Bible reading and prayer. Few issues show such a collision of majority sentiment with minority sensitivity. Perhaps the best commentary comes from Justice Robert Jackson. His classic opinion in 1943 upheld the rights of students who belong to religious minorities: "The very purpose of a Bill of Rights," he said, "was to withdraw certain subjects from . . . political controversy, to place them beyond the reach of majorities." Jackson understood that matters of faith cannot be decided by majority vote.

EDITED SUPREME COURT OPINIONS
Abington School Dist. v. Schempp.

MR. JUSTICE CLARK delivered the opinion of the Court.

Once again we are called upon to consider the scope of the provision of the First Amendment to the United States Constitution which declares that "Congress shall make no law respecting an establishment of religion, or prohibiting the free exercise thereof . . ." In light of the history of the First Amendment and of our cases interpreting and applying its requirements, we hold that the practices at issue and the laws requiring them are unconstitutional under the Establishment Clause, as applied to the States through the Fourteenth Amendment. . . .

The Commonwealth of Pennsylvania by law, . . . requires that "At least ten verses from the Holy Bible shall be read, without comment, at the opening of each public school on each school day. Any child shall be excused from such Bible reading, or attending such Bible reading, upon the written request of his parent or guardian." The Schempp family, husband and wife and two of their three children, brought suit to enjoin enforcement of the statute, contending that their rights under the Fourteenth Amendment to the Constitution of the United States are, have been, and will continue to be violated unless this statute be declared unconstitutional as violative of these provisions of the First Amendment. . . . A three-judge statutory District Court for the Eastern District of Pennsylvania held that the statute is violative of the Establishment Clause of the First Amendment as applied to the States by the Due Process Clause of the Fourteenth Amendment and directed that appropriate injunctive relief issue. . . .

The appellees Edward Lewis Schempp, his wife Sidney, and their children, Roger and Donna, are of the Unitarian faith and are members of the Unitarian Church in Germantown, Philadelphia, Pennsylvania, where they, as well as another son, Ellory, regularly attend religious services. . . .

At the first trial Edward Schempp and the children testified as to specific religious doctrines purveyed by a literal reading of the Bible "which were contrary to the religious beliefs which they held and to their familial teaching." . . . The children testified that all of the doctrines to which they referred were read to them at various times as part of the exercises. Edward Schempp testified at the second trial that he had considered having Roger and Donna excused from attendance at the exercises but decided against it for several reasons, including his belief that the children's relationships with their teachers and classmates would be adversely affected. . . .

The trial court, in striking down the practices and the statute requiring them, made specific findings of fact that the children's attendance at Abington Senior High School is compulsory and that the practice of reading 10 verses from the Bible is also compelled by law. It also found that: . . .

"The fact that some pupils, or theoretically all pupils, might be excused from attendance at the exercises does not mitigate the obligatory nature of the ceremony. . . . The record demonstrates that it was the intention of . . . the Commonwealth . . . to introduce a religious ceremony into the public schools of the Commonwealth." . . .

It is true that religion has been closely identified with our history and government. As we said in *Engel* v. *Vitale* (1962), "The history of man is inseparable from the history of religion. And . . . since the beginning of that history many people have devoutly believed that 'More things are wrought by prayer than this world dreams of.' " . . . We gave specific recognition to the proposition that "[w]e are a religious people whose institutions presuppose a Supreme Being." The fact that the Founding Fathers believed devotedly that there was a God and that the unalienable rights of man were rooted in Him is clearly evidenced in their writings, from the Mayflower Compact to the Constitution itself. This background is evidenced today in our public life through the continuance in our oaths of office from the Presidency to the Alderman of the final supplication, "So help me God." Likewise each House of the Congress provides through its Chaplain an opening prayer, and the sessions of this Court are declared open by the crier in a short ceremony, the final phrase of which invokes the grace of God. . . . It can be truly said, therefore, that today, as in the beginning, our national life reflects a religious people who, in the words of Madison, are "earnestly praying, as . . . in duty bound, that the Supreme Lawgiver of the Universe . . . guide them into every measure which may be worthy of his [blessing. . . .]" . . .

This is not to say, however, that religion has been so identified with our history and government that religious freedom is not likewise as strongly imbedded in our public and private life. Nothing but the most telling of personal experiences in religious persecution suffered by our forebears, . . . could have planted our belief in liberty of religious opinion any more deeply in our heritage. . . . [T]he views of Madison and Jefferson, preceded by Roger Williams, came to be incorporated not only in the Federal Constitution but likewise in those of most of our States. This freedom to worship was indispensable in a country whose people came from the four quarters of the earth and brought with them a diversity of religious opinion. Today authorities list eighty-three separate religious bodies, each with membership exceeding fifty thousand, existing among our people, as well as innumerable smaller groups. . . .

First, this Court has decisively settled that the First Amendment's mandate that "Congress shall make no law respecting an establishment of religion, or prohibiting the free exercise thereof" has been made wholly applicable to the States by the Fourteenth Amendment. . . .

Second, this Court has rejected unequivocally the contention that the Establishment Clause forbids only governmental preference of one religion over another. . . .

Finally, in *Engel* v. *Vitale*, only last year, these principles were so universally recognized that the Court . . . held that "it is no part of the business of government to compose official prayers for any group of the American people to recite as a part of a religious program carried on by government." . . . In discussing the reach of the Establishment and Free Exercise Clauses of the First Amendment the Court said: . . .

> "When the power, prestige and financial support of government is placed behind a particular religious belief, the indirect coercive pressure upon religious minorities to conform to the prevailing officially approved religion is plain." . . .

And in further elaboration the Court found that the "first and most immediate purposeof the Establishment Clauserested on the belief that a union of government and religion tends to destroy government and to degrade religion." . . .

The conclusion follows that . . . the laws require religious exercises and such exercises are being conducted in direct violation of the rights of the appellees and petitioners. Nor are these required exercises mitigated by the fact that individual students may absent themselves upon parental request, for that fact furnishes no defense to a claim of unconstitutionality under the Establishment Clause. . . . Further, it is no defense to urge that the religious practices here may be relatively minor encroachments on the First Amendment. The breach of neutrality that is today a trickling stream may all too soon become a raging torrent . . .

The place of religion in our society is an exalted one, achieved through a long tradition of reliance on the home, the church and the inviolable citadel of the individual heart and mind. We have come to recognize through bitter experience that it is not within the power of government to invade that citadel, whether its purpose or effect be to aid or oppose, to advance or retard. In the relationship between man and religion, the State is firmly committed to a position of neutrality. Though the application of that rule requires interpretation of a delicate sort, the rule itself is clearly and concisely stated in the words of the First Amendment. Applying that rule to the facts of these cases, we affirm the judgment. . . .

MR. JUSTICE STEWART, dissenting.

The First Amendment declares that "Congress shall make no law respecting an establishment of religion, or prohibiting the free exercise thereof. . . ." It is, I think, a fallacious oversimplification to regard these two provisions as establishing a single constitutional standard of "separation of church and state," which can be mechanically applied in every case to delineate the required boundaries between government and religion. We err in the first place if we do not recognize, as a matter of history and as a matter of the imperatives of our free society, that religion and government must necessarily interact in countless ways. Secondly, the fact is that while in many contexts the Establishment Clause and the Free Exercise Clause fully complement each other, there are areas in which a doctrinaire reading of the Establishment Clause leads to irreconcilable conflict with the Free Exercise Clause.

A single obvious example should suffice to make the point. Spending federal funds to employ chaplains for the armed forces might be said to violate the Establishment Clause. Yet a lonely soldier stationed at some faraway outpost could surely complain that a government which did *not* provide him the opportunity for pastoral guidance was affirmatively prohibiting the free exercise of his religion. And such examples could readily be multiplied. The short of the matter is simply that the two relevant clauses of the First Amendment cannot accurately be reflected in a sterile metaphor which by its very nature may distort rather than illumine the problems involved in a particular case. . . .

Unlike other First Amendment guarantees, there is an inherent limitation upon the applicability of the Establishment Clause's ban on state support to religion. . . .

That the central value embodied in the First Amendment—and, more particularly, in the guarantee of "liberty" contained in the Fourteenth—is the safeguarding of an individual's right to free exercise of his religion has been consistently recognized. . . .

It is this concept of constitutional protection embodied in our decisions which makes the cases before us such difficult ones for me. For there is involved in this case a substantial free exercise claim on the part of those who affirmatively desire to have their children's school day open with the reading of passages from the Bible. . . . It might be argued here that parents who wanted their children to be exposed to religious influences in school could . . . send their children to private or parochial schools. But the consideration which renders this contention too facile to be determinative has already been recognized by the Court: "Freedom of speech, freedom of the press, freedom of religion are available to all, not merely to those who can pay their own way." (*Murdock* v. *Pennsylvania*) . . .

It might also be argued that parents who want their children exposed to religious influences can adequately fulfill that wish off school property and outside school time. With all its surface persuasiveness, however, this argument seriously misconceives the basic constitutional justification for permitting the exercises at issue in these cases. For a compulsory state educational system so structures a child's life that if religious exercises are held to be an impermissible activity in schools, religion is placed at an artificial and state-created disadvantage. Viewed in this light, permission of such exercises for those who want them is necessary if the schools are truly to be neutral in the matter of religion. And a refusal to permit religious exercises thus is seen, not as the realization of state neutrality, but rather as the establishment of a religion of secularism, or at the least, as government support of the beliefs of those who think that religious exercises should be conducted only in private. . . .

In the *Schempp* case the record shows no more than a subjective prophecy by a parent of what he thought would happen if a request were made to be excused from participation in the exercises under the amended statute. No such request was ever made, and there is no evidence whatever as to what might or would actually happen, nor of what administrative arrangements the school actually might or could make to free from pressure of any kind those who do not want to participate in the exercises. . . .

What our Constitution indispensably protects is the freedom of each of us, be he Jew or Agnostic, Christian or Atheist, Buddhist or Freethinker, to believe or disbelieve, to worship or not worship, to pray or keep silent, according to his own conscience, uncoerced and unrestrained by government. It is conceivable that these school boards, or even all school boards, might eventually find it impossible to administer a system of religious exercises during school hours in such a way as to meet this constitutional standard—in such a way as completely to free from any kind of official coercion those who do not affirmatively want to participate. But I think we must not assume that school boards so lack the qualities of inventiveness and good will as to make impossible the achievement of that goal.

BIBLIOGRAPHY

KEYNES, EDWARD. *The Court v. Congress.* Duke University Press, 1989.

LAUBACH, JOHN H. *School Prayers: Congress, the Courts, and the Public.* Public Affairs Press, 1969.

POLLAK, LOUIS H. "The Supreme Court 1962 Term—Foreword: Public Prayers in Public Schools." *Harvard Law Review* 77, no. 1 (November 1963): 62.

SCANLON, JOHN. "Prayer or Pluralism in the Schools?" *The Saturday Review.* July 18, 1964, p. 41.

"The Bible—Better in School than in Court." *Life.* April 12, 1963, p. 62.

SMITH, RODNEY K. *Public Prayer and the Constitution.* Scholarly Resources, 1987.

Edwards v. Aguillard

482 U.S. 578 (1987)

High school biology teachers have long had trouble with fundamentalist critics of Darwin's theory of evolution. The 1925 trial of John Scopes in Tennessee pitted Clarence Darrow against William Jennings Bryan in a battle of legal giants, but the case never reached the Supreme Court. In 1968, Little Rock teacher Susan Epperson won a Supreme Court ruling that laws against teaching evolution reflect religious dogma and violate the First Amendment's establishment clause. Evolution opponents in 1982 persuaded Louisiana lawmakers to require "balanced treatment" of "evolution science" and "creation science" in biology classes. Don Aguillard, a Lafayette teacher, challenged the law. Ruling in 1987, the Supreme Court held that states may not "restructure the science curriculum to conform with a particular religious viewpoint."

TRANSCRIPT OF EDITED AND NARRATED ARGUMENTS IN
Edwards v. *Aguillard*, 482 U.S. 578 (1987)

Counsel for petitioner: Wendell Bird, Atlanta, Georgia
Counsel for respondent: Jay Topkis, New York, New York

Chief Justice Rehnquist: We will hear arguments first this morning in No. 85-1513, Edwin W. Edwards, appellant, versus Don Aguillard, respondent.

Narrator: It's December 10th, 1986. Chief Justice William Rehnquist has called a case that began in Louisiana in 1981. But the case really goes back to 1859, when Charles Darwin published his book, *The Origin of Species.* Darwin argued that all living things, including humans, evolved into their present forms over millions of years through a process of natural selection. Since Darwin's time, most scientists agree that evolution best explains how species develop and change.

Many religious leaders also agree that evolution does not conflict with the Bible. But some believe in a literal reading of the creation story in the book of Genesis. They argue that God created all species, including humans, at one time and in one unchanging form. During this century, evolution's defenders and opponents have fought many battles that began in classrooms and ended in courtrooms. The first and most famous was the Scopes trial in 1925. John Scopes, a high school biology teacher, challenged a Tennessee law against teaching evolution. Two legal giants, Clarence Darrow and William Jennings Bryan, debated Darwin and Genesis in a classic legal duel. Scopes was convicted, but his case never reached the Supreme Court.

Forty years later another biology teacher, Susan Epperson, challenged an Arkansas law against evolution. The First Amendment to the Constitution prohibits any "establishment of religion" by government. In the *Epperson* case, the Supreme Court ruled unanimously in 1968 that states could not allow religious "fundamentalists" to dictate the biology curriculum.

Evolution opponents shifted tactics after the *Epperson* decision. They claimed that "creationism" was not religious doctrine but science, based on biology and geology. In the early 1980s, creationists convinced lawmakers in Arkansas and Louisiana to force teachers to give, in their words, "balanced treatment" to both "evolution science" and "creation science." In 1982, a federal judge threw out the Arkansas law.

Another biology teacher, Don Aguillard of Lafayette, Louisiana, filed a lawsuit against the state's governor, Edwin Edwards. Wendell Bird, a young lawyer who drafted the Louisiana law for creationist groups, defends his statute as the state's special counsel. Chief Justice Rehnquist welcomes him.

Rehnquist: Mr. Bird, you may proceed whenever you're ready.

Bird: Mr. Chief Justice, and may it please the Court.

This case is an appeal from an eight-to-seven decision of the U.S. Court of Appeals for the Fifth Circuit. It involves a facial constitutional challenge to Louisiana's law for balanced treatment of creation science and evolution in public schools. That law defines "evolution" as scientific evidences supporting evolution, and inferences from those scientific evidences. In parallel, it defines "creation science" as scientific evidences supporting creation, and inferences from those scientific evidences.

Narrator: The legal issues are complicated. Lower court judges decided the case without a trial. They ruled on the basis of written statements, or "affidavits," from experts on both sides. This is called "summary judgment." They decided constitutional issues on a Supreme Court standard called the "tripartite"—or three-part—test. This requires proof of a "secular," or nonreligious, purpose behind the law. Bird faced both issues.

Bird: The state today hopes to address two key questions: first, the procedural question of the material factual issues, and particularly, the uncontroverted affidavits, which must be addressed in order to apply the tripart test and which preclude summary judgment; and then, second, the constitutional question, particularly of the abundant evidence in the record of a secular purpose, although not an exclusively secular purpose, we concede.

The facts in regard to this procedural issue are that the state filed affidavits by creationist and evolutionist scientists; by a creationist philosopher; an evolutionist theologian; and a creationist educator. They were not only Protestants, but two Roman Catholics and one agnostic.

Narrator: Justice John Paul Stevens had a question.

Stevens: Mr. Bird, what would you say was the factual issue that had to be resolved?

Bird: Your honor, the definition of "creation science" is one very important factual issue, what the statute's about.

Stevens: You don't think the statute defines the term adequately?

Bird: Well, your honor, it does give a definition that's highly scientific, in referring only to scientific evidences, and inferences from those scientific evidences.

Narrator: Bird argued that religious objections to evolution were not the first or second reasons but "tertiary," or third, in the minds of lawmakers. Justice Stevens was skeptical.

Bird: It's also critical that the standard applied by this Court at all times in the past for "purpose" review be applied; that it is not necessary to have an exclusively secular purpose; but instead, it is sufficient to have *a* secular purpose. In fact, I think the legislative history in this case indicates a primary secular purpose, although the state does recognize that there are tertiary religious purposes indicated in the record. We would suggest that the appellee's highly selective . . .

Stevens: What are those religious purposes that you acknowledge are indicated in the record?

Bird: Your Honor, we'd suggest that the legislative history indicates that there were a variety of reasons for this act being passed.

Stevens: I just asked you what were the religious purposes that are—that you acknowledge are present?

Bird: As a tertiary purpose only, not as the primary or even the secondary purpose, we'd recognize that doubtless, some legislators had a desire to teach religious doctrine in the classroom. We feel that was a small minority of the legislators, as indicated by the record. But certainly there's no question that in this mixture of many different purposes, that would certainly be a tertiary or less important purpose, along with basic concepts of fairness; the academic freedom concern of students' right to receive . . .

Stevens: Do you think there was also a purpose—do you think there was also a purpose to exclude the teaching of evolutionary science, or whatever you might call it?

Bird: No, sir, I don't. It is true that there are . . .

Stevens: So to the extent that there's a religious purpose, it's to add to the curriculum, rather than to subtract from it?

Bird: Yes, sir. And if that were the case, I'd suggest that the courts could properly address that issue if any—if they saw that issue as being a sufficiently significant purpose—simply by stating what the state agrees wholeheartedly with: that the teaching of the Bible, as part of implementing this statute, would be unconstitutional. The state has consistently taken the position that that, in a science classroom, would not be appropriate under the Constitution or under the statute.

Narrator: Justice Sandra O'Connor pressed the religion issue.

O'Connor: Mr. Bird, do you think that it is constitutional within the establishment clause to teach a purely religious concept in public school in order to balance other concepts that are perceived to be antireligious?

Bird: Your Honor, not in this case, and not in the general . . .

O'Connor: Well, in general. (Bird: Only in the general . . .) In general. Is that —is that valid?

Bird: No. Only in the limited context this Court has recognized, in *Schempp* and other decisions, of an objective, neutral discussion of a wide variety of religious views. We don't believe that that is even applicable to this case. The state has consistently taken the position that to teach religious doctrine would not only violate the establishment clause in science classes but would violate the terms of the statute.

Narrator: Justice Antonin Scalia asked about the religious purposes of the law.

Scalia: Does it necessarily require the teaching of a God, a personal God, as opposed to a first cause that may be quite impersonal, or a giant slug, for all we know?

Bird: Your Honor, teaching creation science does not entail, necessarily, the teaching of any of those concepts. In other words, with creation science consisting of scientific evidence, such as the abrupt appearance of complex life in the fossil record, the systematic gaps between fossil categories, the mathematical improbability of evolution, the vast information content of all living forms, the genetic limits on viable change—in none of that is there any concept of a creator, and certainly no concept of Genesis. That is scientific data. In fact, the term "creation" is used in much scientific discussion without any reference to a creator.

Narrator: Bird questioned the claims of scientists like Carl Sagan that the universe and the evolutionary process began—billions of years ago—with a "Big Bang." Justice Scalia had more questions.

Stevens: Mr. Bird, can I ask you, you gave an example a moment ago of a "Big Bang" theory to mention the evolutionary process. Supposing there was a "Big Bang" a million years ago that created much of what we know on the Earth, but— everything except man. And then after that, there was evolution to what we now know as man. Would a person who believed that be an evolutionist or a creation scientist?

Bird: Well, your honor, we have taken the position that the "Big Bang" theory would be an evolutionary explanation of cosmic evolution, as described by Carl Sagan . . .

Scalia: Can you tell me which theory—which category my example falls under?

Bird: Probably the evolutionary category, though some people would differ.

Scalia: Well, what if the—what if I included, say, Neanderthal man, and then —but say that it was a lower form of life than present man? Would it still be— then would that be a creationist or an evolutionist?

Bird: That would probably be categorized as an evolutionist view, with the creationist scientists at trial anticipating testimony that Neanderthal man certainly existed, but that the physical evidence is that it was simply someone comparable to modern humans with bone disease, causing a bowing of the bones.

Scalia: All of your examples of people who are creation scientists would deny any evolutionary process at all?

Bird: Your Honor, I guess my point, to try to say it more clearly, is that many evolutionists do recognize creation science and evolution as mutually exclusive on each issue, as a logical matter. Some people disagree. That's an area where the scientific community does appear to disagree.

Scalia: Well, but do you have a position? Do the people supporting this legislation say it draws such a distinction?

Narrator: Bird's answer took the Court into textbook issues.

Bird: Yes, Your Honor, we—the state has taken the position consistently that creation science and evolution do reflect two separate positions . . .

Scalia: Mutually exclusive positions, and if there's any evolution at all, then you're in the evolutionary category?

Bird: Well, if you define evolution as being macroevolutionary change, yes. But creationist scientists recognize the occurrence of change; microevolution, without any question. So to say that change occurs certainly is not an evolutionary statement. It's a statement that essentially every scientist on either side would agree to. The question is whether evolution occurred from one or a few simple single-celled living forms, through fish, amphibia, reptiles, primates, and so forth.

Scalia: Well, if that's the test, your answer to my question is easy. The example I gave is that you're a creationist.

Bird: Yes, yes, Your Honor, I suppose so.

Scalia: Even though there's a very definite process of evolution from the Neanderthal man to the present society.

Bird: And that's an area of disputed fact.

Narrator: Bird appealed to principles of academic freedom.

Bird: I guess the point is that the Louisiana legislature determined that students were not receiving all of the scientific information on the subject; they were receiving, in general, only that which supported evolution; and that those students were entitled to receive additional scientific information, however those students chose to categorize it. That's the issue in this case, when we get into the constitutional question.

Narrator: Chief Justice Rehnquist.

Rehnquist: Thank you, Mr. Bird. We'll hear now from you, Mr. Topkis.

Narrator: Jay Topkis, a volunteer for the American Civil Liberties Union, defended Don Aguillard.

Topkis: Mr. Chief Justice, if the Court please.
   Mr. Bird was complaining at some length about how the Court of Appeals ignored the legislative history. I'm perfectly content to discuss the legislative history, but I'd like to take as my starting point Justice Frankfurter's dictum that

when there's some uncertainty about the legislative history, it's not forbidden to look at the plain language of the statute. *(laughter)*

What's all this talk about technical terms? These are not polysyllabic scientific words beginning with polymicro-something-or-another. These are words that we've all heard since we were kids. "Creation." "Creation"—that's a word we're all familiar with. Let me just go to the dictionary quickly. *Webster's Third International.* And what the word means, according to Webster, is the act of bringing into existence, from nothing, the universe or the world or the living and nonliving things in it.

Now, the statute, of course, also uses the term "creationism." And Webster defines that, too: "A doctrine or theory of creation holding that matter, the various forms of life, and the world were created by a transcendent God out of nothing." That's what *Webster's Third*, published in 1981, the year this statute was adopted, gave as the definitions of these two key words.

Narrator: Justice Scalia jumped in.

Scalia: What about Aristotle's view of a first cause, an unmoved mover? (Topkis: Yes, Your Honor.) Would that be a creationist view? I don't think Aristotle considered himself a theologian as opposed to a philosopher. In fact, a scientist.

Topkis: No, but Aquinas had a somewhat similar view.

Scalia: No, I want to go back earlier. *(laughter)* That's because my next question is going to be whether you considered Aristotelianism a religion?

Topkis: Of course not.

Scalia: Well, then, you could believe in a first cause, an unmoved mover, that may be impersonal, and has no obligation of obedience or veneration from men, and in fact, doesn't care what's happening to mankind. (Topkis: Right) And believe in creation.

Topkis: Well, believe in creation? Not when creation means creation by a divine creator. That's the test.

Narrator: Chief Justice Rehnquist broke in.

Rehnquist: If the statute was passed for religious purposes, say, fairly broadly interpreted like, "love thy neighbor as thyself," the statute might be bad. You wouldn't go that far, would you?

Topkis: The statute might be . . .

Rehnquist: The statute might be unconstitutional as being an establishment of religion.

Topkis: I would not regard "love thy neighbor as thyself" as a necessarily religious doctrine. I would think of it as a proposition in morality.

Rehnquist: Well, but supposing it's a morality subscribed to by many religious faiths?

Topkis: Well, there are lots of propositions that are subscribed to by religious faiths, but they do not become religious, as I understand it, merely by virtue of that subscription. For example, most religions forbid or speak against homicide. But a civil—pardon me, a criminal statute making homicide criminal is not a religious statute.

Rehnquist: Even though, perhaps, a number of church people go down and say, we want this statute passed because it's consistent with our religious beliefs?

Topkis: Even though.

Narrator: Justice Scalia joined the debate.

Scalia: And here, do we know that the state is acting out of religious motivation?

Topkis: By every index that we can possibly have, Your Honor, yes.

Scalia: Which is what?

Topkis: We take a look at the vocabulary of the statute; it is religious. We take a look at what the legislators said at the time they acted; it is nothing *but* religion. We can go through this entire record without finding anybody talking about a secular purpose. They talk about how terrible evolution is. Why? Because it's godless evolution, and what we got to do is bring God into balance with evolution.

Scalia: Once you say that what they're doing is teaching religion, it's a different ballgame. If that is motivated by a religious purpose, then I think you're quite right. But that is an essential part of what you have to establish, though, isn't it? Not just that a secular action is ultimately motivated by some religious concern?

Topkis: Quite so, quite so.

Scalia: Okay, I'm with you.

Topkis: All right. Now, I said before that this definition that Mr. Bird is so fond of, and I quote it—"origin through abrupt appearance in complex form of biological life, life itself, and the physical universe"—one thing we know about that collection of words is that it has never before been seen upon the face of the earth except in Mr. Bird's briefs. . . .

Narrator: Topkis and Chief Justice Rehnquist traded jokes.

Topkis: Mr. Bird is a little slender to play Tweedledum, but that's what he's trying to do. He wants words to mean what *he* says they mean. That didn't fool Alice, and I doubt very much that it will fool this Court.

Rehnquist: Don't overestimate us. *(laughter)*

Narrator: Topkis moved to a serious issue.

Topkis: Your Honors, I'd like now to go to another of Mr. Bird's buzzwords, "academic freedom." The idea of academic freedom that is advanced here is, again, unlike any previous notion of that term. It's not a term; it's an incantation, as he uses it.

   This statute calls for the very antithesis of academic freedom. It says that the teacher *must* give balanced treatment, regardless of whether the evidence is balanced. It says the teacher may teach evolution *only* at the price of teaching what he or she knows to be pseudoscience. And the teacher may teach *only* the evidences for creation; none against. I can't imagine anything farther from the idea of academic freedom.

Narrator: Topkis returned to the Court's "secular purpose" test. Justice Scalia had more questions.

Topkis: There is nothing in the legislative history which speaks of a secular purpose. No sponsor of the legislature—of the legislation; no witness; nobody.

   The one witness I love is a Ms. Babs Minhinette, who said: "I think if you teach children that they are evolved from apes, then they will start acting like apes. If we teach them possibly that they were created by an Almighty God, then they will believe that they were a creature of God and start acting like one of

God's children." That's what she told the Senate before the Senate voted. Now, I don't, of course, take issue . . .

Scalia: Mr. Topkis, let me just be sure. Is there nothing in the legislative history supporting the—this academic freedom argument?

Topkis: Oh, sure, your honor. Academic freedom. We got to give God equal time. That's their idea of academic freedom.

Narrator: Topkis and Justice Scalia debated the law's purpose.

Topkis: There isn't a single word in this history of secular interest.

Scalia: But isn't righting what the state legislature considered an imbalance in instruction a secular purpose; that only one side of an issue is being presented?

Topkis: Not, Your Honor, with respect, when the complaint is: "They're teaching *that* religion; why don't they teach *my* religion?" And that's what the legislators said, and that's what the witnesses said, over and over again. There's nobody coming forward and taking any other position.

Narrator: Topkis argued that Bird had religious motives in drafting the Louisiana law.

Topkis: This bill was, of course, drafted by a theologian, or somebody versed in apologetics. There's an amusing bit of evidence on that subject in the very language of the bill. The bill keeps using—the act keeps using the term "evidences" in the plural. We lawyers never speak of "evidences" in the plural; we speak of "evidence," the singular. And I got nagged by it, and I looked it up the other day. And of course the only dictionary reference to "evidences" is to Christian apologetics: the "evidences" for Christianity. This is a matter of theological disputation.

Narrator: On June 19th, 1987, the Supreme Court ruled that Don Aguillard did not have to teach "creation science" in his biology classes. By a seven-to-two vote, the justices agreed with Jay Topkis that the case involved a theological dispute. The law violated the establishment clause of the First Amendment.

Justice William Brennan wrote for the Court. He quoted the law's sponsor that "a creator was responsible for everything that is in this world." Brennan concluded, in his words, that "the preeminent purpose of the Louisiana legislature was clearly to advance the religious viewpoint that a supernatural being created humankind." Lawmakers, he said, cannot force "the science curriculum to conform with a particular religious viewpoint."

Justice Scalia joined Chief Justice Rehnquist in dissent. Scalia disputed Brennan's claim that the law had religious motivations. "The legislature," he wrote, "wanted to ensure that students would be free to decide for themselves how life began, based upon a fair and balanced presentation of the scientific evidence" on both sides. Even if the law had religious motives, Scalia was not bothered. "Christian fundamentalists," he said, are entitled "to have whatever scientific evidence there may be against evolution presented in their schools."

Since the *Aguillard* decision, few battles over evolution versus creation made headlines. But local skirmishes continue across the country. How life began, how it changes, and how teachers should talk about evolution are still controversial in many cities and towns.

EDITED SUPREME COURT OPINIONS
Edwards v. *Aguillard*

JUSTICE BRENNAN delivered the opinion of the Court.

The question for decision is whether Louisiana's "Balanced Treatment for Creation-Science and Evolution-Science in Public School Instruction" Act (Creationism Act), . . . is facially invalid as violative of the Establishment Clause of the First Amendment.

The Creationism Act forbids the teaching of the theory of evolution in public schools unless accompanied by instruction in "creation science." . . . No school is required to teach evolution or creation science. If either is taught, however, the other must also be taught. The theories of evolution and creation science are statutorily defined as "the scientific evidences forcreation or evolutionand inferences from those scientific evidences." . . .

Appellees, who include parents of children attending Louisiana public schools, Louisiana teachers, and religious leaders, challenged the constitutionality of the Act in District Court, seeking an injunction and declaratory relief. Appellants, Louisiana officials charged with implementing the Act, defended on the ground that the purpose of the Act is to protect a legitimate secular interest, namely, academic freedom. Appellees attacked the Act as facially invalid because it violated the Establishment Clause. . . . The court held that there can be no valid secular reason for prohibiting the teaching of evolution, a theory historically opposed by some religious denominations. The court further concluded that "the teaching of 'creation-science' and 'creationism,' as contemplated by the statute, involves teaching 'tailored to the principles' of a particular religious sect or group of sects." . . . (citing *Epperson* v. *Arkansas*, 393 U. S. 97, 106 (1968)). The District Court therefore held that the Creationism Act violated the Establishment

Clause either because it prohibited the teaching of evolution or because it required the teaching of creation science with the purpose of advancing a particular religious doctrine.

The Establishment Clause forbids the enactment of any law "respecting an establishment of religion." The Court has applied a three-pronged test to determine whether legislation comports with the Establishment Clause. First, the legislature must have adopted the law with a secular purpose. Second, the statute's principal or primary effect must be one that neither advances nor inhibits religion. Third, the statute must not result in an excessive entanglement of government with religion. *Lemon* v. *Kurtzman*, 403 U. S. 602, 612–613 (1971). State action violates the Establishment Clause if it fails to satisfy any of these prongs. . . .

The Court has been particularly vigilant in monitoring compliance with the Establishment Clause in elementary and secondary schools. Families entrust public schools with the education of their children, but condition their trust on the understanding that the classroom will not purposely be used to advance religious views that may conflict with the private beliefs of the student and his or her family. Students in such institutions are impressionable and their attendance is involuntary. . . .

Lemon's first prong focuses on the purpose that animated adoption of the Act. . . . A governmental intention to promote religion is clear when the State enacts a law to serve a religious purpose. . . . If the law was enacted for the purpose of endorsing religion, "no consideration of the second or third criteria [of *Lemon*] is necessary." . . . In this case, appellants have identified no clear secular purpose for the Louisiana Act.

True, the Act's stated purpose is to protect academic freedom. . . . Even if "academic freedom" is read to mean "teaching all of the evidence" with respect to the origin of human beings, the Act does not further this purpose. The goal of providing a more comprehensive science curriculum is not furthered either by outlawing the teaching of evolution or by requiring the teaching of creation science.

While the Court is normally deferential to a State's articulation of a secular purpose, it is required that the statement of such purpose be sincere and not a sham. . . . The preeminent purpose of the Louisiana Legislature was clearly to advance the religious viewpoint that a supernatural being created humankind. The term "creation science" was defined as embracing this particular religious doctrine by those responsible for the passage of the Creationism Act. Senator Keith's leading expert on creation science, Edward Boudreaux, testified at the legislative hearings that the theory of creation science included belief in the existence of a supernatural creator. . . . Senator Keith also cited testimony from other experts to support the creation-science view that "a creatorwasresponsible for the universe and everything in it." . . . The legislative history therefore reveals that the term "creation science," as contemplated by the legislature that adopted this Act, embodies the religious belief that a supernatural creator was responsible for the creation of humankind.

Furthermore, it is not happenstance that the legislature required the teaching of a theory that coincided with this religious view. The legislative history documents that the Act's primary purpose was to change the science curriculum of public schools in order to provide persuasive advantage to a particular religious doctrine that rejects the factual basis of evolution in its entirety. The sponsor of the Creationism Act, Senator Keith, explained during the legislative hearings that his disdain for the theory of evolution resulted from the support that evolution supplied to views contrary to his own religious beliefs. According to Senator Keith, the theory of evolution was consonant with the "cardinal principle[s]of religious humanism, secular humanism, theological liberalism, aetheistism [sic]." . . . The state senator repeatedly stated that scientific evidence supporting his religious views should be included in the public school curriculum to redress the fact that the theory of evolution incidentally coincided with what he characterized as religious beliefs antithetical to his own. The legislation therefore sought to alter the science curriculum to reflect endorsement of a religious view that is antagonistic to the theory of evolution. . . .

The Louisiana Creationism Act advances a religious doctrine by requiring either the banishment of the theory of evolution from public school classrooms or the presentation of a religious viewpoint that rejects evolution in its entirety. The Act violates the Establishment Clause of the First Amendment because it seeks to employ the symbolic and financial support of government to achieve a religious purpose. The judgment of the Court of Appeals therefore is

Affirmed.

JUSTICE SCALIA, with whom THE CHIEF JUSTICE joins, dissenting.

Even if I agreed with the questionable premise that legislation can be invalidated under the Establishment Clause on the basis of its motivation alone, without regard to its effects, I would still find no justification for today's decision. The Louisiana legislators who passed the "Balanced Treatment for Creation-Science and Evolution-Science Act" . . . each of whom had sworn to support the Constitution, were well aware of the potential Establishment Clause problems and considered that aspect of the legislation with great care. After seven hearings and several months of study, resulting in substantial revision of the original proposal, they approved the Act overwhelmingly and specifically articulated the secular purpose they meant it to serve. Although the record contains abundant evidence of the sincerity of that purpose (the only issue pertinent to this case), the Court today holds, essentially on the basis of "its visceral knowledge regarding what *must* have motivated the legislators," . . . that the members of the Louisiana Legislature knowingly violated their oaths and then lied about it. I dissent. Had requirements of the Balanced Treatment Act that are not apparent on its face been clarified by an interpretation of the Louisiana Supreme Court, or by the manner of its implementation, the Act might well be found unconstitutional; but the question of its constitutionality cannot rightly be disposed of on the gallop, by impugning the motives of its supporters.

. . . Our cases in no way imply that the Establishment Clause forbids legislators merely to act upon their religious convictions. We surely would not strike down a law providing money to feed the hungry or shelter the homeless if it could be demonstrated that, but for the religious beliefs of the legislators, the funds would not have been approved. Also, political activism by the religiously motivated is part of our heritage. Notwithstanding the majority's implication to the contrary, . . . we do not presume that the sole purpose of a law is to advance religion merely because it was supported strongly by organized religions or by adherents of particular faiths. . . . To do so would deprive religious men and women of their right to participate in the political process. Today's religious activism may give us the Balanced Treatment Act, but yesterday's resulted in the abolition of slavery, and tomorrow's may bring relief for famine victims. . . .

With the foregoing in mind, I now turn to the purposes underlying adoption of the Balanced Treatment Act.

We have relatively little information upon which to judge the motives of those who supported the Act. About the only direct evidence is the statute itself and transcripts of the seven committee hearings at which it was considered. . . . We have no committee reports, no floor debates, no remarks inserted into the legislative history, no statement from the Governor, and no postenactment statements or testimony from the bill's sponsor or any other legislators. . . . Nevertheless, there is ample evidence that the majority is wrong in holding that the Balanced Treatment Act is without secular purpose.

At the outset, it is important to note that the Balanced Treatment Act did not fly through the Louisiana Legislature on wings of fundamentalist religious fervor —which would be unlikely, in any event, since only a small minority of the State's citizens belong to fundamentalist religious denominations. . . . Our task is not to judge the debate about teaching the origins of life, but to ascertain what the members of the Louisiana Legislature believed. The vast majority of them voted to approve a bill which explicitly stated a secular purpose; what is crucial is not their *wisdom* in believing that purpose would be achieved by the bill, but their *sincerity* in believing it would be.

Most of the testimony in support of Senator Keith's bill came from the Senator himself and from scientists and educators he presented, many of whom enjoyed academic credentials that may have been regarded as quite impressive by members of the Louisiana Legislature. To a substantial extent, their testimony was devoted to lengthy, and, to the layman, seemingly expert scientific expositions on the origin of life. . . .

We have no way of knowing, of course, how many legislators believed the testimony of Senator Keith and his witnesses. But in the absence of evidence to the contrary, we have to assume that many of them did. Given that assumption, the Court today plainly errs in holding that the Louisiana Legislature passed the Balanced Treatment Act for exclusively religious purposes.

Even with nothing more than this legislative history to go on, I think it would be extraordinary to invalidate the Balanced Treatment Act for lack of a valid secular purpose. Striking down a law approved by the democratically elected representatives of the people is no minor matter. . . .

The Court cites three provisions of the Act which, it argues, demonstrate a "discriminatory preference for the teaching of creation science" and no interest in "academic freedom." . . . First, the Act prohibits discrimination only against creation scientists and those who teach creation science. Second, the Act requires local school boards to develop and provide to science teachers "a curriculum guide on presentation of creation-science." . . . Finally, the Act requires the Governor to designate seven creation scientists who shall, upon request, assist local school boards in developing the curriculum guides. . . . But none of these provisions casts doubt upon the sincerity of the legislators' articulated purpose of "academic freedom"—unless, of course, one gives that term the obviously erroneous meanings preferred by the Court. The Louisiana legislators had been told repeatedly that creation scientists were scorned by most educators and scientists, who themselves had an almost religious faith in evolution. It is hardly surprising, then, that in seeking to achieve a balanced, "non-indoctrinating" curriculum, the legislators protected from discrimination only those teachers whom they thought were *suffering* from discrimination. . . .

In sum, even if one concedes, for the sake of argument, that a majority of the Louisiana Legislature voted for the Balanced Treatment Act partly in order to foster (rather than merely eliminate discrimination against) Christian fundamentalist beliefs, our cases establish that that alone would not suffice to invalidate the Act, so long as there was a genuine secular purpose as well. We have, moreover, no adequate basis for disbelieving the secular purpose set forth in the Act itself, or for concluding that it is a sham enacted to conceal the legislators' violation of their oaths of office. I am astonished by the Court's unprecedented readiness to reach such a conclusion, which I can only attribute to . . . an instinctive reaction that any governmentally imposed requirements bearing upon the teaching of evolution must be a manifestation of Christian fundamentalist repression. In this case, however, it seems to me the Court's position is the repressive one. The people of Louisiana, including those who are Christian fundamentalists, are quite entitled, as a secular matter, to have whatever scientific evidence there may be against evolution presented in their schools, just as Mr. Scopes was entitled to present whatever scientific evidence there was for it. . . .

Because I believe that the Balanced Treatment Act had a secular purpose, which is all the first component of the *Lemon* test requires, I would reverse the judgment of the Court of Appeals and remand for further consideration. . . .

BIBLIOGRAPHY

FREIDHEIM, ELIZABETH. "Science in School: From Antireligion to Scientific Cult." *John Marshall Law Review* 21, no. 4 (Summer 1988): 449.

GILKEY, LANGDON B. *Creationism on Trial.* Winston, 1985.

LA FOLLETTE, MARCEL. *Creationism, Science, and the Law.* MIT Press, 1983.

LARSON, EDWARD J. *Trial and Error.* Oxford University Press, 1985.

"The Supreme Court—Leading Cases." *Harvard Law Review* 101, no. 1 (November 1987): 189.

"You Decide: Should Public Schools Teach Creationism?" *Scholastic Update* 121, no. 8 (December 16, 1988): 15.

Wisconsin v. Yoder

406 U.S. 205 (1972)

Jonas Yoder belongs to the Old Order Amish community in Green County, Wisconsin. The Amish faith is based on a rural church community apart from the world, and it rejects formal education beyond the eighth grade. Yoder removed his daughter Frieda from school in 1968. He was tried and found guilty of violating the Wisconsin school attendance law, which requires children to attend school until the age of sixteen. Yoder appealed his conviction on the ground that the school attendance law violated his rights, and those of his daughter, under the free exercise clause of the First Amendment. In 1972, the Supreme Court unanimously ruled that Amish children should be exempted from compulsory high school education. "Enforcement of the State's requirement," Chief Justice Burger wrote, "would gravely endanger if not destroy the free exercise ofthe Amishreligious belief."

TRANSCRIPT OF EDITED AND NARRATED ARGUMENTS IN
Wisconsin v. Yoder, 406 U.S. 205 (1972)

Counsel for petitioners: John W. Calhoun, Milwaukee, Wisconsin
Counsel for respondents: William Ball, Harrisburg, Pennsylvania

Narrator: It's December 8th, 1971. Chief Justice Warren Burger has called case 70-110, State of Wisconsin versus Jonas Yoder. Only seven justices sit behind the mahogany bench. Two longtime justices, Hugo Black and John Harlan, died recently and have not yet been replaced.

Today's argument involves the First Amendment and the Amish church. Most Americans associate the Amish with horse-drawn buggies and old-fashioned dress. They are considered "quaint" for living an eighteenth-century life in the twentieth century. But the Amish are hardworking and successful. About fifty thousand live in close-knit farming communities in seventeen states, most in Pennsylvania, Ohio, Indiana, and Wisconsin.

The Amish are part of a larger religious group known as Mennonites and stem from the Protestant Reformation in Europe. They base their religion on the Sermon on the Mount. Their refusal to bear arms and to renounce their beliefs brought persecution and death to hundreds. One history says, "The men were burned and the women buried alive." They sought refuge in Pennsylvania, which granted freedom to all religions. Three centuries later, the Amish remain apart from the modern world, centered on family, farm, and church.

How did the Amish wind up in the Supreme Court? This case began with three children—Frieda Yoder, Barbara Miller, and Vernon Yutzy—in Green County, Wisconsin. They finished the eighth grade in 1968. They were fourteen and fifteen years old. Wisconsin has a compulsory school attendance law that requires education until the age of sixteen. The Amish children did not enroll in high school that fall. The school administrator signed a complaint against their parents. They were tried, convicted, and fined five dollars each.

The Amish believe in education. Their church policy says, "Our children should be trained to read, to write, and to cipher." But they don't believe they need to go past the eighth grade to become good farmers and housekeepers. Their statement says, "We believe . . . the farm and the home are the best school rooms."

The Amish parents appealed their convictions. The Constitution's First Amendment guarantees the "free exercise" of religion. This clause protects religious belief but not every religious act or practice. The Supreme Court ruled in the nineteenth century that Mormons could not practice polygamy, or plural marriage. Amish belief keeps their children out of high school. Can the state prohibit this practice to further educational goals? The Wisconsin Supreme Court ruled the law violated the free exercise clause. John Calhoun, an assistant attorney general, argues the state's appeal.

Calhoun: Mr. Chief Justice, and may it please the Court.

We have absolutely no quarrel with the Amish way of life. In fact, to some of us, in the remorseless daily crunch of living, the grass on the Amish side of the fence looks green, much greener than ours at times. But I submit that retreat to a simpler era may have had some justification two hundred years ago, when Rousseau was extolling the virtues of the Cro-Magnon man, but that too much water has gone through the turbines for that kind of a position. What is needed is more education to cope with the problems of society, more pride in intellect, not less pride. This is what we should be developing in our educational programs. The objection that the Amish have is to an additional two years, at this point, an additional two years of education. And the people before the Court here are Amish.

Narrator: Justice Thurgood Marshall had a question.

Marshall: Do you deny that it is a part of their faith that they should not go to public schools beyond eighth grade?

Calhoun: No, I deny that it—I say this, that the trial court found that this did not interfere with their religious belief as such but with their freedom to act, and that the freedom to act, the restriction on the freedom to act here was a reasonable one which has been imposed since 1642 in this country, that the compulsory school attendance is not a law which has just been recently enforced. We've had it since the beginning of our educational system.

We think there are two issues here, really. First of all, is whether the—let me state them—whether or not respondents may select the time, the extent, and whether or not they will comply with the compulsory school attendance laws. And whether there is, somewhat more broadly stated, a constitutional right to conscientiously object to education.

Narrator: Calhoun faced another question.

Court: Yes, but as I get it, though, or am I wrong, we're not concerned here with whether the children *have* to go to school, Amish or not. We're concerned with whether Amish parents can be compelled, under threat of criminal punishment . . .

Calhoun: Well, of course, we're concerned about the rights of a child to an education. I think we're concerned about that. I don't think we can avoid that as an overriding issue, and I think the dissenting opinion expressed that well. Because the compelling interest of the state is in the education of the children, and the interest of the child in education is important. I don't think—the compelling interest is not in *total* compliance necessarily; the question is whether or not the Court can say that the Amish parents have a constitutional right to conscientiously object to education, to sending their children to school.

Court: You don't, does the state challenge that this is their position about education, is the warp and woof of their religion?

Calhoun: What we have said in that is simply this: that as the trial court said, it interferes with their freedom to act but not with their religious belief as such; and that the cases are clear, and this Court has pronounced time and again, that the freedom to act may be restricted in interpretation of the First Amendment, but the freedom to believe may not.

Narrator: Supreme Court precedent requires states to show a "compelling interest" before restricting First Amendment rights. Calhoun addressed the issue.

Calhoun: What we're saying here is essentially that there is a compelling interest in education. That's essentially our view. And that this Court and the Congress, the people of this country have manifested this compelling interest. The compulsory school attendance laws have been in existence for years. They were part of the established church when this country was founded, when the colonists established the theocratic societies in the prerevolutionary days. When the church became disestablished, the compulsory school attendance laws remained; they remained in a democratic fashion. And they are applied and enacted in a democratic fashion. This is a positive force that we're dealing with, for the benefit of society. And it is the legislature that should determine, in its own area of protection of the liberties of this country, it is the legislature that should determine whether the compulsory school attendance laws are necessary to enact or to obtain the full benefit of education to the individual and society.

Narrator: The Court ruled in the 1920s that states could not ban religious schools. Calhoun raised this case.

Calhoun: Now, what we're concerned about here takes us to *Pierce* against *The Society of Sisters of the Holy Name*, where the Court said that we couldn't compel attendance at public schools, but there was no reason why attendance could not be compelled at public or private, secular or nonsecular schools. And this is the area, when you talk about aid to parochial education, that we get into. We get into a proposition that endeavors to augment this, and that is not really the question here; the question here is, education or no education. It's not a question of private education or public education or how much one should be aided over the other. Yes, there is a First Amendment question, but it's an establishment question rather than a freedom-to-worship question.

Narrator: Wisconsin school officials had not approved the program that Amish children used to study farming. Calhoun faced a final question about this.

Court: I take it if, I think you said earlier in answer to Mr. Justice Douglas, that the Amish do have their own schools? (Calhoun: Yes) And I take it, it's like Roman Catholic parochial schools, or any other parochial schools. If the standards of education in those schools met the state standards, you wouldn't be here, would you?

Calhoun: That's right, we would not.

Narrator: William Ball, a Pennsylvania lawyer, represents the Amish community.

Ball: My argument, may it please the Court, will pursue two points. One, the free exercise claim, and secondly, the question of danger to interests of the state, which the state of Wisconsin has said exist in so substantial a degree.

The free exercise point is extremely important. That is, it's extremely important that I try to develop this at some length, because here we're not talking about one tenet of a religion being at stake; for example, observance of the Sabbath or opposition to military training. We're not talking here about one particular practice, say, spreading the Gospel through speech or press or assembly as has appeared in a number of cases. We're not talking about one forced exercise, such as the salute to a graven image or recitation of prayers or Bible reading. But we're talking about a whole complex of religious interests, religious interests in rights in education, in worship, in parental nurture, in individual religious choice, in vocation, in communal association, with respect to teaching and learning, with respect to privacy, as we have tried to spell out in our brief. And indeed, we're talking about—as will appear—the continued existence of the Amish faith community in the United States.

Narrator: Ball explained the basis of Amish belief.

Ball: They believe that their lives had to be governed completely by the Sermon on the Mount. And this would be, therefore, the call for the creating of a community of love, of mutual help, of simplicity, closeness to nature, animals, soil, plants, and so on, turning the other cheek. And extremely importantly, perhaps the most critical point in the understanding of the Amish religion, separation from the world. They believe that education's aim should be the life of goodness, not the life of the intellect, the making of a good man, not the making of the good American life.

Therefore, they reject what many of the rest of us accept, a world of knowledge, and they believe that the education in writing and reading and arithmetic which a child can acquire up until the time of adolescence is sufficient education. The Amish do not want their children, and they do not want themselves, to be exposed to the spirit of luxury, of ostentation, of strife, consumerism, competition, speed, violence, other such elements as are commonly found in our American life. Therefore, education for them embraces a rejection of the higher learning and a positive emphasis upon the learning of the agricultural life. It rejects the concept of exposure to, and service in, the ways of the world. And when you add to this the factor of adolescence, you will see why an Amish person—whether we would agree with him or not—may not, from a religious point of view, attend school beyond the eighth grade.

Narrator: Ball stressed the trial testimony of Dr. Donald Erickson, a noted educator. Justice Potter Stewart had a question.

Ball: Now, when you take a child from Amish life at adolescence and place him in a high school, he is naturally going to be exposed to those values which his parents' religion rejects. He is going to be exposed to those ways of life which typify high school today. And this alienation, which is abundant testimony in the record, this alienation of the child, who has been raised as he has a right to be raised in the Amish faith community up until adolescence—there's no disagreement with that on the part of the state—he has been raised in that atmosphere up until then, to be suddenly placed in a high school where there is different dress, different speech, very, very different people with very, very different backgrounds—this is extremely traumatic to the person. And this alienation is psychologically damaging to such a person.

Stewart: Why is that so much more traumatic than the eighth grade would be?

Ball: In the eighth grade, our particular defendants were in parochial schools, Amish parochial schools until the eighth grade. They attend an eighth grade, they attended up to that time, whether they are in a public or an Amish school, to be at least in part associated with other Amish children.

The state has talked loosely about the disease of ignorance, of opening the gateways of opportunity to these children. But we introduced positive evidence which shows that Amish education produces good people; we cited the testimony of Dr. Erickson of the University of Chicago, and we specifically asked him questions concerning Amish education, which he had very carefully studied, and his comment was this: "The Amish definitely provide for their children of high school age what could be called an education. I would be inclined to say that they do a better job of this than most of the rest of us do. The Amish are in a fortunate position respecting schooling which they conduct for children beyond the eighth grade. It is learning by doing, an ideal system."

Narrator: Ball summed up.

Ball: I think that what we are talking about here are really great achievers. They've been in the education business for three hundred years. They're the finest natural farmers in the Western hemisphere. You go up, members of the Court, you go up to Lancaster County in Pennsylvania and you're to see these people, see them in actuality. You would find young men who are heads of families and managers of large farms, experts in husbandry. You would find in their women, very model women, managers of households, very fine people. And I think it's quite surprising that these people are singled out as not having an education, denying their people an education. For three hundred years these people have done superbly; for three hundred years these people have performed very well in our society.

The question before the Court, then, is whether the state may destroy— because that's what it will come to if these children are forced into high school —a peaceable, self-sustaining community, two hundred and fifty years on this soil, on the ground that the parents in that community cannot send their children, on account of the clear mandate of their religion, to one or two years of high school. The Amish do not come here as fearful supplicants to this Court. They come here with confidence, believing in this Court as their brothers in justice, in love, in goodness, in belief in constitutional liberty.

Narrator: The Court decided the case on May 15th, 1972. The justices agreed that Wisconsin could not force Amish children to attend high school. Chief Justice Burger wrote for the Court. He praised the Amish for "their devotion to a life in harmony with nature and the soil." They continue to lead, he said, "the simple life of the early Christian era" and to "insulate themselves from the modern world."

Burger cited Dr. Erickson's testimony that Amish education produces "good farmers and citizens." They enter adult life with skills "perhaps superior to ordinary high school education." Burger agreed that Amish children might face "great psychological harm" in public high schools. He also agreed that states have a legitimate interest in educating children. The Court's job was to balance the conflicting claims: religious freedom to lead a simple life and educating children for the modern world.

Burger did not doubt which claim had more weight. Forcing Amish children into high school, he said, posed "a very real threat of undermining the Amish community and religious practice." Ruling for Wisconsin "would gravely endanger if not destroy the free exercise" of Amish religious beliefs.

All seven justices who voted supported the Amish position. But four had reservations about Burger's opinion. They felt children had rights of their own. Justice Byron White asked about Amish children who "may wish to become nuclear physicists, ballet dancers, computer programmers." He noted evidence that "many children desert the Amish faith when they come of age." They should be able to choose further education. Justice William Douglas agreed. "I think the children should be . . . heard," he said. "It is the future of the student, not the future of the parents, that is imperiled by today's decision."

Judicial decisions on religion raise more questions than they answer. Matters of faith cannot be decided in courtrooms. No one doubts the sincerity of the Amish. But what about other religious practices? The use of drugs like peyote in Native American ceremonies? Keeping children from medical treatment? Teaching children that some races are inferior? These are hard questions, and the Constitution has no easy answers.

EDITED SUPREME COURT OPINIONS
Wisconsin v. *Yoder*

MR. CHIEF JUSTICE BURGER delivered the opinion of the Court.

On petition of the State of Wisconsin, we granted the writ of certiorari in this case to review a decision of the Wisconsin Supreme Court holding that respondents' convictions of violating the State's compulsory school-attendance law were invalid under the Free Exercise Clause of the First Amendment to the United States Constitution made applicable to the States by the Fourteenth Amendment. For the reasons hereafter stated we affirm the judgment of the Supreme Court of Wisconsin.

Respondents Jonas Yoder and Wallace Miller are members of the Old Order Amish religion, and respondent Adin Yutzy is a member of the Conservative Amish Mennonite Church. They and their families are residents of Green County, Wisconsin. Wisconsin's compulsory school-attendance law required them to cause their children to attend public or private school until reaching age 16 but the respondents declined to send their children, ages fourteen and fifteen, to public school after they completed the eighth grade. The children were not enrolled in any private school, or within any recognized exception to the compulsory-attendance law, and they are conceded to be subject to the Wisconsin statute.

On complaint of the school district administrator for the public schools, respondents were charged, tried, and convicted of violating the compulsory-attendance law in Green County Court and were fined the sum of five dollars each. Respondents defended on the ground that the application of the compulsory-attendance law violated their rights under the First and Fourteenth Amendments. The trial testimony showed that respondents believed, in accordance with the tenets of Old Order Amish communities generally, that their children's attendance at high school, public or private, was contrary to the Amish religion and way of life. They believed that by sending their children to high school, they would not only expose themselves to the danger of the censure of the church community, but, as found by the county court, also endanger their own salvation and that of their children. The State stipulated that respondents' religious beliefs were sincere.

. . . Old Order Amish communities today are characterized by a fundamental belief that salvation requires life in a church community separate and apart from the world and worldly influence. This concept of life aloof from the world and its values is central to their faith. . . . They object to the high school, and higher education generally, because the values they teach are in marked variance with Amish values and the Amish way of life; they view secondary school education as an impermissible exposure of their children to a "worldly" influence in conflict with their beliefs. The high school tends to emphasize intellectual and scientific accomplishments, self-distinction, competitiveness, worldly success, and social life with other students. Amish society emphasizes informal learning-through-doing; a life of "goodness," rather than a life of intellect; wisdom, rather than technical knowledge; community welfare, rather than competition; and separation from, rather than integration with, contemporary worldly society.

Formal high-school education beyond the eighth grade is contrary to Amish beliefs, not only because it places Amish children in an environment hostile to Amish beliefs . . . but also because it takes them away from their community, physically and emotionally, during the crucial and formative adolescent period of life. During this period, the children must acquire Amish attitudes favoring manual work and self-reliance and the specific skills needed to perform the adult role of an Amish farmer or housewife. They must learn to enjoy physical labor. Once a child has learned basic reading, writing, and elementary mathematics, these traits, skills, and attitudes admittedly fall within the category of those best learned through example and "doing" rather than in a classroom. And, at this time in life, the Amish child must also grow in his faith and his relationship to the Amish community if he is to be prepared to accept the heavy obligations imposed by adult baptism. . . .

The record shows that the respondents' religious beliefs and attitude toward life, family, and home have remained constant—perhaps some would say static —in a period of unparalleled progress in human knowledge generally and great changes in education. The respondents freely concede, and indeed assert as an article of faith, that their religious beliefs and what we would today call "life style" have not altered in fundamentals for centuries. Their way of life in a church-oriented community, separated from the outside world and "worldly" influences, their attachment to nature and the soil, is a way inherently simple and uncomplicated, albeit difficult to preserve against the pressure to conform. Their rejection of telephones, automobiles, radios, and television, their mode of dress, of speech, their habits of manual work do indeed set them apart from much of contemporary society; these customs are both symbolic and practical. . . .

The conclusion is inescapable that secondary schooling, by exposing Amish children to worldly influences in terms of attitudes, goals, and values contrary to beliefs, and by substantially interfering with the religious development of the Amish child and his integration into the way of life of the Amish faith community at the crucial adolescent stage of development, contravenes the basic religious tenets and practice of the Amish faith, both as to the parent and the child. . . .

In sum, the unchallenged testimony of acknowledged experts in education and religious history, almost three hundred years of consistent practice, and strong evidence of a sustained faith pervading and regulating respondents' entire mode of life support the claim that enforcement of the State's requirement of compulsory formal education after eighth grade would gravely endanger if not destroy the free exercise of respondents' religious beliefs. . . .

Insofar as the State's claim rests on the view that a brief additional period of formal education is imperative to enable the Amish to participate effectively and intelligently in our democratic process, it must fall. The Amish alternative to formal secondary school education has enabled them to function effectively in their day-to-day life under self-imposed limitations on relations with the world, and to survive and prosper in contemporary society as a separate, sharply identifiable and highly self-sufficient community for more than two hundred years in this country.

. . . In itself this is strong evidence that they are capable of fulfilling the social and political responsibilities of citizenship without compelled attendance beyond the eighth grade at the price of jeopardizing their free exercise of religious belief. When Thomas Jefferson emphasized the need for education as a bulwark of a free people against tyranny, there is nothing to indicate he had in mind compulsory education through any fixed age beyond a basic education. Indeed, the Amish communities singularly parallel and reflect many of the virtues of Jefferson's ideal of the "sturdy yeoman" who would form the basis of what he considered as the ideal of a democratic society. Even their idiosyncratic separateness exemplifies the diversity we profess to admire and encourage. . . .

For the reasons stated we hold, with the Supreme Court of Wisconsin, that the First and Fourteenth Amendments prevent the State from compelling respondents to cause their children to attend formal high school to age sixteen. Our disposition of this case, however, in no way alters our recognition of the obvious fact that courts are not school boards or legislatures, and are ill-equipped to determine the "necessity" of discrete aspects of a State's program of compulsory education. This should suggest that courts must move with great circumspection in performing the sensitive and delicate task of weighing a State's legitimate social concern when faced with religious claims for exemption from generally applicable educational requirements. . . .

Affirmed.

MR. JUSTICE WHITE, with whom MR. JUSTICE BRENNAN and MR. JUSTICE STEWART join, concurring.

. . . In the present case, the State is not concerned with the maintenance of an educational system as an end in itself, it is rather attempting to nurture and develop the human potential of its children, whether Amish or non-Amish: to expand their knowledge, broaden their sensibilities, kindle their imagination, foster a spirit of free inquiry, and increase their human understanding and tolerance. It is possible that most Amish children will wish to continue living the rural life of their parents, in which case their training at home will adequately equip them for their future role. Others, however, may wish to become nuclear physicists, ballet dancers, computer programmers, or historians, and for these occupations, formal training will be necessary. There is evidence in the record that many children desert the Amish faith when they come of age. A State has a legitimate interest not only in seeking to develop the latent talents of its children but also in seeking to prepare them for the life style that they may later choose, or at least to provide them with an option other than the life they have led in the past. In the circumstances of this case, although the question is close, I am unable to say that the State has demonstrated that Amish children who leave school in the eighth grade will be intellectually stultified or unable to acquire new academic skills later. The statutory minimum school attendance age set by the State is, after all, only sixteen. . . .

MR. JUSTICE DOUGLAS, dissenting in part.

On this important and vital matter of education, I think the children should be entitled to be heard. While the parents, absent dissent, normally speak for the entire family, the education of the child is a matter on which the child will often have decided views. He may want to be a pianist or an astronaut or an oceanographer. To do so he will have to break from the Amish tradition.

It is the future of the student, not the future of the parents, that is imperiled by today's decision. If a parent keeps his child out of school beyond the grade school, then the child will be forever barred from entry into the new and amazing world of diversity that we have today. The child may decide that that is the preferred course, or he may rebel. It is the student's judgment, not his parents', that is essential if we are to give full meaning to what we have said about the Bill of Rights and of the right of students to be masters of their own destiny. If he is harnessed to the Amish way of life by those in authority over him and if his education is truncated, his entire life may be stunted and deformed. The child, therefore, should be given an opportunity to be heard before the State gives the exemption which we honor today. . . .

BIBLIOGRAPHY

"Constitutional Law: Free Exercise of Religion v. Compulsory Education." *Minnesota Law Review* 56, no. 1 (November 1971): 111.

"Court Upholds Amish Exemption . . ." *Christian Century* 89 (May 31, 1972): 627.

"First Amendment—Freedom of Religion . . ." *Georgetown Law Journal* 61 (October 1972): 236.

HOSTETLER, JOHN. *Amish Society.* Johns Hopkins Press, 1968.

HOSTETLER, JOHN, and GERTRUDE ENDERS HUNTINGTON. *Children in the Amish Society.* Holt, Rinehart & Winston; 1971.

KIRK, R. "Amish Case." *National Review* 24 (July 7, 1972): 747.

Cox v. Louisiana

379 U.S. 536, 559 (1965)

In December 1961, twenty-three black students were arrested in Baton Rouge, Louisiana, for picketing stores that maintained segregated lunch counters. The following morning, the Reverend B. Elton Cox led a march to the courthouse, where two thousand students gathered to protest the arrests. Cox urged them to conclude the demonstration with sit-ins in the segregated stores. The police immediately dispersed the crowd, using tear gas. Cox was arrested and convicted under laws against disturbing the peace, obstructing public passages, and courthouse picketing. He appealed his twenty-one-month sentence, claiming that his First Amendment rights of free speech and assembly had been violated. In 1965, the Supreme Court declared Louisiana's laws unconstitutional. "We reaffirm," Justice Arthur Goldberg wrote, "that our constitutional command of free speech and assembly is fundamental and encompasses peaceful social protest."

TRANSCRIPT OF EDITED AND NARRATED ARGUMENTS IN
Cox v. Louisiana, 379 U.S. 536, 559 (1965)

Counsel for petitioner: Carl Rachlin, New York, New York; Nils Douglas, New Orleans, Louisiana
Counsel for respondent: Ralph Roy, Baton Rouge, Louisiana

Chief Justice Earl Warren: Number 24, B. Elton Cox, appellant, versus Louisiana.

Narrator: It's October 21st, 1964. Chief Justice Earl Warren has called a case that began with a noisy demonstration on the streets of Baton Rouge, Louisiana.

The civil rights struggle of the 1950s and '60s brought dozens of cases before the Court. Beginning with *Brown versus Board of Education* in 1954, the justices ruled consistently that racial segregation violates the Constitution. The Court struck down segregation in schools, buses, hotels, and restaurants. But the justices had more trouble with cases that involved civil rights marches and rallies on public property.

The Constitution's First Amendment guarantees "freedom of speech" and "the right of the people peaceably to assemble, and to petition the Government for a redress of grievances." Does the right of free speech allow noisy demonstrations? Can the police arrest protest leaders who urge their followers to break segregation laws? Does the First Amendment protect demonstrators who block streets and sidewalks? Can those who petition the government gather outside courthouses and jails? These are the questions before the Court today.

The Civil War ended slavery, but it did not end segregation in Louisiana. A century later, the state's capital of Baton Rouge was ruled by Jim Crow laws. Black residents could shop in downtown stores. But they could not eat at "whites-only" restaurants and lunch counters. Civil rights workers organized a protest campaign during the Christmas season of 1961. Their slogan was "Don't shop where you can't eat." They backed up the boycott with picketing and sit-ins at segregated eating places.

The Baton Rouge campaign was led by college students who belonged to CORE, the Congress on Racial Equality. CORE was a "direct-action" group that organized the "Freedom Rides" across the South. Students from Southern University in Baton Rouge invited Reverend B. Elton Cox, a CORE field secretary, to lead their protest marches. Reverend Cox arrived just after twenty-three students were arrested for violating a law against picketing. They were locked up in the Baton Rouge jail, in the same building as the courthouse.

The next day, Reverend Cox led a march of two thousand students from the campus to the courthouse. They pledged allegiance to the American flag, prayed for justice and equality, and sang the civil rights anthem, "We Shall Overcome." The police responded with dogs and tear gas, and the students fled in fear. Reverend Cox was arrested and convicted of violating three laws— "disturbing the peace," "obstructing public passages," and "picketing near a courthouse." He was sentenced to twenty-one months in prison. The Louisiana Supreme Court upheld all three convictions.

Reverend Cox has two lawyers before the Supreme Court, Carl Rachlin and Nils Douglas. Chief Justice Warren welcomes Rachlin to the podium.

Warren: Mr. Rachlin?

Rachlin: Mr. Chief Justice, and may it please the Court.

On December 14th, 1961, twenty-three youngsters were arrested for peaceful picketing in downtown Baton Rouge. The purpose of their picketing was to protest against the discrimination of Negroes and the segregation of Negroes. On December 15th, Southern University students—and Southern University is a few miles outside of the city of Baton Rouge—began to hold a demonstration and decided to make a protest against the arrest of these twenty-three and to protest the segregation and discrimination that existed in Baton Rouge at the time, by coming into Baton Rouge to point out their protest. And by various means, some on foot, some by auto, some by bus, they arrived a couple of blocks from the scene of the incidents which we are concerned with here. And at some point, about noontime of that day, they were met by the chief of police, Mr. Wingate White, and by the sheriff, Mr. Clemmons.

Narrator: Rachlin described the agreement between Reverend Cox and the police officials.

Rachlin: Cox advised them they were going to have some songs, some prayers, and he would make a short speech. He was directed to hold his demonstration on the west side of the street, approximately 103 feet from the courthouse, and on the opposite side of the sidewalk adjoining the courthouse. And this meeting then went on, pursuant to his instructions by the chief of police and the sheriff to meet on the west side, that is, the side away from the court. At this very moment, of course, the two thousand people approximately were visible to the police and to the sheriff and to the mayor, and everybody knew it was approximately noontime.

Narrator: Sheriff Clemmons testified that Reverend Cox was arrested for an "inflammatory" speech to the students. Rachlin told the Court what happened.

Rachlin: When Cox said, and it came to a point, "It's now noontime. You must be hungry. Why don't you go sit down and demand to be fed," referring to the restaurants in downtown Baton Rouge.

At the moment Cox said, "Let's go have lunch," Sheriff Clemmons says: "I grabbed a power microphone. I didn't grab. Sergeant Ritrek was standing by and I took this power microphone, and I said: 'Now, you have been allowed to demonstrate. Up until now your demonstration has been more or less peaceful, but what you are doing now is a direct violation of the law, a disturbance of the peace, and it has got to be broken up immediately!' "

Narrator: Prosecution witnesses testified that Reverend Cox told the students, "Don't move!" Rachlin blamed the sheriff for the resulting panic.

Rachlin: Well, whether Cox did or did not say, "Don't move," within approximately forty seconds to a minute—the time varies slightly from witness to witness—off goes the tear gas, and then utter chaos was created.

Narrator: Rachlin argued that the trial judge was racially biased. He quoted his opinion to the Court.

Rachlin (Reading from trial judge's opinion): "It must be recognized to be inherently dangerous and a breach of the peace to bring fifteen hundred people, colored people, down in the predominantly white business district in the city of Baton Rouge and congregate across the street from the courthouse and sing songs as described to me by the defendant as the CORECongress on Racial Equalitynational anthem, carrying lines such as, quote, black and white together, and to urge those fifteen hundred people to descend upon our lunch counters and sit there until they are served."

Narrator: Justice Hugo Black supported free speech rights, but he opposed sitins on private property. He and Rachlin debated these tough questions. Rachlin claimed Reverend Cox was arrested only because of his speech.

Rachlin: He made a perfectly peaceful statement which offended the sheriff, and that's what—not that Cox *did* anything or *said* anything which was wrong or violated any of the principles of any of the cases previously decided by this Court. The sheriff interrupted not because Cox took too long or there was any serious problem. He interrupted because he didn't like what Cox said at that given moment.

Black: Suppose Cox had said to a crowd of two thousand, "I want you to go down immediately and sit in for two hours in a number of stores." Would you say that was, or was not, constitutionally protected?

Rachlin: Well, fortunately, I can answer that question academically, since that isn't the facts in these cases. Speaking for myself, Your Honor, if people behave in a peaceful manner and cause no other disturbance other than their sitting there quietly and do not do any—commit any violence against the property other than sitting there, as far as I'm concerned that should be a constitutionally protected right. But I know this Court has not yet said that. I hope someday it will.

Black: You are not basing this defense on that grounds?

Rachlin: Not at all, not at all. We're saying he said something absolutely peaceful, and he should not have been interrupted, and the order of the police was illegal, even if Cox said, "Don't move," which we dispute. Even if Cox said, "Don't move," this was an illegal order, and I think as citizens we have an obligation to refuse to obey an obviously illegal and discriminatory order issued by the police.

Narrator: Chief Justice Warren welcomed the state's lawyer, Ralph Roy.

Warren: Mr. Roy?

Roy: Mr. Chief Justice, may it please the Court.

Narrator: Roy painted a different scene of the demonstration.

Roy: The twenty-three who had been incarcerated up in the jail and who were about a hundred feet, I would imagine, from where the demonstrators were, started yelling and screaming and beating on the jail walls. And a response in turn was had by the two thousand people downstairs, and quite a commotion developed. Plenty of noise. No physical violence, but plenty of noise. And the sheriff then informed appellant that this thing is getting out of hand, you better disperse. And he did tell him twice. The record will show this. And some of the evidence says that the appellant told his members, "Don't move." In any event, when this thing that the sheriff said got to be ripe for a riot, and you could feel the tenseness in the atmosphere, that the bombs were used to disperse the crowd.

Court: What'd you say?

Roy: Tear gas bombs.

Narrator: The Civil Rights Act of 1964 outlawed restaurant segregation. Roy was asked if Reverend Cox could be convicted of "breach of the peace" for his statements before that law was passed.

Court: Are you claiming that he could be convicted for what he said alone?

Roy: No, sir, not alone. Of course, we are claiming also that this statement to the effect—and this was, of course, prior to the Civil Rights Act—the statement to the effect, to go to the eating places where they won't serve you, and if they refuse, to stay there, was not a lawful statement.

Court: Not a lawful what?

Roy: It was encouraging people to . . .

Court: Was he convicted under one of the statutes for saying that to them, for saying that alone?

Roy: No, sir, he was not.

Warren: Isn't it quite clear that the trial court convicted the defendant precisely for what he said? Didn't the trial court make that very clear?

Roy: Yes, I think the trial judge did that.

Warren: That's the basis of the conviction.

Roy: I think that's right.

Warren: The statement.

Roy: I think that statement—from that statement, the trial court found the intent to commit a breach of the peace.

Narrator: Reverend Cox was sentenced to a year in prison for picketing near a courthouse. Nils Douglas based his argument on Supreme Court rulings that only a "clear and present danger" could justify restrictions on speech or assembly.

Douglas: My argument consists of three points. The first point is that there was no clear and present danger requiring the conviction of the appellant in this case. The second point is that neither one of the state courts which passed on this action applied the clear and present danger rule. And the third portion of my argument is that there was no evidence upon which to convict the appellant herein.

Narrator: Justice Potter Stewart had a question.

Stewart: Let's just say there's a "Keep Off the Grass" ordinance, and people insist on congregating there to assemble and express their ideas. Is it your contention that there has to be a clear and present danger of damage to the government . . .

Douglas: In every instance, Your Honor, it is our contention . . .

Stewart: . . . or only a clear and present danger of damage to the grass? That's a limited, specific ordinance with a precise purpose. Is it your contention that such an ordinance would be entirely invalid unless you can show a clear and present danger to public safety?

Douglas: It's our position, Your Honor, that in every instance where free speech is being exercised, that it must be shown as a matter of fact that there was a clear and present danger, and of course . . .

Stewart: Clear and present danger to what? To what?

Douglas: To substantial interests that the state has a right to protect.

Narrator: Douglas defended the right of demonstration.

Douglas: If this were a case of the evenhanded administration of justice, many of the issues raised here would not be as perplexing as they are. However, our basic position is that the streets and sidewalks are natural places for people to express their views, and they have no less right to express the view of antisegregation than they have a right to express their views on anything else. Much has been made of the fact that the activities took on an aspect of picketing. I might suggest that there were other areas of the demonstration which took up the aspect, a greater aspect, of free speech—the pledging allegiance to the flag. This would suggest a support of the government, rather than an attempt to destruct it. The singing of patriotic songs likewise, the singing of religious songs, would seem to me to suggest that this was to be nonviolent.

Narrator: Ralph Roy defended Reverend Cox's conviction for picketing near the courthouse. His argument prompted a lengthy debate with Chief Justice Warren.

Roy: Substantially, these acts prohibit the picketing or parading in or near a courthouse or in or near a building or residence occupied or used by a judge, juror, witness, or court official, with the intent of interfering with, obstructing or impeding the administration of justice, or with the intent of influencing any such official. As pointed out by the state Supreme Court and as is known by everyone, picketing factually is not the equivalent of speech, and consequently, as this Court has said, it is not equal in legal equivalent.

Warren: You think that the mere presence of these people at the place where they were at this time was a violation of the law?

Roy: Not this particular law, because it requires not only their presence at this particular place in the manner suggested, crowding or picketing in or near a courthouse—not only is that required, but there also is required an intent to influence a court official or to impede the administration of justice. This is required, and we get this requirement from their proclaimed design and object to go out there and protest this illegal arrest, as they called it.

Warren: Then the mere fact that they agreed to protest is in itself a part of this crime?

Roy: Yes, sir. I think you have to utilize that to get the intent.

Narrator: Roy cited the testimony of Ronnie Moore, a student leader who faced a ten-year sentence for "criminal anarchy." Chief Justice Warren had more questions.

Roy: The trial judge went to great lengths in asking Ronnie Moore on the witness stand, "Why the courthouse? Why did you come down here? Why not on the old State Capitol grounds or some other part of town, some public park? Why here?" And he says, "Here's where they were arrested and we came to protest it; we came here."

"Well, what did you hope to gain by doing this? What did you hope to gain?" I think he said something about love—love, or the hearts of men, or words to that effect.

Warren: Do I understand, Mr. Roy, that it's your position that even if the chief of police did give them permission to be on this side of the street with their people and to give the pledge of allegiance, as they did, and to sing religious songs, as they did, and to speak, as Mr. Cox did, that they're still guilty, without more, of violating this particular statute?

Roy: As I said, I think so. In fact, I feel rather sure they would, because I know of no law that would grant immunity to a person who violates the law by virtue of the fact that some police officer acquiesced in it or gave him permission.

Warren: In other words, you think the conduct before the chief of police told them to disband and move on was in itself sufficient to sustain a conviction, even though the chief of police had told them, after knowing that they intended to do these things, that if they kept on one side of the street, which they did, that it was all right.

Roy: I think they could have been arrested, clearly, at the old State Capitol for blocking that sidewalk, before they ever got to the courthouse. And, as the chief of police said, the only reason he tolerated it was—well, of course, as I have just read from the transcript, he was asked to disperse before he ever got two blocks from the courthouse, which he refused to do. And the only reason that this tolerance or acquiescence on the part of the public officials was had was because they were trying to get out of a bad situation as easily as possible.

Narrator: Reverend Cox urged the students to "move on" from the courthouse to the downtown stores. In his rebuttal, Carl Rachlin blamed Sheriff Clemmons for the panic that followed this statement.

Rachlin: I don't know what "move on" means to people of two thousand, when two thousand people are congregated in a small area. I don't know what "move on" means, frankly, and I don't think the sheriff knew what he was saying. He was just so mad because Cox was suggesting that they have a sit-in. Because— you read everybody's testimony. This was the sticking point in every single witness's mind, that Cox said, "Let's eat," and the place blew apart so far as the police were concerned. And when you have that kind of a sequence of events, if the sheriff had not interrupted, that meeting would have ended a moment or two later in a peaceful fashion. There would have been no problem whatsoever.

It was the police that caused the trouble in the situation, and they caused it, we say, for a discriminatory, illegal, unconstitutional reason.

Narrator: The Supreme Court decided the case on January 18th, 1965. The justices issued two rulings. By a seven-to-two vote, they reversed the convictions for "breach of the peace" and "obstructing public passages." And Reverend Cox escaped a year in prison for "picketing near a courthouse" by a single vote, five-to-four.

Cases that mix speech and assembly with noise and commotion are difficult. Back in 1919, Justice Oliver Wendell Holmes wrote that the lawfulness "of every act depends on the circumstances in which it is done." The justices looked closely at the circumstances of this demonstration. They even looked at television film of the singing and clapping. The majority agreed that "the entire meeting from the beginning to its dispersal by tear gas was orderly and not riotous." It was not Reverend Cox but the police who breached the peace.

The students clearly obstructed the sidewalk and violated Louisiana law. But the issue wasn't that simple. Public places are designed both for traffic and protest. The balance again depends on circumstances. "The rights of free speech and assembly," the Court held, do not protect marches "in the middle of Times Square at the rush hour." But the police can't use traffic laws to censor ideas they don't like. They can't allow the American Legion to march and stop Reverend Cox with tear gas. The Court held that giving the police "uncontrolled discretion" to "permit or prohibit" marches violates the First Amendment.

Reverend Cox didn't know how close he came to prison walls. Justice Arthur Goldberg first wrote an opinion upholding the conviction for "picketing near a courthouse." Louisiana was entitled to protect its courts from coercion. But the television film changed Goldberg's mind. It showed Sheriff Clemmons pointing to where the students could stand on the sidewalk. Goldberg's final opinion said the sheriff agreed the demonstration would not be "near" the courthouse.

Justice Hugo Black was outraged by Goldberg's desertion. His dissenting opinion deplored the "fanatical, threatening, lawless mob" that would apply "coercive pressures" to the courts. Black evened the score after Goldberg left the Court in 1965. The next year, Black wrote for a new majority that upheld the convictions of students who marched outside a jail in Tallahassee, Florida. One vote made the difference between protest and prison.

The scales of justice still balance free speech against public order. How the courts weigh these rights in the circumstances of each case will decide how loudly we can shout and sing.

EDITED SUPREME COURT OPINIONS
Cox v. Louisiana

No. 24

MR. JUSTICE GOLDBERG delivered the opinion of the Court.

Appellant, the Reverend Mr. B. Elton Cox, the leader of a civil rights demonstration, was arrested and charged with four offenses under Louisiana law —criminal conspiracy, disturbing the peace, obstructing public passages, and picketing before a courthouse. In a consolidated trial before a judge without a jury, and on the same set of facts, he was acquitted of criminal conspiracy but convicted of the other three offenses. He was sentenced to serve four months in jail and pay a two hundred dollar fine for disturbing the peace, to serve five months in jail and pay a five hundred dollar fine for obstructing public passages, and to serve one year in jail and pay a five thousand dollar fine for picketing before a courthouse. The sentences were cumulative. . . .

Appellant was convicted of violating a Louisiana "disturbing the peace" statute, which provides:

"Whoever with intent to provoke a breach of the peace, or under circumstances such that a breach of the peace may be occasioned thereby . . . crowds or congregates with others . . . in or upon . . . a public street or public highway, or upon a public sidewalk, or any other public place or building . . . and who fails or refuses to disperse and move on . . . when ordered so to do by any law enforcement officer of any municipality, or parish, in which such act or acts are committed, or by any law enforcement officer of the state of Louisiana, or any other authorized person . . . shall be guilty of disturbing the peace." La. Rev. Stat. § 14:103.1 (Cum. Supp. 1962).

It is clear to us that on the facts of this case . . . Louisiana infringed appellant's rights of free speech and free assembly by convicting him under this statute. . . .

Appellant led a group of young college students who wished "to protest segregation" and discrimination against Negroes and the arrest of twenty-three fellow students. They assembled peaceably at the State Capitol building and marched to the courthouse where they sang, prayed and listened to a speech. A reading of the record reveals agreement on the part of the State's witnesses that Cox had the demonstration "very well controlled," and until the end of Cox's speech, the group was perfectly "orderly." Sheriff Clemmons testified that the crowd's activities were not "objectionable" before that time. They became objectionable, according to the Sheriff himself, when Cox, concluding his speech, urged the students to go uptown and sit in at lunch counters. The Sheriff testified that the sole aspect of the program to which he objected was "[t]he inflammatory manner in which he [Cox] addressed that crowd and told them to go on up town, go to four places on the protest list, sit down and if they don't feed you, sit there for one hour." Yet this part of Cox's speech obviously did not deprive the demonstration of its protected character under the Constitution as free speech and assembly. . . .

There is an additional reason why this conviction cannot be sustained. The statute at issue in this case, as authoritatively interpreted by the Louisiana Supreme Court, is unconstitutionally vague in its overly broad scope. The statutory crime consists of two elements: (1) congregating with others "with intent to provoke a breach of the peace, or under circumstances such that a breach of the peace may be occasioned," and (2) a refusal to move on after having been ordered to do so by a law enforcement officer. While the second part of this offense is narrow and specific, the first element is not. The Louisiana Supreme Court in this case defined the term "breach of the peace" as "to agitate, to arouse from a state of repose, to molest, to interrupt, to hinder, to disquiet." . . . Both definitions would allow persons to be punished merely for peacefully expressing unpopular views. Yet, a "function of free speech under our system of government is to invite dispute. It may indeed best serve its high purpose when it induces a condition of unrest, creates dissatisfaction with conditions as they are, or even stirs people to anger. Speech is often provocative and challenging. It may strike at prejudices and preconceptions and have profound unsettling effects as it presses for acceptance of an idea. That is why freedom of speech . . . is . . . protected against censorship or punishment. . . . There is no room under our Constitution for a more restrictive view. For the alternative would lead to standardization of ideas either by legislatures, courts, or dominant political or community groups." *Terminiello* v. *Chicago,* 337 U. S. 1, 4–5 . . .

For all these reasons we hold that appellant's freedoms of speech and assembly, secured to him by the First Amendment, as applied to the States by the Fourteenth Amendment, were denied by his conviction for disturbing the peace. The conviction on this charge cannot stand.

We now turn to the issue of the validity of appellant's conviction for violating the Louisiana statute, La. Rev. Stat. § 14:100.1 . . . , which provides:

"Obstructing Public Passages"

"No person shall wilfully obstruct the free, convenient and normal use of any public sidewalk, street, highway, bridge, alley, road, or other passageway, or the entrance, corridor or passage of any public building, structure, watercraft or ferry, by impeding, hindering, stifling, retarding or restraining traffic or passage thereon or therein.

"Providing however nothing herein contained shall apply to a bona fide legitimate labor organization or to any of its legal activities such as picketing, lawful assembly or concerted activity in the interest of its members for the purpose of accomplishing or securing more favorable wage standards, hours of employment and working conditions."

Appellant was convicted under this statute, not for leading the march to the vicinity of the courthouse, which the Louisiana Supreme Court stated to have been "orderly," . . . but for leading the meeting on the sidewalk across the street from the courthouse. . . .

It is clearly unconstitutional to enable a public official to determine which expressions of view will be permitted and which will not or to engage in invidious discrimination among persons or groups either by use of a statute providing a system of broad discretionary licensing power or, as in this case, the equivalent of such a system by selective enforcement of an extremely broad prohibitory statute.

. . . [H]ere it is clear that the practice in Baton Rouge allowing unfettered discretion in local officials in the regulation of the use of the streets for peaceful parades and meetings is an unwarranted abridgment of appellant's freedom of speech and assembly secured to him by the First Amendment, as applied to the States by the Fourteenth Amendment. It follows, therefore, that appellant's conviction for violating the statute as so applied and enforced must be reversed.

No. 49

MR. JUSTICE GOLDBERG delivered the opinion of the Court.

Appellant was convicted of violating a Louisiana statute which provides:

"Whoever, with the intent of interfering with, obstructing, or impeding the administration of justice, or with the intent of influencing any judge, juror, witness, or court officer, in the discharge of his duty pickets or parades in or near a building housing a court of the State of Louisiana . . . shall be fined not more than five thousand dollars or imprisoned not more than one year, or both." La. Rev. Stat. § 14:401 (Cum. Supp. 1962). . . .

There can be no question that a State has a legitimate interest in protecting its judicial system from the pressures which picketing near a courthouse might create. Since we are committed to a government of laws and not of men, it is of the utmost importance that the administration of justice be absolutely fair and orderly. This Court has recognized that the unhindered and untrammeled functioning of our courts is part of the very foundation of our constitutional democracy. . . .

We hold that this statute on its face is a valid law dealing with conduct subject to regulation so as to vindicate important interests of society and that the fact that free speech is intermingled with such conduct does not bring with it constitutional protection. . . .

There are, however, more substantial constitutional objections arising from appellant's conviction on the particular facts of this case. Appellant was convicted for demonstrating not "in," but "near" the courthouse. It is undisputed that the demonstration took place on the west sidewalk, the far side of the street, exactly 101 feet from the courthouse steps and, judging from the pictures in the record, approximately 125 feet from the courthouse itself. The question is raised as to whether the failure of the statute to define the word "near" renders it unconstitutionally vague. . . .

The record here clearly shows that the officials present gave permission for the demonstration to take place across the street from the courthouse. Cox testified that they gave him permission to conduct the demonstration on the far side of the street. This testimony is not only uncontradicted but is corroborated by the State's witnesses who were present. . . .

Liberty can only be exercised in a system of law which safeguards order. We reaffirm the repeated holdings of this Court that our constitutional command of free speech and assembly is basic and fundamental and encompasses peaceful social protest, so important to the preservation of the freedoms treasured in a democratic society. We also reaffirm the repeated decisions of this Court that there is no place for violence in a democratic society dedicated to liberty under law, and that the right of peaceful protest does not mean that everyone with opinions or beliefs to express may do so at any time and at any place. There is a proper time and place for even the most peaceful protest and a plain duty and responsibility on the part of all citizens to obey all valid laws and regulations. There is an equally plain requirement for laws and regulations to be drawn so as to give citizens fair warning as to what is illegal . . .

The application of these principles requires us to reverse the judgment of the Supreme Court of Louisiana.

Reversed.

MR. JUSTICE BLACK dissenting in No. 49

I would sustain the conviction of appellant for violation of Louisiana's Rev. Stat. § 14:401 which makes it an offense for anyone, under any conditions, to picket or parade near a courthouse, residence or other building used by a judge, juror, witness, or court officer, "with the intent of influencing" any of them. Certainly the record shows beyond all doubt that the purpose of the two thousand or more people who stood right across the street from the courthouse and jail was to protest the arrest of members of their group who were then in jail. As the Court's opinion states, appellant Cox so testified. Certainly the most obvious reason for their protest at the courthouse was to influence the judge and other court officials who used the courthouse and performed their official duties there. . . .

This statute . . . was enacted to protect courts and court officials from the intimidation and dangers that inhere in huge gatherings at courthouse doors and jail doors to protest arrests and to influence court officials in performing their duties. The very purpose of a court system is to adjudicate controversies, both criminal and civil, in the calmness and solemnity of the courtroom according to legal procedures. Justice cannot be rightly administered, nor are the lives and safety of prisoners secure, where throngs of people clamor against the processes of justice right outside the courthouse or jailhouse doors. The streets are not now and never have been the proper place to administer justice. Use of the streets for such purposes has always proved disastrous to individual liberty in the long run, whatever fleeting benefits may have appeared to have been achieved. And minority groups, I venture to suggest, are the ones who always have suffered and always will suffer most when street multitudes are allowed to substitute their pressures for the less glamorous but more dependable and temperate processes of the law. Experience demonstrates that it is not a far step from what to many seems the earnest, honest, patriotic, kind-spirited multitude of today, to the fanatical, threatening, lawless mob of tomorrow. And the crowds that press in the streets for noble goals today can be supplanted tomorrow by street mobs pressuring the courts for precisely opposite ends.

Minority groups in particular need always to bear in mind that the Constitution, while it requires States to treat all citizens equally and protect them in the exercise of rights granted by the Federal Constitution and laws, does not take away the State's power, indeed its duty, to keep order and to do justice according to law. Those who encourage minority groups to believe that the United States Constitution and federal laws give them a right to patrol and picket in the streets whenever they choose, in order to advance what they think to be a just and noble end, do no service to those minority groups, their cause, or their country. I am confident from this record that this appellant violated the Louisiana statute because of a mistaken belief that he and his followers had a constitutional right to do so, because of what they believed were just grievances. But the history of the past twenty-five years if it shows nothing else shows that his group's constitutional and statutory rights have to be protected by the courts, which must be kept free from intimidation and coercive pressures of any kind. Government under law as ordained by our Constitution is too precious, too sacred, to be jeopardized by subjecting the courts to intimidatory practices that have been fatal to individual liberty and minority rights wherever and whenever such practices have been allowed to poison the streams of justice. I would be wholly unwilling to join in moving this country a single step in that direction.

BIBLIOGRAPHY

CARSON, CLAYBORNE. *In Struggle*. Harvard University Press, 1981.

CARSON, CLAYBORNE. *The Movement*. Meckler, 1989.

"Civil Rights . . ." *American Bar Association Journal* 51, no. 4 (April 1965): 369.

FREEMAN, HARROP A. "Civil Disobedience, Law, and Democracy." *Law in Transition*, Winter, 1966, p. 13.

FREEMAN, HARROP A. "The Right to Protest and Civil Disobedience." *Indiana Law Journal* 41, no. 2 (Winter 1966): 228.

GLASSER, IRA. *Visions of Liberty*. Arcade, 1991.

Tinker v. Des Moines

393 U.S. 503 (1969)

In 1965, Mary Beth Tinker was an eighth grader at Warren Harding Junior High in Des Moines, Iowa. In December, she and students from other schools decided to support a Christmas truce and bombing halt in the Vietnam War by wearing black armbands to school. Hearing of this plan, the Des Moines public school principals immediately enacted a policy prohibiting students from wearing armbands, claiming that protest would lead to disruption. They subsequently suspended five students who wore armbands. Mary Beth Tinker challenged the policy as violating the free speech clause of the First Amendment. In 1969, the Supreme Court ruled that the Constitution guarantees public school students a right to symbolic, nondisruptive political expression. Students, Justice Abe Fortas wrote, do not "shed their constitutional rights to freedom of speech or expression at the schoolhouse gate."

TRANSCRIPT OF EDITED AND NARRATED ARGUMENTS IN
Tinker v. *Des Moines*, 393 U.S. 503 (1969)

Counsel for petitioners: Dan Johnston, Des Moines, Iowa
Counsel for respondents: Allen Herrick, Des Moines, Iowa

Narrator: It's November 12th, 1968. Chief Justice Earl Warren has called for argument a case—*"Tinker versus Des Moines"*—that stemmed from domestic conflict over the Vietnam War. For the past four years, since Congress authorized President Lyndon Johnson to unleash bombing attacks on North Vietnam, the war split the nation into hawks and doves. Support for the war eroded as thousands of American troops came home in body bags. Johnson's critics— both hawks and doves—shot down his reelection plans. Just a week before this argument, Richard Nixon was narrowly elected President, promising a "secret plan" to end the war.

The *Tinker* case began in America's heartland, the farm country of Iowa, in December 1965. In broadest terms, it placed free speech claims under the Constitution's First Amendment against the powers of government. More narrowly, it questioned the authority of school officials to censor symbolic speech in classrooms. And finally, it challenged the right of Des Moines principals to suspend five students, including Mary Beth Tinker, for wearing black armbands to class. A federal judge upheld the suspensions, ruling that the armbands, in his words, "would be likely to disturb the disciplined atmosphere required for any classroom." Mary Beth's lawyer, Dan Johnston, argues her appeal to the Supreme Court.

Warren: Mr. Johnston.

Johnston: Mr. Chief Justice, and may it please the Court.

The conduct of the students essentially was this. That at Christmastime in 1965, they decided that they would wear small black armbands to express certain views which they had in regard to the war in Vietnam. Specifically, the views were that they mourned the dead of both sides, both civilian and military in that war, and they supported the proposal that had been made by United States Senator Robert Kennedy that the truce which had been proposed for that war over the Christmas period be made an open-ended or an indefinite truce. This was the purpose that the students gave for wearing the armbands during this period.

During this period of time, of course, there were school days and they wore the armbands to school. Prior to the time when any of these petitioners wore the armbands to school, it came to the attention of the school authorities that perhaps there would be some students who would express views related to the war in Vietnam in this manner during school time.

Narrator: Johnston explained what happened when school officials were informed of the armband protest.

Johnston: The principals of the secondary schools, the high schools, and perhaps the junior high schools in the City of Des Moines public school system met prior to the time that any of the armbands had been worn and enacted a policy which was not written but which was agreed upon among themselves, that no student could wear an armband in the Des Moines public school system for this purpose; that if the student came to school wearing the armband he would be asked to remove it; failing that, the student's parents would be contacted and their assistance would be solicited in getting the students to remove the armbands; failing that, the students would be sent home—would be in effect suspended from school until such time as they were willing to return to school without the armbands.

Narrator: Johnston introduced the justices to his three clients.

Johnston: The three students who are petitioners in this case—Christopher Eckhardt, who was sixteen and in the tenth grade at Roosevelt High School in Des Moines at the time; John Tinker, who was fifteen and in the eleventh grade at another high school; Mary Beth Tinker, who was thirteen and in the eighth grade—determined that in spite of the policy that had been announced through the schools, they would wear the armbands as a matter of conscience to express the views that they had.

Narrator: The vice-principal suspended Chris Eckhardt even before he got to his first class. Mary Beth Tinker, at Warren Harding Junior High, was next.

Johnston: Mary Beth Tinker also wore her armband on that first day. However, she wore it throughout the entire morning without any incident related to it that in any way disrupted the school or distracted. She wore it at lunch and she wore it—where there was, by the way, some conversation between herself and other students in the lunchroom about why she was wearing the armband and whether or not she should be wearing it—and then wore it into the first class in the afternoon. And it was in the first class in the afternoon that she was called to the office and the procedure was followed for contacting her parents, apparently asking her to remove it, and she did remove the armband and then returned to class. However, in spite of the fact that she had removed the armband and was returned to class, she was later called out of class and suspended nevertheless.

Narrator: Justice Byron White broke in.

White: What if the student had gotten up from the class he went to and delivered the message orally that his armband was intended to convey and insisted on doing it all through the hour?

Johnston: In that case, Your Honor, we would not be here, even if he insisted on doing it only for a second, because he would clearly be—although he would be expressing his views, he would be doing something else.

White: Why did they wear the armband to class, to express that message?

Johnston: To express the message, yes.

White: To everybody in the class?

Johnston: To everyone in the class, yes, Your Honor.

White: Everybody while they were listening to some other subject matter was supposed to be looking at the armband and taking in that message?

Johnston: Well, to the extent that they would see it. But I don't believe there was any—I don't believe that the . . .

White: Well, they were intended to see it, weren't they?

Johnston: They were intended to see it in a way that would not be distracting . . .

White: And to understand it.

Johnston: And to understand it.

White: And to absorb that message . . .

Johnston: And to absorb the message . . .

White: While they're studying arithmetic or mathematics, they're supposed to be taking in this message about Vietnam?

Johnston: Well, except that, Your Honor, I believe that the method that the students chose in this particular instance was specifically designed in such a way that it would not cause that kind of disruption.

Narrator: Justice White pressed Dan Johnston on classroom disruption.

White: Again, why did they wear the armband?

Johnston: They wore the armband to . . .

White: . . . convey a message.

Johnston: . . . convey the message; that's right.

White: They anticipated students would see it and understand it and think about it?

Johnston: That's correct.

White: And when they did it in class, they intended the students to do it *in* class?

Johnston: I think it's a fair assumption that the method of expression . . .

White: They intended the students to think about it outside of class but not in class?

Johnston: I think they intended, I think they chose a message, chose a method of expression, Your Honor, which would not be distracting . . .

White: . . . physically; it wouldn't make a noise, it wouldn't cause a commotion, but don't you think it would cause some people to direct their attention to the armband and the Vietnam War and think about that, rather than what they were thinking about, supposed to be thinking about in the classroom?

Johnston: I think perhaps, Your Honor, it might for a few moments have done that, and I think it perhaps might have distracted some students, just as many other things do in the classroom which are allowed, from time to time.

Narrator: Johnston accused the school board of violating the First Amendment.

Johnston: Our contention is that the policy as it was adopted, it was a broad policy which did not distinguish, not in any way was directed toward disruption or distraction. It is a policy which will not stand the test of freedom of expression under the First Amendment.

Narrator: Another justice moved to the *method* of expressing a message.

Brennan: Suppose it had been a button—Stop the Bombing.

Johnston: Well, as a matter of fact, a number of political buttons were worn at this school.

Court: That is, I'm for Humphrey, or I'm for Wallace?

Johnston: I'm for Humphrey—well, we didn't have at that time—I'm for Humphrey, or I'm for Nixon, I'm for Goldwater. The record also shows that . . .

Brennan: Suppose it was just, Stop the Bombing?

Johnston: That, to me, would not be the sort of thing which would be designed to disrupt the class.

Brennan: Suppose it was a placard, with a message?

Johnston: The situation, I think, and the problem that we have, is this specific regulation, directed only toward one specific kind of conduct. The difficulty we have with this particular policy as it was enacted is that there was no indication, no testimony by teachers, by administrators or anyone else, of any reason to believe that it would be disruptive. And when the students in fact did wear the armbands, the record quite clearly shows that it was not in fact disruptive.

Narrator: Chief Justice Warren pushed Johnston on the disruption issue.

Warren: I suppose you would concede that if it started fistfights, or something of that kind, and disrupted the school, that the principal could prevent the use of them?

Johnston: The suggestion I believe we're making, Your Honor, is that there should not be any special rule for freedom of expression cases for schools. I would like to make a distinction, if I may, between the, an expression of an opinion which might itself disrupt a class, and the expression of an opinion which might cause someone else to disrupt the class. And I believe those are perhaps two separate cases. I would also like to make a distinction between the expression of an opinion which is coupled with something else, like marching in the hallway, or standing up in the class and making a speech about the war in Vietnam during mathematics class. That kind of thing, I think the court can prohibit.

Narrator: Dan Johnston concluded.

Johnston: I should not think that there would have to be a special rule for schools or any other part of our society for the First Amendment. Now the evidence of disruption might be different. But as far as the principles applied, we'd like to have the same principles applied in the school or perhaps especially in the school that are applied elsewhere.

Narrator: Allan Herrick represented the school board. Born at the end of the nineteenth century, he reflected the values of an older generation.

Herrick: The respondents believe that there are two basic issues involved here. The first, Do school administrators or school boards have to wait until violence, disorder, and disruption break out and the scholarly discipline of the school is disrupted, or may they act when in good faith, in their reasonable discretion and judgment, disorder and disruption of the scholarly atmosphere of the schoolroom will result unless they act firmly and promptly?

The second issue, it seems to me, is that this Court must determine how far it wants to go under the constitutional amendments for free speech in reviewing every decision of every school district made in good faith, in its reasonable discretion and judgment, as necessary to maintain order and a scholarly, disciplined atmosphere within the classroom.

A third issue might be added. Are disturbances or threatened disturbances in the schools to be measured by identical standards with disturbances or threatened disturbances on the streets?

Narrator: Herrick defended the school board's decision to ban the armbands.

Herrick: Now, it's the position of the respondents that the decision of the school administration and of the school board, made in good faith, under the circumstances existing when that decision was made, was the reasonable exercise of discretion on the part of the school authorities and did not deprive petitioners of their constitutional right of free speech.

Narrator: Herrick cited a recent Supreme Court decision upholding criminal convictions of black students who marched to support jailed sit-in demonstrators. Justice Thurgood Marshall had defended black students as a civil rights lawyer.

Herrick: The case of *Adderly versus the State of Florida* seems particularly pertinent, where the students went from the university to the jail grounds to protest the arrest of students who had been arrested the day before, and their claim was . . .

Marshall: Mr. Herrick, how many students were involved in the *Addersly (sic)* case?

Herrick: In the *Adderly* case?

Marshall: Uh, huh. Several hundred, wasn't it?

Herrick: It was quite a large number.

Marshall: How many were involved in this one?

Herrick: Well, there were. . . . That's a question, Your Honor, what do you mean by "involved"?

Marshall: How many were wearing armbands?

Herrick: Well, there were five suspended for wearing armbands.

Marshall: Well, were any wearing armbands who were not suspended?

Herrick: Yes, I think there were two.

Marshall: That makes seven.

Herrick: They weren't excepted, and I'll refer to that a little later; they were . . .

Marshall: Seven out of eighteen thousand, and the school board was afraid that seven students wearing armbands would disrupt eighteen thousand. Am I correct?

Herrick: I think, if the Court please, that that doesn't give us the entire background that builds up to what was existing in the Des Moines schools at the time the armbands were worn.

Narrator: Three months before this argument, antiwar rallies at the Democratic Party convention in Chicago provoked a violent police response. It shocked the nation. Herrick tried to link the Des Moines protestors to a controversial group, Students for a Democratic Society, that sponsored the Chicago rallies and earlier antiwar marches.

Herrick: In the background of this case, in November of 1965, the petitioner, Christopher Eckhardt, with his mother, who was president of the Des Moines chapter of the Women's International League for Peace and Freedom, had come to Washington, D.C., to participate with the Students for a Democratic Society, Dr. Spock, and others, in the march, which I'm sure this Court's familiar with, from the White House to the Washington Monument.

Now, that was in November, I think, about the Thanksgiving holiday. On Saturday, December 11th, 1965, following this march, a group which included students related to the Students for a Democratic Society, and some adults, met at the Eckhardt home, and one of the proposals that developed at this meeting was the wearing of these black armbands.

Narrator: Herrick quoted the trial judge's opinion in the *Tinker* case.

Herrick: "The Vietnam war and the involvement of the United States therein has been the subject of a major controversy for some time. When the armband regulation involved herein was promulgated, debate over the Vietnam War had become vehement in many localities. A protest march against the war had recently been held in Washington, D.C. A wave of draft card burning incidents protesting the war had swept the country. At that time, two highly publicized draft card burning cases were pending in this court. Both individuals supporting the war and those opposing it were quite vocal in expressing their views. This was demonstrated during the school board's hearing on the armband regulation."

And that appears also in the record. I think some two hundred had gathered who were, many of them, outsiders, at the time of the school board hearing. At this hearing the school board voted in support of the rule prohibiting the wearing of the black armbands, the wearing of armbands, in school premises. It is against this background the Court must review the reasonableness of the regulation.

Narrator: During the armband controversy, a Des Moines soldier, Private James Flagg, died in Vietnam. Herrick said his death created an "explosive situation" in the schools. Justice Marshall raised sharp questions.

Herrick: This thing had been extensively exploited in the press. We had a situation here where it was explosive.

Marshall: And that explosive situation was that they had a meeting in Washington, D.C. What else besides that?

Herrick: All right. This is page 70, at the top of the Appendix. "A former student at one of our high schools was killed in Vietnam. Some of his friends are still in school. It was felt that if any kind of a demonstration existed, it might evolve into something which would be difficult to control."

Marshall: Do we have a city in this country that hasn't had someone killed in Vietnam?

Herrick: No, I think not, Your Honor, but I don't think it would be an explosive situation in most cases. But if someone is going to appear in court with an armband here, protesting the thing, that it could be explosive. That is the situation we find ourselves in.

Marshall: It *could* be.

Herrick: What?

Marshall: It *could* be. Is that your position? And there is no evidence that it *would* be? Is that the rule you want us to adopt?

Herrick: No, not at all, Your Honor.

Narrator: Herrick asked the justices to tell Mary Beth Tinker where she could *not* wear her armband.

Herrick: Not at every time, not at every place, and particularly not under the circumstances that existed in this case, not in the school room at a time when it might result in disruption and might even result in violence.

Now, in substance, if we understand the petitioners' position in this case, it is that the school officials are powerless to act until the disruption occurs. Respondents believe that should not be the rule. Sometimes an ounce of prevention is a lot better than a pound of cure, and I think the subsequent history of such activities bear out the judgment of the school officials in their discretion.

Narrator: Three months later, on February 24th, 1969, Mary Beth Tinker won the right to wear her black armband. Justice Abe Fortas wrote the opinion in the seven-to-two decision. Neither students nor teachers, he wrote, "shed their constitutional rights to freedom of speech or expression at the schoolhouse gate." In Fortas's words, public schools "may not be enclaves of totalitarianism."

"Fear or apprehension of disturbance" cannot overcome the First Amendment. He admitted that speech on controversial issues may start arguments or cause disturbance. But in his words, "our Constitution says we must take this risk."

The Court's oldest member, Hugo Black, was known for his absolute defense of the First Amendment. But he rebelled in the *Tinker* case, endorsing, in his words, "the old-fashioned slogan that 'children are to be seen not heard.' " He warned that the Court's approval of armbands marked "the beginning of a new revolutionary era of permissiveness in this country."

Since the *Tinker* decision, the Supreme Court has trimmed the First Amendment rights of students. In 1988, a five-to-four majority ruled that officials could censor articles in school newspapers that—in Justice Byron White's words—are "unsuitable for immature audiences." In *Hazelwood School District* v. *Kuhlmeier* he cited Justice Black's dissent in the Tinker case.

Mary Beth Tinker is proud of her stand in junior high. She now works as a VA hospital nurse and treats Vietnam veterans. And she's still a peace activist. "I'm really proud that we had a part in ending the crazy Vietnam war," she says.

EDITED SUPREME COURT OPINIONS
Tinker v. Des Moines

MR. JUSTICE FORTAS delivered the opinion of the Court.

First Amendment rights, applied in light of the special characteristics of the school environment, are available to teachers and students. It can hardly be argued that either students or teachers shed their constitutional rights to freedom of speech or expression at the schoolhouse gate. This has been the unmistakable holding of this Court for almost fifty years. . . .

In *West Virginia* v. *Barnette*, . . . this Court held that under the First Amendment, the student in public school may not be compelled to salute the flag. Speaking through Mr. Justice Jackson, the Court said:

> "The Fourteenth Amendment, as now applied to the States, protects the citizen against the State itself and all of its creatures—Boards of Education not excepted. These have, of course, important, delicate, and highly

discretionary functions, but none that they may not perform within the limits of the Bill of Rights. That they are educating the young for citizenship is reason for scrupulous protection of Constitutional freedoms of the individual, if we are not to strangle the free mind at its source and teach youth to discount important principles of our government as mere platitudes." 319 U. S., at 637.

On the other hand, the Court has repeatedly emphasized the need for affirming the comprehensive authority of the States and of school officials, consistent with fundamental constitutional safeguards, to prescribe and control conduct in the schools. . . . Our problem lies in the area where students in the exercise of First Amendment rights collide with the rules of the school authorities.

The problem posed by the present case does not relate to regulation of the length of skirts or the type of clothing, to hair style, or deportment. . . . It does not concern aggressive, disruptive action or even group demonstrations. Our problem involves direct, primary First Amendment rights akin to "pure speech."

The school officials banned and sought to punish petitioners for a silent, passive expression of opinion, unaccompanied by any disorder or disturbance on the part of petitioners. There is here no evidence whatever of petitioners' interference, actual or nascent, with the schools' work or of collision with the rights of other students to be secure and to be let alone. Accordingly, this case does not concern speech or action that intrudes upon the work of the schools or the rights of other students.

Only a few of the eighteen thousand students in the school system wore the black armbands. Only five students were suspended for wearing them. There is no indication that the work of the schools or any class was disrupted. Outside the classrooms, a few students made hostile remarks to the children wearing armbands, but there were no threats or acts of violence on school premises.

The District Court concluded that the action of the school authorities was reasonable because it was based upon their fear of a disturbance from the wearing of the armbands. But, in our system, undifferentiated fear or apprehension of disturbance is not enough to overcome the right to freedom of expression. Any departure from absolute regimentation may cause trouble. Any variation from the majority's opinion may inspire fear. Any word spoken, in class, in the lunchroom, or on the campus, that deviates from the views of another person may start an argument or cause a disturbance. But our Constitution says we must take this risk, . . . and our history says that it is this sort of hazardous freedom—this kind of openness—that is the basis of our national strength and of the independence and vigor of Americans who grow up and live in this relatively permissive, often disputatious, society.

In order for the State in the person of school officials to justify prohibition of a particular expression of opinion, it must be able to show that its action was caused by something more than a mere desire to avoid the discomfort and unpleasantness that always accompany an unpopular viewpoint. Certainly where there is no finding and no showing that engaging in the forbidden conduct would "materially and substantially interfere with the requirements of appropriate discipline in the operation of the school," the prohibition cannot be sustained. . . .

It is also relevant that the school authorities did not purport to prohibit the wearing of all symbols of political or controversial significance. The record shows that students in some of the schools wore buttons relating to national political campaigns, and some even wore the Iron Cross, traditionally a symbol of Nazism. The order prohibiting the wearing of armbands did not extend to these. Instead, a particular symbol—black armbands worn to exhibit opposition to this Nation's involvement in Vietnam—was singled out for prohibition. Clearly, the prohibition of expression of one particular opinion, at least without evidence that it is necessary to avoid material and substantial interference with schoolwork or discipline, is not constitutionally permissible.

In our system, state-operated schools may not be enclaves of totalitarianism. School officials do not possess absolute authority over their students. Students in school as well as out of school are "persons" under our Constitution. They are possessed of fundamental rights which the State must respect, just as they themselves must respect their obligations to the State. In our system, students may not be regarded as closed-circuit recipients of only that which the State chooses to communicate. They may not be confined to the expression of those sentiments that are officially approved. In the absence of a specific showing of constitutionally valid reasons to regulate their speech, students are entitled to freedom of expression of their views.

. . . We reverse and remand for further proceedings consistent with this opinion.

Reversed and remanded.

MR. JUSTICE BLACK, dissenting.

While the record does not show that any of these armband students shouted, used profane language, or were violent in any manner, detailed testimony by some of them shows their armbands caused comments, warnings by other students, the poking of fun at them, and a warning by an older football player that other, nonprotesting students had better let them alone. There is also evidence that a teacher of mathematics had his lesson period practically "wrecked" chiefly by disputes with Mary Beth Tinker, who wore her armband for her "demonstration." Even a casual reading of the record shows that this armband did divert students' minds from their regular lessons, and that talk, comments, etc., made John Tinker "self-conscious" in attending school with his armband. While the absence of obscene remarks or boisterous and loud disorder perhaps justifies the Court's statement that the few armband students did not actually "disrupt" the classwork, I think the record overwhelmingly shows that the armbands did exactly what the elected school officials and principals foresaw they would, that is, took the students' minds off their classwork and diverted them to thoughts about the highly emotional subject of the Vietnam War. And I repeat that if the time has come when pupils of state-supported schools, kindergartens, grammar schools, or high schools, can defy and flout orders of school officials to keep their minds on their own schoolwork, it is the beginning of a new revolutionary era of permissiveness in this country fostered by the judiciary. . . .

Change has been said to be truly the law of life but sometimes the old and the tried and true are worth holding. The schools of this Nation have undoubtedly contributed to giving us tranquility and to making us a more law-abiding people. Uncontrolled and uncontrollable liberty is an enemy to domestic peace. We cannot close our eyes to the fact that some of the country's greatest problems are crimes committed by the youth, too many of school age. School discipline, like parental discipline, is an integral and important part of training our children to be good citizens—to be better citizens. Here a very small number of students have crisply and summarily refused to obey a school order designed to give pupils who want to learn the opportunity to do so. One does not need to be a prophet or the son of a prophet to know that after the Court's holding today some students in Iowa schools and indeed in all schools will be ready, able, and willing to defy their teachers on practically all orders. This is the more unfortunate for the schools since groups of students all over the land are already running loose, conducting break-ins, sit-ins, lie-ins, and smash-ins. Many of these student groups, as is all too familiar to all who read the newspapers and watch the television news programs, have already engaged in rioting, property seizures, and destruction. They have picketed schools to force students not to cross their picket lines and have too often violently attacked earnest but frightened students who wanted an education that the pickets did not want them to get. Students engaged in such activities are apparently confident that they know far more about how to operate public school systems than do their parents, teachers, and elected school officials. It is no answer to say that the particular students here have not yet reached such high points in their demands to attend classes in order to exercise their political pressures. Turned loose with lawsuits for damages and injunctions against their teachers as they are here, it is nothing but wishful thinking to imagine that young, immature students will not soon believe it is their right to control the schools rather than the right of the States that collect the taxes to hire the teachers for the benefit of the pupils. This case, therefore, wholly without constitutional reasons in my judgment, subjects all the public schools in the country to the whims and caprices of their loudest-mouthed, but maybe not their brightest, students. I, for one, am not fully persuaded that school pupils are wise enough, even with this Court's expert help from Washington, to run the 23,390 public school systems in our fifty States. I wish, therefore, wholly to disclaim any purpose on my part to hold that the Federal Constitution compels the teachers, parents, and elected school officials to surrender control of the American public school system to public school students. I dissent.

BIBLIOGRAPHY

CUTLIP, JAMES. "Symbolic Speech, High School Protest and the First Amendment." *Journal of Family Law* 9, no. 1 (1969): 119.

"Free to Speak Out—With Limits" *Senior Scholastic* 94, no. 7 (March 14, 1969): 14.

IRONS, PETER. *The Courage of Their Convictions*, ch. 10. Penguin, 1990.

NAHMOD, S. H. "Beyond Tinker . . ." *Harvard Civil Rights-Civil Liberties Law Review* 5 (April 1970): 278.

"School Protest: Is It a 'Right'?" *U. S. News & World Report*, March 10, 1969, p. 12.

SHEPLEY, JAMES R. "Demonstrations, Not Disruption." *Time*, March 7, 1969, p. 47.

Communist Party v. Subversive Activities Control Board

351 U.S. 115 (1956)

In 1950, prompted by the Korean War and the Soviet hydrogen bomb, Congress passed the Internal Security Act. This law set rules to control "communist-action" organizations and created the Subversive Activities Control Board to enforce these rules. After a lengthy hearing, the board in 1952 ordered the Communist Party to register with the government and to open its financial and membership records. The party appealed, arguing that the law violated the freedom of association guaranteed by the First Amendment. It also claimed that the board's findings relied on perjured testimony. The Supreme Court in 1956 declined to decide the constitutionality of the act. But it remanded the case to the board for a new hearing, "to make certain," Justice Felix Frankfurter wrote, "that it bases its findings upon untainted evidence." Later decisions undermined the law, and Congress finally abolished the powerless board.

TRANSCRIPT OF EDITED AND NARRATED ARGUMENTS IN
Communist Party v. *Subversive Activities Control Board*, 351 U.S. 115 (1956)

Counsel for petitioner: John Abt, New York City; Joseph Forer, Washington, D.C.

Counsel for respondent: Solicitor General Simon Sobeloff, Washington, D.C.

Chief Justice Earl Warren: Number 48, *Communist Party of the United States of America versus Subversive Activities Control Board.*

Narrator: It's November 17th, 1955. Chief Justice Earl Warren has called a case involving one of the most feared and hated groups in American history: the Communist Party. The justices must weigh claims of First and Fifth Amendment rights against those of national security.

In 1919, American supporters of the Soviet Revolution founded the Communist Party. Within months, officials launched a campaign against the party. Federal agents rounded up ten thousand Communists and other radicals. Hundreds who were not American citizens were deported. Many party members went underground, changing names and working in secret cells.

The Great Depression brought the party out of hiding and attracted thousands of new members. During World War Two, the United States and Soviet Union fought as allies against fascism. Communists supported the war effort with enthusiasm. American and Soviet troops joined hands as Germany surrendered in 1945. The atomic bomb ended the Pacific war and gave America a fearsome new weapon. But the nuclear age turned wartime allies into Cold War adversaries. The Soviets raised an Iron Curtain around Eastern Europe. The U.S. answered with a North Atlantic military alliance. American Communists denounced their country's foreign policy.

The hard-line Communist stand brought new calls to punish the party and its members. In 1949, a federal jury convicted ten party leaders under a prewar law, making it a crime to advocate the violent overthrow of the government. The Supreme Court rejected claims the law violated First Amendment rights to free speech and association. The justices ruled the Communist Party was a criminal conspiracy and posed a "clear and present danger" to American security.

1950 was a momentous year. In Korea, the Cold War became a shooting war. The Soviets tested a hydrogen bomb. Senator Joseph McCarthy's crusade against communism started another "-ism," McCarthyism. And Congress passed another law, the Internal Security Act. This law set up a Subversive Activities Control Board. Communist groups must register with the board and disclose their members and finances. Failure to comply exposed party members to heavy fines and loss of passports and government jobs. President Harry Truman vetoed the bill. "We need not fear the expression of ideas," he said, "we do need to fear their suppression." But Congress overrode his veto with little opposition.

After lengthy hearings, the Subversive Activities Board ordered the Communist Party to register. A lower court upheld the board's order. The party's appeal brought about today's argument. Chief Justice Warren welcomes the party's longtime lawyer, John Abt.

Warren: Mr. Abt.

Abt: May it please the Court.

The first point that I shall argue here today is that the act, on its face and as applied, violate the First Amendment. I shall show that under the guise of a registration statute, the act in fact represents an attempt, I submit without precedent in this country, to coerce conformity by suppressing advocacy, association, and collective activity for wholly legitimate purposes.

Narrator: Congress labeled the Communist Party as part of a "world-wide conspiracy" against America. Abt described the consequences of registration.

Abt: If the organization registers as a criminal conspirator, it not only destroys itself but it jeopardizes the livelihood and the liberty of its members, its contributors, and even those with whom it does business, by listing their names for public scrutiny. If a member registers as a criminal conspirator, he destroys himself. Hence the act makes, and we think was obviously intended to make, registration impossible.

On the other hand, nonregistration exposes the officers and members to astronomical criminal penalties for nonregistration. The order thus offers a Hobson's choice between suicide by registration and governmental execution for nonregistration. Far from accomplishing disclosure, the act compels concealment, the only sanctuary left to the organization and its members. The registration order thus results not in information but in proscription. Its function is to outlaw the petitioner, lay a foundation for the mass prosecution of its members, and establish a basis for proscribing other organizations, including trade unions, as Communist front or Communist infiltrated.

The respondent argues that the act is valid because it strikes at a great evil, and Congress could reasonably find that the Communists, the alleged source of the evil, are a danger to American security. The inference from that argument is, that once an organization like petitioner has legislatively been declared to be a danger, all of its advocacy and collective activity may be suppressed, including the concededly nondangerous. This justification of the act rests on an H-bomb theory of congressional power. The theory is that, whenever Congress finds the existence of a danger, it may throw an H-bomb in its general direction. That, of course, is a very easy way to get rid of the danger, if one isn't squeamish about the Constitution. The Court, however, putting the Constitution first, has flatly rejected this H-bomb theory in cases which dealt specifically with the Communist Party and its members.

Narrator: In earlier cases dealing with Communists, the Court drew a line between protected advocacy of ideas and criminal acts. Abt emphasized this distinction.

Abt: The act is condemned by the First Amendment, not only because it proscribes peaceable advocacy and association but also because, on its face and as applied by the board and the court below, its sanctions are imposed as penalties for the exercise of rights protected by the First Amendment. For example, section 13(e)(2) of the act required the board to consider the extent to which petitioner's views and policies did not deviate from those of the Soviet Union. These views and policies need be neither seditious, dangerous, or even false. They may be patently valid and in the best interests of the American people. Yet they provide one of the bases for the imposition of the liabilities and penalties of the act, simply because they are similar to Soviet views and policies.

Narrator: Abt noted Communist support for the admission of China to the United Nations and the banning of atomic weapons.

Abt: Now, if the Court please, we submit that if the heresy of nondeviation from Soviet views such as these can be penalized, then indeed governmental control over political association and expression is completely unlimited. This is a technique which was refined and perfected by McCarthyism. What the act does is to enshrine it, freeze it into law, and arm it with intolerable sanctions.

Narrator: Another party lawyer, Joseph Forer, continued the argument. He claimed the law imposed criminal penalties on party members without trial and violated the due process clause of the Fifth Amendment.

Warren: Mr. Forer.

Forer: If the Court please, I will first take up another aspect of the act's denial of due process to the members of an organization ordered to register. As Mr. Abt has already pointed out, a registration order automatically inflicts on every member of the organization certain intolerable sanctions, including the defamation which occurs from being listed, and loss of employment, loss of passports, and so forth.

What the act does is to conclusively presume that every member of an organization is a disloyal person who should, on that account, be excluded from access to vital privileges. This presumption applies whether or not the member knows or believes that the organization is subversive. And, furthermore, the member never has an opportunity to prove that, no matter what you say about the organization, he personally is not disloyal. This, we say, clearly violates due process.

Narrator: Chief Justice Warren interrupted.

Forer: This Court, in two recent decisions . . .

Warren: The only remedy is to withdraw from the organization?

Forer: If you mean . . . yes, he can withdraw from the organization. That's a violation of his right of association. In other words, the remedy that you're suggesting that he cure . . .

Warren: I just asked if that was the sole remedy?

Forer: That is his sole remedy, if you can call it a remedy. In other words, in order to get due process he has to sacrifice his First Amendment right.

The point is that a man may honestly remain a member of the organization after the board's order is sustained, because he honestly disagrees with the board and he honestly disagrees with the decisions of the courts. In that case, he's not disloyal, he's just stubborn. Maybe he's also right. And the government cannot constitutionally brand a man as disloyal, and deprive him of vital privileges on account of disloyalty, merely on the grounds that he's stubborn. That is confusing disloyalty with nonconformity.

Narrator: Solicitor General Simon Sobeloff defended the law for the government.

Warren: Mr. Solicitor General.

Sobeloff: May it please the Court.

The arguments that you've just heard seek to cast the question in terms of a violation of the First Amendment. We do not see the case in that light, and we'd like to be understood at the outset to agree, nay, to insist, that utterance, however it may diverge from popular opinion or from official opinion, and no matter how false or odious, is permitted and protected. And efforts to change people's minds and beliefs are immune from any interference under the protection of the First Amendment to the Constitution. And a man is free to preach any doctrine. But if, in preaching doctrine, he couples that with conspiratorial plans to employ illegal means to subvert and destroy this government, Congress may deal with it and the First Amendment does not stand in the way.

Narrator: Sobeloff linked Soviet aggression around the world to American Communists.

Sobeloff: Now, what is the history and background of this statute? We can't consider the thing in a vacuum. Let me review briefly what led to this enactment. What was the world situation in 1950, when Congress enacted this law? For a generation or more, Congress as well as the rest of the world had been observing the activities of a world Communist movement that has its center in Moscow. Congress had beheld a whole series of coups d'etat in Europe. They had seen successively the swallowing up by the Soviet Union, through military aggression, of some of its neighbors like Latvia, Lithuania, Estonia, parts of Poland and Finland. And Congress had also witnessed, as had the whole world, that this world Communist movement, directed by the Soviet Union, had by infiltration, by subversion, by fraud, deceit, and the threat of force, where force was not necessary, they had taken Czechoslovakia and Hungary, Rumania, Albania, and for a time Yugoslavia and Bulgaria. And they had seen strong attempts made by the same methods to dominate Greece and Iran and Italy and France.

Moreover, Congress had, only three months before the passage of this law, voted funds to raise an army, to send it to Korea to resist aggression of the same, from the same source.

And Congress was not unaware what was going on at home. In 1949, the year before the passage of this act, there had been the conviction of the ten leading officials of this Communist Party of the U.S.A., the very men who are leading this movement. And that conviction had been affirmed only a month before the act was passed.

Narrator: Sobeloff added Grimm's Fairy Tales to his argument.

Sobeloff: Now Congress, whatever else may be said about them, they don't have to be naive as Little Red Riding Hood, who wondered about grandma's big ears. They have a perfect right to view the facts and to make their appraisal and to draw their inferences. Now, with this body of knowledge and experience, Congress declared the existence of a danger. And the validity of these congressional findings, that is, the existence of the peril, I respectfully submit, must be accepted by this Court if there is any rational basis for Congress to believe. I submit it's almost difficult to imagine a rational basis for disbelieving it.

Narrator: Sobeloff answered John Abt on the consequences of registration.

Sobeloff: Now, what is the sanction against this petitioner? That it register. I say it's a very mild requirement, if any faith is to be given to these findings. Nothing could be more reasonable than an organization that has been duly, and in an orderly way, shown to be the handmaiden of a foreign power, and whose objective it has been to destroy this government, nothing could be more mild or reasonable than to say that such an organization shall at least register and make disclosure of its members and of its funds, and that, though it isn't silenced even now, it shall at least tell the public who's speaking.

When you have someone speaking as the secret agent of a foreign government, whose purpose it is to subvert this government, Congress has a right to say that one who has been proven such shall at least label its contribution to the public discussion so that people can know how to evaluate it.

Narrator: Sobeloff responded to Joseph Forer on the penalties for party membership.

Sobeloff: We in a democracy have great tolerance for stubborn people. But I think it's carrying stubbornness to a great extreme to say that a man may go on and persist in membership in an organization after it has been adjudicated by this board, created for the purpose of considering the matter, and with the affirmance of the court of appeals, and after this Court has considered the matter, and he can say, "I *still* don't believe that it's a foreign-dominated organization, that it has these nefarious purposes that have been attributed to it, I insist on belonging to it." I think that's carrying it too far.

Narrator: Communist Party members could be prosecuted for failure to register. But they couldn't challenge the government's claim they belonged to a criminal conspiracy. Sobeloff debated this crucial issue with Justice Hugo Black.

Sobeloff: An individual here would be entitled to a jury trial if he were indicted . . .

Black: Would he be entitled to have a jury trial of the issues which the board had decided?

Soboloff: He would be entitled to a jury trial on his own affiliation with that condemned organization.

Black: That's right. Would he be entitled to a jury trial on the . . . (Soboloff: nature of the organization?) That's right.

Soboloff: No, sir. And Your Honor, I want to face that frankly. I don't think it's practical or necessary under the Constitution to do that. It's simply impossible to have a fifteen-month trial on this side issue in the case of everybody that's going to be proceeded against. You don't go into the nature of the Communist movement all over again. You don't have to prove all over again, each time, that the sun rises in the east. You do have to prove in each case, fully, beyond a reasonable doubt, the connection of the particular defendant with the movement, and that he knew what he was doing. Trial by jury of any individual . . .

Black: Do you think that gives Congress—the mere fact that they're unpopular, they're not liked, that they're dangerous—the right to have them tried without the benefit of a trial by jury, where they try the facts?

Soboloff: In this law, all that is determined by the Board is the nature of the Communist Party. So far as individuals are concerned, they have the right of a trial by jury on all other issues.

Black: That's right. But that is foreclosed when they get there, because the board has passed on it.

Soboloff: That one issue is foreclosed.

Black: And you of course wouldn't say that that was justified, because they're Communists, rather than . . .

Soboloff: Not because, not because they are Communists, but because they are conspirators against the government.

Narrator: John Abt had the final word.

Abt: As I understand the solicitor general, he now in substance concedes that a registration order against an accused organization, for all practical purposes, will destroy it, or cripple it, proscribe it, outlaw it, put it out of business, call it what you will. Nevertheless, he says this is not a First Amendment case. He says nobody has a constitutional right to engage in a conspiracy to overthrow the government. Of course that's true. And I put aside for the moment the question that there was no proof of such a conspiracy in this case. Let's assume there was proof. Let's assume it was proved that the Communist Party is a conspiracy to overthrow the government of the United States. You can punish that conspiracy, if the Court please. But you can't prohibit a conspirator from engaging in legitimate, peaceful advocacy. The solicitor general says, "but none of their advocacy is legitimate or peaceful because it's all for a bad motive." As soon as the government has the power to punish a legitimate activity because it labels that activity as being done for a bad purpose, you've armed government with the power to suppress all legitimate activity.

Narrator: Both sides argued important constitutional issues. Did the law violate the First and Fifth Amendments? The Supreme Court evaded these tough questions. In April 1956, the Court sent the case back to the Subversive Activities Board. Justice Felix Frankfurter wrote for the Court. He based his ruling on charges by Communist Party lawyers that three government witnesses had lied in testimony to the board. The Court could decide constitutional issues, Frankfurter said, only on a record free of "tainted evidence."

After further hearings, the board again ordered the Communists to register, and lower courts upheld the order. Five years passed before the Supreme Court finally ruled in 1961. It was a narrow, five-to-four decision. Justice Frankfurter wrote a second opinion. He upheld the board's two major findings. American Communists were "controlled" by the Soviets and shared their "objectives" of worldwide revolution.

Frankfurter rejected the party's First Amendment argument. He took a winding path around recent precedent. The Court protected civil rights groups from disclosing their members because of public hostility in southern states. Frankfurter saw a difference. Congress was entitled, he said, to strip the "mask of anonymity" from Communists, because of the party's foreign control and subversive intent. But Frankfurter again ducked the Fifth Amendment issue. It would be "premature" to decide until party members refused to register.

The four dissenters, including Chief Justice Warren, differed on First Amendment issues, but agreed the law violated the Fifth Amendment. By 1965, after Frankfurter's death, the Court's minority became a majority. A party leader, William Albertson, challenged a registration order. The Court ruled that admission of party membership subjected Communists to prosecution and violated the self-incrimination clause.

The Communist Party never obeyed the registration order. And Congress abolished the Subversive Activities Control Board in 1973. Both extremes of American politics, hard-line Communism and McCarthyism, have almost disappeared. But Americans still face political dissent and pressures for conformity.

The issues are different, but passions still run high. The words of Justice Hugo Black still ring true: "The freedoms guaranteed by the First Amendment must be accorded to the ideas we hate or sooner or later they will be denied to the ideas we cherish."

EDITED SUPREME COURT OPINIONS
Communist Party of the United States v. Subversive Activities Control Board

MR. JUSTICE FRANKFURTER delivered the opinion of the Court.

This case is here to review the judgment of the Court of Appeals for the District of Columbia affirming an order of the Subversive Activities Control Board that petitioner register with the Attorney General as a "Communist-action" organization, as required by the Subversive Activities Control Act of 1950, Title I of the Internal Security Act of 1950 . . . That Act sets forth a comprehensive plan for regulation of "Communist-action" organizations. Section 2 of the Act describes a world Communist movement directed from abroad and designed to overthrow the Government of the United States by any means available, including violence. Section 7 requires all Communist-action organizations to register as such with the Attorney General. If the Attorney General has reason to believe that an organization, which has not registered, is a Communist-action organization, he is required . . . to bring a proceeding to determine that fact before the Subversive Activities Control Board, a five-man board appointed by the President with the advice and consent of the Senate and created for the purpose of holding hearings and making such determinations. . . .

Proceeding under . . . this statute, the Attorney General, on November 22, 1950, petitioned the Board for an order directing a petitioner to register pursuant to § 7 of the Act. . . . The hearing began on April 23, 1951, before three members of the Board, later reduce to two, sitting as a hearing panel, and it terminated on July 1, 1952. Proposed findings of fact and briefs were filed by both parties, and oral argument was held before the hearing panel in August 1952. In October 1952 the hearing panel issued a recommended decision that the Board order petitioner to register as a Communist-action organization. Exceptions to the panel's findings were filed by both parties, and oral argument was held before the Board in January 1953. The Board filed its report, which occupies 251 pages of the record in this case, on April 20, 1953.

In its report the Board found that there existed a world Communist movement, substantially as described in § 2 of the Act, organized and directed by a foreign government. The Board detailed the history of the Communist Party of the United States and its close relation to the world Communist movement. It then set forth illustrative evidence and made findings with respect to the statutory criteria . . . On the basis of these findings the Board concluded that petitioner was a Communist-action organization . . . and ordered it to register as such with the Attorney General.

Petitioner brought this order to the Court of Appeals for the District of Columbia for review. While the case was pending, it filed a motion. . . . The basis of the motion was that . . . additional material evidence became available to the petitioner subsequent to the administrative proceeding and that this evidence would

> "establish that the testimony of three of the witnesses for the Attorney General, on whichthe Boardrelied extensively and heavily in making findings which are of key importance to the order now under review, was false. . . . In summary, this evidence will establish that Crouch, Johnson and Matusow, all professional informers heretofore employed by the Department of Justice as witnesses in numerous proceedings, have committed perjury, are completely untrustworthy and should be accorded no credence; that at least two of them are now being investigated for perjury by the Department of Justice, and that because their character as professional perjurorssichas now been conclusively and publicly demonstrated, the Attorney General has ceased to employ any of them as witnesses." . . .

The Government did not deny these allegations. It . . . asserted that the hearing should not be reopened for the receipt of evidence merely questioning, as it claimed, the credibility of some witnesses, but not any fact at issue, and it maintained that the findings of the Board were amply supported by evidence apart from the testimony of the three witnesses sought to be discredited. . . . The court . . . found that the Board's conclusion was supported by the basic findings which it had affirmed. . . .

The challenge to the Act on which the order was based plainly raises constitutional questions appropriate for this Court's consideration, and so we brought the case here. . . . At the threshold we are, however, confronted by a particular claim that the Court of Appeals erred in refusing to return the case to the Board for consideration of the new evidence proffered by petitioner's motion and affidavit. This non-constitutional issue must be met at the outset, because the case must be decided on a non-constitutional issue, if the record calls for it, without reaching constitutional problems. . . .

In considering this non-constitutional issue raised by denial of petitioner's motion, we must avoid any intimation with respect to the other issues raised by petitioner. We do not so intimate by concluding that the testimony of the three witnesses, against whom the uncontested challenge of perjury was made, was not inconsequential in relation to the issues on which the Board had to pass. No doubt a large part of the record consisted of documentary evidence. However, not only was the human testimony significant but the documentary evidence was also linked to the activities of the petitioner and to the ultimate finding of the Board by human testimony, and such testimony was in part that of these three witnesses. The facts bearing on the issue are not in controversy.

. . . The annotated report of the Board, in which citations to the evidence were made to illustrate the support for its findings, contained thirty-six references to the testimony of Crouch, twenty-five references to the testimony of Johnson, and twenty-four references to the testimony of Matusow. These references were made in support of every finding . . . and it is also not to be assumed that the evidence given by these three witnesses played no role in the Board's findings of fact even when not specifically cited. Testimony, for example, directed toward proving that the Communist Party of the United States was an agency utilized by a foreign government to undermine the loyalty of the armed forces, and to be in a position to paralyze shipping and prevent transportation of soldiers and war supplies through the Panama Canal, Hawaii, and the ports of San Francisco and New York in time of war, cannot be deemed insignificant in such a determination as that which the Board made in this proceeding.

This is a proceeding under an Act which Congress conceived necessary for "the security of the United States and to the existence of free American institutions. . . ." 64 Stat., at 989. The untainted administration of justice is certainly one of the most cherished aspects of our institutions. Its observance is one of our proudest boasts. This Court is charged with supervisory functions in relation to proceedings in the federal courts. . . . Therefore, fastidious regard for the honor of the administration of justice requires the Court to make certain that the doing of justice be made so manifest that only irrational or perverse claims of its disregard can be asserted.

When uncontested challenge is made that a finding of subversive design by petitioner was in part the product of three perjurious witnesses, it does not remove the taint for a reviewing court to find that there is ample innocent testimony to support the Board's findings. If these witnesses in fact committed perjury in testifying in other cases on subject matter substantially like that of their testimony in the present proceedings, their testimony in this proceeding is inevitably discredited and the Board's determination must duly take this fact into account. We cannot pass upon a record containing such challenged testimony. We find it necessary to dispose of the case on the grounds we do, not in order to avoid a constitutional adjudication but because the fair administration of the justice system requires it. Since reversal is thus demanded, however, we do not reach the constitutional issues.

The basis for challenging the testimony was not in existence when the proceedings were concluded before the Board. Petitioner should therefore be given leave to make its allegations before the Board in a proceeding . . . The issue on which the case must be returned to the Board lies within a narrow compass and the Board has ample scope of discretion in passing upon petitioner's motion. The purpose of this remand, as is its reason, is to make certain that the Board bases its findings upon untainted evidence. To that end it may hold a hearing to ascertain the truth of petitioner's allegations, and if the testimony of the three witnesses is discredited, it must not leave that testimony part of the record. Alternatively, the Board may choose to assume the truth of petitioner's allegations and, without further hearing, expunge the testimony of these witnesses from the record. In either event, the Board must then reconsider its original determination in the light of the record as freed from the challenge that now beclouds it.

The case is reversed and remanded for proceedings in conformity with this opinion.

Reversed and remanded.

MR. JUSTICE CLARK, with whom MR. JUSTICE REED and MR. JUSTICE MINTON join, dissenting.

I have not found any case in the history of the Court where important constitutional issues have been avoided on such a pretext. . . . Here the case will be finally decided only *after* our decision on the constitutional questions. The action today is taken merely for delay and can result only in the Board reaffirming the action. In fact it so advised the Court of Appeals and that court found that all of the testimony of the questionable witnesses was supported by "masses of other evidence."

The allegations of the motion itself are entirely inadequate in that they point to no particular testimony before the Board as being false. There is no offer to disprove any testimony given, and no fact at issue in the proceeding is controverted. As to Crouch and Johnson, the motion merely cites additional cases in which it is alleged that their testimony was conflicting. These allegations are purely cumulative of the witnesses' cross-examination before the Board. With regard to Matusow, the motion mentions only newspaper reports and a press release referring to the statements of certain persons that Matusow had told them that he had lied. . . .

I abhor the use of perjured testimony as much as anyone, but we must recognize that never before have mere allegations of perjury, so flimsily supported, been considered grounds for reopening a proceeding or granting a new trial. The Communist Party makes no claim that the Government knowingly used false testimony, and it is far too realistic to contend that the Board's action will be any different on remand. The only purpose of this procedural maneuver is to gain additional time before the order to register can become effective. This proceeding has dragged out for many years now, and the function of the Board remains suspended and the congressional purpose frustrated at a most critical time in world history.

Ironically enough, we are returning the case to a Board whose very existence is challenged on constitutional grounds. We are asking the Board to pass on the credibility of witnesses after we have refused to say whether it has the power to do so. The constitutional questions are fairly presented here for our decision. If all or any part of the Act is unconstitutional, it should be declared so on the record before us. If not, the Nation is entitled to effective operation of the statute deemed to be of vital importance to its well-being at the time it was passed by the Congress. I would decide the questions presented by this record.

BIBLIOGRAPHY

CHAFFEE, ZECHARIAH, JR. "Freedom to Think." *The Atlantic* 195, no. 3 (March 1955): 23.

GUTTMAN, ALLEN. *Communism, the Courts, and the Constitution.* D.C. Heath, 1965.

OBER, FRANK B. "Communism and the Court: An Examination of Recent Developments." *American Bar Association Journal* 44, no. 1 (January 1958): 35.

REEVES, THOMAS C. *McCarthyism.* Dryden, 1973.

SOMMERVILLE, JOHN. *The Communist Trials and the American Tradition.* Cameron, 1956.

WEISSMAN D. L. "Issue: Freedom; Place: The Court." *Nation*, November 26, 1955, p. 450.

Texas v. Johnson

491 U.S. 397 (1989)

During the 1984 Republican National Convention in Dallas, Texas, Gregory Lee Johnson joined a demonstration against the Reagan administration's policies. At the end of the march, while protesters chanted, Johnson burned an American flag. He was convicted of "desecration of a venerated object" protected by Texas law and sentenced to a year in prison. Johnson appealed, claiming that his actions were protected by the First Amendment as symbolic political speech. In 1989, the Supreme Court ruled by one vote that the state's interest in protecting the flag as a symbol of national unity does not justify restrictions of political expression. "We do not consecrate the flag by punishing its desecration," Justice William Brennan wrote, "for in doing so we dilute the freedom that this cherished symbol represents." The next year, the Court also rejected a congressional attempt to punish flag burners.

TRANSCRIPT OF EDITED AND NARRATED ARGUMENTS IN
Texas v. *Johnson*, 491 U.S. 397 (1989)

Counsel for petitioner: Kathi Alyce Drew, Dallas, Texas
Counsel for respondent: William Kunstler, New York, New York

Chief Justice Rehnquist: Number 88-155, *Texas versus Gregory Lee Johnson.*

Narrator: It's March 21st, 1989. Chief Justice William Rehnquist has called a
case that involves the symbol of our country: the American flag. The flag stands
beside the justices in the courtroom. It flies over the Capitol; over the White
House; at the Tomb of the Unknown Soldier. Millions of Americans have
pledged their allegiance to the flag and to the principles it symbolizes: liberty
and justice for all.

But, does that liberty include the right to burn the flag? Can a state punish
acts of flag desecration with criminal penalties? Does the free speech clause of
the First Amendment protect those who destroy our national symbol? These
questions provoke heated answers on both sides.

Justice Hugo Black once wrote that "emotions bubble and tempers flare"
when protest spills into the streets. This case began in the streets of Dallas,
Texas, on a hot August day. The 1984 Republican National Convention attracted thousands of delegates and hundreds of demonstrators. One small protest
group, the Revolutionary Communist Youth Brigade, marched through downtown Dallas. Gregory Johnson led the march and shouted slogans—some obscene—over a bullhorn. When his group reached City Hall, Johnson held up
an American flag, soaked it with lighter fluid, and set it on fire. While the flag
burned, protesters chanted, "Red, white, and blue, we spit on you!"

The flag burning drew a crowd. One man, Daniel Walker, gathered up the
charred remains, took them home, and buried them in his backyard. Prosecutors
said Gregory Johnson violated a Texas law punishing anyone who "desecrates"
a state or national flag. The state must prove the act "will seriously offend one
or more persons" who observe it. Walker told the jury the flag burning offended
his feelings. The prosecutor also claimed Johnson breached the peace. Johnson
posed a danger to Texas, he said, "by what he does and the way he thinks." The
jurors agreed and sentenced Johnson to a year in prison.

The state's highest court struck down his conviction. The judges ruled that
flag burning was a form of "symbolic speech." They applied three legal tests;
Texas failed each one. First, the state had not shown a "compelling interest" in
protecting the flag. Second, states cannot punish the content of speech, however
offensive. Third, even if Johnson caused "serious offense" to Daniel Walker,

hurt feelings alone do not breach the peace. Kathi Drew, an assistant district attorney in Dallas, argues the state's appeal.

Drew: Mr. Chief Justice, and may it please the Court.

The issue before this Court is whether the public burning of an American flag which occurred as part of a demonstration with political overtones is entitled to First Amendment protection.

For purposes of this argument today and with the Court's indulgence, the state will assume the symbolic speech standard and proceed directly to the question of Texas's compelling interests in regulating this type of conduct.

Throughout the course of the appellate history in this case, Texas has advanced two compelling state interests. One is the preservation of the flag as a symbol of nationhood and national unity. The second is the preservation*sic*of a breach of the peace.

I would like to address first the nationhood interest. We believe that preservation of the flag as a symbol of nationhood and national unity is a compelling and valid state interest. We feel very certain that Congress has the power to both adopt a national symbol and to take steps to prevent the destruction of that symbol, to protect the symbol.

Narrator: Justice Antonin Scalia broke in.

Scalia: Why does the—why did the defendant's actions here destroy the symbol? His actions would have been useless unless the flag was a very good symbol for what he intended to show contempt for. His action does not make it any less a symbol.

Drew: Your Honor, we believe that if a symbol over a period of time is ignored or abused that it can, in fact, lose its symbolic effect.

Scalia: I think not at all. I think when somebody does that to the flag, the flag becomes even more a symbol of the country. I mean, it seems to me you're running quite a different argument—not that he's destroying its symbolic character, but that he is showing disrespect for it, that you not just want a symbol, but you want a venerated symbol, and you don't make that argument because then you're getting into a sort of content preference. I don't see how you can argue that he's making it any less of a symbol than it was.

Drew: Your Honor, I'm forced to disagree with you. Because I believe that every desecration of the flag carried out in the manner that he did here—and certainly I don't think there can be any question that Mr. Johnson is a hard-core violator of this statute—if his actions in this case, under the facts of this case, do not constitute flag desecration, then I really am not quite certain what *would* constitute flag desecration.

Scalia: They desecrate the flag indeed, but do they make it—do they destroy the symbol? Do they make it any less symbolic of the country? That's the argument I thought you were running, that we have a right to have a national symbol. And if you let the people desecrate the flag, we won't have a national symbol. I don't see how that follows. We may not have a respected national symbol, but that's a different argument. Now, if you want to run that argument that we have the right to insist upon respect for the flag, that's a different argument.

Drew: Texas is not suggesting that we can insist on respect. We are suggesting that we have the right to preserve the physical integrity of the flag so that it may serve as a symbol because its symbolic effect is diluted by certain flagrant public acts of flag desecration.

Narrator: Justice Sandra O'Connor shifted from Gregory Johnson to Daniel Walker. She forced a concession from Drew.

O'Connor: I thought this statute only applied if the desecration were done in a way that the actor knows will offend one or more other people likely to discover it.

Drew: That is correct, Your Honor.

O'Connor: There is that little added requirement, is there not?

Drew: Yes, Your Honor, that is correct.

O'Connor: Well, I thought that the Court had held that it's firmly settled under the Constitution, that the public expression of ideas may not be prohibited merely because the ideas are themselves offensive to some of their hearers.

Drew: That's correct, Your Honor.

O'Connor: And this statute seems to try to achieve exactly that.

Drew: I don't believe that it does, Your Honor, because I believe that the pivotal point is, in a way, how is the conduct effectuated, how is it done, not what an individual may be trying to say, not how onlookers perceive the action, not how the crowd reacts, but how is it done. If you take your flag into your basement in the dead of night, soak it with lighter fluid and ignite it, you probably have not violated this statute, because the Texas statute is restricted to certain limited forms of flag desecration.

Narrator: Justice Scalia continued his debate with Drew.

Kennedy: What is the juridical category you're asking us to adopt in order to say we can punish this kind of speech? Just an exception for flags? It's just a—there's just a flag exception of the First Amendment?

Drew: To a certain extent, we have made that argument in our brief. With respect to the symbolic speech standard, we believe that there are compelling state interests that will in a balancing posture override this individual's symbolic speech rights, and that preserving the flag as a symbol, because it is such a national property, is one of those.

Scalia: I understand that. But we up to now have never allowed such an item to be declared a national symbol and to be usable symbolically only in one direction, which is essentially what you're arguing. You can honor it all you like, but you can't dishonor it as a sign of disrespect for the country.

Drew: No, Your Honor. We're not arguing that at all. (Scalia: Oh?) Not at all. We are in no way arguing that one cannot dishonor the flag or that one cannot demonstrate disrespect for the flag. Individuals have that right. What we are arguing is that you may not publicly desecrate a flag, regardless of the motivation for your action.

Narrator: Justice O'Connor started another exchange.

O'Connor: Do you suppose Patrick Henry and any of the Founding Fathers ever showed disrespect to the Union Jack?

Drew: Quite possibly, Your Honor.

O'Connor: You think they had in mind then in drafting the First Amendment that it should be a prosecutable offense?

Drew: Of course, Your Honor, one has no way of knowing whether it would be or not.

Scalia: I think your response is that they were willing to go to jail, just as they were when they signed the Declaration.

White: They were hoping they wouldn't get caught. (*laughter*)

Drew: Yes, Your Honor, I believe the classic line is: "We hang together or separately."

Court: That's right.

Narrator: Drew concluded.

Drew: I'd like to turn very briefly, if I may, to the breach of the peace interest. We do feel that preventing a breach of the peace is a legitimate state interest. And, indeed, the Texas court of criminal appeals recognized that preventing a breach of the peace is a legitimate state interest. Again, the Texas legislature has made a judgment in this area that public desecration is likely to lead to violence, that it can lead to violence. And I think the record in this case is abundantly clear that it is merely fortuitous; it is our good luck that a breach of the peace did not occur as a result of this particular flag desecration.

I think the flag is this nation's cherished property, that every individual has a certain interest. The government may maintain a residual interest, but so do the people. And you protect the flag because it is such an important symbol of national unity.

Narrator: William Kunstler argues for Gregory Johnson. He has defended many controversial clients. Kunstler jumps on Drew's concession to Justice O'Connor.

Kunstler: Mr. Chief Justice, may it please the Court.

Some of the steam has been taken out of me by some of the questions and some of the responses and the concession by the state. The state now apparently concedes that you can write out of the statute what Justice O'Connor referred to, the question of whether the actor knows or means that what he's doing will seriously offend one or more persons likely to observe or destroy*sic*, or discover his particular act.

That's out of the statute, apparently, according to the argument, because in the reply brief and today she has said essentially what is in the reply brief. Like Gertrude Stein, "A rose is a rose," they now say, "A flag burning is a flag burning." And they read out of the statute under which he was convicted and which went to the jury and the charge on the question of seriously offend, that's all out as far as Ms. Drew is concerned. But it's *not* out as far as this Court is concerned. That's what the conviction was about, that's what the argument to the jury was about, that's what the charge was about.

I think that what you have here is a statute that depends solely and exclusively on communicative impact on the audience, whether they're there or they read it in the newspaper or they see it on the screen in the evening.

Narrator: Kunstler raised two questions. Is the flag a sacred symbol? And just what *is* a flag?

Kunstler: And when you use the word "desecrate," you don't mean really in essence praising the flag. Desecrate has a meaning, and I just looked in *Webster's Second International* about it, and desecrate means "to divest of a sacred character or office, to divert from a sacred purpose, to violate the sanctity of, to profane, the opposite of consecrate."

It's used all over for commercial purposes. I notice that Barbara Bush wore a flag scarf, for example. There are flag bikinis, there are flag everything. There are little cocktail flags that you put into a hot dog or meatball and then throw in the garbage pail. They're flags under the Texas statute, something made out of cloth, but I think there are all sorts of flags used commercially. I'm not sure in my heart whether I think there's any control over the use of the flag, not on the criminal side anyway.

By the way, "national flag" does not just mean the American flag. There is a presidential flag—they don't put it in capitals—there is a presidential flag that is flown. The secretary of state has a flag that's a national flag. There are many national flags. I counted seventeen national flags. Each department here in Washington has a flag. They're national flags, and the state of Texas would also include those as national flags, certainly the president's flag. So, I think that the word "national" flag needs definition in itself.

Narrator: Under Supreme Court precedent, speech cannot be punished unless it poses a "clear and present danger" to society. Kunstler attacked the Texas law.

Kunstler: I think you must at least show some clear and present danger, some imminence. The statute here is not limited to an imminent breach, by the way. It doesn't say imminent breach of the peace at all. It just says "likely" or "might" or "the actor could reasonably believe that someone might be seriously offended by it."

The Texas court of appeals treated this, I think, in its opinion. It said, "This statute is so broad that it may be used to punish protected conduct which has no propensity to result in breaches of the peace." Serious offense does not always result in a breach of the peace. The protest in this case did not lead to violence. And, I might add, in this protest they had policemen right along with them, undercover police officers. The crowd was not a large crowd. They estimate between 100, 110, and Texas went on to say, as with most other protests of this nature, police were present at the scene.

A witness was obviously seriously offended by appellant's conduct because he gathered the burned flag and buried it at his home. Nevertheless so seriously offended, this man was not moved to violence. Serious offense occurred, but there was no breach of the peace, nor does the record reflect that the situation was potentially explosive. One cannot equate serious offense with incitement to breach the peace.

Narrator: Another Supreme Court precedent—*West Virginia versus Barnette*—ruled that schools could not force students to salute the flag. Kunstler debated the case with Chief Justice Rehnquist.

Kunstler: With reference to the nationhood and national unity, which Ms. Drew raised and which is filled in the brief, both the reply brief and the main brief of the state, I think—I thought *Barnette* set that to rest. I thought when Justice Jackson said that, "If there is any fixed star in our constitutional constellation, it is that no official, high or petty, can prescribe what shall be orthodox in politics, nationalism . . ."

Rehnquist: Well, the facts of *West Virginia* v. *Barnette* were quite different from this. There the students were required to salute the flag.

Kunstler: And here, Chief Justice, you're asking—people are required *not* to do something.

Rehnquist: Yes.

Kunstler: And I think that's a comparable situation. We order you—we can't order you to salute the flag, we can't order you to do all these obeisances with reference to the flag. Can we order you *not* to do something to show something about the flag?

Can you say you can't force them to salute the flag or pledge allegiance to the flag, but can you then say we can force them *not* to show other means of disrespect for the flag, other means of protest over the flag by saying you can't burn the flag? I think they're the same, in all due deference. I don't know if I've convinced you, but . . .

Rehnquist: Well, you may have convinced others. (*laughter*)

Narrator: Kunstler summed up.

Kunstler: I would just like to end my argument—I think this is a fundamental First Amendment case, that the First Amendment to the written Constitution is in jeopardy by statutes like this. And I wanted to essentially close with two remarks. One, Justice Jackson said in *Barnette,* "Those who begin coercive elimination of dissent soon find themselves eliminating dissenters. Compulsory unification of opinion achieves only the unanimity of the graveyard. The First Amendment was designed to avoid these ends by avoiding these beginnings." And I think that's an important statement over the years from Justice Jackson.

And I understand that this flag has serious important meanings. The Chief has mentioned many times that it's not just pieces of material, blue and white and red. That it has real meaning to real people out there. But that does not mean that it may have different meanings to other people out there and that they may not under the First Amendment show their feelings by what Texas calls desecration of a venerated object.

I think it's a most important case. I sense that it goes to the heart of the First Amendment, to hear things or to see things that we hate tests the First Amendment more than seeing or hearing things that we like. It wasn't designed for things we like. They never needed a First Amendment. This statute, or this amendment was designed so that the things we hate can have a place in the marketplace of ideas and can have an area where protest can find itself. I submit that this Court should on whatever ground it feels right, should affirm the Texas court of criminal appeals with reference to this statute and this conviction. Thank you very much.

Narrator: On June 21st, 1989, the justices struck down the Texas law by a vote of five-to-four. Justice William Brennan wrote for the majority. He agreed that "there is a special place reserved for the flag in this Nation." It is because of that special place that burning a flag conveys a powerful message, however hateful to most Americans. Gregory Johnson was punished, Brennan said, "because of the content" of his message. The Constitution does not permit such punishment.

Brennan put the case in these words: "If there is a bedrock principle underlying the First Amendment, it is that the Government may not prohibit the expression of an idea because society finds the idea . . . offensive." Brennan suggested an answer to Johnson. "We can imagine no more appropriate response to burning a flag than waving one's own."

This was a hard case for justices on both sides. The Court's newest member, Anthony Kennedy, joined the majority with a brief concurrence. "The hard fact," he said, "is that sometimes we must make decisions we do not like. We make them because they are right, right in the sense that the law and the Constitution, as we see them, compel the result."

The four dissenters disagreed. Chief Justice Rehnquist did not see the flag as "just another symbol," Johnson's act as just another message. The flag was more than special to Rehnquist. Millions of Americans, he said, regard the flag "with an almost mystical reverence." He cited the Marines who raised the flag over Iwo Jima in World War Two. The government tells Americans, Rehnquist said, "they must fight and perhaps die for the flag." States can certainly protect it from burning.

The Court's decision ignited a political fire storm. President George Bush called for a constitutional amendment to overrule the Court. Congress declined to tamper with the Constitution, but it passed a federal law against flag burning. Once again, Gregory Johnson burned a flag, this time on the Capitol steps. Once again, he was arrested. And once again, the Supreme Court struck down the law.

Early in this century, Justice Oliver Wendell Holmes made a profound statement. "We live by symbols," he said. But symbols only reflect our values. And America's basic values—liberty and justice for all—are embodied in our Constitution.

EDITED SUPREME COURT OPINIONS
Texas v. Gregory Lee Johnson

JUSTICE BRENNAN delivered the opinion of the Court.

After publicly burning an American flag as a means of political protest, Gregory Lee Johnson was convicted of desecrating a flag in violation of Texas law. This case presents the question whether his conviction is consistent with the First Amendment. We hold that it is not.

While the Republican National Convention was taking place in Dallas in 1984, respondent Johnson participated in a political demonstration dubbed the "Republican War Chest Tour." As explained in literature distributed by the demonstrators and in speeches made by them, the purpose of this event was to protest the policies of the Reagan administration and of certain Dallas-based corporations. The demonstrators marched through the Dallas streets, chanting political slogans and stopping at several corporate locations to stage "die-ins" intended to dramatize the consequences of nuclear war. On several occasions they spray-painted the walls of buildings and overturned potted plants, but Johnson himself took no part in such activities. He did, however, accept an American flag handed to him by a fellow protestor who had taken it from a flag pole outside one of the targeted buildings.

The demonstration ended in front of Dallas City Hall, where Johnson unfurled the American flag, doused it with kerosene, and set it on fire. While the flag burned, the protestors chanted, "America, the red, white, and blue, we spit on you." After the demonstrators dispersed, a witness to the flag burning collected the flag's remains and buried them in his backyard. No one was physically injured or threatened with injury, though several witnesses testified that they had been seriously offended by the flag burning.

Of the approximately one hundred demonstrators, Johnson alone was charged with a crime. The only criminal offense with which he was charged was the desecration of a venerated object in violation of Tex. Penal Code Ann. §42.09 (a)(3) (1989).After a trial, he was convicted, sentenced to one year in prison, and fined two thousand dollars. . . .

The State of Texas conceded for purposes of its oral argument in this case that Johnson's conduct was expressive conduct . . . Johnson burned an American flag as part—indeed, as the culmination—of a political demonstration that coincided with the convening of the Republican Party and its renomination of Ronald Reagan for President. The expressive, overtly political nature of this conduct was both intentional and overwhelmingly apparent. At his trial, Johnson explained his reasons for burning the flag as follows: "The American Flag was burned as Ronald Reagan was being renominated as President. And a more powerful statement of symbolic speech, whether you agree with it or not, couldn't have been made at that time. It's quite a just positionjuxtaposition. We had new patriotism and no patriotism." . . . In these circumstances, Johnson's burning of the flag was conduct "sufficiently imbued with elements of communication . . . to implicate the First Amendment."

. . . The State offers two separate interests to justify this conviction: preventing breaches of the peace, and preserving the flag as a symbol of nationhood and national unity. We hold that the first interest is not implicated on this record and that the second is related to the suppression of expression.

Texas claims that its interest in preventing breaches of the peace justifies Johnson's conviction for flag desecration. However, no disturbance of the peace actually occurred or threatened to occur because of Johnson's burning of the flag. Although the State stresses the disruptive behavior of the protestors during their march toward City Hall, . . . it admits that "no actual breach of the peace occurred at the time of the flag burning or in response to the flag burning." . . . The State's emphasis on the protestors' disorderly actions prior to arriving at City Hall is not only somewhat surprising given that no charges were brought on the basis of this conduct, but it also fails to show that a disturbance of the peace was a likely reaction to Johnson's conduct. The only evidence offered by the State at trial to show the reaction to Johnson's actions was the testimony of several persons who had been seriously offended by the flag burning. . . .

The State's position, therefore, amounts to a claim that an audience that takes serious offense at particular expression is necessarily likely to disturb the peace and that the expression may be prohibited on this basis. Our precedents do not countenance such a presumption. On the contrary, they recognize that a principal "function of free speech under our system of government is to invite dispute. It may indeed best serve its high purpose when it induces a condition of unrest, creates dissatisfaction with conditions as they are, or even stirs people to anger." *Terminiello* v. *Chicago*, 337 U. S. 1, 4 (1949) . . .

Texas' focus on the precise nature of Johnson's expression, moreover, misses the point of our prior decisions: their enduring lesson, that the Government may not prohibit expression simply because it disagrees with its message, is not dependent on the particular mode in which one chooses to express an idea. If we were to hold that a State may forbid flag burning wherever it is likely to endanger the flag's symbolic role, but allow it wherever burning a flag promotes that role— as where, for example, a person ceremoniously burns a dirty flag—we would be saying that when it comes to impairing the flag's physical integrity, the flag itself may be used as a symbol—as a substitute for the written or spoken word or a "short cut from mind to mind"—only in one direction. We would be permitting a State to "prescribe what shall be orthodox" by saying that one may burn the flag to convey one's attitude toward it and its referents only if one does not endanger the flag's representation of nationhood and national unity.

. . . It is not the State's ends, but its means, to which we object. It cannot be gainsaid that there is a special place reserved for the flag in this Nation, and thus we do not doubt that the Government has a legitimate interest in making efforts to "preserv[e] the national flag as an unalloyed symbol of our country." *Spence*, 418 U. S., at 412. We reject the suggestion, urged at oral argument by counsel for Johnson, that the Government lacks "any state interest whatsoever" in regulating the manner in which the flag may be displayed. . . .

To say that the Government has an interest in encouraging proper treatment of the flag, however, is not to say that it may criminally punish a person for burning a flag as a means of political protest. "National unity as an end which officials may foster by persuasion and example is not in question. The problem is whether under our Constitution compulsion as here employed is a permissible means for its achievement." *Barnette*, 319 U. S., at 640. . . .

The way to preserve the flag's special role is not to punish those who feel differently about these matters. It is to persuade them that they are wrong. . . . And, precisely because it is our flag that is involved, one's response to the flag burner may exploit the uniquely persuasive power of the flag itself. We can imagine no more appropriate response to burning a flag than waving one's own, no better way to counter a flag burner's message than by saluting the flag that burns, no surer means of preserving the dignity even of the flag that burned than by—as one witness here did—according its remains a respectful burial. We do not consecrate the flag by punishing its desecration, for in doing so we dilute the freedom that this cherished emblem represents.

Johnson was convicted for engaging in expressive conduct. The State's interest in preventing breaches of the peace does not support his conviction because Johnson's conduct did not threaten to disturb the peace. Nor does the State's interest in preserving the flag as a symbol of nationhood and national unity justify his criminal conviction for engaging in political expression. The judgment of the Texas Court of Criminal Appeals is therefore

Affirmed.

JUSTICE KENNEDY, concurring . . .

The case before us illustrates better than most that the judicial power is often difficult in its exercise. We cannot here ask another branch to share responsibility, as when the argument is made that a statute is flawed or incomplete. For we are presented with a clear and simple statute to be judged against a pure command of the Constitution. The outcome can be laid at no door but ours.

The hard fact is that sometimes we must make decisions we do not like. We make them because they are right, right in the sense that the law and the Constitution, as we see them, compel the result. And so great is our commitment to the process that, except in the rare case, we do not pause to express distaste for the result, perhaps for fear of undermining a valued principle that dictates the decision. This is one of those rare cases.

Our colleagues in dissent advance powerful arguments why respondent may be convicted for his expression, reminding us that among those who will be dismayed by our holding will be some who have had the singular honor of carrying the flag in battle. And I agree that the flag holds a lonely place of honor in an age when absolutes are distrusted and simple truths are burdened by unneeded apologetics.

With all respect to those views, I do not believe the Constitution gives us the right to rule as the dissenting members of the Court urge, however painful this judgment is to announce. Though symbols often are what we ourselves make of them, the flag is constant in expressing beliefs Americans share, beliefs in law and peace and that freedom which sustains the human spirit. The case here today forces recognition of the costs to which those beliefs commit us. It is poignant but fundamental that the flag protects those who hold it in contempt.

For all the record shows, this respondent was not a philosopher and perhaps did not even possess the ability to comprehend how repellent his statements must be to the Republic itself. But whether or not he could appreciate the enormity of the offense he gave, the fact remains that his acts were speech, in both the technical and the fundamental meaning of the Constitution. So I agree with the Court that he must go free.

CHIEF JUSTICE REHNQUIST, with whom JUSTICE WHITE and JUSTICE O'CONNOR join, dissenting.

In holding this Texas statute unconstitutional, the Court ignores Justice Holmes' familiar aphorism that "a page of history is worth a volume of logic." . . . For more than two hundred years, the American flag has occupied a unique position as the symbol of our Nation, a uniqueness that justifies a governmental prohibition against flag burning in the way respondent Johnson did here.

At the time of the American Revolution, the flag served to unify the Thirteen Colonies at home, while obtaining recognition of national sovereignty abroad. . . .

The American flag played a central role in our Nation's most tragic conflict, when the North fought against the South. The lowering of the American flag at Fort Sumter was viewed as the start of the war. . . . The Southern States, to formalize their separation from the Union, adopted the "Stars and Bars" of the Confederacy. The Union troops marched to the sound of "Yes We'll Rally Round The Flag Boys, We'll Rally Once Again." President Abraham Lincoln refused proposals to remove from the American flag the stars representing the rebel States, because he considered the conflict not a war between two nations but an attack by eleven States against the National Government. . . . By war's end, the American flag again flew over "an indestructible union, composed of indestructible states." . . .

In the First and Second World Wars, thousands of our countrymen died on foreign soil fighting for the American cause. At Iwo Jima in the Second World War, United States Marines fought hand-to-hand against thousands of Japanese. By the time the Marines reached the top of Mount Suribachi, they raised a piece of pipe upright and from one end fluttered a flag. That ascent had cost nearly six thousand American lives. . . .

During the Korean War, the successful amphibious landing of American troops at Inchon was marked by the raising of an American flag within an hour of the event. Impetus for the enactment of the Federal Flag Desecration Statute in 1967 came from the impact of flag burnings in the United States on troop morale in Vietnam. . . .

The flag symbolizes the Nation in peace as well as in war. It signifies our national presence on battleships, airplanes, military installations, and public buildings from the United States Capitol to the thousands of county courthouses and city halls throughout the country. Two flags are prominently placed in our courtroom. Countless flags are placed by the graves of loved ones each year on what was first called Decoration Day, and is now called Memorial Day. . . .

The American flag, then, throughout more than two hundred years of our history, has come to be the visible symbol embodying our Nation. It does not represent the views of any particular political party, and it does not represent any particular political philosophy. The flag is not simply another "idea" or "point of view" competing for recognition in the marketplace of ideas. Millions and millions of Americans regard it with an almost mystical reverence regardless of what sort of social, political, or philosophical beliefs they may have. I cannot agree that the First Amendment invalidates the Act of Congress, and the laws of forty-eight of the fifty States, which make criminal the public burning of the flag. . . .

The Court concludes its opinion with a regrettably patronizing civics lecture, presumably addressed to the Members of both Houses of Congress, the members of the forty-eight state legislatures that enacted prohibitions against flag burning, and the troops fighting under that flag in Vietnam who objected to its being burned: "The way to preserve the flag's special role is not to punish those who feel differently about these matters. It is to persuade them that they are wrong." . . . The Court's role as the final expositor of the Constitution is well established, but its role as a platonic guardian admonishing those responsible to public opinion as if they were truant school children has no similar place in our system of government. . . . Uncritical extension of constitutional protection to the burning of the flag risks the frustration of the very purpose for which organized governments are instituted. The Court decides that the American flag is just another symbol, about which not only must opinions pro and con be tolerated, but for which the most minimal public respect may not be enjoined. The government may conscript men into the Armed Forces where they must fight and perhaps die for the flag, but the government may not prohibit the public burning of the banner under which they fight. I would uphold the Texas statute as applied in this case.

BIBLIOGRAPHY

BERNS, WALTER. "Flag-Burning and Other Modes of Expression."
    Commentary 88, no. 4 (October 1989): 37.

BUCKLEY, WILLIAM F. "The Court and the Flag Decision."
    National Review, August 4, 1989, p. 13.

GARBUS, M. "The 'Crime' of Flag Burning." *Nation*, March 20,
    1989, p. 369.

LOEWY, A. H. "The Flag Burning Case." *North Carolina Law
    Review* 68 (November 1989): 165.

TUSHNET, MARK V. "The Flag Burning Episode." *University of Colorado Law Review* 61, no. 1 (Winter 1990): 39.

WOOD, JAMES E., JR. "Making the Nation's Flag a Sacred Symbol." *Journal of Church and State* 31, no. 3 (Autumn 1989): 375.

New York Times v. United States

403 U.S. 713 (1971)

The Pentagon Papers case began on June 13, 1971, when the *New York Times* published six pages of articles and documents from a top-secret Defense Department history of the Vietnam War. The *Washington Post* soon followed the *Times*. Government lawyers quickly asked federal judges to bar the two newspapers from printing further excerpts from the Pentagon Papers. This unprecedented case raised the issue of prior restraint of the press, the primary target of the First Amendment. Solicitor General Griswold argued to the Supreme Court that publication of the Pentagon Papers would "materially affect the security of the United States." Two weeks after the case began, the Supreme Court rejected his argument and ruled that the government had not met the "heavy burden" of proving that national security claims outweighed the First Amendment.

TRANSCRIPT OF EDITED AND NARRATED ARGUMENTS IN
New York Times v. *United States*, 403 U.S. 713 (1971)

Counsel for petitioners: Alexander Bickel, Yale Law School (*New York Times*);
William Glendon, Washington, D.C. (*Washington Post*)
Counsel for respondent: Solicitor General Erwin Griswold, Washington, D.C.

Narrator: It's June 26th, 1971. The Court's regular term has ended. Chief
Justice Warren Burger presides at this special session. It normally takes at least
two years for a case to reach the Supreme Court. These cases started only two
weeks ago. On Sunday, June 13th, the *New York Times* printed articles and
documents from a top-secret Defense Department history of the Vietnam War.
And the *Washington Post* soon printed other documents from the forty-seven
volumes known as the Pentagon Papers.

Daniel Ellsberg initiated this unprecedented confrontation. Ellsberg graduated from Harvard during the Korean War and served in the Marine Corps. He
worked for the Defense Department in Vietnam as a military analyst and helped
prepare the Pentagon Papers. Ellsberg's Vietnam experience, and his exposure
to secret documents, turned him from a hawk to a dove. He felt Americans
should learn how their country was sucked into a war it could not win. But his
speeches and articles against the war failed to change policy. So Ellsberg gave
the Pentagon Papers to the *New York Times* and *Washington Post*. He wanted
to stir up debate on the war, and he succeeded.

After the first article, government lawyers asked federal judges in New York
and Washington for injunctions to block further publication. Judges in both
cities held emergency hearings and issued conflicting rulings. Confronted with
legal confusion, the Supreme Court voted to hear both cases.

The Pentagon Papers case tests the limits of the Constitution's First Amendment, which protects freedom of the press. It also involves the issue of prior
restraint, the doctrine that bars government censorship *before* publication. More
narrowly, it raises the government's claim for an exception to prior restraint,
when publication might endanger "national security."

Solicitor General Erwin Griswold will argue for the government in both
cases. A former dean of Harvard Law School, he speaks first for *all* the lawyers
on the pressures they faced in preparing for this argument. Chief Justice Burger
welcomes him.

Chief Justice Burger: Mr. Solicitor General, you may proceed.

Griswold: Mr. Chief Justice, and may it please the Court.

I am told that the law students of today are indignantly opposed to final examinations because they say that no lawyer ever has to work under such pressure that he has to get things out in three or four hours. I can only say that I think it's perhaps fortunate that Mr. Glendon and Mr. Bickel and I went to law school under an earlier dispensation.

Narrator: Griswold outlined the government's position.

Griswold: It is important, I think, to get this case in perspective. The case, of course, raises important and difficult problems about the constitutional right of free speech and of the free press, and we've heard much about that from the press in the last two weeks. But it also raises important questions of the equally fundamental and important right of the Government to function.

Great emphasis has been put on the First Amendment, and rightly so. But there is also involved here a fundamental question of separation of powers in the sense of the power and authority which the Constitution allocates to the president, as chief executive and as commander-in-chief of the Army and Navy. And, involved in that, there is also the question of the integrity of the institution of the presidency: whether that institution—one of the three great powers under the separation of powers—can function effectively.

Narrator: Griswold addressed the prior restraint issue.

Griswold: The problem lies on a wide spectrum and, like all questions of constitutional law, involves the resolution of competing principles. In the first place, it seems to me that it will be helpful to make some preliminary observations. If we start out with the assumption that never—under any circumstances—can the press be subjected to prior restraints, never—under any circumstances—can the press be enjoined from publication, of course we come out with the conclusion that there can be no injunction here. But I suggest, not as necessarily conclusive in this case, but I suggest that there is no such constitutional rule, and never has been such a constitutional rule.

Narrator: Griswold claimed that "top secret" stamps on ten items in the Pentagon Papers justified injunctions against their publication. Justice Potter Stewart was skeptical.

White: Mr. Solicitor General, I don't want to bring in a red herring in this case—or which might be—but do you also say that the ten items you have talked about fully justify the classification that has been given them and still remains on them?

Griswold: My position would be that as to those ten items—it's more than ten documents—as to those ten items, that they are properly classified "top secret."

White: Thank you. As I understand . . .

Griswold: One of the items, I should make plain, is four volumes of the forty-seven volumes. Four related volumes, all dealing with one specific subject, the broaching of which to the entire world at this time would be of extraordinary seriousness to the security of the United States.

Narrator: Four volumes of the Pentagon Papers dealt with diplomatic efforts to negotiate between North Vietnam and the United States. Griswold did not know that Ellsberg withheld these volumes from the press, to protect the diplomats. He faced more questions on judicial standards for injunctions.

Stewart: As I understand it, Mr. Solicitor General—and you tell me, please, if I misunderstand it—your case doesn't really depend upon the classification of this material, whether it's classified or how it's classified?

Griswold: Well I think, Mr. Justice, that is true. But I also think the heart of our case is that the publication of the material specified in my closed brief will, as I have tried to argue there, materially affect the security of the United States. It will affect lives. It will affect the process of the termination of the war. It will affect the process of recovering prisoners of war. I cannot say that the termination of the war, or recovering prisoners of war, is something which has an "immediate" effect on the security of the United States. I say that it has such an effect on the security of the United States that it ought to be the basis of an injunction in this case.

Narrator: Griswold offered a concession.

Griswold: If this material had never been classified, I think we would have a considerably greater difficulty in coming in and saying—well, for example, suppose the material had been included in a public speech made by the president of the United States.

Stewart: Well, then it would be in the public domain already. That's something else.

Griswold: All right. But we come in and say, "You can't print this because it will gravely affect the security of the United States." I think we would plainly be out.

Stewart: And a very shaky case on the facts. And that's . . .

Griswold: Or suppose it had been . . . (*laughter*)

Stewart: And this, therefore, is a fact case, isn't it? Until we can decide this case, we have to look at the facts, the evidence in this case that's been submitted under seal.

Griswold: In large part, yes, Mr. Justice.

Narrator: Griswold criticized Judge Gerhard Gesell, who ruled in the *Washington Post* case that the government must prove "immediate harm" to the United States to justify prior restraint.

Griswold: If the standard is that we cannot prevent the publication of improperly acquired material unless we can show in substance and effect—because that's what he really meant—that there will be a break in diplomatic relations, or that there will be an armed attack on the United States, I suggest that the standard which Judge Gesell used is far too narrow. And, as I've said, that the standard should be "great and irreparable harm to the security of the United States."

Narrator: Griswold raised an alarm about diplomatic efforts to end the war.

Griswold: In the whole diplomatic area the things don't happen at 8:15 tomorrow morning. It may be weeks, or months. People tell me that already channels of communication on which great hope had been placed have dried up. I haven't the slightest doubt, myself, that the material which has already been published, and the publication of the other materials, affects American lives, and is a thoroughly serious matter. And I think that to say that it can only be enjoined if there will be a war tomorrow morning, when there's a war now going on, is much too narrow.

Narrator: Chief Justice Burger.

Burger: Thank you, Mr. Solicitor General. Mr. Bickel.

Narrator: Alexander Bickel, a Yale Law School professor, argued for the *New York Times*.

Bickel: Mr. Chief Justice, may it please the Court.

I don't, for a moment, argue that the president doesn't have full inherent power to establish a system of classification; that he doesn't have the fullest inherent power to administer that system and its procedures within the executive branch. He has his means of guarding security at the source. In some measure, he's aided by the criminal sanction, but in any event he has full inherent power. And the scope of judicial review of the exercise of that power will presumably vary with the case in which it comes up.

Narrator: Bickel made a strategic concession.

Bickel: We concede—we have all along in this case conceded—for purposes of the argument, that the prohibition against prior restraint, like so much else in the Constitution, is not an absolute. But beyond that, Mr. Justice, our position is a little more complicated than that.

   Rather, our position is twofold. First, on principles as we view them with the separation of powers, which we believe deny the existence of inherent presidential authority on which an injunction can be based, first on those. And, secondly, on First Amendment principles which are interconnected on both and which involve the question of a standard before one reaches the facts—a standard on which we differ greatly from the solicitor general.

Narrator: Bickel's support for the "immediate harm" standard for prior restraint led to questions.

White: I take it, then, that you could easily concede that there may be documents in these forty-seven volumes which would satisfy the definition of "top secret" in the Executive Order and, nevertheless, would not satisfy your standard?

Bickel: That would be chiefly for the reason that, as is notorious, classifications are imposed . . .

White: No, no, my question was, let's concede for the moment that there are some documents . . . (Bickel: Which are properly?) . . . properly classified "top secret." You would say that does not necessarily mean that you standard is satisfied?

Bickel: That's correct, Mr. Justice. I would say that . . .

White: Well, I think—I haven't read anything in any of your documents, or in any of these cases, which the newspapers suggest for a moment that there is *no* document in these forty-seven volumes which satisfies properly the definition of "top secret."

Bickel: Having read the submissions of the government, I am flatly persuaded that there's nothing in there. Because if there—nothing that would meet my standard in there for a statute or for independent executive action—because if there were it surely should have turned up by now.

Narrator: Justice Potter Stewart asked a tough question.

Stewart: Now, Mr. Bickel, it's understandably and inevitably true that in a case like this, particularly when so many of the facts are under seal, it's necessary to speak in abstract terms. (Bickel: Yes, sir.) But let me give you a hypothetical case. Let us assume that when the members of the Court go back and open up this sealed record, we find something there that absolutely convinces us that its disclosure would result in the sentencing to death of a hundred young men whose only offense had been that they were nineteen years old and had low draft numbers. What should we do?

Bickel: Mr. Justice, I wish there were a statute that covered it.

Stewart: Well, there isn't, we agree—or you submit—so I'm asking you in this case, what should we do? You would say the Constitution requires that it be published and that these men die. Is that it?

Bickel: No. No, I'm afraid I'd have, I'm afraid that my, the inclinations of humanity overcome the somewhat more abstract devotion to the First Amendment, in a case of that sort.

Narrator: Justice Hugo Black asked if Congress could impose prior restraint on the press.

Bickel: We don't face it in this case and I really don't know. I'd have to face that if I saw it—if I saw the statute—if I saw how definite it was.

Douglas: Why would the statute make a difference? Because the First Amendment provides that "Congress shall make no law abridging freedom of the press." (Bickel: Well . . .) And you can read that to mean Congress may make "some laws" abridging freedom of the press?

Bickel: No, sir—only in that I have conceded for purposes of this argument that some limitations, some impairment of the absoluteness of that prohibition, is possible. And I argue that whatever that may be—whatever that may be—it is surely at its very least when the president acts without statutory authority, because that inserts into it, as well as separation of powers . . .

Douglas: That's a very strange argument for the *Times* to be making, that the Congress can make all of this illegal by passing laws.

Bickel: Well, I didn't really argue that, Mr. Justice. At least I hope not.

Douglas: That was the strong impression you left in my mind.

Narrator: William Glendon argued for the *Washington Post*. Chief Justice Burger asked about the "immediate harm" standard.

Burger: Mr. Glendon, how does a government meet the burden of proof in the sense that Judge Gesell laid it down? That doesn't bring any battleships to the outer limits of New York Harbor, or set off any missiles, but would you say that it's not a very grave matter?

Glendon: Your Honor, I think if we are to place possibilities or conjecture against suspension or abridgment of the First Amendment, the answer is obvious. The fact, the possibility, the conjecture of the hypothesis, that diplomatic negotiations would be made more difficult or embarrassing, does not justify— and this is what we have in this case, I think, it's all we have—does not justify suspending the First Amendment.

Burger: You are now in the position of making demands on the First Amendment . . . (Glendon: That's right) . . . and you say the newspaper has a right to protect its sources, but the government does not?

Glendon: I see no conflict, Your Honor. I see no conflict at all. We're in the position of asking that there not be a prior restraint, in violation of the Constitution, imposed on us, and that equity should not do that. We are also in the position of saying that under the First Amendment we are entitled to protect our sources. And I find—frankly, I just don't find any conflict there, Your Honor.

Narrator: Glendon reminded the Court of the stakes in the case.

Glendon: It isn't just that the United States has been injured. Judge Gesell made a point, which I think is a very good one, and I think perhaps the government may forget, that the interests of the United States are the people's interest. And you're weighing here—and this is why, I suppose, we're here—you're weighing here an abridgment of the First Amendment, the people's right to know. And that may be an abstraction, but it's one that's kept this country and made it great for some two hundred years, and you're being asked to approve something that the government has never done before. We were told by the attorney general to stop publishing this news. We didn't obey that order, and we were brought into court, and we ended up being enjoined.

Narrator: Solicitor General Griswold spoke in rebuttal. Justices Thurgood Marshall and Hugo Black had questions.

Griswold: I think that if properly classified materials are improperly acquired, and that it can be shown that they do have an immediate, or current impact, on the security of the United States that there ought to be an injunction. Now I think it is relevant, at this point . . .

Marshall: Well, wouldn't we then be—the federal courts—be the censorship board? (Griswold: Uh, that's . . .) As to whether this does . . .

Griswold: That's a pejorative way to put it, Mr. Justice. I don't know what the alternative is.

Black: The First Amendment might be. (*laughter*)

Griswold: Yes, Mr. Justice. And we are, of course, fully supporting the First Amendment. We do not claim, or suggest, any exception to the First Amendment. And we do not agree with Mr. Glendon when he says that we have set aside the First Amendment, or that Judge Gesell or the two Courts of Appeals in this case have set aside the First Amendment by issuing the injunction which they have.

The problem in this case is the construction of the First Amendment. Now, Mr. Justice Black, your construction of that is well known, and I certainly respect it. You say that "no law" means "no law," and that should be obvious.

Black: I rather thought that.

Griswold: And I can only say, Mr. Justice, that to me it is equally obvious that "no law" does *not* mean "no law." And I would seek to persuade the Court that that is true.

Narrator: On June 30th, 1971, only four days after this argument, the Supreme Court decided the Pentagon Papers case. In a three-paragraph opinion, six justices agreed that the government had not met the First Amendment's "heavy presumption" against prior restraints on the press. This short opinion was all the majority agreed on.

Reflecting the nation's division over the Vietnam War, each of the nine justices wrote a separate opinion. Justice Hugo Black blasted the government for what he called "a flagrant, indefensible, and continuing violation of the First Amendment."

Only Justice William Douglas agreed with Black that the Constitution barred *any* prior restraint. Four justices would allow the government to restrain publication of material that would cause, as Justice Potter Stewart wrote, "direct, immediate, and irreparable damage" to the United States. But the Pentagon Papers had not caused such damage.

Chief Justice Burger led the three dissenters. He blamed the newspapers for rushing into print and pressuring the Courts. "Free from unwarranted deadlines and frenetic pressures," he wrote, judges might have found documents that justified prior restraint.

Freed from judicial orders to stop the presses, newspapers across the country resumed publication of the Pentagon Papers. The Vietnam War ended four years later with an American defeat. Some critics blame the press for "losing" the war. The Persian Gulf War in 1991 again raised First Amendment issues of military censorship and media access to war zones. As long as bombs fall and presses roll, the Constitution will take hits from both sides. Whether it survives is up to the American people.

EDITED SUPREME COURT OPINION
New York Times v. *United States*

PER CURIAM.

We granted certiorari in these cases in which the United States seeks to enjoin the *New York Times* and the *Washington Post* from publishing the contents of a classified study entitled "History of U. S. Decision-Making Process on Viet Nam Policy." *Post*, pp. 942, 943.

"Any system of prior restraints of expression comes to this Court bearing a heavy presumption against its constitutional validity." *Bantam Books, Inc.* v. *Sullivan*, 372 U.S. 58, 70 (1963) . . . The Government "thus carries a heavy burden of showing justification for the imposition of such a restraint." *Organization for a Better Austin* v. *Keefe*, 402 U. S. 415, 419 (1971). The District Court for the Southern District of New York in the *New York Times* case and the District Court for the District of Columbia and the Court of Appeals for the District of

Columbia Circuit in the *Washington Post* case held that the Government had not met that burden. We agree.

The judgment of the Court of Appeals for the District of Columbia Circuit is therefore affirmed. The order of the Court of Appeals for the Second Circuit is reversed and the case is remanded with directions to enter a judgment affirming the judgment of the District Court for the Southern District of New York. The stays entered June 25, 1971, by the Court are vacated. The judgments shall issue forthwith.

So ordered.

MR. JUSTICE BLACK, with whom MR. JUSTICE DOUGLAS joins, concurring.

I adhere to the view that the Government's case against the *Washington Post* should have been dismissed and that the injunction against the *New York Times* should have been vacated without oral argument when the cases were first presented to this Court. I believe that every moment's continuance of the injunctions against these newspapers amounts to a flagrant, indefensible, and continuing violation of the First Amendment. . . . In my view it is unfortunate that some of my Brethren are apparently willing to hold that the publication of news may sometimes be enjoined. Such a holding would make a shambles of the First Amendment.

Our Government was launched in 1789 with the adoption of the Constitution. The Bill of Rights, including the First Amendment, followed in 1791. Now, for the first time in the 182 years since the founding of the Republic, the federal courts are asked to hold that the First Amendment does not mean what it says, but rather means that the Government can halt the publication of current news of vital importance to the people of this country.

. . . The Bill of Rights changed the original Constitution into a new charter under which no branch of government could abridge the people's freedoms of press, speech, religion, and assembly. Yet the Solicitor General argues and some members of the Court appear to agree that the general powers of the Government adopted in the original Constitution should be interpreted to limit and restrict the specific and emphatic guarantees of the Bill of Rights adopted later. I can imagine no greater perversion of history. Madison and the other Framers of the First Amendment, able men that they were, wrote in language they earnestly believed could never be misunderstood: "Congress shall make no law . . . abridging the freedom . . . of the press . . . ." Both the history and language of the First Amendment support the view that the press must be left free to publish news, whatever the source, without censorship, injunctions, or prior restraints.

In the First Amendment the Founding Fathers gave the free press the protection it must have to fulfill its essential role in our democracy. The press was to serve the governed, not the governors. The Government's power to censor the press was abolished so that the press would remain forever free to censure the Government. The press was protected so that it could bare the secrets of government and inform the people. Only a free and unrestrained press can effectively expose deception in government. And paramount among the responsibilities of a free press is the duty to prevent any part of the government from deceiving the people and sending them off to distant lands to die of foreign fevers and foreign shot and shell. In my view, far from deserving condemnation for their courageous reporting, the *New York Times*, the *Washington Post*, and other newspapers should be commended for serving the purpose that the Founding Fathers saw so clearly. In revealing the workings of government that led to the Vietnam War, the newspapers nobly did precisely that which the Founders hoped and trusted they would do. . . .

The word "security" is a broad, vague generality whose contours should not be invoked to abrogate the fundamental law embodied in the First Amendment. The guarding of military and diplomatic secrets at the expense of informed representative government provides no real security for our Republic. The Framers of the First Amendment, fully aware of both the need to defend a new nation and the abuses of the English and Colonial governments, sought to give this new society strength and security by providing that freedom of speech, press, religion, and assembly should not be abridged. This thought was eloquently expressed in 1937 by Mr. Chief Justice Hughes—great man and great Chief Justice that he was—when the Court held a man could not be punished for attending a meeting run by Communists.

> "The greater the importance of safeguarding the community from incitements to the overthrow of our institutions by force and violence, the more imperative is the need to preserve inviolate the constitutional rights of free speech, free press and free assembly in order to maintain the opportunity for free political discussion, to the end that government may be responsive to the will of the people and that changes, if desired, may be obtained by peaceful means. Therein lies the security of the Republic, the very foundation of constitutional government." *De Jonge* v. *Oregon*, 299 U. S. 353, 365.

MR. CHIEF JUSTICE BURGER, dissenting.

So clear are the constitutional limitations on prior restraint against expression, that . . . we have had little occasion to be concerned with cases involving prior restraints against news reporting on matters of public interest. There is, therefore, little variation among the members of the Court in terms of resistance to prior restraints against publication. Adherence to this basic constitutional principle, however, does not make these cases simple. In these cases, the imperative of a free and unfettered press comes into collision with another imperative, the effective functioning of a complex modern government and specifically the effective exercise of certain constitutional powers of the Executive. Only those who view the First Amendment as an absolute in all circumstances—a view I respect, but reject—can find such cases as these to be simple or easy.

These cases are not simple for another and more immediate reason. We do not know the facts of the cases. No District Judge knew all the facts. No Court of Appeals judge knew all the facts. No member of this Court knows all the facts.

Why are we in this posture, in which only those judges to whom the First Amendment is absolute and permits of no restraint in any circumstances or for any reason, are really in a position to act?

I suggest we are in this posture because these cases have been conducted in unseemly haste. . . . The prompt setting of these cases reflects our universal abhorrence of prior restraint. But prompt judicial action does not mean unjudicial haste.

Here, moreover, the frenetic haste is due in large part to the manner in which the *Times* proceeded from the date it obtained the purloined documents. It seems reasonably clear now that the haste precluded reasonable and deliberate judicial treatment of these cases and was not warranted. The precipitate action of this Court aborting trials not yet completed is not the kind of judicial conduct that ought to attend the disposition of a great issue.

The newspapers make a derivative claim under the First Amendment; they denominate this right as the public "right to know" . . .

It is not disputed that the *Times* has had unauthorized possession of the documents for three to four months, during which it has had its expert analysts studying them, presumably digesting them and preparing the material for publication. During all of this time, the *Times*, presumably in its capacity as trustee of the public's "right to know," has held up publication for purposes it considered proper and thus public knowledge was delayed. No doubt this was for a good reason; the analysis of seven thousand pages of complex material drawn from a vastly greater volume of material would inevitably take time and the writing of good news stories takes time. But why should the United States Government, from whom this information was illegally acquired by someone, along with all the counsel, trial judges, and appellate judges be placed under needless pressure? After these months of deferral, the alleged "right to know" has somehow and suddenly become a right that must be vindicated instanter.

Would it have been unreasonable, since the newspaper could anticipate the Government's objections to release of secret material, to give the Government an opportunity to review the entire collection and determine whether agreement could be reached on publication? . . .

. . . To me it is hardly believable that a newspaper long regarded as a great institution in American life would fail to perform one of the basic and simple duties of every citizen with respect to the discovery or possession of stolen property or secret government documents. That duty, I had thought—perhaps naively—was to report forthwith, to responsible public officers. This duty rests on taxi drivers, Justices, and the *New York Times*. The course followed by the *Times*, whether so calculated or not, removed any possibility of orderly litigation of the issues. . . .

The consequence of all this melancholy series of events is that we literally do not know what we are acting on. As I see it, we have been forced to deal with litigation concerning rights of great magnitude without an adequate record, and surely without time for adequate treatment either in the prior proceedings or in this Court. It is interesting to note that counsel on both sides, in oral argument before this Court, were frequently unable to respond to questions on factual points. Not surprisingly they pointed out that they had been working literally "around the clock" and simply were unable to review the documents that give rise to these cases and were not familiar with them. This Court is in no better posture. . . .

We all crave speedier judicial processes but when judges are pressured as in these cases the result is a parody of the judicial function.

BIBLIOGRAPHY

Gelb, Leslie H. "Today's Lessons from the Pentagon Papers." *Life*, September 17, 1971, p. 34.

Konig, Hans. "Did the Pentagon Papers Make Any Difference?" *Saturday Review*, June 10, 1972, p. 13.

McGovern, George, and John R. Roche. "The Pentagon Papers—A Discussion." *Political Science Quarterly* 87, no. 2 (June 1972): 173.

Schrag, Peter. *Test of Loyalty*. Touchstone, 1974.

"The Counter-Government and the Pentagon Papers." *National Review*, July 13, 1971, p. 739.

"The First Amendment on Trial." *Columbia Journalism Review*, September/October 1971, p. 7.

Ungar, Sanford J. *The Papers and the Papers*. Dutton, 1972.

PART THREE:

"In All Criminal Prosecutions"

AMERICANS ARE JUSTLY concerned about crime. The foundation of our society rests on the protection of personal safety and the security of our property. We expect the police to patrol our streets, to keep an eye on suspicious persons, to investigate crimes, and to apprehend those who commit criminal acts. We also expect the courts to bring the accused to trial and to impose punishment on those who are convicted. Most people believe that criminals should be punished severely, and a substantial majority of Americans support capital punishment.

Fear of crime and hostility toward criminals have prompted many persons to advocate shortcuts to arrests and convictions. Politicians often loudly call for "law and order" during election campaigns. Richard Nixon attacked the Supreme Court in 1968 for decisions he said "have gone too far in weakening the peace forces as against the criminal forces in this country." Attorney General Edwin Meese, who served under President Ronald Reagan, denounced Supreme Court decisions that allowed criminal suspects to remain silent, saying that "you don't have many suspects who are innocent."

Debates over the rights of criminal suspects go back to colonial days. The British authorities enforced laws with little regard for "due process" and conducted "drumhead" trials before military tribunals. Homes and shops were searched for contraband under "general warrants" that imposed no limits on revenue agents. Suspects could be held in jail for months—sometimes years—before indictment or trial. And punishments were harsh. Conviction of petty crimes often brought whipping or branding with red-hot irons. And the list of crimes punishable by death in colonial Massachusetts—more than twenty offenses—included blasphemy, adultery, and the refusal of children to obey their parents. As late as 1775, the death penalty was carried out by "burning alive" the convicted felon.

The men who framed the Bill of Rights were determined to protect Americans from the abuses they suffered under British rule. The framers had no desire to let criminals escape from prosecution or punishment, but they gave real meaning to the historic principle of "due process" as a guarantee of fairness to criminal defendants. They believed that when *any* person was falsely charged, unfairly tried, or brutally punished, no person felt safe from police, prosecutors, or prison. It is no accident that four of the first eight amendments to the Constitution established a code of criminal procedure. For there is no greater power of the government that requires protection against abuse than the power to take away a person's liberty or even life.

Unless the police actually witness a crime, the first step they usually take against a criminal suspect is a "stop" for questioning. Depending on the answers or the suspect's behavior, the police may conduct a search, not only for illicit evidence but also to protect themselves. They may also search pockets, bags, cars, or buildings. But the Constitution limits the police. The Fourth Amendment protects "the right of the people to be secure in their persons, houses, papers, and effects, against unreasonable searches and seizures." A "seizure" includes not only physical evidence but also an "arrest" of a suspect.

The Fourth Amendment also requires that police, before they conduct a search or arrest a suspect, first obtain a "warrant" that is based on "probable cause" and describes "the place to be searched, and the persons or things to be seized." Judges must answer tough questions when suspects claim their Fourth Amendment rights are violated. What is an "unreasonable" search or arrest? Are there circumstances in which police can act without a warrant? And what constitutes "probable cause" to justify a search or arrest? Is it "unreasonable" for police to "stop and frisk" someone because they are walking back and forth in front of a jewelry store? Can the police dig into pockets to look for guns, or knives, or drugs? Does an anonymous "tip" over the telephone constitute "probable cause" to search a house for criminal evidence?

Over the past fifty years, defense lawyers and prosecutors have argued hundreds of Fourth Amendment cases before the Supreme Court. Each side has won significant victories, but the justices have struggled to define the meaning of words like "unreasonable" and "probable cause." Each criminal case has different facts, and general rules can't cover every situation. But police officers and citizens are both entitled to know the "rules of engagement" when crimes are committed and suspects are searched.

Once the police arrest a suspect, he or she is deprived of "liberty" and protected by the "due process" clause of the Fifth Amendment against unfair practices. The Supreme Court has interpreted that clause to include *all* the protections the Bill of Rights gives to criminal defendants. The Fifth Amendment also provides that no person "shall be compelled in any criminal case to be a witness against himself." This right protects suspects against police coercion in securing confessions. In 1936, the Supreme Court reversed the death sentences of black defendants who confessed to rape and murder after being whipped and hanged until near death. "It would be difficult to conceive of methods more revolting to the sense of justice," the Court wrote in *Brown v. Mississippi.*

Most people agree the Fifth Amendment protects suspects against physical or mental torture. But does the right against self-incrimination also prevent the police from questioning suspects after their arrest? Many people reason that only a guilty person would refuse to answer questions. The innocent have nothing to hide and no reason to remain silent. Physical torture is outlawed, but police officers have developed subtle psychological methods to obtain confessions. The Supreme Court has heard many arguments on the limits of interrogation. Does the Fifth Amendment push the right against self-incrimination back from trial to the moment of arrest? At what stage of interrogation are suspects allowed to consult a lawyer? Can prosecutors comment on a defendant's decision not to testify? Supreme Court decisions on these questions have provoked public debate and political heat.

Once a criminal trial begins, the Sixth Amendment provides defendants with significant protections. Every defendant is entitled to a "speedy and public trial, by an impartial jury," to knowledge "of the nature and cause of the accusation" against him, to "be confronted with the witnesses against him," to "have compulsory process for obtaining witnesses in his behalf, and to have the Assistance of Counsel for his defense." The last of these protections is probably the most important. Can a criminal defendant receive a fair trial without a defense lawyer to answer the prosecutor? Today, the answer seems obvious to most people, but it took the Supreme Court until 1963 to decide this basic question.

The final question in criminal law is punishment. Do we punish the crime or the criminal? Is the purpose of punishment deterrence, rehabilitation, or retribution? Should sentences be uniform, or should judges have discretion in setting prison terms? The Constitution has only one clause that provides judges with guidance on these hard questions. The Eighth Amendment prohibits "cruel and unusual punishments." The Supreme Court has agreed that this clause outlaws whipping and branding of criminals. But the most difficult question in the Constitution is capital punishment. Does the death penalty violate the Eighth Amendment? Does the answer to this question come from history or from the "evolving standards of decency" in civilized society? Do racial disparities in seeking and imposing capital punishment have constitutional significance? The Supreme Court has heard impassioned argument on both sides of these questions. The justices have never held that capital punishment violates the Constitution, but they have limited the powers of juries and judges to impose the death penalty.

Americans differ on many issues, but they are virtually unanimous that crime is a serious problem and that criminals should be punished. Beyond this agreement, opinions differ on the rights of criminal defendants. Many believe the Constitution should not stand between criminals and prison bars. Others argue that the Constitution is all that stands between democracy and a police state. The argument will continue as long as crime afflicts our society, and the Supreme Court will continue to hear arguments in criminal cases.

Gideon v. Wainwright

372 U.S. 335 (1963)

In 1961, Clarence Earl Gideon was arrested in Florida for stealing change and cigarettes from a poolroom. He had a long record of petty crimes and couldn't afford a lawyer. Gideon told the judge that "the United States Supreme Court says I am entitled to be represented by counsel." But Florida gave poor people lawyers only in capital cases, and Gideon was forced to defend himself. He was convicted and sent to prison for five years. From his cell, he penciled a petition to the Supreme Court, which appointed Abe Fortas—a future Justice—to argue his case. The Court had ruled in 1942 that states were not bound by the Sixth Amendment guarantee of "the assistance of counsel" in federal cases. In Gideon's case, the Court held that fair trials were impossible "if the poor man charged with crime has to face his accusers without a lawyer to assist him." Granted a new trial and a lawyer, Gideon won acquittal and his freedom.

TRANSCRIPT OF EDITED AND NARRATED ARGUMENTS IN
Gideon v. *Wainwright*, 372 U.S. 335 (1963)

Counsel for petitioner: Abe Fortas, Washington, D.C.
Counsel for respondent: Bruce Jacob, Tallahassee, Florida

Chief Justice Earl Warren: Number 155, Clarence Earl Gideon, petitioner, versus H. G. Cochran, director, Division of Corrections.

Narrator: It's January 15th, 1963. Chief Justice Earl Warren has called for argument a case that raises the most basic issue in our justice system: Can a criminal defendant get a fair trial without a lawyer?

Most Americans think of trials as courtroom battles, with Perry Mason or the lawyers of "L.A. Law" on one side and prosecutors on the other. We've all seen defense lawyers on TV and movie screens. They shout objections, badger witnesses, and use every legal trick to get their clients off. Courtroom reality is far different. For every F. Lee Bailey, there are hundreds of overworked public defenders. They are the last line of defense between poor people and prison cells.

Before 1963, many criminal defendants—too poor to hire lawyers—were forced to defend themselves at trial. Most wound up in prison. Back in 1942, a Maryland farmhand named Smith Betts was charged with robbery. The judge denied his request for a lawyer. Betts did his best to defend himself, but he went to prison for eight years. His appeal to the Supreme Court rested on the Sixth Amendment to the Constitution: "In all criminal prosecutions, the accused shall enjoy the right . . . to have the assistance of Counsel for his defense."

The Court ruled in *Betts versus Brady* that the Sixth Amendment applied only in federal cases. "Appointment of counsel" in state courts "is not a fundamental right, essential to a fair trial," the Court said. Twenty years later, most states did provide lawyers to poor defendants. But Florida and other southern states didn't go along.

Today's arguments began with a small-time crime in a small-town bar. On June 3d, 1961, somebody broke into the Bay Harbor Poolroom in Panama City, Florida. The burglar stole some wine bottles and change from the cigarette machine and juke box. A witness told police he recognized Clarence Earl Gideon coming out of the bar. Gideon had a prior record for gambling and theft. His life, he confessed, was "no cause for pride." But he knew his rights, or thought he did. "The United States Supreme Court says I am entitled to be represented by counsel," he argued. The judge denied his request. Gideon did his best to defend himself but was convicted and sentenced to five years in prison.

From his prison cell, Gideon sent a handwritten petition to the Supreme Court. He again claimed the Constitution gave him the right to a lawyer. The Court grants very few prisoners' petitions, but the justices voted to hear this case. They asked a prominent Washington lawyer, Abe Fortas, to argue for Gideon. Most of his clients were powerful companies, but Fortas eagerly accepted this case. The big-time lawyer and his small-time client were both 51. They were both southerners. Their families went through hard times in the Great Depression. Maybe these facts explain why Fortas fought the case so hard. He read the transcript of Gideon's trial, and as a tough lawyer, he was appalled. Chief Justice Warren welcomes Fortas to the podium.

Warren: Mr. Fortas.

Fortas: Mr. Chief Justice; may it please the Court.

If you will look at this transcript of the record, perhaps you will share my feeling, which is a feeling of despondency. This record does not indicate that Clarence Earl Gideon is a man of inferior natural talents. This record does not indicate that Clarence Earl Gideon is a moron or a person of low intelligence. This record does not indicate that the judge of the trial court in the state of Florida, or that the prosecuting attorney in the state of Florida, was derelict in his duty. On the contrary, it indicates that they tried to help Gideon. But to me, if the Court please, this record indicates the basic difficulty with *Betts* against *Brady*. And the basic difficulty with *Betts* against *Brady* is that no man, certainly no layman, can conduct a trial in his own defense so that the trial is a fair trial.

Narrator: The justices asked both sides to argue whether *Betts versus Brady* should be overruled. Fortas had no doubt.

Fortas: I believe that this case dramatically illustrates the point that you cannot have a fair trial without counsel. Indeed, I believe that the right way to look at this, if I may put it that way, is that a court, a criminal court, is not properly constituted—and this has been said in some of your own opinions—under our adversary system of law, unless there is a judge and unless there is a counsel for the prosecution and unless there is a counsel for the defense. Without that, how can a civilized nation pretend that it is having a fair trial, under our adversary system, which means that counsel for the state will do his best within the limits of fairness and honor and decency to present the case for the state, and counsel for the defense will do his best, similarly, to present the best case possible for the defendant, and from that clash there will emerge the truth. That is our concept, and how can we say, how can it be suggested that a court is properly constituted, that a trial is fair, unless those conditions exist.

Narrator: Fortas moved to the concept of federalism, and argued that letting each state set trial rules was unfair to people like Gideon.

Fortas: I may be wrong about this, but I do believe that in some of this Court's decisions there has been a tendency from time to time, because of the pull of federalism, to forget, to forget the realities of what happens downstairs, of what happens to these poor, miserable, indigent people when they are arrested and they are brought into the jail and they are questioned and later on they are brought in these strange and awesome circumstances before a magistrate, and then later on they are brought before a court; and there, Clarence Earl Gideon, defend yourself.

Narrator: Fortas aimed his words at a skeptical justice, John Harlan, who generally supported state powers.

Fortas: I think that, in some of the Court's opinions, if I may say so, Mr. Justice Harlan, this element, this failure to remember what happens downstairs, has crept in. Not because of an insensitivity of the judges but because of the understandable pull of the sensitivity about the states' old jurisdiction. And that's why I want to analyze that. I don't think that it stands the test of logic, and I don't think that the argument of federalism here is either correct or soundly founded or stands the test of experience, and that's what I want to come to. Now, first . . .

Harlan: "Understandable sensitivity" to describe a basic principle of our government doesn't seem to me to be a very happy expression.

Fortas: Well, I'm sorry, sir. I meant that a regard, which I myself share, for the principles of federalism. But I believe that those principles are misapplied here. First, they are misapplied, if I may respectfully say so, when they are used for the purpose of negating a Fourteenth Amendment right to a fair trial. Second, they are misapplied here because a true regard, in my judgment, Mr. Justice Harlan, for federalism here means that this Court will lay down a principle, will establish a principle, and that this Court will not exercise the kind of minute, detailed, *ex post facto* supervision over state court trials that you have been exercising for these past years and which, in my opinion, is the most corrosive possible way to administer our federal-state system.

Narrator: Fortas was followed by J. Lee Rankin, former solicitor general of the United States. Rankin appears today as "friend of the Court" for the American Civil Liberties Union.

Rankin: It is enough of a fiction to be able to claim that the ordinary lawyer, with the greatest diligence and skill, is able to present fairly a case on behalf of a defendant against this skilled prosecutor that's had hundreds of cases behind him and understands the reaction of the court, in addition to knowing right off every case that could have a bearing upon the question. But when you take the poor layman and put him against those odds, there isn't the remotest possibility that you can get a fair trial except by pure accident.

Narrator: Justice Harlan remained skeptical.

Harlan: That's a terribly broad generalization, Mr. Rankin. I'm not saying that there isn't force to your argument, but to make a sweeping generalization as a dogmatic piece of, a dogmatic assertion that there can be no fair trial without a counsel ignores the facts of life that every lawyer knows.

Rankin: I say the rule has got to be turned around according to the facts; that generally you can't have a fair trial without counsel and the exception is the case that you and I know about, where some skilled layman has been able to get a fair trial despite not having counsel. But *Betts* against *Brady* is built upon the premise that generally you can get a fair trial without counsel. And that's where I think it's unsound.

Narrator: Justice Potter Stewart lightened the courtroom atmosphere.

Stewart: Florida wouldn't let Gideon represent anybody else on trial in that state, would it? *(laughter)*

Rankin: And it's rarely, as we lawyers all know, that a man does as well, because we have a saying, as you all know, that when he represents himself he has a fool for counsel, and it's often true.

Narrator: Bruce Jacob, a young assistant attorney general in Florida, argued his first case in the Supreme Court.

Jacob: Mr. Chief Justice, may it please the members of the Court, I am Bruce Jacob from the attorney general's office of Florida, representing the respondent.

Since our brief has been printed, I've received a letter from the trial judge who handled this case. I asked him what happened at arraignment because I just couldn't believe that a judge would make this statement at the trial without examining the man and finding out whether he really was incompetent or unable to handle his own defense. And Judge McCurry wrote back and said this:

He said, "I do remember the arraignment of this defendant, and also that he asked for counsel at arraignment and on the date of trial. He was advised that when a person appears to have the mental ability to interview witnesses and present testimony to the jury, the practice of appointing counsel is not followed except in capital cases. After talking with this defendant, it was my opinion that he had both the mental capacity and the experience in the courtroom at previous trials to adequately conduct his defense. This was later borne out at the trial, as you can determine from examination of the record in this case."

Narrator: Jacob answered Fortas's argument that the states must apply federal rights under the Fourteenth Amendment.

Jacob: Before getting into the argument on *Betts versus Brady,* I'd like to briefly outline our argument on this point.

   First of all, I'm going to point out that historically there is no basis whatsoever for including the right to automatic appointment of counsel in noncapital cases in the due process clause. Secondly, I'd like to indicate to the Court that due process, the term "due process," as it has been developed by this Court in many cases since the Civil War, is a relative and not an absolute concept; and therefore, this Court cannot impose an inflexible rule requiring appointment in all felony cases or in all criminal cases, for that matter.

   Next, I'll discuss the question of federalism and attempt to show the Court that imposition of an inflexible rule in this area would be an unwarranted intrusion into the historic rights of the states to determine their own rules of criminal procedure. I'll also point out that although the majority of states now do provide for automatic appointment in cases less than capital, the states that do that do so by court rule and by statute and not by constitutional construction.

Narrator: Justice Hugo Black had dissented in *Betts versus Brady.* He hadn't changed his mind in twenty years.

Black: One of my objections to *Betts* and *Brady* is that it does impose an unfair burden on the states in that it leaves them uncertain in every criminal case whether it will come up here and the facts will be viewed differently to the way the facts were viewed by the state courts. And so far as the injury to federalism is concerned, injury to the states, one of my objections to *Betts* and *Brady* has been just that, that the state's entitled to know with some degree of certainty what they can do to comply with what this Court says the Constitution requires.

Jacob: Your Honor, I don't think *Betts versus Brady* is that unclear. I think it's inconsistent in the same way that the entire common law is inconsistent.

Narrator: Chief Justice Warren had been a county prosecutor in California, which provided lawyers to poor defendants. He asked Jacob about practices in Florida's courts.

Warren: Mr. Jacob, I suppose out of those fifty-two hundred prisoners now in your jails who were not represented by counsel, that a vast majority of them are not only poor but are illiterate. Would that be a fair observation?

Jacob: Your Honor, I don't know.

Warren: Well, what's your observation?

Jacob: My observation is that—in all honesty, my observation is that there are some (Warren: "some?") but I have no idea how many. But I think in general the judges in Florida do make a very careful observation of every defendant that comes before them. And as I said, many judges are now at the point where they provide counsel in every single instance.

Warren: Even if they're illiterate? If they're just poor and illiterate, you think they always give them a lawyer in Florida?

Jacob: I can't say they always do, Your Honor, because there are some—they do . . .

Warren: Well, do they, as a general rule, give them?

Jacob: If the judge knows that he's illiterate or incompetent in some way, from his own observation, he does appoint counsel.

Warren: Well, do they, do they try to find out whether . . .

Jacob: Yes, they do, and here's the way they do it: They spend perhaps fifteen, twenty minutes asking him questions about his work experience, about his past history, his education, his experience in life, whether he's been convicted before and how much experience he's had in court; in other words, they try to follow the rules that have been set down by this Court in the cases since *Betts versus Brady.*

Narrator: Justice Stewart repeated the question he asked Lee Rankin. Another member of the Court joined in.

Stewart: I suppose I am right in my assumption that I made earlier that Florida wouldn't permit Gideon or any other layman to defend anyone else in the state on trial, would it?

Jacob: No, it wouldn't, Your Honor. Gideon could—if a man came into court and said, I want to be defended by Gideon, then certainly the court would not object.

Stewart: Wouldn't Gideon maybe get in trouble for practicing law without a license? (*laughter*)

Court: With the local bar association.

Jacob: I'm sorry, Your Honor, that was a stupid answer. (*laughter*)

Narrator: Jacob recovered his composure for his closing argument.

Jacob: By imposing an inflexible rule in all criminal cases, we feel that this Court would be intruding into a field that has been historically reserved for the states. Ever since the Fourteenth Amendment was adopted, this Court has in one case after another pointed out that a state can abolish the jury trial, trial by jury, if it wishes. It doesn't have to follow the specific guarantees of the Sixth Amendment. There's one case that says that a state can adopt a civil law if it wishes. A state should be free to adopt any system it wants. If it wants, it should be able to do away with the need for a prosecutor. Perhaps a judge could handle the whole trial. I'm not urging this, but I'm saying that the Court—that the states have the right to do this.

Narrator: Twenty-two states filed a friend of the court brief supporting Gideon. Only two southern states, Alabama and North Carolina, supported Florida. A lawyer for Alabama briefly defended his state's position. Abe Fortas had the last word.

Fortas: I think that *Betts* against *Brady* was wrong when decided; I think time has illuminated that fact. But I think that perhaps time has also done a service, because time has prepared the way so that the rule, the correct rule, the civilized rule, the rule of American constitutionalism, the rule of due process, may now be stated by this Court.

Narrator: Chief Justice Warren had gracious words for the lawyers on both sides.

Warren: Mr. Fortas, before you sit down, I should like to say this: This is a very important case, it's a very fundamental case. It's important to the state of Florida, to the state of Alabama and the other states that have that same rule; it's important to thousands and thousands of poor litigants throughout our country.

I want to say that we're always indebted to members of the bar who are willing to undertake cases of this kind as a public service, and we're grateful to you for having done so for this indigent defendant. We're very grateful to you, General Rankin, for having appeared as a friend of the court in the same cause. And of course, gentlemen of the attorney general's offices of Florida and of Alabama, we realize the great burden that you have in representing your state, and we appreciate the fair, frank, and earnest manner in which you have represented your states here. We've had a good argument and we thank all of you.

Narrator: Clarence Gideon waited only two months for a decision. On March 18th, 1963, the justices ruled unanimously that all states must provide lawyers to poor defendants in felony cases.

Justice Hugo Black argued for more than twenty years—mostly in dissent—that states must obey the federal Constitution. Gideon's case gave Black the satisfaction of turning his *Betts* dissent into law. He got quickly to the point: "We conclude that *Betts versus Brady* should be overruled." Even Justice Harlan agreed but grumbled that the *Betts* case should get "a more respectful burial."

Like Chief Justice Warren, Black had been a county prosecutor. He understood courtroom reality. States "spend vast sums of money," he wrote, to hire police and prosecutors. Defendants with money, he added, "hire the best lawyers they can get." Black wanted to make the courtroom battle a fair fight. The ideal of equal justice, he said, "cannot be realized if the poor man charged with crime has to face his accusers without a lawyer to assist him."

Black's opinion gave Clarence Gideon another chance to face his accusers. This time a lawyer assisted him. A surprise witness said the most likely poolroom burglar was the prosecution's chief witness. Gideon took the stand this time. "I'm not guilty," he told the jurors. "I know nothing about it." The jurors deliberated for an hour. When they returned, Clarence Gideon was a free man. After two years in prison, he could see his six children.

The Gideon case is a success story for the Bill of Rights. States must now provide lawyers for all criminal defendants who cannot afford them. But trials are still not fair fights in many courtrooms. Public defenders are still overworked and outspent by prosecutors and police. But they remain, for many poor people, the last line of defense in our justice system.

EDITED SUPREME COURT OPINIONS
Gideon v. Wainwright.

MR. JUSTICE BLACK delivered the opinion of the Court.

Petitioner was charged in a Florida state court with having broken and entered a poolroom with intent to commit a misdemeanor. This offense is a felony under Florida law. Appearing in court without funds and without a lawyer, petitioner asked the court to appoint counsel for him, whereupon the following colloquy took place:

> "The COURT: Mr. Gideon, I am sorry, but I cannot appoint Counsel to represent you in this case. Under the laws of the State of Florida, the only time the Court can appoint Counsel to represent a Defendant is when that person is charged with a capital offense. I am sorry, but I will have to deny your request to appoint Counsel to defend you in this case.

> "The DEFENDANT: The United States Supreme Court says I am entitled to be represented by Counsel."

Put to trial before a jury, Gideon conducted his defense about as well as could be expected from a layman. He made an opening statement to the jury, cross-examined the State's witnesses, presented witnesses in his own defense, declined to testify himself, and made a short argument "emphasizing his innocence to the charge contained in the Information filed in this case." The jury returned a verdict of guilty, and petitioner was sentenced to serve five years in the state prison. Later, petitioner filed in the Florida Supreme Court this habeas corpus petition attacking his conviction and sentence on the ground that the trial court's refusal to appoint counsel for him denied him rights "guaranteed by the Constitution and the Bill of Rights by the United States Government." Treating the petition for habeas corpus as properly before it, the State Supreme Court, "upon consideration thereof" but without an opinion, denied all relief. Since 1942, when *Betts* v. *Brady*, 316 U. S. 455, was decided by a divided Court, the problem of a defendant's federal constitutional right to counsel in a state court has been a continuing source of controversy and litigation in both state and federal courts. To give this problem another review here, we granted certiorari. . . . Since Gideon was proceeding *in forma pauperis*, we appointed counsel to represent him and requested both sides to discuss in their briefs and oral arguments the following: "Should this Court's holding in *Betts* v. *Brady* be reconsidered?"

. . . Since the facts and circumstances of the two cases are so nearly indistinguishable, we think the *Betts* v. *Brady* holding if left standing would require us to reject Gideon's claim that the Constitution guarantees him the assistance of counsel. Upon full reconsideration we conclude that *Betts* v. *Brady* should be overruled.

The Sixth Amendment provides, "In all criminal prosecutions, the accused shall enjoy the right . . . to have the Assistance of Counsel for his defence." We have construed this to mean that in federal courts counsel must be provided for defendants unable to employ counsel unless the right is competently and intelligently waived. Betts argued that this right is extended to indigent defendants in state courts by the Fourteenth Amendment. . . .

[T]he Court concluded that "appointment of counsel is not a fundamental right, essential to a fair trial." . . . It was for this reason the *Betts* Court refused to accept the contention that the Sixth Amendment's guarantee of counsel for indigent federal defendants was extended to or, in the words of that Court, "made obligatory upon the States by the Fourteenth Amendment." Plainly, had the Court concluded that appointment of counsel for an indigent criminal defendant was "a fundamental right, essential to a fair trial," it would have held that the Fourteenth Amendment requires appointment of counsel in a state court, just as the Sixth Amendment requires in a federal court.

We think the Court in *Betts* had ample precedent for acknowledging that those guarantees of the Bill of Rights which are fundamental safeguards of liberty immune from federal abridgment are equally protected against state invasion by the Due Process Clause of the Fourteenth Amendment. . . . [T]his Court has looked to the fundamental nature of original Bill of Rights guarantees to decide whether the Fourteenth Amendment makes them obligatory on the States. Explicitly recognized to be of this "fundamental nature" and therefore made immune from state invasion by the Fourteenth, or some part of it, are the First Amendment's freedoms of speech, press, religion, assembly, association, and petition for redress of grievances. For the same reason, though not always in precisely the same terminology, the Court has made obligatory on the States the Fifth Amendment's command that private property shall not be taken for public use without just compensation, the Fourth Amendment's prohibition of unreasonable searches and seizures, and the Eighth's ban on cruel and unusual punishment. On the other hand, this Court . . . refused to hold that the Fourteenth Amendment made the double jeopardy provision of the Fifth Amendment obligatory on the States. . . .

We accept *Betts* v. *Brady's* assumption, based as it was on our prior cases, that a provision of the Bill of Rights which is "fundamental and essential to a fair trial" is made obligatory upon the States by the Fourteenth Amendment. We think the Court in *Betts* was wrong, however, in concluding that the Sixth Amendment's guarantee of counsel is not one of these fundamental rights. Ten years before *Betts* v. *Brady*, this Court, after full consideration of all the historical data examined in *Betts*, had unequivocally declared that "the right to the aid of counsel is of this fundamental character." *Powell* v. *Alabama*, 287 U. S. 45, 68 (1932). While the Court at the close of its *Powell* opinion did by its language, as this Court frequently does, limit its holding to the particular facts and circumstances of that case, its conclusions about the fundamental nature of the right to counsel are unmistakable. . . . The fact is that in deciding as it did—that "appointment of counsel is not a fundamental right, essential to a fair trial"—the Court in *Betts* v. *Brady* made an abrupt break with its own well-considered precedents. In returning to these old precedents, sounder we believe than the new, we but restore constitutional principles established to achieve a fair system of justice. Not only these precedents but also reason and reflection require us to recognize that in our adversary system of criminal justice, any person haled into court, who is too poor to hire a lawyer, cannot be assured a fair trial unless counsel is provided for him. This seems to us to be an obvious truth. Governments, both state and federal, quite properly spend vast sums of money to establish machinery to try defendants accused of crime. Lawyers to prosecute are everywhere deemed essential to protect the public's interest in an orderly society. Similarly, there are few defendants charged with crime, few indeed, who fail to hire the best lawyers they can get to prepare and present their defenses. That government hires lawyers to prosecute and defendants who have the money hire lawyers to defend are the strongest indications of the widespread belief that lawyers in criminal courts are necessities, not luxuries. The right of one charged with crime to counsel may not be deemed fundamental and essential to fair trials in some countries, but it is in ours. From the very beginning, our state and national constitutions and laws have laid great emphasis on procedural and substantive safeguards designed to assure fair trials before impartial tribunals in which every defendant stands equal before the law. This noble ideal cannot be realized if the poor man charged with crime has to face his accusers without a lawyer to assist him. . . .

The judgment is reversed and the cause is remanded to the Supreme Court of Florida for further action not inconsistent with this opinion.

Reversed.

MR. JUSTICE HARLAN, concurring.

I agree that *Betts* v. *Brady* should be overruled, but consider it entitled to a more respectful burial than has been accorded, at least on the part of those of us who were not on the Court when that case was decided.

I cannot subscribe to the view that *Betts* v. *Brady* represented "an abrupt break with its own well-considered precedents." . . . In 1932, in *Powell* v. *Alabama*, . . . a capital case, this Court declared that under the particular facts there presented—"the ignorance and illiteracy of the defendants, their youth, the circumstances of public hostility . . . and above all that they stood in deadly peril of their lives" (287 U. S., at 71)—the state court had a duty to assign counsel for the trial as a necessary requisite of due process of law. It is evident that these limiting facts were not added to the opinion as an afterthought; they were repeat-edly emphasized, . . . and were clearly regarded as important to the result.

Thus when this Court, a decade later, decided *Betts v. Brady*, it did no more than to admit of the possible existence of special circumstances in noncapital as well as capital trials, while at the same time insisting that such circumstances be shown in order to establish a denial of due process. The right to appointed counsel had been recognized as being considerably broader in federal prosecutions, see *Johnson v. Zerbst*, 304 U. S. 458, but to have imposed these requirements on the States would indeed have been "an abrupt break" with the almost immediate past. The declaration that the right to appointed counsel in state prosecutions, as established in *Powell v. Alabama*, was not limited to capital cases was in truth not a departure from, but an extension of, existing precedent.

The principles declared in *Powell* and in *Betts*, however, have had a troubled journey throughout the years that have followed first the one case and then the other. . . .

In noncapital cases, the "special circumstances" rule has continued to exist in form while its substance has been substantially and steadily eroded. In the first decade after *Betts*, there were cases in which the Court found special circum-stances to be lacking, but usually by a sharply divided vote. . . . At the same time, there have been not a few cases in which special circumstances were found in little or nothing more than the "complexity" of the legal questions presented, although those questions were often of only routine difficulty. The Court has come to recognize, in other words, that the mere existence of a serious criminal charge constituted in itself special circumstances requiring the services of counsel at trial. In truth the *Betts v. Brady* rule is no longer a reality.

This evolution, however, appears not to have been fully recognized by many state courts, in this instance charged with the front-line responsibility for the enforcement of constitutional rights. To continue a rule which is honored by this Court only with lip service is not a healthy thing and in the long run will do disservice to the federal system.

The special circumstances rule has been formally abandoned in capital cases, and the time has now come when it should be similarly abandoned in noncapital cases, at least as to offenses which, as the one involved here, carry the possibility of a substantial prison sentence. (Whether the rule should extend to *all* criminal cases need not now be decided.) This indeed does no more than to make explicit something that has long since been foreshadowed in our decisions.

In agreeing with the Court that the right to counsel in a case such as this should now be expressly recognized as a fundamental right embraced in the Fourteenth Amendment, I wish to make a further observation. When we hold a right or immunity, valid against the Federal Government, to be "implicit in the concept of ordered liberty" and thus valid against the States, I do not read our past decisions to suggest that by so holding, we automatically carry over an entire body of federal law and apply it in full sweep to the States. Any such concept would disregard the frequently wide disparity between the legitimate interests of the States and of the Federal Government, the divergent problems that they face, and the significantly different consequences of their actions. . . .

On these premises I join in the judgment of the Court.

BIBLIOGRAPHY

KAMISAR, Y. "Right to Counsel." *University of Chicago Law Review* 30 (Autumn 1965): 1.

LEWIS, ANTHONY. *Gideon's Trumpet*. Vintage, 1966.

MAZOR, L. J. "Right to Be Provided Counsel." *Utah Law Review* 9 (Summer 1965): 50.

SCHIEFFER, B. "Lawyers Are for Poor People, Too." *Texas Bar Journal* 28 (April 1965): 275.

SILVERSTEIN, LEE. "The Continuing Impact of Gideon v. Wainwright on the States." *American Bar Association Journal* 51, no. 11 (November 1965): 1023.

TEMPLE, DAVID G. "Facing Up to Gideon." *National Civic Review* 54 (July 1965): 354.

Terry v. Ohio

392 U.S. 1 (1968)

Police officer Martin McFadden was patrolling the streets in down-town Cleveland, Ohio, on a fall day in 1963 when he spotted two men behaving suspiciously near a jewelry store. Suspecting them of "casing a job, a stick-up," the officer stopped John Terry and Richard Tilton and proceeded to "frisk" them in a pat-down search. He removed two guns from their overcoats. Terry and Chilton were later convicted of carrying concealed weapons and sentenced to prison. Terry appealed his conviction, charging that it violated his right against unreasonable searches and seizures under the Fourth Amendment. The Supreme Court ruled against him in 1968, holding that a police officer is entitled by the Constitution to "stop and frisk" individuals for weapons, when he has an "articulable" suspicion of criminal activity and a "reasonable fear for his own or others' safety."

TRANSCRIPT OF EDITED AND NARRATED ARGUMENTS IN
Terry v. *Ohio*, 392 U.S. 1 (1968)

Counsel for petitioner: Louis Stokes, Cleveland, Ohio
Counsel for respondent: Reuben Payne, Cleveland, Ohio

Chief Justice Earl Warren: Number 67, John W. Terry, et al., petitioners, versus Ohio.

Narrator: It's December 12th, 1967. Chief Justice Earl Warren has called a case that began on a street corner in Cleveland, Ohio. This is not an unusual or complicated case. It's what police call a "stop and frisk." A police officer observed three men who looked suspicious. He patted them down, found pistols on two suspects, and arrested them for carrying concealed weapons. The trial judge denied a motion to exclude the guns as evidence. The two men were convicted and sent to prison. There's no question they violated the law. The question is, Did the officer violate the Constitution?

The Supreme Court is asked every year to review hundreds of criminal convictions. Many are for serious crimes like murder. Only a handful are picked for argument and decision. Why did the justices choose this case? The Constitution is written in broad phrases, like "due process of law." Judges look to precedent in applying these phrases. But old cases don't always cover new facts. The Supreme Court picks cases like this to fill gaps in the law.

This case involves two broad phrases in the Constitution's Fourth Amendment. The first protects us against "unreasonable searches and seizures" by the police. The other requires police to have "probable cause" to believe someone has committed a crime before an arrest. The police search and arrest thousands of people every day. How does an officer know if a search is "unreasonable"? Or if he has "probable cause" for an arrest? John Terry's case will help police answer these tough questions.

Every case begins with a place and time. This one begins in downtown Cleveland. It's 2:30 in the afternoon, October 31st, 1963. Police Detective Martin McFadden is patrolling the area in plain clothes. He's patrolled this area for thirty years, looking for shoplifters and pickpockets. He sees two black men on the corner of Fourteenth Street and Euclid Avenue. "They didn't look right to me," he says later. So McFadden watches them for about ten minutes. They walk back and forth, one at a time, looking in store windows. A short, white man comes up and talks to them. They start walking and stop in front of Zucker's clothing store. McFadden approaches the three men. He testified later about what happened next.

John Terry's lawyer continues the story. Louis Stokes is an experienced criminal defense lawyer; he was later elected to Congress. Chief Justice Warren welcomes him.

Warren: Mr. Stokes.

Stokes: Mr. Chief Justice; may it please the Court.

His testimony was that their backs were to the plate glass windows. They were facing the street. And when interrogated with reference to what they were doing, he said they were merely standing there talking. He described their gait away from Fourteenth Street as they walked down to the haberdashery as a normal walk—nothing unusual about it.

The police officer then says, "I then went over to the three men. I said to them, 'I'm a police officer. What are your names?' " In the first instance, he said: "They gave it to me quick." In all other places in the record, he says: "They mumbled something." He said, at this: "I then reached and got Terry. I spun him around, holding him in front of me. I then began to pat him down." Once he had patted—patted this man down—he says: "I felt inside of his topcoat what felt to be the handle of a gun. I then reached inside the coat and tried to remove the gun. I could not remove the gun. I therefore took the entire coat off of him and then took the gun out of the coat."

Narrator: The two men with Terry were Richard Chilton and Carl Katz. Stokes continues with McFadden's testimony.

Stokes: At this point, he says: "I ordered the three of them into the store. As I walked through the doorway, I said to the store personnel, 'Order the wagon.' " He later explained that "ordering the wagon" means you are then under arrest. Once inside the store, the three men were ordered up against the wall, whereupon he then searched Chilton. Inside of Chilton's topcoat, he also found a loaded revolver. He searched the third male, Katz, upon whom he found nothing.

The police officer testified further with reference to questions propounded to him having to bear on the question of probable cause. We asked him, "Did you know any of these men?" "No." "Had you ever seen any of these men previously?" "No." "Had anyone given you any information regarding them?" "No."

He was then asked what had attracted his attention to them. He said, "Well, to tell you the truth, I didn't like them. And I was attracted to their actions up there on Fourteenth Street."

This officer testified further, though, that he felt that they might be "casing" the place for a stick-up. And by the way, this police officer had been a police officer for thirty-nine years, and a detective for thirty-five years.

The court specifically asked him if he had, during his thirty-nine years as a police officer, ever previously observed anyone casing a place. He said no, he had not. When asked if he had arrested anyone for casing a place, in his thirty-nine years, he said that he had not.

Narrator: Justice Abe Fortas had a question.

Fortas: There is nothing in the record to indicate that the policeman had any reason to fear bodily harm to himself?

Stokes: Well, we're saying that; and we're saying, in addition, this, Your Honor: We are saying that, at the point this police officer approached these men, and at the point that he lay his hands on the citizen, that he had—he did not have the probable cause that is required. He had stated that all he had, at that point, was this intuitive sixth sense, and that he had never in his long experience as a police officer ever arrested anyone for this purpose.

Narrator: Justice William Brennan continued the questioning.

Brennan: Up to the point where he spun Terry around, had he done anything outside what a policeman might properly do?

Stokes: No. He had done nothing outside of what a policeman might ordinarily do.

Brennan: Now, if then at that juncture he had reason to believe they might be armed, did he have to complete his questioning first? Or could he frisk them?

Stokes: I would say under the circumstances presented to me, that he did not under those circumstances have the right to lay hands on this citizen and to spin him around.

Brennan: And this would be because you do not think the record shows that he had any reason to believe they had weapons?

Stokes: No, I am saying that at the point that you lay your hands on the citizen, and you begin to exercise dominion over that citizen on the street by spinning him around, I am saying, in order for you to do this that you must have the probable cause that is required to place a person under arrest, because if the person is substantially under your custody, your dominion . . .

Brennan: Then you mean he can't frisk for weapons, without probable cause to arrest? Is that what you're saying?

Stokes: Yes.

Narrator: Chief Justice Warren expressed concern.

Warren: Police officers are very often in a position where they might not be able to make an actual arrest, but they are in a position of great danger. Now, where they are in a position of great danger, are they in a position to protect themselves from violence, by looking into the situation to see if anyone is armed to do them violence?

Stokes: The average police officer would do this under these circumstances. If he felt himself to be in any type of danger, that he would conduct a search, for the purpose of protecting his own life in a possibly dangerous situation. But I am saying that we cannot—merely because of that type of situation, and it not being what is required under the Fourth Amendment—we can't give sanctity to it by way of saying: Since you did find this product, we're going to permit it into the evidence.

Another thing I think the Court has to take into consideration here, of course, is the impossibility that this Court has of standardizing such a subjective thing as "intuition."

Narrator: The state asked the Court to equate "probable cause" with "reasonable suspicion" by an officer. Stokes disagreed.

Stokes: Now experience has already taught us, if the Court please, that policemen have had enough difficulty being able to grapple with and to determine for themselves what is tantamount to probable cause, as it has been enunciated in decisions by this Court. Now they're saying to this Court: Give us another standard. Give us this "reasonably suspects," or "based upon suspicion," or whatever the standard is that's less than probable cause. And we think that we're just compounding the policeman's problem if the Court does permit this type of a thing to occur.

And I think, through *Terry*, that we look at the hundreds of people walking the street by the day, because a police officer finds himself observing a situation where he says, as he did in this case, "Well, to tell you the truth, I just didn't like them and then I began watching them." And then the fact that he wants to go further—and at that point, I think we're subjecting all of the people who have this inviolate right of privacy, to this type of activity on the public streets throughout our nation.

Narrator: Chief Justice Warren welcomes Reuben Payne. He argues for the state of Ohio.

Warren: Mr. Payne.

Payne: Mr. Chief Justice; if it please the members of the Court.

A question has been asked here, What is the difference between "reasonable suspicion" and "probable cause"? I cannot see any basic difference in having a reasonable suspicion and equating it with the term "probable cause," in and of itself. It has been indicated that we have asked for a different standard here, as to probable cause. I find no problem with this, particularly, because I do not ask for a different standard of probable cause, as it may relate to the right to lawfully arrest a person.

I think that the quantum of evidence that is basic and essential under the circumstances to establish probable cause for the officer to arrest, or to stop a person and to ask him questions, may be somewhat lesser in degree but, by the same token, it is probable cause under any circumstances.

Narrator: Justice Thurgood Marshall debated "probable cause" with Reuben Payne.

Marshall: When did he get probable cause to arrest?

Payne: He received probable cause for arrest when he turned Terry around and ran his hands over the outside of his clothing and, feeling a gun in the upper left breast pocket, and indicating emphatically at that time that, "What I felt was a gun, a weapon."

Marshall: Well, he didn't have it, as counsel for petitioner says, he didn't have it when he laid hands on him and turned him around?

Payne: I would agree with—he did not have probable cause to arrest. (Marshall: Right) I would agree that he would have probable cause to frisk, or to lay hands on him, at this point.

Marshall: Why?

Payne: Because of the nature of the circumstances and protection of his own life.

Narrator: Marshall shifted his questions.

Marshall: Mr. Payne, in this case this arresting officer testified, did he not, that he had never seen anybody "case a joint"?

Payne: That is correct; he did so testify.

Marshall: He also testified that he had been on that same area for some thirty years, doing the following things: checking for pickpockets and shoplifters?

Payne: That is correct.

Marshall: So where did he get his expertise about somebody's about to commit a robbery?

Payne: I think that he would get his expertise by virtue of the fact that he had been a member of the police department for forty years, and by being a member of the police department for forty years, I am quite sure that, even if by osmosis, some knowledge would have to come to him of the various degrees of crime . . .

Marshall: Now we're getting intuition by osmosis? (*laughter*)

Payne: Not at all, sir; not at all. Not at all. I didn't mean to imply that (Marshall: I'm sorry) nor did I mean any disrespect by so using that particular term. I think that, for example, if I as a lawyer am around a particular office for a number of years, that I certainly must gain knowledge about various concepts of law that may come about from time to time.

Marshall: There are exceptions to this. (*laughter*)

Payne: I would agree with the Court, in these circumstances also.

Narrator: Marshall did not let up. He wanted to know when McFadden arrested Terry.

Marshall: Couldn't you say that when he laid hands on him and swung him around that petitioner's freedom of movement was arrested?

Payne: I would agree that his freedom of movement was arrested.

Marshall: But that's not an arrest?

Payne: I do not agree that his freedom of movement was arrested in a significant way.

Marshall: He only turned him around. It didn't take long to turn him around?

Payne: No, no. I mean in the sense of the circumstances involved at that particular time.

Marshall: Well, in this particular case he laid hands on him, and swung him around. How many days later was Payne [*sic*] free to go, from that moment on, in this case?

Payne: If there had been no more . . .

Marshall: No. In this particular case, when did he next get out? When did Terry get his freedom?

Payne: Some time after he was convicted of the crime of carrying a concealed weapon.

Marshall: So his freedom was arrested for quite a while.

Narrator: Payne's argument prompted Justice Brennan to break in.

Payne: So the arrest took place the moment that he ordered them into the store itself. Their freedom of movement was interfered with, significantly, at that time so that they could not . . .

Brennan: Let's use the Fourth Amendment language, then. When was the first "seizure" of the person?

Payne: The first seizure of the person—the first seizure of the person was at the time that he ordered them into the store.

Brennan: You mean when he took Terry and swung him around there was no seizure of the person?

Payne: I think there was a temporary detaining, or interference with his person.

Brennan: Well, he had his hands on him and he switched him around. Surely —there was no seizure of the person?

Payne: All right. But here again we're dealing in simply semantic words.

Brennan: I'm asking, that word is in the Fourth Amendment, isn't it?

Payne: I agree that it is, sir.

Narrator: Payne returned to the point where Officer McFadden approached the suspects in front of Zucker's store.

Payne: At this point, taking into consideration the nature of the crime which he has concluded—a stick-up—and the use of weapons as they are characteristically used in a stick-up, there is only one course of conduct then open to a prudent police officer. And that is, to frisk or pat for weapons, for the protection of his life.

Under these circumstances that he was confronted with at this time, I believe that it is in the interest of public safety; I believe it is in the interest of the welfare of the community and society, that he have the right, based on these probable cause circumstances, to frisk this man, to temporarily detain him, to ascertain that which he has observed, and to confiscate any weapons which he may find on his person at that particular time; and, that they are admissible in the evidence of his trial subsequently thereto. I think that the affirmance of the conviction of the petitioners on the law in the instant case is reasonable, is necessary, and is appropriate to secure the safety and the welfare and the best interest of the public of the state of Ohio.

Narrator: The Court decided the case on June 10th, 1968. Chief Justice Warren spoke for all but one justice. Some of his opinions were criticized as "soft on criminals." The loudest complaints came from the *Miranda* decision that forced police to tell suspects they could remain silent. But the Chief started as a county prosecutor and considered himself a supporter of police. He just wanted them to do their jobs within constitutional bounds.

Warren looked closely at the encounter between Officer McFadden and the suspects. There's nothing unusual, he said, about standing on a corner. Or strolling up and down the street. Or looking in windows. Warren noted that store windows "are made to be looked in." Then he viewed the scene through McFadden's eyes. He saw Terry and Chilton looking in the same window about twenty-four times, conferring after each trip, meeting Katz, then proceeding to Zucker's store. McFadden concluded "these men were contemplating a daytime robbery." It was reasonable for McFadden to question the suspects and to pat them down for weapons. "It would have been poor police work indeed," Warren said, if McFadden had *not* conducted the "stop and frisk."

Warren took pains to limit the scope of his ruling. He cautioned that each case must "be decided on its own facts." Warren noted that most encounters between citizens and police begin and end without trouble or danger. But police need protection when the answer to questions may be a bullet. A brief stop and a "carefully limited search" of outer clothing do not violate the Constitution.

The only dissent came from Justice William Douglas. He accused the majority of abandoning the "probable cause" standard for searches and seizures. Changing the standard to "reasonable suspicion" may help prevent crime, Douglas said. But it takes us "a long step down the totalitarian path."

Chief Justice Warren wrote his opinion against a backdrop of urban violence. Every ghetto explosion in the mid-sixties, from Newark to Watts, began with a police incident. Warren expressed concern about the "wholesale harassment of minority groups" by police. Tempers that flare during a "stop and frisk" can spark violence, even rioting.

Warren believed strongly that we need not choose between effective policing and constitutional rights. Lawless police and lawless citizens both endanger society. Courts must be ready, as Warren said many times, to enforce the Constitution against anyone who violates its commands.

EDITED SUPREME COURT OPINIONS
Terry v. *Ohio.*

MR. CHIEF JUSTICE WARREN delivered the opinion of the Court.

This case presents serious questions concerning the role of the Fourth Amendment in the confrontation on the street between the citizen and the policeman investigating suspicious circumstances. . . .

The Fourth Amendment provides that "the right of the people to be secure in their persons, houses, papers, and effects, against unreasonable searches and seizures, shall not be violated. . . ." This inestimable right of personal security belongs as much to the citizen on the streets of our cities as to the homeowner closeted in his study to dispose of his secret affairs. For, as this Court has always recognized,

> "No right is held more sacred, or is more carefully guarded, by the common law, than the right of every individual to the possession and control of his own person, free from all restraint or interference of others, unless by

clear and unquestionable authority of law." *Union Pac. R. Co. v. Botsford,* 141 U. S. 250, 251 (1891) . . .

Of course, the specific content and incidents of this right must be shaped by the context in which it is asserted. For "what the Constitution forbids is not all searches and seizures, but unreasonable searches and seizures." . . . Unquestionably petitioner was entitled to the protection of the Fourth Amendment as he walked down the street in Cleveland. . . . The question is whether in all the circumstances of this on-the-street encounter, his right to personal security was violated by an unreasonable search and seizure. . . .

On the one hand, it is frequently argued that in dealing with the rapidly unfolding and often dangerous situations on city streets the police are in need of an escalating set of flexible responses, graduated in relation to the amount of information they possess. For this purpose it is urged that distinctions should be made between a "stop" and an "arrest" (or a "seizure" of a person), and between a "frisk" and a "search." Thus, it is argued, the police should be allowed to "stop" a person and detain him briefly for questioning upon suspicion that he may be connected with criminal activity. Upon suspicion that the person may be armed, the police should have the power to "frisk" him for weapons. If the "stop" and the "frisk" give rise to probable cause to believe that the suspect has committed a crime, then the police should be empowered to make a formal "arrest," and a full incident "search" of the person. This scheme is justified in part upon the notion that a "stop" and a "frisk" amount to a mere "minor inconvenience and petty indignity," which can properly be imposed upon the citizen in the interest of effective law enforcement on the basis of a police officer's suspicion.

On the other side the argument is made that the authority of the police must be strictly circumscribed by the law of arrest and search as it has developed to date in the traditional jurisprudence of the Fourth Amendment. It is contended with some force that there is not—and cannot be—a variety of police activity which does not depend solely upon the voluntary cooperation of the citizen and yet which stops short of an arrest based upon probable cause to make such an arrest. The heart of the Fourth Amendment, the argument runs, is a severe requirement of specific justification for any intrusion upon protected personal security, coupled with a highly developed system of judicial controls to enforce upon the agents of the State the commands of the Constitution. . . .

Our first task is to establish at what point in this encounter the Fourth Amendment becomes relevant. That is, we must decide whether and when Officer McFadden "seized" Terry and whether and when he conducted a "search." There is some suggestion in the use of such terms as "stop" and "frisk" that such police conduct is outside the purview of the Fourth Amendment because neither action rises to the level of a "search" or "seizure" within the meaning of the Constitution. We emphatically reject this notion. It is quite plain that the Fourth

Amendment governs "seizures" of the person which do not eventuate in a trip to the station house and prosecution for crime—"arrests" in traditional terminology. It must be recognized that whenever a police officer accosts an individual and restrains his freedom to walk away, he has "seized" that person. And it is nothing less than sheer torture of the English language to suggest that a careful exploration of the outer surfaces of a person's clothing all over his or her body in an attempt to find weapons is not a "search." Moreover, it is simply fantastic to urge that such a procedure performed in public by a policeman while the citizen stands helpless, perhaps facing a wall with his hands raised, is a "petty indignity." It is a serious intrusion upon the sanctity of the person, which may inflict great indignity and arouse strong resentment, and it is not to be undertaken lightly. . . .

Applying these principles to this case, we consider first the nature and extent of the governmental interests involved. One general interest is of course that of effective crime prevention and detection; it is this interest which underlies the recognition that a police officer may in appropriate circumstances and in an appropriate manner approach a person for purposes of investigating possibly criminal behavior even though there is no probable cause to make an arrest. It was this legitimate investigative function Officer McFadden was discharging when he decided to approach petitioner and his companions. He had observed Terry, Chilton, and Katz go through a series of acts, each of them perhaps innocent in itself, but which taken together warranted further investigation. There is nothing unusual in two men standing together on a street corner, perhaps waiting for someone. Nor is there anything suspicious about people in such circumstances strolling up and down the street, singly or in pairs. Store windows, moreover, are made to be looked in. But the story is quite different where, as here, two men hover about a street corner for an extended period of time, at the end of which it becomes apparent that they are not waiting for anyone or anything; where these men pace alternately along an identical route, pausing to stare in the same store window roughly twenty-four times; where each completion of this route is followed immediately by a conference between the two men on the corner; where they are joined in one of these conferences by a third man who leaves swiftly; and where the two men finally follow the third and rejoin him a couple of blocks away. It would have been poor police work indeed for an officer of thirty years' experience in the detection of thievery from stores in this same neighborhood to have failed to investigate this behavior further. . . .

We conclude that the revolver seized from Terry was properly admitted in evidence against him. At the time he seized petitioner and searched him for weapons, Officer McFadden had reasonable grounds to believe that petitioner was armed and dangerous, and it was necessary for the protection of himself and others to take swift measures to discover the true facts and neutralize the threat of harm if it materialized. The policeman carefully restricted his search to what was appropriate to the discovery of the particular items which he sought. Each case of this sort will, of course, have to be decided on its own facts. We merely hold today that where a police officer observes unusual conduct which leads him reasonably to conclude in light of his experience that criminal activity may be afoot and that the persons with whom he is dealing may be armed and presently dangerous, where in the course of investigating this behavior he identifies himself as a policeman and makes reasonable inquiries, and where nothing in the initial stages of the encounter serves to dispel his reasonable fear for his own or others' safety, he is entitled for the protection of himself and others in the area to conduct a carefully limited search of the outer clothing of such persons in an attempt to discover weapons which might be used to assault him. Such a search is a reasonable search under the Fourth Amendment, and any weapons seized may properly be introduced in evidence against the person from whom they were taken.

Affirmed.

MR. JUSTICE DOUGLAS, dissenting.

I agree that petitioner was "seized" within the meaning of the Fourth Amendment. I also agree that frisking petitioner and his companions for guns was a "search." But it is a mystery how that "search" and that "seizure" can be constitutional by Fourth Amendment standards, unless there was "probable cause" to believe that (1) a crime had been committed or (2) a crime was in the process of being committed or (3) a crime was about to be committed.

The opinion of the Court disclaims the existence of "probable cause." If loitering were an issue and that was the offense charged, there would be "probable cause" shown. But the crime here is carrying concealed weapons; and there is no basis for concluding that the officer had "probable cause" for believing that that crime was being committed. Had a warrant been sought, a magistrate would, therefore, have been unauthorized to issue one, for he can act only if there is a showing of "probable cause." We hold today that the police have greater authority to make a "seizure" and conduct a "search" than a judge has to authorize such action. We have said precisely the opposite over and over again.

In other words, police officers up to today have been permitted to effect arrests or searches without warrants only when the facts within their personal knowledge would satisfy the constitutional standard of *probable cause*. At the time of their "seizure" without a warrant they must possess facts concerning the person arrested that would have satisfied a magistrate that "probable cause" was indeed present. The term "probable cause" rings a bell of certainty that is not sounded by phrases such as "reasonable suspicion." Moreover, the meaning of "probable cause" is deeply imbedded in our constitutional history. . . .

To give the police greater power than a magistrate is to take a long step down the totalitarian path. Perhaps such a step is desirable to cope with modern forms of lawlessness. But if it is taken, it should be the deliberate choice of the people through a constitutional amendment. Until the Fourth Amendment, which is closely allied with the Fifth, is rewritten, the person and the effects of the individual are beyond the reach of all government agencies until there are reasonable grounds to believe (probable cause) that a criminal venture has been launched or is about to be launched.

There have been powerful hydraulic pressures throughout our history that bear heavily on the Court to water down constitutional guarantees and give the police the upper hand. That hydraulic pressure has probably never been greater than it is today.

Yet if the individual is no longer to be sovereign, if the police can pick him up whenever they do not like the cut of his jib, if they can "seize" and "search" him in their discretion, we enter a new regime. The decision to enter it should be made only after a full debate by the people of this country.

BIBLIOGRAPHY

" 'Frisking' Ruling—Boon to Police." *U.S. News & World Report,* June 24, 1968, p. 12.

"Search and Seizure . . . 'Stop and Frisk.' " *American Bar Association Journal* 54 (September 1968): 914.

SILVER, ISIDORE. "Eroding the Fourth Amendment—Stop and Frisk." *Commonweal* 88, no. 16 (July 12, 1968): 455.

"Stop and Frisk: Dilemma for the Courts." *Southern California Law Review* 41 (1967–68): 161.

YOUNGER, ESTELLE J. "Stop and Frisk: 'Tell It Like It Is.' " *Journal of Criminal Law, Criminology and Police Science* 58, no. 3 (September 1967): 293.

Miranda v. Arizona

384 U.S. 436 (1966)

On March 2, 1963, a young woman in Phoenix, Arizona, was forced into a 1953 Packard automobile, driven into the desert, and raped. Eleven days later, police arrested Ernest Miranda. They traced the car to Miranda through a license plate the victim's brother had seen. After two hours of interrogation in the police station, Miranda confessed to kidnapping and rape. He was not offered a chance to consult a lawyer. The state's only exhibit at Miranda's trial was his confession. After being sentenced to a twenty-year prison term, Miranda sent a petition to the Supreme Court. His argument linked the Fifth Amendment protection against self-incrimination with the Sixth Amendment guarantee of "the assistance of counsel" for criminal defendants. Ruling in 1966, the Supreme Court agreed and granted Miranda a new trial. Ironically, without his confession as evidence, Miranda was again convicted and given another twenty- year sentence.

TRANSCRIPT OF EDITED AND NARRATED ARGUMENTS IN
Miranda v. *Arizona*, 384 U.S. 436 (1966)

Counsel for petitioner: John Flynn, Phoenix, Arizona
Counsel for respondent: Gary Nelson, Assistant Attorney General, State of Arizona, Phoenix
Counsel for National Association of District Attorneys as amicus curiae, Duane Nedrud, Chicago, Illinois

Narrator: It's February 28th, 1966. Chief Justice Earl Warren has called for argument in *Miranda versus Arizona,* a case that will be closely watched not only in the courtroom but in police stations and cellblocks across the country.

On March 2d, 1963, a young woman was kidnapped and raped in Phoenix, Arizona. Eleven days later, police officers Carroll Cooley and Wilfred Young found a 1953 Packard. They traced the car to 2525 West Mariposa Street through a licence plate identified by the victim's brother. They went inside and arrested Ernest Miranda. He fit the victim's description and had a lengthy criminal record, including charges of attempted rape.

The victim identified Miranda in a police lineup. Officers Cooley and Young took him into interrogation room two. Miranda signed his confession to kidnapping and rape two hours later. He also confessed to another robbery. After Miranda was charged, the judge appointed counsel for him. His lawyer was paid one hundred dollars. He called no witnesses. The state's only exhibit was Miranda's confession. The jury found him guilty and the judge sent him to prison.

The state supreme court upheld his conviction. From his cell, Miranda petitioned the United States Supreme Court. The Court receives thousands of prisoners' petitions each year and grants only a handful. Ernest Miranda's case raised an issue the justices wanted to tackle. In 1964, the Court ruled five-to-four in *Escobedo versus Illinois* that police must allow a suspect to consult his lawyer after a specific request. Refusal of this request violated Danny Escobedo's Fifth Amendment right to remain silent and his Sixth Amendment right to assistance of counsel. Miranda argued that police should tell *all* suspects—even those without lawyers—of these basic rights.

The American Civil Liberties Union in Phoenix recruited an experienced criminal lawyer to argue Miranda's case. Chief Justice Warren welcomes John Flynn to the lawyers' podium.

Warren: Mr. Flynn, you may proceed now.

John Flynn: Mr. Chief Justice, may it please the Court.
This case concerns itself with the conviction of a defendant of two crimes

of rape and kidnapping, the sentences on each count of twenty to thirty years to run concurrently. I should point out to the Court, in an effort to avoid possible confusion, that the defendant was convicted in a companion case of the crime of robbery in a completely separate and independent act.

Now the issue before the Court is the admission in evidence of the defendant's confession, under the facts and circumstances of this case, over the specific objection of his trial counsel that it had been given in the absence of counsel.

Narrator: Flynn described Miranda's arrest.

Flynn: The facts in the case indicate that the defendant was a twenty-three-year-old, Spanish-American extraction; that on the morning of March 13th, 1963, he was arrested at his home, taken down to the police station by two officers named Young and Cooley; that at the police station he was immediately placed in a lineup. He was there identified by the prosecutrix in this case and later identified by the prosecutrix in the robbery case. And immediately after the interrogations, he was taken into the police confessional at approximately 11:30 A.M. and by 1:30 they had obtained from him an oral confession.

He had denied his guilt, according to the officers, at the commencement of the interrogation; by 1:30 he had confessed. I believe that the record indicates that at no time during the interrogation and prior to his confession, his oral confession, was he advised either of his rights to remain silent, of his right to counsel, or of his right to consult with counsel.

Narrator: Flynn explained what happened after Miranda confessed.

Flynn: The defendant was then asked to sign a confession, to which he agreed. The form handed to him to write on contained a typed statement as follows, which preceded his handwritten confession: "I, Ernest A. Miranda, do hereby swear that I make this statement voluntarily and of my own free will, with no threats, coercion, or promises of immunity, and with full knowledge of my legal rights, understanding any statement I make may be used against me."

This statement was read to him by the officers, and he confessed in his own handwriting. Throughout the interrogation the defendant did not request counsel at any time. In due course the trial court appointed counsel to defend him in both cases, and defense counsel requested a psychiatric examination, which has been made—and the medical report—has been made a portion of the transcript of the record in this case, as it enlightens us to a portion of some of the factual information surrounding the defendant.

The further history relating to this defendant found in the psychiatric examination would indicate that he had an eighth-grade education, and it was found by the Supreme Court that he had a prior criminal record and that he was mentally abnormal. He was found, however, to be competent to stand trial and legally sane at the time of the commission of the alleged acts.

Narrator: Flynn read from the cross-examination of Officer Young by Miranda's trial lawyer.

Flynn: (reading transcript): "Did you state to the defendant at any time before he made the statement you are about to answer to, that anything he said would be held against him?"
"Answer: No, sir."
"Question: You didn't warn him of that?"
"Answer: No, sir."
"Question: Did you warn him of his rights to an attorney?"
"Answer: No, sir."
"Question: You never warned him he was entitled to an attorney nor anything he said would be held against him, did you?"
"Answer: We told him anything he said would be used against him; he wasn't required by law to tell us anything."

Narrator: Justice Potter Stewart asked what police should do when they focus on a particular suspect.

Stewart: What do you think is the result of the adversary process coming into being when this focusing takes place? What follows from that? Is there then, what, a right to a lawyer?

Flynn: I think that the man at that time has the right to exercise, if he knows, and under the present state of the law in Arizona, if he's rich enough, and if he's educated enough, to assert his Fifth Amendment right, and if he recognizes that he has a Fifth Amendment right, to request counsel. But I simply say that at that stage of the proceeding, under the facts and circumstances in *Miranda* of a man of limited education, of a man who certainly is mentally abnormal, who is certainly an indigent, that when that adversary process came into being that the police, at the very least, had an obligation to extend to this man not only his clear Fifth Amendment right, but to afford to him the right of counsel.

Narrator: Justice Stewart gave John Flynn an opening to make his case.

Stewart: Again, I don't mean to quibble, and I apologize, but I think it's first important to define what those rights are—what his rights under the Constitution are at that point. He can't be advised of his rights unless somebody knows what those rights are.

Flynn: Precisely my point. And the only person that can adequately advise Ernest Miranda is a lawyer.

Stewart: And what would the lawyer advise him that his rights then were?

Flynn: That he had the right not to incriminate himself; that he had a right not to make any statement; that he had the right to be free from further questioning by the police department; that he had the right, at an ultimate time, to be represented adequately by counsel in court; and that if he was too indigent, too poor to employ counsel, that the state would furnish him counsel.

Narrator: Justice Stewart's next question prompted an exchange between Justices Hugo Black and Byron White.

Stewart: Is there any claim in this case that this confession was compelled—was involuntary?

Flynn: No, Your Honor.

Stewart: None at all?

Flynn: None at all. We have raised no question that he was compelled to give this statement, in the sense that anyone forced him to do it by coercion, by threats, by promises, or compulsion of that kind.

Black: He doesn't have to have a gun pointed at his head, does he?

White: Of course he doesn't. So he was compelled to do it, wasn't he, according to your theory?

Flynn: Not by gunpoint, as Mr. Justice Black has indicated. He was called upon to surrender a right that he didn't fully realize and appreciate that he had.

Narrator: Chief Justice Warren, a former criminal prosecutor, asked a leading question.

Warren: I suppose, Mr. Flynn, you would say that if the police had said to this young man, "Now, you're a nice young man, and we don't want to hurt you, and so forth; we're your friends and if you'll just tell us how you committed this crime, we'll let you go home and we won't prosecute you," that that would be a violation of the Fifth Amendment, and that, technically speaking, would not be "compelling" him to do it. It would be an inducement, wouldn't it?

Flynn: That is correct.

Warren: I suppose you would argue that that is still within the Fifth Amendment, wouldn't you?

Flynn: It's an abdication of the Fifth Amendment right, simply because . . .

Warren: That's what I mean.

Narrator: Justice Black asked Flynn if the Constitution protected *all* Americans.

Flynn: It certainly does protect the rich, the educated, and the strong—those rich enough to hire counsel, those who are educated enough to know what their rights are, and those who are strong enough to withstand police interrogation and assert those rights.

Narrator: Flynn argued that the Constitution had not protected Ernest Miranda, who was neither rich nor educated.

Flynn: In view of the interrogation and the facts and circumstances of *Miranda,* it simply had no application because of the facts and circumstances in that particular case, and that's what I am attempting to express to the Court.

Narrator: Gary Nelson, an assistant attorney general for Arizona, argued for the state. Justice Abe Fortas asked about Miranda's rights to remain silent and to consult a lawyer.

Fortas: Let us assume that he was advised of these rights. In your opinion, does it make any difference when he was advised? That is, whether he was advised at the commencement of the interrogation, or at an early stage of the interrogation, or whether he was advised only when he was ready to sign the confession—the written confession? Does that make any difference in terms of the issues before us?

Nelson: Assuming for a moment that some warning is going to be required, or should have been given, then I would think to be of any effect it must be given before he'd made any statement.

Narrator: Nelson backed away from this concession.

Fortas: Now, do you believe that, is it your submission to us that a warning is necessary before a confession, in the absence of counsel, can be taken and subsequently introduced in the trial?

Nelson: No.

Fortas: What is your position on that?

Nelson: No. My position basically is—concerning the warning—is that each case presents a factual situation in which the court would have to determine, or a court or a judge or prosecutor at some level, would have to make a determination as to whether or not a defendant, because of the circumstances surrounding his confession, was denied a specific right—whether it be right to counsel, the right to not be compelled to testify against himself—and that the warning, or age or literacy, the circumstances, the length of the questioning, all these factors would be important.

Fortas: I suppose it's quite arguable that Miranda, the petitioner here, was entitled to a warning. Would you agree to that?

Nelson: Oh, it's arguable. I have extensively argued the facts that he wasn't of such a nature as an individual, because of his mental condition or his educational background, as to require any more than he got. He got every—in other words, I'm saying he got every warning except the right, the warning, the specific warning of the right to counsel. He didn't have counsel. Counsel wasn't specifically denied to him, on the basis of a request to retain counsel. The only possible thing that happened to Mr. Miranda that, in my light, assuming that he had the capability of understanding at all, is the fact that he did not get the specific warning of his right to counsel.

Narrator: Nelson asked the Court to avoid the "extreme" position of giving suspects access to counsel during an interrogation.

Nelson: I think if the extreme position is adopted that says he has to either have counsel at this stage, or intelligently waive counsel, that a serious problem in the enforcement of our criminal law will occur. First of all, let us make one thing certain. We need no empirical data as to one factor: what counsel will do if he is actually introduced. I am talking now about counsel for defendant. At least among lawyers there can be no doubt as to what counsel for the defendant is to do. He is to represent him one hundred percent, win, lose, or draw, guilty or innocent. That's our system. When counsel is introduced at interrogation, interrogation ceases.

Narrator: The justices also heard Duane Nedrud, from the National District Attorneys Association. After quoting an earlier Supreme Court decision, he moved his argument from Washington to Vietnam.

Chief Justice Warren: Mr. Nedrud.

Nedrud: Mr. Chief Justice, if it please the Court.
 "If we are talking about equality between the rich and the poor, we are striving for a worthy objective. If we are talking about equality between the policeman and the criminal, we are on dangerous ground."
 I would remind this Court that we are not talking about the police versus the defendant. We are talking about the people versus the defendant. In the same way that we would not talk about the Army or the Marine Corps versus the Viet Cong, but we would talk about the United States versus the Viet Cong.

Narrator: Nedrud asked the justices not to handcuff the police.

Nedrud: If this is to be our objective—to limit the use of the confession in criminal cases—then you are taking from the police the most important piece of evidence in every case that they bring before a court of justice. Police officers are public servants. They are not attempting to put innocent people in jail. They want to follow the dictates of this Court, and they will follow them to the best of their ability, but they too are human beings. They do have, however, an experience and knowledge which many of us lack, because this is their job—in investigation of crime—and we have not, as lawyers, paid attention to their problems. We have seldom been down to the police station and asked, "What can we do to assist you in your problems?"

Narrator: Chief Justice Warren, skilled in cross-examination, put Nedrud in the witness box.

Warren: May I ask you this, please, Mr. Nedrud. What would you say as to the man who did not have a lawyer but who said he wanted a lawyer before he talked?

Nedrud: If he asked for a lawyer, and he does not waive his right to counsel, I think that he should have a lawyer. I think that even the state should—I would go so far as to say I think the state should appoint him a lawyer, if he asks for a lawyer. I do not think, however, that we should in effect encourage him to have a lawyer.

Warren: And why do you say we should not encourage him to have a lawyer? Are lawyers a menace?

Nedrud: Mr. Chief Justice, a lawyer must, in our system of justice, *must* attempt to free the defendant. This is his job.

Warren: Because it's his professional duty to raise any defenses the man has?

Nedrud: Yes, sir.

Warren: Do you think, in doing that, he's a menace to our administration of justice?

Nedrud: I think that he is not a menace at the trial level. He is not a menace, per se, but he is, in doing his duty, is going to prevent a confession from being obtained.

Warren: When does he cease being a menace?

Nedrud: Mr. Chief Justice, I did not say he was a menace.

Warren: Well, you said he did, he did if he injected himself into it before the trial level.

Nedrud: I merely said that he in effect will prevent a confession from being obtained. And if this is what we are looking for, then we should appoint a counsel even *before* the arrest stage, because the moment that a murder takes place the government is out looking for the criminal.

Narrator: Justice William Douglas pressed Nedrud.

Douglas: Very important rights can be lost many days, many weeks prior to the trial. (Nedrud: Mr. Justice Douglas) We come down to the question as to, dealing with the Constitution, that concededly—I think we'd say "concededly" —everyone is entitled to a lawyer at the trial, and also at some point anterior to the trial.

Nedrud: The question comes, I think, Mr. Justice Douglas, whether or not we are going to allow the trial court to determine the guilt or innocence, or the defense counsel. If the defense counsel comes in at the arrest stage, he will, as he should, prevent the defendant from confessing to his crime, and you will have fewer convictions. If this is what is wanted, this is what will occur.

Narrator: The Supreme Court decided the Miranda case on June 13th, 1966. Once again, the justices were sharply divided on the rights of criminal defendants. Ernest Miranda won the right to a new trial by one vote. The Court's divisions prompted more than a hundred pages of opinions.

Chief Justice Warren, a former D.A. who proudly called himself a "hard prosecutor," wrote the majority opinion. He covered the brutal history of forcing confessions with fists and whips, and modern techniques of psychological coercion. To prevent tainted confessions, police must give suspects in custody the following warnings, in Warren's words: "Prior to any questioning, the person must be warned that he has a right to remain silent, that any statement he does make may be used as evidence against him, and that he has the right to the presence of an attorney." Only if suspects intelligently waive their Miranda rights can confessions be used against them.

Justice Byron White was the most critical of the four dissenters. Warren's opinion, he predicted, "will return a killer, a rapist or other criminal to the streets . . . to repeat his crime whenever it pleases him."

But the Court's decision did not return Ernest Miranda to the streets. A second trial, without his confession to the police, produced a second conviction and another twenty-year sentence. Four years after his parole, Miranda was stabbed to death in a Phoenix bar. The police arrested the man who provided the knife and read his Miranda rights in both English and Spanish.

The *Miranda* case remains controversial. But studies show that Miranda warnings have not reduced confessions or freed criminals. Even Justice White joined an opinion in 1990 that reaffirmed the *Escobedo* and *Miranda* decisions. Over the past quarter-century, police officers have learned to live with the Bill of Rights.

EDITED SUPREME COURT OPINIONS
Miranda v. *Arizona*

MR. CHIEF JUSTICE WARREN delivered the opinion of the Court.

The cases before us raise questions which go to the roots of our concepts of American criminal jurisprudence: the restraints society must observe consistent with the Federal Constitution in prosecuting individuals for crime. More specifically, we deal with the admissibility of statements obtained from an individual who is subjected to custodial police interrogation and the necessity for procedures which assure that the individual is accorded his privilege under the Fifth Amendment to the Constitution not to be compelled to incriminate himself. . . .

An understanding of the nature and setting of this in-custody interrogation is essential to our decisions today. The difficulty in depicting what transpires at such interrogations stems from the fact that in this country they have largely taken place incommunicado. From extensive factual studies undertaken in the early 1930's, including the famous Wickersham Report to Congress by a Presidential Commission, it is clear that police violence and the "third degree" flourished at that time. . . .

Again we stress that the modern practice of in-custody interrogation is psychologically rather than physically oriented. As we have stated before, "Since *Chambers* v. *Florida*, 309 U. S. 227, this Court has recognized that coercion can be mental as well as physical, and that the blood of the accused is not the only hallmark of an unconstitutional inquisition." *Blackburn* v. *Alabama*, 361 U. S. 199, 206 (1960). Interrogation still takes place in privacy. Privacy results in secrecy and this in turn results in a gap in our knowledge as to what in fact goes on in the interrogation rooms. A valuable source of information about present police practices, however, may be found in various police manuals and texts which document procedures employed with success in the past, and which recommend various other effective tactics. . . .

To highlight the isolation and unfamiliar surroundings, the manuals instruct the police to display an air of confidence in the suspect's guilt and from outward appearance to maintain only an interest in confirming certain details. The guilt of the subject is to be posited as a fact. The interrogator should direct his comments toward the reasons why the subject committed the act, rather than court failure by asking the subject whether he did it. Like other men, perhaps the subject has had a bad family life, had an unhappy childhood, had too much to drink, had an unrequited desire for women. The officers are instructed to minimize the moral seriousness of the offense, to cast blame on the victim or on society. These tactics are designed to put the subject in a psychological state where his story is but an elaboration of what the police purport to know already—that he is guilty. Explanations to the contrary are dismissed and discouraged. . . .

It is obvious that such an interrogation environment is created for no purpose other than to subjugate the individual to the will of his examiner. This atmosphere carries its own badge of intimidation. To be sure, this is not physical intimidation, but it is equally destructive of human dignity. The current practice of incommunicado interrogation is at odds with one of our Nation's most cherished principles— that the individual may not be compelled to incriminate himself. Unless adequate protective devices are employed to dispel the compulsion inherent in custodial surroundings, no statement obtained from the defendant can truly be the product of his free choice. . . .

At the outset, if a person in custody is to be subjected to interrogation, he must first be informed in clear and unequivocal terms that he has the right to remain silent. For those unaware of the privilege, the warning is needed simply to make them aware of it—the threshold requirement for an intelligent decision as to its exercise. More important, such a warning is an absolute prerequisite in overcoming the inherent pressures of the interrogation atmosphere. It is not just the subnormal or woefully ignorant who succumb to an interrogator's imprecations, whether implied or expressly stated, that the interrogation will continue until a confession is obtained or that silence in the face of accusation is itself damning and will bode ill when presented to a jury. Further, the warning will show the individual that his interrogators are prepared to recognize his privilege should he choose to exercise it. . . .

The circumstances surrounding in-custody interrogation can operate very quickly to overbear the will of one merely made aware of his privilege by his interrogators. Therefore, the right to have counsel present at the interrogation is indispensable to the protection of the Fifth Amendment privilege under the system we delineate today. Our aim is to assure that the individual's right to choose between silence and speech remains unfettered throughout the interrogation process. A once-stated warning, delivered by those who will conduct the interrogation, cannot itself suffice to that end among those who most require knowledge of their rights. A mere warning given by the interrogators is not alone sufficient to accomplish that end. . . .

In order fully to apprise a person interrogated of the extent of his rights under this system then, it is necessary to warn him not only that he has the right to consult with an attorney, but also that if he is indigent a lawyer will be appointed to represent him. Without this additional warning, the admonition of the right to consult with counsel would often be understood as meaning only that he can consult with a lawyer if he has one or has the funds to obtain one. The warning of a right to counsel would be hollow if not couched in terms that would convey to the indigent—the person most often subjected to interrogation—the knowledge that he too has a right to have counsel present. As with the warnings of the right to remain silent and of the general right to counsel, only by effective and express explanation to the indigent of this right can there be assurance that he was truly in a position to exercise it.

Once warnings have been given, the subsequent procedure is clear. If the individual indicates in any manner, at any time prior to or during questioning, that he wishes to remain silent, the interrogation must cease. At this point he has shown that he intends to exercise his Fifth Amendment privilege; any statement taken after the person invokes his privilege cannot be other than the product of compulsion, subtle or otherwise. Without the right to cut off questioning, the setting of in-custody interrogation operates on the individual to overcome free choice in producing a statement after the privilege has been once invoked. If the individual states that he wants an attorney, the interrogation must cease until an attorney is present. . . .

To summarize, we hold that when an individual is taken into custody or otherwise deprived of his freedom by the authorities in any significant way and is subjected to questioning, the privilege against self-incrimination is jeopardized. Procedural safeguards must be employed to protect the privilege, and unless other fully effective means are adopted to notify the person of his right of silence and to assure that the exercise of the right will be scrupulously honored, the following measures are required. He must be warned prior to any questioning that he has the right to remain silent, that anything he says can be used against him in a court of law, that he has the right to the presence of an attorney, and that if he cannot afford an attorney one will be appointed for him prior to any questioning if he so desires. Opportunity to exercise these rights must be afforded to him throughout the interrogation. After such warnings have been given, and such opportunity afforded him, the individual may knowingly and intelligently waive these rights and agree to answer questions or make a statement. But unless and until such warnings and waiver are demonstrated by the prosecution at trial, no evidence obtained as a result of interrogation can be used against him.

MR. JUSTICE HARLAN, whom MR. JUSTICE STEWART and MR. JUSTICE WHITE join, dissenting.

I believe the decision of the Court represents poor constitutional law and entails harmful consequences for the country at large. How serious these consequences may prove to be only time can tell. But the basic flaws in the Court's justification seem to me readily apparent now once all sides of the problem are considered. . . .

While passing over the costs and risks of its experiment, the Court portrays the evils of normal police questioning in terms which I think are exaggerated. Albeit stringently confined by the due process standards interrogation is no doubt often inconvenient and unpleasant for the suspect. However, it is no less so for a man to be arrested and jailed, to have his house searched, or to stand trial in court, yet all this may properly happen to the most innocent given probable cause, a warrant, or an indictment. Society has always paid a stiff price for law and order, and peaceful interrogation is not one of the dark moments of the law. . . .

Miranda's oral and written confessions are now held inadmissible under the Court's new rules. One is entitled to feel astonished that the Constitution can be read to produce this result. These confessions were obtained during brief, daytime questioning conducted by two officers and unmarked by any of the traditional indicia of coercion. They assured a conviction for a brutal and unsettling crime, for which the police had and quite possibly could obtain little evidence other than the victim's identifications, evidence which is frequently unreliable. There was, in sum, a legitimate purpose, no perceptible unfairness, and certainly little risk of injustice in the interrogation. Yet the resulting confessions, and the responsible course of police practice they represent, are to be sacrificed to the Court's own finespun conception of fairness which I seriously doubt is shared by many thinking citizens in this country. . . .

MR. JUSTICE WHITE, with whom MR. JUSTICE HARLAN and MR. JUSTICE STEWART join, dissenting.

The proposition that the privilege against self-incrimination forbids in-custody interrogation without the warnings specified in the majority opinion and without a clear waiver of counsel has no significant support in the history of the privilege or in the language of the Fifth Amendment. . . .

The obvious underpinning of the Court's decision is a deep-seated distrust of all confessions. As the Court declares that the accused may not be interrogated without counsel present, absent a waiver of the right to counsel, and as the Court all but admonishes the lawyer to advise the accused to remain silent, the result adds up to a judicial judgment that evidence from the accused should not be used against him in any way, whether compelled or not. This is the not so subtle overtone of the opinion—that it is inherently wrong for the police to gather evidence from the accused himself. And this is precisely the hub of this dissent. I see nothing wrong or immoral, and certainly nothing unconstitutional, in the police's asking a suspect whom they have reasonable cause to arrest whether or not he killed his wife or in confronting him with the evidence on which the arrest was based, at least where he has been plainly advised that he may remain completely silent . . .

. . . There is, in my view, every reason to believe that a good many criminal defendants who otherwise would have been convicted on what this Court has previously thought to be the most satisfactory kind of evidence will now, under this new version of the Fifth Amendment, either not be tried at all or will be acquitted if the State's evidence, minus the confession, is put to the test of litigation.

I have no desire whatsoever to share the responsibility for any such impact on the present criminal process.

In some unknown number of cases the Court's rule will return a killer, a rapist or other criminal to the streets and to the environment which produced him, to repeat his crime whenever it pleases him. As a consequence, there will not be a gain, but a loss, in human dignity. The real concern is not the unfortunate consequences of this new decision on the criminal law as an abstract, disembodied series of authoritative proscriptions, but the impact on those who rely on the public authority for protection and who without it can only engage in violent self-help with guns, knives and the help of their neighbors similarly inclined. There is, of course, a saving factor: the next victims are uncertain, unnamed and unrepresented in this case.

Nor can this decision do other than have a corrosive effect on the criminal law as an effective device to prevent crime. A major component in its effectiveness in this regard is its swift and sure enforcement. The easier it is to get away with rape and murder, the less the deterrent effect on those who are inclined to attempt it. This is still good common sense. If it were not, we should posthaste liquidate the whole law enforcement establishment as a useless, misguided effort to control human conduct. . . .

BIBLIOGRAPHY

BAKER, LIVA. *Miranda—Crime, Law and Politics.* Atheneum, 1983.

"Court v. the Cops . . ." *Saturday Evening Post,* July 30, 1966, p. 82.

DESMOND, CHARLES S. "Reflections of a State Reviewing Court Judge upon the Supreme Court's Mandates in Criminal Cases." *Journal of Criminal Law, Criminology and Police Science* 57, no. 3 (September 1966): 301.

GIVENS, RICHARD A. "Reconciling the Fifth Amendment with the Need for More Effective Law Enforcement." *American Bar Association Journal* 42, no. 5 (May 1966): 443.

MCKAY, R. B. "Self-Incrimination and The New Privacy." *Supreme Court Review* 1967, p. 193.

"Uproar as Confessed Rapists and Murderers Go Free." *Life* 61, no. 17 (October 21, 1966): 34.

Gregg v. Georgia

428 U.S. 153 (1976)

Capital punishment has remained controversial throughout American history. The Supreme Court has never held that the death penalty violates the Eighth Amendment ban on "cruel and unusual punishment," but in 1972 the Court struck down laws that gave jurors "arbitrary" power to impose the death sentence. The Court's ruling spared hundreds of condemned prisoners and added this volatile issue to a presidential campaign. More than thirty-five states responded with laws that listed "aggravating" and "mitigating" factors to guide jurors in capital cases. Upholding in 1976 the death sentence on Troy Gregg for two murders, the Court held that "capital punishment is an expression of society's moral outrage" at murderers and that Georgia's new law prevented jurors from "wantonly and freakishly" imposing the ultimate penalty.

TRANSCRIPT OF EDITED AND NARRATED ARGUMENTS IN
Gregg v. *Georgia* (consolidated capital punishment cases), 428 U.S. 153 (1976)

Counsel for appellants: Anthony G. Amsterdam, New York, New York
Counsel for United States, as *amicus curiae:* Solicitor General Robert H. Bork,
Washington, D.C.

Narrator: It's March 30th, 1976. Lawyers, reporters, and spectators crowd the
courtroom. For two days, the justices will hear arguments by ten lawyers in
cases from five different states. The lives of six men are at stake in these arguments. Each was convicted of murder and sentenced to die. And each has
challenged the state law under which the sentence was imposed.

Capital punishment raises strong opinions and emotions on both sides.
Some supporters claim the death penalty is a deterrent to homicide. Others rely
on biblical notions of retribution: "an eye for an eye, a tooth for a tooth." They
say a death for a death is a just punishment. Some opponents point to studies
that executions do not deter homicides, but may actually stimulate "copy cat"
killers. And others cite the biblical command: "Thou shalt not kill." They say it
is equally unjust for the state to kill.

Public support for capital punishment has shifted dramatically over the past
quarter-century. In the 1960s, a majority of Americans opposed the death penalty. But in the 1990s, support for executions moved above 75 percent. This
change in opinion has more to do with politics than statistics. Homicide rates
are affected by economic and other factors. They actually declined since the
1920s. During the 1980s, murders went down by 14 percent. But politicians
listen to voters, and voters are concerned about crime, especially murders. The
easy question is whether to pass death penalty laws. The hard question is how to
apply them, how to decide who lives and who dies.

The Constitution is not decided by polls or elections, and capital punishment raises significant legal issues. Opponents claim the death penalty violates
the Eighth Amendment's ban on "cruel and unusual punishment." They also
argue that juries have few guidelines for sentencing and discriminate against
black and poor defendants. The Supreme Court considered these questions in
1972, in the case of *Furman versus Georgia.* The justices split, five-to-four,
striking down laws that did not provide guidelines for "individualized determinations" in sentencing.

Four years after the *Furman* decision, thirty-five states had revised their
laws to provide guidelines for juries. Most of these laws required juries to consider "aggravating" and "mitigating" factors about the crime and the defendant.
Only if "aggravating" factors outweigh "mitigating" factors can the jury recommend the death penalty.

Each of the five cases being argued today involves a different state law and different lawyers. Two of these lawyers will argue the basic issue of whether the new laws satisfy the standard of the *Furman* case. Anthony Amsterdam is a noted law professor and opponent of capital punishment who argued and won the *Furman* case. Robert Bork, the solicitor general of the United States, will argue for the federal government in all five cases as *amicus curiae*, a "friend of the court." Amsterdam focuses on the Texas law and tells the justices there are two reasons it violates the Constitution.

Amsterdam: First, that death sentences imposed pursuant to systems of arbitrary selectivity of this sort are unconstitutional under *Furman*. The square holding of the *Furman* decision, rightly conceded, compels that result. And, secondly, that apart from the specific holding in *Furman*, the death penalty as it is used or as it is proposed to be used today is an excessively cruel punishment when it is assessed against the history of this country's use of the punishment in this century.

We are challenging in our second contention the forms of law under which it is now proposed to execute people in the United States.

Narrator: Justice Potter Stewart had a question.

Stewart: I thought your second contention was broader, that the execution of a death sentence upon conviction in any state of a person of any crime is cruel and unusual punishment, no matter what the technique—whether it be electrocution or hanging or shooting or the gas chamber—and no matter how serious the offense, and no matter how completely a fair trial he may have been given. Now, isn't that your point?

Amsterdam: That is precisely the second contention, yes.

Narrator: Texas requires a "death qualified" jury in capital cases. Opponents of the death penalty are excluded from these juries. Amsterdam argues this is unfair to defendants.

Amsterdam: The first thing I want to note is that at the outset of a Texas capital trial, the jury is death qualified, it's required to be death qualified by statute, and it's required to be told prior to trial that the question of life or death is in issue.

The fact remains that the jury will know that their answers to the specific questions submitted at the penalty phase will determine whether the defendant is to be punished by death or life imprisonment. To say that the jury's answers would not be affected by their attitude toward the death penalty as a punishment for crime simply because they will not bring forth the ultimate verdict, simply because the law attaches death to the answer to factual questions, would be to disregard the obvious.

Narrator: The defendant in the Texas case was sentenced to die for the kidnap and murder of a ten-year-old girl, the daughter of a police officer. Texas allows the death penalty if the jury finds the defendant would likely commit acts of violence if released. Amsterdam questioned this finding.

Amsterdam: In this case, the evidence on which the jury solemnly decided that the defendant, that there was a probability that the defendant would commit criminal acts of violence that would constitute a continuing threat to society, that evidence consisted of: one, the fact that the defendant had committed a capital murder, which, of course, is true in all cases; and two, the one-line hearsay opinions of four local citizens in the community that the defendant's reputation for peace and good order was bad. The state's position was simple: the defendant is a reprobate; the defendant killed the daughter of a local peace officer; the defendant ought to die.

Narrator: Amsterdam argued that death penalty laws remained unfair after the *Furman* decision because they allow "arbitrary discretion" in deciding who would live and who would die. Justice Stewart remained skeptical.

Stewart: Doesn't your argument prove too much? In other words, in our system of adversary criminal justice, we have prosecutorial discretion; we have jury discretion, including jury nullification, as it's known; we have the practice of submitting to the jury the option of returning verdicts of lesser included offenses; we have appellate review; and we have the possibility of executive clemency. And that's true throughout our adversary system of justice. And if a person is sentenced to anything as the end product of that system, under your argument, his sentence, be it life imprisonment or five years imprisonment, is a cruel and unusual punishment because it's the product of this system. That's your argument, isn't it?

Amsterdam: No.

Stewart: And why not?

Amsterdam: It is not. Our argument is essentially that death is different. If you don't accept the view that for constitutional purposes death is different, we lose this case, let me make that very clear. There is nothing that we argue in this case that will touch imprisonment, life imprisonment, any of those things.

Narrator: Amsterdam summed up.

Amsterdam: Now, why do we say death is different? Our legal system as a whole has always treated death differently. We allow more peremptory challenges; we allow automatic appeals; we have different rules of harmless error; we have indictment requirements; unanimous verdict requirements in some jurisdictions, because death is different.

Death is factually different. Death is final. Death is irremediable. Death is unknowable; it goes beyond this world. It is a legislative decision to do something, and we know not what we do. Death is different because even if exactly the same discretionary procedures are used to decide issues of five years versus ten years, or life versus death, the result will be more arbitrary on the life or death choice.

Narrator: Solicitor General Bork speaks for the federal government.

Bork: Mr. Chief Justice; may it please the Court.

The United States appears as *amicus curiae* in these cases because the Congress has enacted and various presidents have signed into law statutes that permit capital punishment for various serious crimes.

Narrator: Bork argues that the Constitution's framers approved of capital punishment.

Bork: To begin with, we know as a fact that the men who framed the Eighth Amendment did not mean—did not intend as an original matter to outlaw capital punishment because, as has been mentioned, they prescribed the procedures that must be used in inflicting it in the Fifth Amendment. We know that the men who framed and ratified the Fourteenth Amendment did not intend to outlaw capital punishment, because they also discussed and framed the procedures which must be followed in inflicting it. So we know that as an original matter, as a matter of original intention, it is quite certain that the Eighth Amendment was not intended to bar the death penalty and that the Constitution contemplates its infliction.

Narrator: Bork responded to three of Amsterdam's objections.

Bork: I will suggest first that capital punishment is rationally related to legitimate legislative goals of the deterrence of crime and the expression of moral outrage among them; secondly, that capital punishment has not been shown to be inflicted on the basis of race, and that in any event, that question is irrelevant to the issue of the type of punishment; and, thirdly, I will argue that capital punishment is not outlawed because the criminal justice system, which is mandated and permitted by the Constitution, has elements of discretion in it which are intended to be a safeguard of the system.

Narrator: Justice Stewart had a question about "cruel and unusual punishment."

Stewart: What if a state said for the most heinous kind of first-degree murders we are going to inflict breaking a man on the wheel and then disemboweling him while he is still alive and then burning him up: What would you say to that?

Bork: I would say that that practice is so out of step with modern morality and modern jurisprudence that the state cannot return to it. That kind of torture was precisely what the framers thought they were outlawing when they wrote the cruel and unusual punishments clause.

Narrator: Amsterdam claimed that prosecutors and juries have too much discretion in deciding to seek or impose the death penalty. Bork answered his argument.

Bork: I would like to discuss the element of discretion, because that seems to me to be the crucial part of petitioners' counsel's argument. And the argument appears to be that the fact that at various stages in the criminal justice system people are entitled to make judgments renders the death penalty unconstitutional. I don't think there's any logic to that claim, and I don't think it's a constitutional proposition.

Counsel made it plain that he objects to every element of discretion in the system, not just jury discretion. He objects to them collectively and, if I understood him correctly yesterday, he objects—he would object to them singly. The power of an executive to exercise clemency alone would render—if that were the only element of discretion—would render the death penalty unconstitutional.

There is apparently no way, according to this argument, that anybody could devise a system of justice in which anybody used any judgment about the thing which could then inflict the death penalty. The system—the only system that would meet counsel's objections would be one that was so rigid and automatic and insensitive that it would be morally reprehensible, and then apparently it would meet the moral standards of the Constitution.

Narrator: Justice Stewart wrote in the *Furman* case that capital punishment could be imposed "freakishly" if juries had no guidelines. Amsterdam claimed the new laws did not cure this defect. Bork answered his claim.

Bork: Counsel's real complaint is not that anybody is freakishly convicted and executed but, rather, that some murderers are freakishly spared and given life imprisonment. In other words, the fault in the system which makes it unconstitutional to inflict the death penalty is that it errs, if it errs at all, on the side of mercy and the side of safety, and that is what we are told makes it unconstitutional.

Narrator: Bork answered the argument that "death is different."

Bork: These arguments that are made against the death penalty could be made against any other form of punishment. There is not one of them that does not apply to life imprisonment. Now, the sole answer that counsel gives to this is that capital punishment is unique, it's different. Of course, it is different. Life imprisonment is different from a year in prison. Life imprisonment is different from a fine.

Capital punishment is also different in one other respect. It's different in that it deters more than any other punishment. There are some categories of criminals who cannot be deterred any other way. For example, a man serving life imprisonment—and he knows it is a real life term—has no incentive *not* to kill, and some of them have done so. A man who has committed an offense which carries life imprisonment, but has not yet been apprehended, has no incentive not to kill to escape or commit other crimes, except the prospect of a death penalty. So that, as the ultimate sanction, capital punishment is unique; it is different in the sense that it deters more and thereby saves more innocent lives; and it is unique in that it upholds the basic values of our society symbolically and internalizes them for us more than any other punishment.

Narrator: Justice Lewis Powell asked Bork to compare homicide statistics to casualties in the Vietnam War. Bork was glad to reply.

Powell: I have before me the 1973 report of the Federal Bureau of Investigation. It states that in 1968, 13,720 people were murdered in this country; in 1973, the latest year recorded in this report, 19,510 people were murdered—that's an increase of 42 percent.

It is perfectly obvious from these figures that we need some way to deter the slaughter of Americans. I use the word "slaughter" because that word was used in connection with the disaster in Vietnam, in which 55,000 Americans were killed over a six- to seven-year period. If the FBI figures are correct, there were more Americans killed in this country, murdered, than there were on the battlefields of Vietnam. Would you care to comment, elaborate, or state your views with respect to the deterrent effect, if any, of the death sentence?

Bork: Mr. Justice Powell, it seems to me that it cannot rationally be questioned that the death penalty has a deterrent effect. Mankind has always thought that throughout its history. We know it as a matter of common sense and common observation—we know that in all other aspects of human behavior, as you raise the cost and the risk, the amount of the activity goes down. I don't know why murder should be any different.

And I must say, at a time when international and domestic terrorism is going up, at a time when brutal murders are going up, it's an awesome responsibility to take from the states what they think is a necessary deterrent and save a few hundred guilty people and thereby probably condemn to death thousands of innocent people. That is truly an awesome responsibility.

Narrator: Bork put the ultimate decision in the voting booth.

Bork: This case is merely the latest in a continuing series seeking to obtain from this Court a political judgment that the opponents of capital punishment have been unable to obtain from the political branches of government. The United States asks that the constitutionality of the death penalty be upheld.

Narrator: Anthony Amsterdam had two minutes for rebuttal. He denied Bork's claim that public opinion should decide whether capital punishment is constitutional. Chief Justice Burger posed a question.

Burger: Suppose over a period of time, six months or a year, the Gallup Poll and the Harris Poll and all the other polls that are conducted showed 90 percent of the people in this country in favor of capital punishment, 3 percent undecided, and the balance against it. Do you think that enters into the constitutionality appraisal?

Amsterdam: No, Your Honor.

Burger: And the converse of that would be true?

Amsterdam: I don't think that the plebiscites cut one way or the other.

Burger: Well, I got the impression from either what you said yesterday or this morning that in some way we have to evaluate the standards of the people of this country today in light of what people think.

Amsterdam: I think that's true, but not as a matter of plebiscite.

Narrator: Amsterdam made his second summation.

Amsterdam: I simply want to make two points very clear. First of all, to attack the death penalty on Eighth Amendment grounds is not to express sympathy for crime. It is not to express callousness with regard to victims. The death penalty may be the greatest obstacle to adequate enforcement of crime in this country today because it sops public conscience and makes you think we're doing something about serious crime instead of devising other methods of dealing with it.

Secondly, we are taxed in this case and have been throughout our Eighth Amendment presentation with the notion that it is we who are seeking to have this Court use subjective gut feelings, to be a superlegislature. That is not true. Our position is the only coherent analytic position on the Eighth Amendment. The Government says that the death penalty for jaywalking would be bad. Why? Because there is an emotional feeling that's being invited that that's too much. It can't be that it's a comparative test, such as Solicitor General Bork suggests. The Eighth Amendment was written to apply only to the federal government, not to the states; it couldn't be asking a comparative question.

We submit simply that our argument has a coherent Eighth Amendment base adequately and properly based on the facts; it accounts for the needs of law enforcement and protection of victims; and under that view, the death penalty is a violation of the Eighth Amendment.

Narrator: On July 2d, 1976, the Supreme Court handed down decisions in the five cases. The opinions covered more than two hundred pages and reflected the complexity of the different state laws. The justices upheld the death sentences of three men and spared another three from execution. The Court struck down laws that required mandatory death sentences and approved those that provided jury guidelines.

Justice Potter Stewart had questioned both Anthony Amsterdam and Robert Bork about the Eighth Amendment's ban on "cruel and unusual punishment." In the leading case, *Gregg versus Georgia*, Stewart concluded that "the existence of capital punishment was accepted by the Framers" of the Constitution and, in his words, "was a common sanction in every state."

Stewart cited public opinion polls and election results since the *Furman* decision to show that voters and lawmakers supported capital punishment. He concluded that the death penalty is an acceptable "expression of society's moral outrage" at murder.

Only two justices dissented. William Brennan and Thurgood Marshall opposed the death penalty because, they said, it was "degrading to human dignity."

Their retirements in 1990 and '91 removed the only voices and votes against capital punishment from the Supreme Court. Since the *Gregg* decision, more than twenty-five hundred defendants have been sentenced to death. Most are poor, half are black, many are retarded, and some are juveniles. Critics have charged that the Court is insensitive to these factors. But the Court has rejected claims that poor defendants have a right to good lawyers and that southern white juries are biased against blacks. And the Court has approved the execution of mentally retarded and juvenile defendants.

No country has more prisoners awaiting execution than the United States. Capital punishment has increased both in frequency and controversy since the Supreme Court decided that the death penalty does not offend the Constitution.

EDITED SUPREME COURT OPINIONS
Gregg v. *Georgia*

Judgment of the Court, and opinion of MR. JUSTICE STEWART, MR. JUSTICE POWELL and MR. JUSTICE STEVENS, announced by MR. JUSTICE STEWART.

The issue in this case is whether the imposition of the sentence of death for the crime of murder under the law of Georgia violates the Eighth and Fourteenth Amendments.

The petitioner, Troy Gregg, was charged with committing armed robbery and murder. In accordance with Georgia procedure in capital cases, the trial was in two stages, a guilt stage and a sentencing stage. The evidence at the guilt trial established that on November 21, 1973, the petitioner and a traveling companion, Floyd Allen, while hitchhiking north in Florida were picked up by Fred Simmons and Bob Moore. Their car broke down, but they continued north after Simmons purchased another vehicle with some of the cash he was carrying. While still in Florida, they picked up another hitchhiker, Dennis Weaver, who rode with them to Atlanta, where he was let out about 11 P.M. A short time later the four men interrupted their journey for a rest stop along the highway. The next morning the bodies of Simmons and Moore were discovered in a ditch nearby.

On November 23, after reading about the shootings in an Atlanta newspaper, Weaver communicated with the Gwinnett County police and related information concerning the journey with the victims, including a description of the car. The next afternoon, the petitioner and Allen, while in Simmons' car, were arrested in Asheville, N. C. In the search incident to the arrest a .25-caliber pistol, later shown to be that used to kill Simmons and Moore, was found in the petitioner's pocket. After receiving the warnings required by *Miranda* v. *Arizona* . . . and signing a written waiver of his rights, the petitioner signed a statement in which he admitted shooting, then robbing Simmons and Moore. He justified the slayings on grounds of self-defense. . . .

The trial judge instructed the jury that it could recommend either a death sentence or a life prison sentence on each count. The judge further charged the jury that in determining what sentence was appropriate the jury was free to consider the facts and circumstances, if any, presented by the parties in mitigation or aggravation.

Finally, the judge instructed the jury that it "would not be authorized to considerimposingthe penalty of death" unless it first found beyond a reasonable doubt one of these aggravating circumstances:

"One—That the offense of murder was committed while the offender was engaged in the commission of two other capital felonies, to-wit the armed robbery ofSimmons and Moore.

"Two—That the offender committed the offense of murder for the purpose of receiving money and the automobile described in the indictment.

"Three—The offense of murder was outrageously and wantonly vile, horrible and inhuman, in that they[sic]involved the depravity ofthemind of the defendant."

Finding the first and second of these circumstances, the jury returned verdicts of death on each count. . . .

We granted the petitioner's application for a writ of certiorari limited to his challenge to the imposition of the death sentences in this case as "cruel and unusual" punishment in violation of the Eighth and the Fourteenth Amendments. . . .

We address initially the basic contention that the punishment of death for the crime of murder is, under all circumstances, "cruel and unusual" in violation of the Eighth and Fourteenth Amendments of the Constitution. . . . Although this issue was presented and addressed in *Furman*, it was not resolved by the Court. Four Justices would have held that capital punishment is not unconstitutional *per se*; two Justices would have reached the opposite conclusion; and three Justices, while agreeing that the statutes then before the Court were invalid as applied, left open the question whether such punishment may ever be imposed. We now hold that the punishment of death does not invariably violate the Constitution. . . .

Four years ago, the petitioners in *Furman* and its companion cases predicated their argument primarily upon the asserted proposition that standards of decency had evolved to the point where capital punishment no longer could be tolerated. . . .

The petitioners in the capital cases before the Court today renew the "standards of decency" argument, but developments during the four years since *Furman* have undercut substantially the assumptions upon which their argument rested. Despite the continuing debate, dating back to the nineteenth century, over the morality and utility of capital punishment, it is now evident that a large proportion of American society continues to regard it as an appropriate and necessary criminal sanction.

The most marked indication of society's endorsement of the death penalty for murder is the legislative response to *Furman*. The legislatures of at least thirty-five States have enacted new statutes that provide for the death penalty for at least some crimes that result in the death of another person. . . . All of the post-*Furman* statutes make clear that capital punishment itself has not been rejected by the elected representatives of the people.

In the only statewide referendum occurring since *Furman* and brought to our attention, the people of California adopted a constitutional amendment that authorized capital punishment, in effect negating a prior ruling by the Supreme Court of California. . . .

The death penalty is said to serve two principal social purposes: retribution and deterrence of capital crimes by prospective offenders.

In part, capital punishment is an expression of society's moral outrage at particularly offensive conduct. This function may be unappealing to many, but it is essential in an ordered society that asks its citizens to rely on legal processes rather than self-help to vindicate their wrongs. . . . Indeed, the decision that capital punishment may be the appropriate sanction in extreme cases is an expression of the community's belief that certain crimes are themselves so grievous an affront to humanity that the only adequate response may be the penalty of death. . . .

In sum, we cannot say that the judgment of the Georgia Legislature that capital punishment may be necessary in some cases is clearly wrong. Considerations of federalism, as well as respect for the ability of a legislature to evaluate, in terms of its particular State, the moral consensus concerning the death penalty and its social utility as a sanction, require us to conclude, in the absence of more convincing evidence, that the infliction of death as a punishment for murder is not without justification and thus is not unconstitutionally severe.

Finally, we must consider whether the punishment of death is disproportionate in relation to the crime for which it is imposed. There is no question that death as a punishment is unique in its severity and irrevocability. . . . When a defendant's life is at stake, the Court has been particularly sensitive to insure that every safeguard is observed. . . . But we are concerned here only with the imposition of capital punishment for the crime of murder, and when a life has been taken deliberately by the offender, we cannot say that the punishment is invariably disproportionate to the crime. It is an extreme sanction, suitable to the most extreme of crimes.

We hold that the death penalty is not a form of punishment that may never be imposed, regardless of the circumstances of the offense, regardless of the char-

acter of the offender, and regardless of the procedure followed in reaching the
decision to impose it. . . .

For the reasons expressed in this opinion, we hold that the statutory system
under which Gregg was sentenced to death does not violate the Constitution.
Accordingly, the judgment of the Georgia Supreme Court is affirmed.

It is so ordered.

MR. JUSTICE BRENNAN, dissenting.

In *Furman* v. *Georgia*, . . . (concurring opinion), I read "evolving standards
of decency" as requiring focus upon the essence of the death penalty itself and not
primarily or solely upon the procedures under which the determination to inflict
the penalty upon a particular person was made. I there said:

"From the beginning of our Nation, the punishment of death has stirred
acute public controversy. Although pragmatic arguments for and against the
punishment have been frequently advanced, this longstanding and heated
controversy cannot be explained solely as the result of differences over
the practical wisdom of a particular government policy. At bottom, the battle has been waged on moral grounds. The country has debated whether
a society for which the dignity of the individual is the supreme value
can, without a fundamental inconsistency, follow the practice of deliberately putting some of its members to death. . . . It is this essentially
moral conflict that forms the backdrop for the past changes in and
the present operation of our system of imposing death as a punishment for
crime." . . .

This Court inescapably has the duty, as the ultimate arbiter of the meaning
of our Constitution, to say whether, when individuals condemned to death stand
before our Bar, "moral concepts" require us to hold that the law has progressed to
the point where we should declare that the punishment of death, like punishments
on the rack, the screw, and the wheel, is no longer morally tolerable in our
civilized society. My opinion in *Furman* v. *Georgia* concluded that our civiliza-
tion and the law had progressed to this point and that therefore the punishment of
death, for whatever crime and under all circumstances, is "cruel and unusual" in
violation of the Eighth and Fourteenth Amendments of the Constitution. I shall
not again canvass the reasons that led to that conclusion. I emphasize only that
foremost among the "moral concepts" recognized in our cases and inherent in the
Clause is the primary moral principle that the State, even as it punishes, must
treat its citizens in a manner consistent with their intrinsic worth as human beings
—a punishment must not be so severe as to be degrading to human dignity. A

judicial determination whether the punishment of death comports with human dignity is therefore not only permitted but compelled by the Clause. . . .

. . . Death is not only an unusually severe punishment, unusual in its pain, in its finality, and in its enormity, but it serves no penal purpose more effectively than a less severe punishment; therefore the principle inherent in the Clause that prohibits pointless infliction of excessive punishment when less severe punishment can adequately achieve the same purposes invalidates the punishment.

The fatal constitutional infirmity in the punishment of death is that it treats "members of the human race as nonhumans, as objects to be toyed with and discarded. [It is] thus inconsistent with the fundamental premise of the Clause that even the vilest criminal remains a human being possessed of common human dignity." . . . I therefore would hold, on that ground alone, that death is today a cruel and unusual punishment prohibited by the Clause. "Justice of this kind is obviously no less shocking than the crime itself, and the new 'official' murder, far from offering redress for the offense committed against society, adds instead a second defilement to the first." A. Camus, *Reflections on the Guillotine.*

MR. JUSTICE MARSHALL, dissenting.

In *Furman* v. *Georgia* . . . (concurring opinion), I set forth at some length my views on the basic issue presented to the Court in these cases. The death penalty, I concluded, is a cruel and unusual punishment prohibited by the Eighth and Fourteenth Amendments. That continues to be my view. . . .

The two purposes that sustain the death penalty as nonexcessive in the Court's view are general deterrence and retribution. In *Furman*, I canvassed the relevant data on the deterrent effect of capital punishment. . . . The evidence I reviewed in *Furman* remains convincing, in my view, that "capital punishment is not necessary as a deterrent to crime in our society." . . . The justification for the death penalty must be found elsewhere.

There remains for consideration, however, what might be termed the purely retributive justification for the death penalty—that the death penalty is appropriate, not because of its beneficial effect on society, but because the taking of the murderer's life is itself morally good. Some of the language of the opinion of my Brothers STEWART, POWELL, and STEVENS appears positively to embrace this notion of retribution for its own sake as a justification for capital punishment. They state:

"[The decision that capital punishment may be the appropriate sanction in extreme cases is an expression of the community's belief that certain crimes are themselves so grievous an affront to humanity that the only adequate response may be the penalty of death." . . .

" 'The truth is that some crimes are so outrageous that society insists on adequate punishment, because the wrong-doer deserves it, irrespective of whether it is a deterrent or not.' "

Of course, it may be that these statements are intended as no more than observations as to the popular demands that it is thought must be responded to in order to prevent anarchy. But the implication of the statements appears to me to be quite different—namely, that society's judgment that the murderer "deserves" death must be respected not simply because the preservation of order requires it, but because it is appropriate that society make the judgment and carry it out. It is this latter notion, in particular, that I consider to be fundamentally at odds with the Eighth Amendment. . . .

BIBLIOGRAPHY

BEDAU, HUGO A. "New Life for the Death Penalty." *Nation* 223 (August 28, 1976): 144.

BEDAU, HUGO A. "The Death Penalty: Social Policy and Social Justice." *Arizona State Law Journal* 1977 (1977–78): 767.

BEDAU, HUGO A. and CHESTER M. PIERCE. *Capital Punishment in the United States.* AMS, 1976.

BOROWITZ, ALBERT I. "Under Sentence of Death." *American Bar Association Journal* 64 (August, 1978): 1259.

"The Injustice of The Death Penalty." *America* 135 (December 11, 1976): 409.

VAN DEN HAAG, ERNEST. "A Response to Bedau." *Arizona State Law Journal* 1977 (1977–78): 797.

ZIMRING, FRANKLIN E. *Capital Punishment and the American Agenda.* Cambridge University Press, 1986.

PART FOUR:

"The Equal Protection of the Laws"

AMERICANS LIKE TO THINK of themselves as believers in equal rights for all people, both at home and abroad. We cheer the movements to abolish racial apartheid in South Africa, to secure free elections in the former Soviet Union, and to exercise free speech in China. What few Americans like to remember is that, in their own country, racial segregation was once enforced by law in many states: schools, lunch counters, buses, parks, and motels had signs that read "Whites Only." African-Americans were kept from voting by poll taxes, literacy tests, and intimidation. And those who spoke out against segregation were often fired from their jobs, terrorized by hooded night-riders, or even assaulted with fists, guns, and dynamite bombs. This was not the distant past of the Reconstruction era, but just one generation ago in the 1960s. The promise of "Equal Justice Under Law," chiseled above the entrance to the Supreme Court, was an empty promise to many black Americans and to Native Americans and those of Latino and Asian ancestry.

Official celebrations of the Constitutional Bicentennial in 1987 portrayed that document as a charter of equal rights for all Americans. Its preamble speaks grandly of "We the People of the United States" and their plan to "form a more perfect Union" of the states. Only one person spoke up to remind the nation that "We the People" did not include slaves and that the price of "a more perfect Union" was a compromise that recognized slavery in the Constitution. Thurgood Marshall, the first black justice of the Supreme Court, was himself the grandson of a slave and attended segregated schools. He noted that slaves were counted in the Constitution as "three-fifths" of a free person, that Congress was forbidden to ban the importation of slaves before 1808, and that northern states were forced to comply with Fugitive Slave Laws. Marshall's speech took an edge off the gaiety of the Constitution's birthday party.

The fact is that the Constitution did not offer "the equal protection of the laws" to African-Americans until after a bloody war between the slave states of the South and the "free" states of the North. The Supreme Court had contributed to the political turmoil that preceded the Civil War by ruling in 1857 that blacks were not citizens. The Court held that Dred Scott, whose owner took him from Missouri, a slave state, to the free state of Illinois, could not sue to gain his freedom. The Court's opinion said that blacks were viewed by the Constitution's framers as "beings of an inferior order, and altogether unfit to associate with the white race, either in social or political relations; and so far inferior, that they had no rights which the white man was bound to respect; and that the negro might justly and lawfully be reduced to slavery for his benefit."

The idea that slavery was designed for the "benefit" of slaves would strike most Americans today as absurd. But the prevailing view of blacks as "inferior" lasted well beyond the Civil War. After the fighting ended, Congress and the states added three Civil War amendments to the Constitution. The Thirteenth Amendment abolished slavery, the Fourteenth guaranteed every person "the equal protection of the laws," and the Fifteenth granted former slaves the right to vote. Each amendment gave Congress the power to enforce its provisions "by appropriate legislation." Congress passed a number of civil rights laws, but the Supreme Court ruled in 1875 that the equal protection clause did not outlaw racial discrimination in "public accommodations" like hotels and restaurants that were privately owned.

The end of Reconstruction and the failure of the Supreme Court to enforce civil rights laws prompted a rash of Jim Crow laws that imposed segregation on virtually every aspect of southern life. Louisiana passed a law in 1890 that required separate railroad cars for blacks and whites. Homer Plessy, who described himself as "seven-eighths Caucasian and one-eighth African," challenged the law under the equal protection clause. Forty years after the *Dred Scott* decision, the Supreme Court again endorsed the idea of black "inferiority" to whites. "Legislation is powerless to eradicate racial instincts," the Court wrote, and it placed the "customs and traditions" of segregation above the commands of the Constitution. "Separate but equal" facilities did not offend the Fourteenth Amendment. But they did offend Justice John M. Harlan, who dissented in *Plessy* v. *Ferguson*. "Our Constitution is color-blind," he wrote, "and neither knows nor tolerates classes among citizens."

The struggle for a truly color-blind Constitution lasted more than fifty years before the Supreme Court ruled in 1954 that "in the field of public education the doctrine of 'separate but equal' has no place." The Court did not make the change from apartheid to equality on its own. During the half-century between *Plessy* and *Brown* v. *Board of Education*, African-Americans mounted a determined campaign against Jim Crow laws. The National Association for the Advancement of Colored People, organized in 1909, took the lead. During the 1930s, the NAACP Legal Defense Fund planned a longrange legal strategy against school segregation that began with lawsuits against universities and law schools in border states like Missouri and Oklahoma. Thurgood Marshall became head of the fund in 1940 and argued more than twenty cases before the Supreme Court; he won all but two. The *Brown* case was simply the culmination of a brilliant campaign that Marshall directed for more than two decades before he joined the Supreme Court in 1967.

The *Brown* decision did not end conflict over civil rights. In fact, the Court's ruling provoked a southern campaign of "massive resistance" to school integration. The Court faced a direct challenge to its powers in 1958, after Arkansas governor Orval Faubus called out armed troops to keep nine black students from entering Little Rock's Central High School. The Little Rock school board also refused to comply with a federal court's integration orders. The Court's unanimous and strongly worded opinion in *Cooper* v. *Aaron* ended the Arkansas insurrection, but civil rights cases dominated the Court's docket for the next two decades.

African-Americans met white resistance with a renewed campaign against Jim Crow laws. Rosa Parks refused to move to the rear of a segregated bus in 1955 and spurred the Montgomery, Alabama, bus boycott that brought the Reverend Martin Luther King, Jr., to national prominence as an eloquent leader. Four black students refused to leave a segregated lunch counter in Greensboro, North Carolina, in 1960 and began the sit-in movement. In August 1963, two hundred thousand people flocked to the March on Washington for Jobs and Freedom and were enthralled by King's "dream that my four little children will one day live in a nation" that lives up to its creed of equality. Eighteen days later, that dream turned into a nightmare for the families of four little girls in Birmingham, Alabama, who died in a church that was dynamited by the Ku Klux Klan. The next year, three young men—James Chaney, Andrew Goodman, and Michael Schwerner—were killed by Mississippi Klansmen for helping blacks to register as voters.

Congress responded to civil rights protest and violence with new laws: segregation in public accommodations and employment was outlawed in 1964 and voting rights were strengthened in 1965. These laws provoked new arguments before the Supreme Court. Does any provision of the Constitution reach discrimination in private businesses like motels and restaurants? Can cities avoid judicial integration orders by closing down public facilities like swimming pools? Lawyers on both sides argued these and many other civil rights questions before the justices.

The equal protection clause of the Fourteenth Amendment was invoked during the 1960s and 1970s in hundreds of Supreme Court arguments. One of these cases raised a basic question of equality: can states prohibit the marriage of persons of different races? Another case reflected the growing backlash against "affirmative action" programs to increase minority numbers in jobs and classrooms. Can a state medical school set aside sixteen places in a class of one hundred for "disadvantaged" racial minorities and exclude a white applicant with higher test scores than most minority students? Finally, the Court faced a question about public schools that was harder than segregation in the *Brown* case. Does the equal protection clause require that states provide equal funding to schools in rich and poor districts, measured by property values?

The Court's answers to these difficult questions have not always pleased civil rights advocates. In fact, Justice Thurgood Marshall dissented in several of these cases. The Supreme Court opinion in *Brown* spoke of the "feeling of inferiority" that segregation imposed on black students. The "inferiority" of blacks that was endorsed by the Court in *Dred Scott* and *Plessy* has a legacy that endures in American society. A Constitution that was born in compromise over slavery has not yet redeemed its promise of "equal protection" for *all* Americans. But Rev. King's dream remains alive, the dream that new generations of children—of every race—"will not be judged by the color of their skin, but the content of their character."

Cooper v. Aaron

358 U.S. 1 (1958)

In 1957, the school board of Little Rock, Arkansas, adopted a desegregation plan that assigned black children to a previously all-white high school. Southern resistance to school integration encouraged state and local officials, including Arkansas Governor Orval Faubus, to stir public hostility into an explosive situation. President Dwight Eisenhower, initially reluctant to intervene, finally ordered federal troops to protect the black children and escort them through angry mobs around the school. The school board asked a federal judge to suspend the desegregation plan because it disrupted public order and the educational process. In 1958, the Supreme Court denied this request and ordered school integration to proceed. "Law and order," Chief Justice Earl Warren wrote for a unanimous Court, "are not here to be preserved by depriving the Negro children of their constitutional rights."

TRANSCRIPT OF EDITED AND NARRATED ARGUMENTS IN
Cooper v. *Aaron*, 358 U.S. 1 (1958)

Counsel for petitioners: Richard Butler, Little Rock, Arkansas
Counsel for respondents: Thurgood Marshall, New York, New York
Counsel for the United States, as *amicus curiae:* Solicitor General J. Lee Rankin, Washington, D.C.

Chief Justice Earl Warren: The Court is now reconvened in special term to consider an application by the petitioners for a writ of certiorari to the United States Court of Appeals for the Eighth Circuit in the case of William Cooper, et al., versus John Aaron, et al., Number 1 Miscellaneous.

Narrator: It's September 11th, 1958. The Court's regular term begins in October. But Chief Justice Earl Warren has called a special session for argument of this case. Only three times before have the justices met during their recess. But few cases have raised issues of such legal and political importance.

This case began with the Court's unanimous decision in 1954 in *Brown versus Board of Education.* Racial segregation in public schools violated the Constitution's equal protection clause. The Court ruled the next year that integration should proceed, in their words, with "all deliberate speed." Many southern officials viewed this phrase as an invitation for foot-dragging and delay. The school board in Little Rock, Arkansas, prepared a plan that would begin in 1957 with token integration of the city's elite school, Central High. The plan wouldn't end segregation in Little Rock schools for another ten years.

Black parents refused to wait that long. They asked for legal help from the NAACP—the National Association for the Advancement of Colored People. Their lawyers asked federal judges to speed up integration in Little Rock. All they got was an order to admit nine black students to Central High. Even this limited victory enraged racial bigots, who circled the school on opening day with howling mobs. Arkansas governor Orval Faubus ordered National Guard troops to keep the black kids out of Central High. When they approached the school, soldiers forced them back with bayonets.

After three weeks of violence, President Dwight Eisenhower finally ended the insurrection. He sent Army troops to escort the black students into Central High. For the rest of the school year, they fought harassment every day, in school corridors and on sidewalks. The school board continued to fight the Supreme Court. Federal judge Harry Lemley agreed to delay further integration for more than two years. An appellate court reversed his order, and the Supreme Court accepted the board's appeal.

The Constitution proclaims that its provisions are "the supreme law of the land." State officials may not disobey its commands. This case tests the power of the Supreme Court to enforce constitutional rights. It also tests federal authority over claims of "states' rights." The real contestants are President Eisenhower and Governor Faubus. But the actual parties are virtually unknown. William Cooper is president of the school board. John Aaron is first in alphabetical order of the black children whose parents sued the board. Richard Butler, an experienced Little Rock lawyer, argues for the board.

Butler: We believe that the manner and the methods employed by the United States Supreme Court in the two *Brown* decisions of 1954 and 1955 recognized the complexities of this problem, as had previous courts in determining issues of a similar nature. Both of the *Brown* decisions, in our opinion, reflect an understanding by this Court of the history of the Negro race and of the cultural patterns throughout this land.

We believe that this Court recognized that time was required for certain cultural patterns to change and that obviously this Court recognized the necessity or at least the desirability of referring those matters to the local district courts for innumerable problems which this Court recognized would arise, and some of which were enumerated in the decision.

"Deliberate speed," as used by this Court, is certainly not just a phrase coined on the spur of the moment or developed as a philosophy of opportunism to solve an immediate problem, but instead to us it was a carefully conceived philosophy of deliberation which, along with legal reasons for delay as outlined by this Court in the second *Brown* decision, allows for the flexibility and the delay provided in the decision by District Judge Harry J. Lemley. In effect, it provides for a transition from one era to another or from one set of standards to another.

Narrator: Butler asked for a stay of court orders while Arkansas lawmakers debated ways to block school integration. Chief Justice Warren did not conceal his doubts.

Warren: Has the school board determined what it will do toward desegregation or toward leaving the matter as it was last year, in the event this court declines to grant this stay?

Butler: No, sir. It has not decided because it's almost compelled to see what statutes are passed by the general assembly now in session and various other things, which it has no way of determining, and this school board no doubt will have to meet those situations as they arise, as they have had to do all the past year.

Warren: Well, as to these specific children, have they been assigned to any school?

Butler: It is my information, Mr. Chief Justice, that they have now . . . (Warren: they have *not* been?) Yes sir, they have *now* been assigned to the all-Negro school, the new high school there, Horace Mann.

Warren: Well, isn't that, isn't that action toward segregating them again?

Butler: Oh, yes, sir, it is.

Narrator: Butler restated his appeal for delay.

Butler: It is impossible for the school board of Little Rock to operate a school program for the two thousand students at Central High School on an integrated basis at this time, and that unless the plan of desegregation is postponed for a reasonable length of time, that irreparable harm will be inflicted upon the students of both Negro and white race. Now the broad issue, of course, in this case is simply this: Can a court of equity postpone the enforcement of the plaintiffs' constitutional rights if the immediate enforcement thereof will deprive others—many others, as a matter of fact—of their constitutional rights to an education in a free public school?

In Little Rock as well as throughout the South, and in other places where this problem has arisen, the great mass of people are not law violators as such. They are not people who form mobs, they are not people who defy the law, but we submit, and this school board determined, that they were entitled to know what the law was. And as long as editorialists, popular editorialists in our community, were saying that this was not the law of the land, and that there were ways to get around it, and one court was saying one thing, and another court was saying another, and there were laws on the state statute books of Arkansas as well as other states throughout the South, diametrically opposed, as some people argued, some of them could be reconciled, some of them could not, with the decision in the *Brown* case, but it left the people of our community, as well as the people of many communities, in actual doubt as to what the law was.

Narrator: Justice Felix Frankfurter had little sympathy.

Frankfurter: The governor's calling out troops isn't the same thing as the uncertainty of what the law is. That has nothing to do with the uncertainty of the law. That's the action of the governor under what he thought was his refusal to abide by the law.

Butler: Well, this school board in Little Rock, Arkansas, was not faced with theories, it was faced with actualities which are undermining and which are going to destroy the public school system in Little Rock, and when it's destroyed, it'll be destroyed not just for white students, it'll be destroyed all the way up and down the line, unless they're given an opportunity to work this thing out in a climate of calm rather than in a climate of hysteria.

Narrator: Chief Justice Warren did not want mobs to decide legal questions.

Warren: Mr. Butler, I think there's no member of this Court who fails to recognize the very great problem which your school board has. But, can we defer a program of this kind, merely because there are those elements in the community that will commit violence to prevent it from going into effect?

Butler: Mr. Chief Justice, I think so, but not directed to the people who form mobs, not directed to the people who are law defiers—we're not standing up here taking, trying to argue for their side . . . (Warren: I know you're not) We are arguing for the great mass of people throughout the South, who I say again, and will say again and again, are not law defiers; they want to follow the law, but they—as of this moment—without certain state statutes having been tested in court, do not know just exactly what the law is in a particular given circumstance.

Narrator: Butler's final argument provoked a heated reply from Warren.

Butler: The point I'm making is this: that if the governor of any state says that a United States Supreme Court decision is *not* the law of the land, the people of that state, until it is really resolved, have a doubt in their mind and a right to have a doubt.

Warren: I have never heard such an argument made in a court of justice before, and I've tried many a case, over many a year. I never heard a lawyer say that the statement of a governor, as to what was legal or illegal, should control the action of any court.

Narrator: Thurgood Marshall speaks for Little Rock's black children. Marshall headed the NAACP legal staff for many years. He argued and won many civil rights cases before the Court, including *Brown*. He denounces Butler's appeal for delay.

Marshall: The truth of the matter is, these entire proceedings, starting with the filing of the petition of the school board way back in February, asking for time, the whole purpose of these proceedings is to get time. The objective of the proceedings is that the Little Rock schools be returned from desegregated to segregated status as of September school term.

I think we have to think about these children and their parents, these Negro children that went through this every day, and their parents that stayed at home wondering what was happening to their children, listening to the radio about the bomb threats and all of that business. I don't see how anybody under the sun could say, that after those children and those families went through that for a year to tell them: All you have done is gone. You fought for what you considered to be democracy and you lost. And you go back to the segregated school from which you came. I just don't believe it. And I don't believe you can balance those rights.

Narrator: Marshall spoke to the Court like a teacher.

Marshall: Education is not the teaching of the three R's. Education is the teaching of the overall citizenship, to learn to live together with fellow citizens, and above all to learn to obey the law.

And the damage to the education in Arkansas and in Little Rock and in Central High comes about through the order of Judge Lemley which says that not only the school board and the state can and should submit to mob violence and threats of mob violence but that the federal judiciary likewise should do so.

I don't know of any more horrible destruction of principle of citizenship than to tell young children that, those of you who withdrew, rather than to go to school with Negroes, those of you who were punished last year—the few that the school board did punish: Come back, all is forgiven, you win.

And therefore, I am not worried about the Negro children at this stage. I don't believe they're in this case as such. I worry about the white children in Little Rock who are told, as young people, that the way to get your rights is to violate the law and defy the lawful authorities. I'm worried about their future. I don't worry about those Negro kids' future. They've been struggling with democracy long enough. They know about it.

Narrator: Marshall appealed to the rule of law.

Marshall: The way this case stands, there must be a definitive decision—I hate to use the two together, it's bad English but it's the best way I can do it—that there be no doubt in Arkansas that the orders of that district court down there must be respected and cannot be suspended and cannot be interfered with by the legislature or anybody else. And less than that I don't think will give these young children the protection that they need and they most certainly deserve.

Narrator: The justices also listened to Solicitor General J. Lee Rankin. He speaks for the federal government as a friend of the court.

Rankin: We think that this case involves the question of the maintenance of law and order, not only in this community and the state of Arkansas, but throughout this country.

Now, the desegregation of schools has gone forward in many areas of this country. It has gone ahead in border states, many areas without any difficulties whatever, and in some of the areas even of the deeper South.

What is there in this community, Little Rock, in Arkansas, that's different? Certainly people with pigment in their skin—black or white—were involved in those cases, in those areas, where the schools were desegregated without trouble between them. The element in this case is lawlessness. It is a community, a small number at first at least—maybe more later—who decided they were going to defy the laws of this country. And I say to you that that's a problem that's inherent in every little village, great city, or country area of this United States. There isn't a single policeman that isn't going to watch this Court and what it has to say about this matter that doesn't have to deal with people every day who don't like the law he is trying to administer and enforce. And he has to go against that public feeling and will and do his duty. That's the responsibility of every man in this country that's fit to occupy public office.

Narrator: Like Marshall, Rankin appealed to the rule of law.

Rankin: So I say to you, if this school board has any doubt about what the law is, it can turn to the Constitution that it is under oath to support, just as the members of this Court and myself. They should look first to the Constitution. That's what the Constitution, our basic document, says. And then they can look to any federal laws or treaties. And then they can look down to see if there is anything in the constitution of the state or the state laws or their own regulations that they should enforce.

But I say, I think without any proper challenge, that their obligation before this country, in their own community, and before this Court, is to use all the power that they have and exhaust it to try to perform that oath, and first start out with trying to carry out the obligations of the Constitution of the United States as interpreted by this Court.

And in conclusion, let me say that on this Supreme Court building is carved the inscription, "Equal Justice Under Law." All Americans take pride in this controlling principle of our government. It is there as a reminder of the great objective of this Court in all of its decisions. Now, in the gravity of this new challenge to constitutional rights, I respectfully suggest that each time that it becomes an issue the Court must say, in a manner that cannot be misunderstood, throughout the length and breadth of this land: There can be no equality of justice for our people if the law steps aside, even for a moment, at the command of force and violence.

Narrator: Richard Butler made a final appeal for delay.

Butler: All we're asking, all we're asking at this time, is for time, to try to do those things and work out these problems that may bring peace and harmony, and do it in a period of calm when they can be done and not in a period of turmoil and strife.

Can it be logically argued that the ruling of this Court can be carried out, as this Court said it should, in an effective manner, when schools are closed, or if operated at all, with armed troops parading not only the grounds but the halls and classrooms themselves? Patience and forbearance for a short while might save our public school system in Little Rock.

Narrator: The justices had no patience with appeals for delay. The day after this argument, on September 12th, 1958, the Court issued a three-paragraph opinion. The justices unanimously affirmed the lower court orders that integration of Little Rock schools proceed without delay.

Two weeks later the Court issued a longer, detailed opinion. Normally, one justice writes for the Court. In this case—to emphasize its importance—all nine justices signed the opinion. They agreed that the case "raises questions of the highest importance" to the federal system of government. They rejected the claim that, in their words, "there is no duty on state officials to obey federal court orders resting on this Court's considered interpretation of the United States Constitution."

Arkansas officials attempted, the Court said, "to perpetuate . . . the system of racial segregation which this Court" struck down in the *Brown* case. The opinion documented the record of violence against black students, inside and outside Central High School. The justices wrote that "violent resistance" to integration was "directly traceable" to Governor Faubus and Arkansas lawmakers. The justices did not mince words. "The constitutional rights" of black children, they said, "are not to be sacrificed or yielded to the violence and disorder which have followed upon the actions of the Governor and Legislature."

The justices firmly upheld judicial supremacy over state action. The *Brown* decision "is the supreme law of the land," they said. They expressed contempt for officials like Governor Faubus who waged, in their words, "war against the Constitution."

War over school integration continued after the Court's ruling. Little Rock officials refused to obey court orders and closed all high schools until 1959. Finally, parents and voters who cared more about education than segregation changed the school board. The integration of Little Rock schools resumed.

The Court's decision established an important precedent. But it did not end conflict over racial issues that have divided Americans since the time of slavery. School segregation, a relic of that system, stubbornly refuses to go away. Judges can decide legal issues, but they can't change housing patterns or cultural attitudes. Since its unanimous decision in *Cooper* v. *Aaron*, the Supreme Court has split over cases dealing with school integration. *Brown* remains on the books, but the question remains: Will black children in schools across the country receive the integrated—and equal—education the Constitution commands? It is a fateful question for the country.

EDITED SUPREME COURT OPINION
Cooper v. *Aaron*

Opinion of the Court by THE CHIEF JUSTICE, MR. JUSTICE BLACK, MR. JUS-TICE FRANKFURTER, MR. JUSTICE DOUGLAS, MR. JUSTICE BURTON, MR. JUSTICE CLARK, MR. JUSTICE HARLAN, MR. JUSTICE BRENNAN, and MR. JUS-TICE WHITTAKER.

As this case reaches us it raises questions of the highest importance to the maintenance of our federal system of government. It necessarily involves a claim by the Governor and Legislature of a State that there is no duty on state officials to obey federal court orders resting on this Court's considered interpretation of the United States Constitution. Specifically it involves actions by the Governor and Legislature of Arkansas upon the premise that they are not bound by our holding in *Brown* v. *Board of Education*, 347 U. S. 483. That holding was that the Fourteenth Amendment forbids States to use their governmental powers to bar children on racial grounds from attending schools where there is state participation through any arrangement, management, funds or property. We are urged to uphold a suspension of the Little Rock School Board's plan to do away with segregated public schools in Little Rock until state laws and efforts to upset and nullify our holding in *Brown* v. *Board of Education* have been further challenged and tested in the courts. We reject these contentions. . . .

The following are the facts and circumstances so far as necessary to show how the legal questions are presented. . . .

On May 20, 1954, . . . the Little Rock District School Board adopted, and on May 23, 1954, made public, a statement of policy entitled "Supreme Court Decision—Segregation in Public Schools." In this statement the Board recognized that

"It is our responsibility to comply with Federal Constitutional Requirements and we intend to do so when the Supreme Court of the United States
outlines the method to be followed."

Thereafter the Board undertook studies of the administrative problems confronting the transition to a desegregated public school system at Little Rock. It
instructed the Superintendent of Schools to prepare a plan for desegregation, and
approved such a plan on May 24, 1955, seven days before the second *Brown*
opinion. The plan provided for desegregation at the senior high school level
(grades ten through twelve) as the first stage. Desegregation at the junior high and
elementary levels was to follow. It was contemplated that desegregation at the
high school level would commence in the fall of 1957, and the expectation
was that complete desegregation of the school system would be accomplished by
1963. . . .

While the School Board was thus going forward with its preparation for
desegregating the Little Rock school system, other state authorities, in contrast,
were actively pursuing a program designed to perpetuate in Arkansas the system
of racial segregation which this Court had held violated the Fourteenth Amendment. First came, in November 1956, an amendment to the State Constitution
flatly commanding the Arkansas General Assembly to oppose "in every Constitutional manner the Un-constitutional desegregation decisions of May 17, 1954
and May 31, 1955 of the United States Supreme Court" . . .

The School Board and the Superintendent of Schools nevertheless continued with preparations to carry out the first stage of the desegregation program.
Nine Negro children were scheduled for admission in September 1957 to Central
High School, which has more than two thousand students. Various administrative
measures, designed to assure the smooth transition of this first stage of desegregation, were undertaken.

On September 2, 1957, the day before these Negro students were to enter
Central High, the school authorities were met with drastic opposing action on the
part of the Governor of Arkansas who dispatched units of the Arkansas National
Guard to the Central High School grounds and placed the school "off limits" to
colored students. As found by the District Court in subsequent proceedings, the
Governor's action had not been requested by the school authorities, and was
entirely unheralded. . . . The next day, September 3, 1957, the Board petitioned
the District Court for instructions, and the court, after a hearing, found that
the Board's request of the Negro students to stay away from the high school had
been made because of the stationing of the military guards by the state authorities. The court determined that this was not a reason for departing from the approved plan, and ordered the School Board and Superintendent to proceed with
it.

On the morning of the next day, September 4, 1957, the Negro children attempted to enter the high school but, as the District Court later found, units of the Arkansas National Guard "acting pursuant to the Governor's order, stood shoulder to shoulder at the school grounds and thereby forcibly prevented the nine Negro students . . . from entering," as they continued to do every school day during the following three weeks. . . .

The next school day was Monday, September 23, 1957. The Negro children entered the high school that morning under the protection of the Little Rock Police Department and members of the Arkansas State Police. But the officers caused the children to be removed from the school during the morning because they had difficulty controlling a large and demonstrating crowd which had gathered at the high school. . . . On September 25, however, the President of the United States dispatched federal troops to Central High School and admission of the Negro students to the school was thereby effected. Regular army troops continued at the high school until November 27, 1957. They were then replaced by federalized National Guardsmen who remained throughout the balance of the school year. Eight of the Negro students remained in attendance at the school throughout the school year.

We come now to the aspect of the proceedings presently before us. On February 20, 1958, the School Board and the Superintendent of Schools filed a petition in the District Court seeking a postponement of their program for desegregation. Their position in essence was that because of extreme public hostility, which they stated had been engendered largely by the official attitudes and actions of the Governor and the Legislature, the maintenance of a sound educational program at Central High School, with the Negro students in attendance, would be impossible. The Board therefore proposed that the Negro students already admitted to the school be withdrawn and sent to segregated schools, and that all further steps to carry out the Board's desegregation program be postponed for a period later suggested by the Board to be two and one-half years.

After a hearing the District Court granted the relief requested by the Board. Among other things the court found that the past year at Central High School had been attended by conditions of "chaos, bedlam and turmoil"; that there were "repeated incidents of more or less serious violence directed against the Negro students and their property"; that there was "tension and unrest among the school administrators, the class-room teachers, the pupils, and the latters' parents, which inevitably had an adverse effect upon the educational program"; that a school official was threatened with violence; that a "serious financial burden" had been cast on the School District; that the education of the students had suffered "and under existing conditions will continue to suffer"; that the Board would continue to need "military assistance or its equivalent"; that the local police department would not be able "to detail enough men to afford the necessary protection"; and that the situation was "intolerable." . . . The Negro respondents appealed to the

Court of Appeals for the Eighth Circuit and also sought there a stay of the District Court's judgment. . . .

One may well sympathize with the position of the Board in the face of the frustrating conditions which have confronted it, but . . . [t]he constitutional rights of respondents are not to be sacrificed or yielded to the violence and disorder which have followed upon the actions of the Governor and Legislature. . . . Thus law and order are not here to be preserved by depriving the Negro children of their constitutional rights. . . .

The controlling legal principles are plain. The command of the Fourteenth Amendment is that no "State" shall deny to any person within its jurisdiction the equal protection of the laws . . . [T]he prohibitions of the Fourteenth Amendment extend to all action of the State denying equal protection of the laws; whatever the agency of the State taking the action . . . or whatever the guise in which it is taken . . . In short, the constitutional rights of children not to be discriminated against in school admission on grounds of race or color declared by this Court in the *Brown* case can neither be nullified openly and directly by state legislators or state executive or judicial officers, nor nullified indirectly by them through evasive schemes for segregation whether attempted "ingeniously or ingenuously." . . .

What has been said, in the light of the facts developed, is enough to dispose of the case. However, we should answer the premise of the actions of the Governor and Legislature that they are not bound by our holding in the *Brown* case. It is necessary only to recall some basic constitutional propositions which are settled doctrine.

Article VI of the Constitution makes the Constitution the "supreme Law of the Land." In 1803, Chief Justice Marshall, speaking for a unanimous Court, referring to the Constitution as "the fundamental and paramount law of the nation," declared in the notable case of *Marbury* v. *Madison*, 1 Cranch 137, 177, that "It is emphatically the province and duty of the judicial department to say what the law is." This decision declared the basic principle that the federal judiciary is supreme in the exposition of the law of the Constitution, and that principle has ever since been respected by this Court and the Country as a permanent and indispensable feature of our constitutional system. It follows that the interpretation of the Fourteenth Amendment enunciated by this Court in the *Brown* case is the supreme law of the land, and Art. VI of the Constitution makes it of binding effect on the States "any Thing in the Constitution or Laws of any State to the Contrary notwithstanding." Every state legislator and executive and judicial officer is solemnly committed by oath taken pursuant to Art. VI, cl. 3, "to support this Constitution." . . .

No state legislator or executive or judicial officer can war against the Constitution without violating his undertaking to support it. . . .

It is, of course, quite true that the responsibility for public education is primarily the concern of the States, but it is equally true that such responsibilities, like all other state activity, must be exercised consistently with federal constitutional requirements as they apply to state action. The Constitution created a government dedicated to equal justice under law. The Fourteenth Amendment embodied and emphasized that ideal. State support of segregated schools through any arrangement, management, funds, or property cannot be squared with the Amendment's command that no State shall deny to any person within its jurisdiction the equal protection of the laws. The right of a student not to be segregated on racial grounds in schools so maintained is indeed so fundamental and pervasive that it is embraced in the concept of due process of law. . . .

The basic decision in *Brown* was unanimously reached by this Court only after the case had been briefed and twice argued and the issues had been given the most serious consideration. Since the first *Brown* opinion three new Justices have come to the Court. They are at one with the Justices still on the Court who participated in that basic decision as to its correctness, and that decision is now unanimously reaffirmed. The principles announced in that decision and the obedience of the States to them, according to the command of the Constitution, are indispensable for the protection of the freedoms guaranteed by our fundamental charter for all of us. Our constitutional ideal of equal justice under law is thus made a living truth.

BIBLIOGRAPHY

BATES, DAISY. *The Long Shadow of Little Rock.* University of Arkansas Press, 1987.

FREYER, TONY. *The Little Rock Crisis.* Greenwood, 1984.

HAYS, BROOKS. "Inside Story of Little Rock." *U.S. News & World Report*, March 23, 1959, p. 118.

IRONS, PETER. *The Courage of their Conviction*, ch. 5. Penguin, 1990.

KNEBEL, FLETCHER. "The Real Little Rock Story." *Look*, November 12, 1957, p. 31.

SCHLESSINGER, GARY A. "The Law, the Mob, and Desegregation." *California Law Review* 47 (March 1959): 126.

WOFFORD, HARRIS, JR. "The Supreme Court as an Educator." *Saturday Review*, March 7, 1959, p. 13.

Heart of Atlanta Motel v. United States

379 U.S. 241 (1964)

Atlanta proudly calls itself "the heart of Dixie," and the Heart of Atlanta Motel is located in the city's bustling center, drawing travelers from a busy interstate highway. During the 1960s, Atlanta was at the heart of the black movement for equal rights that won its greatest victory in congressional passage of the Civil Rights Act of 1964. Title II of the act outlawed racial segregation in places of public accommodation, including hotels and motels. Congress based the law on its constitutional power to regulate "commerce among the several states." The Heart of Atlanta Motel, which drew 75 percent of its patrons from other states, challenged the law and claimed that "people are not commerce." But the Supreme Court unanimously upheld the law in December 1964. "Congress, acting with its discretion and judgment," Justice Hugo Black wrote, "has power under the Commerce Clause to ban racial discrimination."

TRANSCRIPT OF EDITED AND NARRATED ARGUMENTS IN
Heart of Atlanta Motel v. *United States*, 379 U.S. 241 (1964)

Counsel for petitioner: Moreton Rolleston, Jr., Atlanta, Georgia
Counsel for respondent: Solicitor General Archibald Cox, Washington, D.C.

Narrator: It's October 5th, 1964. Chief Justice Earl Warren has called the year's first case, *Heart of Atlanta Motel versus the United States.* The motel's owners refuse to rent rooms to black travelers. They deny the Constitution requires them to admit and serve all races. This case reached the Court just months after Congress enacted the most sweeping civil rights act in American history. But the deeper issues—moral, political, and social—have divided Americans since the Constitution was framed.

This case really began with the institution of human slavery. Blacks came to America in chains and were sold as property. The Constitution accepted and protected the slave trade. The Supreme Court ruled in the *Dred Scott* case in 1857 that blacks could not be citizens, were not even persons under the law. More than six hundred thousand people—North and South, black and white— died in a Civil War that ended slavery. Congress added the Fourteenth Amendment to the Constitution, providing blacks with the "privileges and immunities" of other citizens and granting them the "equal protection of the laws."

Congress enforced the Fourteenth Amendment with a civil rights act that banned segregation in places like hotels and restaurants. But the Supreme Court struck down the law. Congress could not prevent segregation on private property. "When a man has emerged from slavery," the Court wrote, he "ceases to be the special favorite of the laws." Southern states responded with Jim Crow laws that barred blacks from railroad cars, hotel rooms, and restaurants. The Supreme Court upheld segregation in *Plessy versus Ferguson* in 1896.

This setback did not end the crusade against Jim Crow. Led by Thurgood Marshall, civil rights lawyers won a great victory in 1954. The Supreme Court ruled that school segregation violated the Constitution. But other forms of legal segregation hung on. In 1960, four black students sat down at a lunch counter in Greensboro, North Carolina. They sparked a sit-in movement that swept across the South. Die-hard segregationists answered with bombs and bullets. Four young black girls died in a church bombing in Alabama. Three civil rights workers were murdered in Mississippi.

Congress responded to national revulsion against racial violence. The Civil Rights Act of 1964 outlawed segregation in public accommodations. The law did not rely on the Fourteenth Amendment but the constitutional clause that gives Congress power to regulate "commerce among the several states." Congress held that segregation disrupts the flow of commerce across state lines. The law was quickly challenged by the Heart of Atlanta Motel and quickly upheld by a lower federal court. Chief Justice Warren welcomes Moreton Rolleston, a prominent Atlanta lawyer who argues the motel's appeal.

Warren: Mr. Rolleston.

Rolleston: Mr. Chief Justice, may it please the Court.

Now, the facts in this case are very simple. As a matter of fact, the parties in the case tried to make them simple. . . . The Heart of Atlanta Motel, Incorporated, is a Georgia corporation which owns a motel in Atlanta named the Heart of Atlanta Motel. It is the only business it operates. It is the only business it has in Atlanta. The motel has 216 rooms. It is located in downtown Atlanta and fronting on an interstate highway. By stipulation we agreed that over 75 percent of all the business in the form of guests comes from out of the state of Georgia, that most of the convention business is solicited from out of the state of Georgia, and that we have highway billboards on roads in Georgia.

Narrator: Rolleston listed his objections to the law.

Rolleston: There are five theories of law that we rely on in this case. Number one, that the law of the land—and any lawyer is delighted to have a "white horse case" that says what the law of the land is, if it is true—is our first one; that is, the decision in the *Civil Rights Cases* which was upheld by this Court in 1883.

Narrator: One justice had never heard of a "white horse case." Rolleston said it was "one that just fits your case exactly." He continued.

Rolleston: The second proposition is that the Fourteenth Amendment—neither the Fourteenth Amendment nor the Constitution prohibit racial discrimination by an individual.

The third proposition, we contend that the Civil Rights Act is an unlawful extension of the power of commerce [Congress] under the commerce clause.

Number five [*sic*], we contend that the act, the Civil Rights Act, violates the Fifth Amendment to the Constitution; and last, that it violates the Thirteenth Amendment to the Constitution.

And we submit, gentlemen, that if we can prevail on *any* theory, any one of those five theories, then this act's got to fail.

Narrator: Rolleston challenged the power of Congress over private property.

Rolleston: The fundamental question, besides the legal question of the constitutionality of the act, the fundamental question, I submit, is whether or not Congress has the power to take away the liberty of an individual to run his business as he sees fit in the selection and choice of his customers. This is the real important issue. And the fact of alleged civil rights of the Negroes involved here is purely incidental, because if Congress can exercise these controls over the right of individuals, it is plausible that there is no limit to Congress's power to appropriate private property and liberty.

It is my contention that any Supreme Court, when a case comes before it —it doesn't make any difference what the people thought that enacted the law or what was the theory of the people who argued the case before the Court. The Court has to look at the Constitution as it stands and any amendments to it, and regardless of whether we have anything to say about them as counsel, to consider the pros and cons of the case, and apply the law as it is, not how it is argued or how the people in Congress thought it should be.

Narrator: Four months earlier, the Supreme Court declined to strike down a sit-in conviction for trespass, sending the case back to state court. Rolleston cited this decision for support.

Rolleston: Of course, if the Constitution does not prohibit racial discrimination by an individual unsupported by any other act—and I grant to the Court that this Civil Rights Act was passed after this decision of June of '64—but if the Constitution and the Fourteenth Amendment don't prohibit it, and Congress gets all this power to enact any legislation from the Constitution, how then can Congress pass an act which would prohibit racial discrimination by an individual? Article Six of the Constitution says the supreme law of this land is the Constitution, laws passed pursuant to it, and treaties. Now, Congress can't pass any law that's not pursuant to some delegation of power under the Constitution. One of them could be the commerce clause. Or they can't do anything that is prohibited by the Constitution.

Narrator: The Court had broadly construed the commerce clause since the 1930s. Rolleston disagreed.

Rolleston: We say that the framers of the Constitution intended to cover commerce as commerce is known in business fields; and that is, it was intended to cover the transportation and movement and production of articles from agriculture, products of industry, methods of transportation, tariffs between states— which we don't have now, thank goodness—and anything else that had to do with commerce.

Now it's true that Congress and decisions of the Supreme Court have enlarged the commerce power beyond which I submit the framers never intended and never thought it would be.

Narrator: Justice William Douglas broke in.

Douglas: You say people are not commerce?

Rolleston: There is a holding of the United States Supreme Court that says that people are not commerce. People engage in commerce. People take part in commerce. But people themselves are not commerce. And it has so been held by this Court, and never been overruled.

Narrator: Rolleston aimed a "states' rights" argument at the justices.

Rolleston: This Constitution set up powers between the states and the federal government and enumerated them, and in the Tenth Amendment it reserved to the states all powers not set forth therein to the states or the people. And the only reason for the existence of this Supreme Court, may it please the Court, is to maintain the balance of powers between those different governments.

And if this Court will let Congress do anything it wants to under the commerce clause—and that's what that argument means—if this Court will let them do anything, then this Court has abdicated and there is no reason for the existence of the Supreme Court to adjust and maintain the balance of powers between the various governments in this country. That is the function of the Supreme Court. That is the very reason for it set up in the Constitution, to balance those powers between the two by declaring the act of a state unconstitutional or declaring an act of Congress unconstitutional. And if you abdicate from that power there will be no reason for the Supreme Court, because Congress then can do anything it wants in any facet of our lives.

Narrator: Solicitor General Archibald Cox defended the law for the federal government. Chief Justice Warren welcomed him.

Warren: Mr. Solicitor General.

Cox: Mr. Chief Justice, may it please the Court.

The Civil Rights Act of 1964 is surely the most important legislation enacted in recent decades. It is one of the half-dozen most important laws, I think, enacted in the last century. No legislation within my memory has been debated as widely, as long, or as thoroughly.

The major premise of our argument is the familiar rule that the powers delegated to Congress by the commerce and necessary and proper clauses authorize Congress to regulate local activities, at least activities that are local when separately considered, even though they are not themselves interstate commerce, if they have such a close and substantial relation to commerce that their regulation may be deemed appropriate or useful to foster or promote such commerce, or to relieve it of burdens and obstructions.

The minor premise of our argument is that Congress, to which the economic question thus raised is primarily committed, had ample basis upon which to find that racial discrimination—inns in the one case, inns and motels in the one case, restaurants in the other—does in fact constitute a source of burden or obstruction to interstate commerce. And, of course, from those premises the conclusion would follow that this is a legitimate exercise of the power under the commerce clause.

Narrator: Cox reminded the justices of the campaign against Jim Crow laws.

Cox: Now, Congress started with the outstanding fact, I think, of national life during the past decade, perhaps longer: the thrust toward the realization for Negroes and, in some instances, other minorities, of the promise that all men are created equal.

Congress heard evidence, for example, for about two months in the spring and early summer of 1963, that there were 634 demonstrations in 174 cities and 32 states and the District of Columbia. About a third of those were concerned solely with discrimination in places of public accommodation. Others had a broader scope. The effect of those demonstrations, picketing, boycotts, other forms of protest, upon business conditions and therefore upon interstate commerce, was dramatic.

We're concerned here with the commercial consequences, which were of nationwide scope and almost incredible proportions. Not unnaturally, much of that pressure that I refer to was centered on racial discrimination in places of public accommodation, a practice that was not confined to any one section of the country or to any particular type of establishment.

Narrator: One black parent asked congressmen to imagine *they* were black and driving through the South. "How far do you drive each day? Where can your family eat? Where can they use a rest room? Will your children be denied an ice cream cone because they are not white?" Cox linked these questions to the commerce clause.

Cox: The testimony before Congress provided literally overwhelming evidence that discrimination by hotels and motels impedes interstate travel, and I suggest that there is no possible doubt that interstate travel by men and women is interstate commerce.

Suffice it to say, because I think it epitomizes the point, that on a motor trip between Washington, D.C., and Miami, Florida, the average distance it was found between accommodations of reasonable quality open to Negroes was 141 miles. And when we think of the frequency with which we go by other hotels and motels open to everyone, the significance of a three- or four-hour drive between the *hope* of accommodation is very significant indeed. And it further appeared that those accommodations that were available to Negroes were, on the whole, likely to be small, so that after driving three or four hours, one might well find a "no vacancy" sign, and have another equally lengthy drive ahead of him.

Plainly this kind of restraint has a most marked effect upon the volume of interstate travel. It won't do to say, well, people will go somewhere else. In the first place, it seems to me that that's unlikely. But in the second place, of course, any practice that distorts the flow of commerce and that prevents it from going, flowing freely where Congress thinks it desirable to flow freely, is itself a restraint on interstate commerce. It's something within the power of Congress to deal under the proposition that I stated earlier.

Narrator: Cox faced the crucial question: Are people commerce?

Cox: I say that the movement of people from state to state is a movement in commerce, yes. I hesitate a little to say that the people *are* commerce, but it's certainly movement in commerce.

We think there was ample evidence on which Congress could conclude that the racial practices in hotels and motels and like places did have a very substantial effect upon the movement of people in interstate commerce and that therefore this statute as applied to them is a measure adapted to freeing interstate commerce from restraints and burdens.

The fact that Congress has prohibited hotels and motels from discriminating against all guests rather than against interstate guests does not invalidate the statute. To require a traveler to carry a cachet to show that he is interstate would itself be a burden on commerce. Furthermore, to require the Negro interstate traveler to prove that he was traveling in interstate commerce would itself be a form of discrimination.

Narrator: Cox denied that Congress had taken the motel's property.

Cox: The argument that Congress violated the Fifth Amendment has equally little merit. Certainly there is no taking of property for a public use. The regulation of the conduct of a business is not a taking. Appellants say that they will lose profits as a result of this regulation. Experience rather indicates the contrary, but assuming that that is true, still it has clearly been held that subjecting a man to regulation otherwise proper along with all other similar businesses does not violate the Fifth Amendment simply because he loses money.

Nor does the prohibition of racial discrimination take liberty or property without due process of law. Over and over again, the Court has sustained and enforced statutes prohibiting various forms of racial discrimination.

Narrator: Cox ended with lofty words.

Cox: We shall solve the problems as one people, and thus escape the consequences of the sins of the past, only if we act in the spirit of Lincoln's Second Inaugural: without malice, with charity, and perhaps above all, without that spirit of false self-righteousness that enables men who are not themselves without fault to point the finger at their fellows.

Narrator: Cox had pointed to civil rights protests in Birmingham, Alabama, and Little Rock, Arkansas. Rolleston answered in his rebuttal.

Rolleston: And if the purpose of the passing of the Civil Rights Act was to relieve the burden on interstate commerce by virtue of reference to the things that happened in Birmingham and Little Rock and so forth—all of which happened some time ago now, thank goodness—if it was to relieve the burden on interstate commerce, has it done so?

Counsel seems to think that the act was passed for the benefit of the people in Birmingham and Little Rock, and other people who had racial disturbances in the South. There are forty-three million white people in the South, and I'll say for all of them so loud that Congress can hear, please don't do us any more favors if it's for us. (*laughter*)

Narrator: Rolleston concluded defiantly.

Rolleston: In my opinion, the argument of counsel and of the Government that this is done to relieve a burden on interstate commerce is so much hogwash, that the purpose of Congress was to pass a law which, some way or other, they could control discrimination by individuals in the whole United States.

I didn't come here to talk about commerce. I didn't come here to argue the question of whether or not this motel has an effect on commerce. Certainly, everything that happens in this country has an effect on commerce. But I did perceive, I hope, that in the writings of members of this Court there is still a great facet of personal liberty that this Court stands for. This Court, under the Constitution, is the last bulwark of personal liberty. Where else can a man go to defend personal liberty?

Congress has the right to remove burdens from interstate commerce if it pertains to commerce. But I believe that the rights of individuals, the rights of people, the personal liberty of a person to do what he wants to, to run his business, is more important and more paramount than the commerce of the United States.

Narrator: On December 14th, 1964, the justices unanimously ruled that the Heart of Atlanta Motel must admit all guests, regardless of race. Justice Tom Clark wrote for the Court. He grew up in a segregated society and knew the indignities it imposed on black citizens. He cited the testimony of the black parent who feared driving through "hostile territory" in search of food and lodging. Congress had "overwhelming evidence," Clark said, "that discrimination by hotels and motels impedes interstate travel."

The next question was whether Congress had power under the commerce clause. Clark had asked Archibald Cox if people were commerce. His opinion gave the answer: commerce includes "the movement of persons through more states than one." Clark did not pretend that segregation was simply an economic issue. Congress was entitled to use its commerce power, he said, to deal with "a moral and social wrong."

The Court struck down the first Civil Rights Act in 1883. Moreton Rolleston cited this decision as his "white horse case." But his horse had left the stable. "Conditions of transportation and commerce," Clark wrote, "have changed dramatically" since the nineteenth century. The Constitution must catch up to the twentieth.

Clark's opinion, like the justice himself, was quiet and matter-of-fact. It had no lofty rhetoric, no ringing phrases. But it did what the Court intended. It gave black families the right to a motel room, to a restaurant booth, to an ice cream cone for their kids. It pulled down the "Whites Only" signs that shamed America. And it restored to all Americans the dignity they deserve.

EDITED SUPREME COURT OPINIONS
Heart of Atlanta Motel v. United States.

MR. JUSTICE CLARK delivered the opinion of the Court. . . .
Appellant owns and operates the Heart of Atlanta Motel which has 216 rooms available to transient guests. The motel is located on Courtland Street, two blocks from downtown Peachtree Street. It is readily accessible to interstate highways 75 and 85 and state highways 23 and 41. Appellant solicits patronage from outside

the State of Georgia through various national advertising media, including magazines of national circulation; it maintains over fifty billboards and highway signs
within the State, soliciting patronage for the motel; it accepts convention trade
from outside Georgia and approximately 75 percent of its registered guests are
from out of State. Prior to passage of the Act the motel had followed a practice of
refusing to rent rooms to Negroes, and it alleged that it intended to continue to do
so. In an effort to perpetuate that policy this suit was filed.

The appellant contends that Congress in passing this Act exceeded its power
to regulate commerce under Art. I, § 8, cl. 3, of the Constitution of the United
States; that the Act violates the Fifth Amendment because appellant is deprived of
the right to choose its customers and operate its business as it wishes, resulting in
a taking of its liberty and property without due process of law and a taking of its
property without just compensation; and, finally, that by requiring appellant to
rent available rooms to Negroes against its will, Congress is subjecting it to involuntary servitude in contravention of the Thirteenth Amendment.

The appellees counter that the unavailability to Negroes of adequate accommodations interferes significantly with interstate travel, and that Congress, under
the Commerce Clause, has power to remove such obstructions and restraints; that
the Fifth Amendment does not forbid reasonable regulation and that consequen-
tial damage does not constitute a "taking" within the meaning of that amendment;
that the Thirteenth Amendment claim fails because it is entirely frivolous to say
that an amendment directed to the abolition of human bondage and the removal
of widespread disabilities associated with slavery places discrimination in public
accommodations beyond the reach of both federal and state law. . . .

The District Court sustained the constitutionality of the sections of the Act
under attack . . . and issued a permanent injunction on the counterclaim of the
appellees. It restrained the appellant from "[r]efusing to accept Negroes as guests
in the motel by reason of their race or color" and from "[m]aking any distinction
whatever upon the basis of race or color in the availability of the goods, services,
facilities, privileges, advantages or accommodations offered or made available to
the guests of the motel, or to the general public, within or upon any of the
premises of the Heart of Atlanta Motel, Inc."

Congress first evidenced its interest in civil rights legislation in the Civil
Rights or Enforcement Act of April 9, 1866. There followed four Acts, with a
fifth, the Civil Rights Act of March 1, 1875, culminating the series. In 1883 this
Court struck down the public accommodations sections of the 1875 Act in the
Civil Rights Cases, 109 U. S. 3. No major legislation in this field had been
enacted by Congress for eighty-two years when the Civil Rights Act of 1957
became law. It was followed by the Civil Rights Act of 1960. Three years later, on
June 19, 1963, the late President Kennedy called for civil rights legislation in a
message to Congress to which he attached a proposed bill. Its stated purpose was

"to promote the general welfare by eliminating discrimination based on race, color, religion, or national origin in . . . public accommodations through the exercise by Congress of the powers conferred upon it . . . to enforce the provisions of the fourteenth and fifteenth amendments, to regulate commerce among the several States, and to make laws necessary and proper to execute the powers conferred upon it by the Constitution." . . .

[I]t was not until July 2, 1964, upon the recommendation of President Johnson, that the Civil Rights Act of 1964, here under attack, was finally passed. . . . Since Title II is the only portion under attack here, we confine our consideration to those public accommodation provisions. . . .

This Title is divided into seven sections beginning with § 201 (a) which provides that:

"All persons shall be entitled to the full and equal enjoyment of the goods, services, facilities, privileges, advantages, and accommodations of any place of public accommodation, as defined in this section, without discrimination or segregation on the ground of race, color, religion, or national origin." . . .

It is admitted that the operation of the motel brings it within the provisions of § 201 (a) of the Act and that appellant refused to provide lodging for transient Negroes because of their race or color and that it intends to continue that policy unless restrained.

The sole question posed is, therefore, the constitutionality of the Civil Rights Act of 1964 as applied to these facts. The legislative history of the Act indicates that Congress based the Act on § 5 and the Equal Protection Clause of the Fourteenth Amendment as well as its power to regulate interstate commerce under Art. I, § 8, cl. 3, of the Constitution. . . .

While the Act as adopted carried no congressional findings the record of its passage through each house is replete with evidence of the burdens that discrimination by race or color places upon interstate commerce. . . . This testimony included the fact that our people have become increasingly mobile with millions of people of all races traveling from State to State; that Negroes in particular have been the subject of discrimination in transient accommodations, having to travel great distances to secure the same; that often they have been unable to obtain accommodations and have had to call upon friends to put them up overnight, . . . and that these conditions had become so acute as to require the listing of available lodging for Negroes in a special guidebook which was itself "dramatic testimony to the difficulties" Negroes encounter in travel. . . . These exclusionary practices were found to be nationwide, the Under Secretary of Commerce testifying that there is "no question that this discrimination in the North still exists to a large degree" and in the West and Midwest as well. . . . This testimony indicated a qualitative as well as quantitative effect on interstate travel by Negroes.

The former was the obvious impairment of the Negro traveler's pleasure and convenience that resulted when he continually was uncertain of finding lodging. As for the latter, there was evidence that this uncertainty stemming from racial discrimination had the effect of discouraging travel on the part of a substantial portion of the Negro community. . . .

[T]he determinative test of the exercise of power by the Congress under the Commerce Clause is simply whether the activity sought to be regulated is "commerce which concerns more States than one" and has a real and substantial relation to the national interest. . . .

The same interest in protecting interstate commerce which led Congress to deal with segregation in interstate carriers and the white-slave traffic has prompted it to extend the exercise of its power to gambling, . . . to deceptive practices in the sale of products; . . . to wages and hours; . . . to members of labor unions; . . . to crop control; . . . to the protection of small business from injurious price cutting, . . . and to racial discrimination by owners and managers of terminal restaurants . . .

That Congress was legislating against moral wrongs in many of these areas rendered its enactments no less valid. In framing Title II of this Act Congress was also dealing with what it considered a moral problem. But that fact does not detract from the overwhelming evidence of the disruptive effect that racial discrimination has had on commercial intercourse. It was this burden which empowered Congress to enact appropriate legislation, and, given this basis for the exercise of its power, Congress was not restricted by the fact that the particular obstruction to interstate commerce with which it was dealing was also deemed a moral and social wrong.

It is said that the operation of the motel here is of a purely local character. But . . . the power of Congress to promote interstate commerce also includes the power to regulate the local incidents thereof, including local activities in both the States of origin and destination, which might have a substantial and harmful effect upon that commerce. . . .

Nor does the Act deprive appellant of liberty or property under the Fifth Amendment. The commerce power invoked here by the Congress is a specific and plenary one authorized by the Constitution itself. The only questions are: (1) whether Congress had a rational basis for finding that racial discrimination by motels affected commerce, and (2) if it had such a basis, whether the means it selected to eliminate that evil are reasonable and appropriate. If they are, appellant has no "right" to select its guests as it sees fit, free from governmental regulation.

. . . Likewise in a long line of cases this Court has rejected the claim that the prohibition of racial discrimination in public accommodations interferes with personal liberty. . . . Neither do we find any merit in the claim that the Act is a taking of property without just compensation. . . .

We find no merit in the remainder of appellant's contentions, including that of "involuntary servitude." . . . [T]hirty-two States prohibit racial discrimination in public accommodations. These laws but codify the common-law innkeeper rule which long predated the Thirteenth Amendment. It is difficult to believe that the Amendment was intended to abrogate this principle. . . . We, therefore, conclude that the action of the Congress in the adoption of the Act as applied here to a motel which concededly serves interstate travelers is within the power granted it by the Commerce Clause of the Constitution, as interpreted by this Court for 140 years. It may be argued that Congress could have pursued other methods to eliminate the obstructions it found in interstate commerce caused by racial discrimination. But this is a matter of policy that rests entirely with the Congress not with the courts. How obstructions in commerce may be removed—what means are to be employed—is within the sound and exclusive discretion of the Congress. It is subject only to one caveat—that the means chosen by it must be reasonably adapted to the end permitted by the Constitution. We cannot say that its choice here was not so adapted. The Constitution requires no more.

Affirmed.

MR. JUSTICE DOUGLAS, concurring.

Though I join the Court's opinion(s), I am somewhat reluctant here . . . to rest solely on the Commerce Clause. My reluctance is not due to any conviction that Congress lacks power to regulate commerce in the interests of human rights. It is rather my belief that the right of people to be free of state action that discriminates against them because of race, like the "right of persons to move freely from State to State" (*Edwards* v. *California, supra*, at 177), "occupies a more protected position in our constitutional system than does the movement of cattle, fruit, steel and coal across state lines." . . .

[T]he result reached by the Court is for me much more obvious as a protective measure under the Fourteenth Amendment than under the Commerce Clause. For the former deals with the constitutional status of the individual not with the impact on commerce of local activities or vice versa.

Hence I would prefer to rest on the assertion of legislative power contained in § 5 of the Fourteenth Amendment which states: "The Congress shall have power to enforce, by appropriate legislation, the provisions of this article"—a power which the Court concedes was exercised at least in part in this Act.

A decision based on the Fourteenth Amendment would have a more settling effect, making unnecessary litigation over whether a particular restaurant or inn is within the commerce definitions of the Act or whether a particular customer is an interstate traveler. Under my construction, the Act would apply to all customers in all the enumerated places of public accommodation. And that construction would put an end to all obstructionist strategies and finally close one door on a bitter chapter in American history. . . .

BIBLIOGRAPHY

RICE, C. E. "Federal Public-Accommodations Law: A Dissent." *Mercer Law Review* 17 (Spring 1966): 338.

"Rights Bill Upheld." *Senior Scholastic*, January 7, 1965, p. 17.

SIMPSON, R. T. "Public Accommodations . . ." *Alabama Lawyer* 25 (July 1964): 305.

"Upholding Title II; U.S. Supreme Court Decision." *Newsweek*, December 28, 1964, p. 16.

WHALEN, CHARLES W. *The Longest Debate*. Seven Locks, 1985.

Loving v. Virginia

388 U.S. 1 (1967)

In 1958, Richard Loving married Mildred Jeter in Washington, D.C. He was white and she was black and native American. The couple moved back to Caroline County, Virginia, where they grew up and met. In 1959, the Lovings were convicted of violating Virginia's ban on interracial marriages and were forced to leave the state under threat of criminal prosecution. Antimiscegenation laws of Virginia and other southern states dated back to slavery days. The Lovings challenged the law, claiming it violated the equal protection and due process clauses of the Fourteenth Amendment. In a unanimous decision, the Supreme Court ruled in 1967 that the freedom to marry is an essential personal right which cannot be infringed by the state. "There can be no doubt," Chief Justice Earl Warren wrote, "that restricting the right to marry solely because of racial classifications violates the central meaning of the Equal Protection Clause."

TRANSCRIPT OF EDITED AND NARRATED ARGUMENTS IN
Loving v. *Virginia*, 388 U.S. 1 (1967)

Counsel for petitioners: Philip J. Hirschkop and Bernard S. Cohen, Alexandria,
Virginia
Counsel for respondent: R. D. McIlwaine III, Richmond, Virginia
Counsel for the Japanese American Citizens League, as amicus curiae, William
M. Marutani, Philadelphia, Pennsylvania

Chief Justice Earl Warren: Number 395, Richard Perry Loving, et al., appellants, versus Virginia.

Narrator: It's April 10th, 1967. Chief Justice Earl Warren has called a case that
began when Richard Loving and Mildred Jeter were married in June 1958. The
newlyweds never expected their marriage to come before the Supreme Court.

Rich Loving worked as a brick mason, but his real passion was drag racing
on country tracks in Virginia and Maryland. Rich and Mildred grew up in
Virginia's rural Caroline County. They met at a dance and dated for a few years.
She was quiet and tall and had a warm smile. After they decided to marry,
Rich and Mildred drove to Washington, D.C., for their wedding and a short
honeymoon. They returned to Caroline County to build a house and raise a
family.

Six weeks later, the Lovings had a terrible shock. Sheriff Garnet Brooks
arrived with a warrant directing him to bring "the body of said Richard Loving"
before a judge. He dragged the Lovings out of bed. They spent the next five days
in jail. And what was their crime? Rich was white and Mildred had mixed black
and Indian ancestry. Their marriage violated a Virginia law providing that "if
any white person intermarry with a colored person"—or vice versa—each party
"shall be guilty of a felony" and face prison terms of five years.

Virginia's law against racially mixed marriages goes back to 1691 and the
slave society. Similar antimiscegenation laws—the Latin words mean "mixing
races"—survived the Civil War in most states, North and South. Thirty-one
states kept their laws alive even after Nazi racism died in World War Two. They
were still enforced in sixteen southern and border states when the Lovings were
arrested.

The Lovings pleaded guilty to avoid prison. Judge Leon Bazile suspended a
one-year sentence if they agreed to leave Virginia for twenty-five years. The
Lovings moved to Washington, but they were country people and couldn't adjust
to city life. They came back to Caroline County and lived a fugitive life for nine
years, sheltered by family and friends and raising three small kids. "I never
expected . . . such a beating," Rich said later. "It was right rough."

Rich appealed for help to Attorney General Robert Kennedy in 1963. Kennedy sent his letter to the American Civil Liberties Union, which recruited two Virginia lawyers, Philip Hirschkop and Bernard Cohen. They argue that the Lovings' convictions violate the Fourteenth Amendment's guarantee of "equal protection of the laws" to Americans of all races. Civil rights and church groups support the appeal as friends of the court. Chief Justice Warren welcomes Philip Hirschkop.

Warren: Mr. Hirschkop.

Hirschkop: Mr. Chief Justice, Associate Justices; may it please the Court.
     You have before you today what we consider the most odious of the segregation laws and the slavery laws. In our view of this law, we hope to clearly show that this is a slavery law. And the issue is: May a state proscribe a marriage between two adult consenting individuals because of their race?

Narrator: Hirschkop cited the Virginia laws against mixed marriages and their impact on the Lovings and their children.

Hirschkop: Sections 20-54 and 20-57 void such marriages. And, if they void such marriages—if you would only decide on 20-58 and 20-59—these people, were they to go back to Virginia—and they are in Virginia now—will be subject to immediate arrest under the fornication statute, and the lewd and lascivious cohabitation statute. And, more than that, there are many, many other problems with these. Their children would be declared bastards under many Virginia decisions. They themselves would lose their rights for insurance, social security, for numerous other things to which they're entitled. So we strongly urge the Court, in considering this, to consider this basic question: May the state proscribe a marriage between such individuals because of their race, and their race alone?

Narrator: Virginia's laws against mixed marriages were revised in 1924. The Ku Klux Klan and other racist groups agitated for laws against blacks, Jews, and all foreign immigrants. Hirschkop cited this history.

Hirschkop: All the registration statutes were enacted in the 1924 period. These are the statutes, basically, in which you have to have a certificate of racial composition in the state of Virginia, the statutes which we find absolutely most odious, the statutes which reflect back to Nazi Germany and to the present South African situation.
     The present bill, as it sits on the books, is that law from 1924, and it was

entitled "A Bill to Preserve the Integrity of the White Race" when it was initially issued. It was passed as a bill for "racial integrity"—to preserve racial integrity. And we would advance the argument very strongly to the Court that they're not concerned with the racial integrity of the Negro race, only with the white race.

Narrator: Hirschkop noted that Virginia imposed criminal penalties only on marriages of blacks and whites.

Hirschkop: In fact, in Virginia it's only a crime for white and Negro to inter-marry, and the law is couched in such terms that they say white may only marry white, in section 20-54 of our law, but it goes on from there to make it a crime only for whites and Negroes to intermarry. There's no crime for a Malaysian to marry a Negro, and it's a valid marriage in Virginia. But it would be a void marriage for a Malaysian or any other race, aside from Negro, to marry a white person. A void marriage, but there would be no criminal penalty against anyone but the white person. They were not concerned with racial integrity, but racial supremacy of the white race.

Narrator: Hirschkop quoted the speeches of the law's supporters.

Hirschkop: Again, they wanted to preserve the racial integrity of their citizens. They wanted not to have a "mongrel" breed of citizens. We find there no requirement that a state shall not legislate to prevent the obliteration of racial pride but must permit the corruption of blood even though it weaken and destroy the quality of its citizenship. These are racial, and equal protection thoroughly proscribes these.

Narrator: Hirschkop also quoted Judge Bazile's opinion in the Loving case.

Hirschkop: He says: "Almighty God created the races white, black, yellow, malay and red, and he placed them on separate continents." And I needn't read the whole quote, but it's a fundamentally ludicrous quote.

Narrator: Hirschkop concluded.

Hirschkop: We fail to see how any reasonable man can but conclude that these laws are slavery laws, were incepted to keep the slaves in their place, were prolonged to keep the slaves in their place, and in truth the Virginia laws still view the Negro race as a slave race. That these are the most odious laws to come before the Court. They rob the Negro race of its dignity, and only a decision which will reach the full body of these laws of the state of Virginia will change that.

Narrator: William Marutani spoke for the Japanese American Citizens League as friend of the court. Several states barred Japanese from marrying whites. Marutani addressed Virginia's definition of race.

Marutani: Now, those who would trace their ancestry to the European cultures where, over the centuries, there have been invasions, cross-invasions, population shifts, with the inevitable crossbreeding which follows, and particularly those same Europeans who have been part of the melting pot of America, I suggest would have a most difficult, if not impossible, task of establishing what Virginia's antimiscegenation statutes require, namely—and I quote—proving that, quote, "no trace whatever of any blood other than Caucasian." This is what Virginia statutes would require.

Now, notwithstanding the fact that anthropologists reject, flatly reject, the concept of any notion of a "pure race," under section 20-53 of Virginia's laws, the clerk, or the deputy clerk, is endowed with the power to determine whether an applicant for a marriage license is, quote, "of pure white race"—the clerk or his deputy.

Moreover, the Commonwealth of Virginia would have laymen—that is, clerks, judges, and juries—take vague and standardless terms such as "colored person," "white person," "Caucasian," and apply them to specific situations, coupled with the power in these laymen to invoke civil and criminal sanctions where in their view and interpretation of these terms the laws of Virginia have been violated. I believe no citation is required to state, or to conclude, that this is vagueness in its grossest sense.

Narrator: R. D. McIlwaine defended the Virginia law for the state's attorney general. He first answered Marutani.

Chief Justice Warren: Mr. McIlwaine.

McIlwaine: Mr. Chief Justice; may it please the Court.

A statute, of course, does not have to apply with mathematical precision, but on the basis of the Virginia population, we respectfully submit that the statute before the Court in this case does apply almost with mathematical precision, since it covers all the dangers which Virginia has a right to apprehend from interracial marriage, in that it prohibits the intermarriage of those two groups which constitute more than ninety-nine percent of the Virginia population.

Now, so far as the particular appellants in this case are concerned, there is no question of constitutional vagueness or doubtful definition. It is a matter of record, agreed to by all counsel during the course of this litigation and in the briefs, that one of the appellants here is a white person within the definition of the Virginia law, the other appellant is a colored person within the definition of Virginia law. Thus, the Court is simply faced with the proposition of whether or not a state may validly forbid the interracial marriage of two groups—the white and the colored—in the context of the present statute.

Narrator: McIlwaine addressed the constitutional issues.

McIlwaine: Now, the appellants, of course, have asserted that the Virginia statute here under attack is violative of the Fourteenth Amendment. We assert that it is not, and we do so on the basis of two contentions and two contentions only. The first contention is that the Fourteenth Amendment, viewed in the light of its legislative history, has no effect whatever upon the power of states to enact antimiscegenation laws, specifically antimiscegenation laws forbidding the intermarriage of white and colored persons, and therefore, as a matter of law, this Court under the Fourteenth Amendment is not authorized to infringe the power of the state; that the Fourteenth Amendment does not, read in the light of its history, touch, much less diminish, the power of the states in this regard.

The second contention, an alternative contention, is that if the Fourteenth Amendment be deemed to apply to state antimiscegenation statutes, then this statute serves a legitimate legislative objective of preventing the sociological and psychological evils which attend interracial marriages, and is an expression—a rational expression—of a policy which Virginia has a right to adopt.

Narrator: McIlwaine moved from the Constitution to social science.

McIlwaine: We start with the proposition, on this connection, that it is the family which constitutes the structural element of society; and that marriage is the legal basis upon which families are formed. Consequently, this Court has held, in numerous decisions over the years, that society is structured on the institution of marriage; that it has more to do with the welfare and civilizations of a people than any other institutions; and that out of the fruits of marriage spring relationships and responsibilities with which the state is necessarily required to deal. Text writers and judicial writers agree that the state has a natural, direct, and vital interest in maximizing the number of successful marriages which lead to stable homes and families and in minimizing those which do not.

It is clear, from the most recent available evidence on the psycho-sociological aspect of this question that intermarried families are subjected to much greater pressures and problems than are those of the intramarried, and that the state's prohibition of interracial marriage, for this reason, stands on the same footing as the prohibition of polygamous marriage, or incestuous marriage, or the prescription of minimum ages at which people may marry, and the prevention of the marriage of people who are mentally incompetent.

Narrator: Chief Justice Warren was skeptical.

Warren: There are people who have the same feeling about interreligious marriages. But because that may be true, would you think that the state could prohibit people from having interreligious marriages?

McIlwaine: I think that the evidence in support of the prohibition of interracial marriages is stronger than that for the prohibition of interreligious marriages; but I think that . . .

Warren: How can you say that?

McIlwaine: Well, we say that principally . . .

Warren: Because you believe that?

McIlwaine: No, sir. We say it principally on the basis of the authority which we have cited in our brief.

Narrator: Warren forced McIlwaine to confess that he didn't personally believe his argument. His only support was a textbook by Dr. Albert Gordon.

McIlwaine: Dr. Gordon has stated it, as his opinion that "it is my conviction that intermarriage is definitely inadvisable; that they are wrong because they are most frequently, if not solely, entered into under present-day circumstances by people who have a rebellious attitude toward society, self-hatred, neurotic tendencies, immaturity, and other detrimental psychological factors."

Narrator: Justice Byron White broke in.

Stewart: Of course, you don't know what is cause, and what is effect. Presuming the validity of these statistics, I suppose it could be argued that one reason that marriages of this kind are sometimes unsuccessful is the existence of the kind of laws that are in issue here, and the attitudes that those laws reflect. Isn't that correct?

McIlwaine: I think it is more the latter, the attitudes that perhaps the laws reflect. I don't find anywhere in this that the existence of the law does it. It is the attitude which society has toward interracial marriages, which in detailing his opposition, he says, "causes a child to have almost insuperable difficulties in identification," and that the problems which the child of an interracial marriage faces are those which no child can come through without damage to himself.

Now, if the state has an interest in marriage, if it has an interest in maximizing the number of stable marriages, and in protecting the progeny of interracial marriages from these problems, then clearly there is scientific evidence available that this is so. It is not infrequent that the children of intermarried parents are referred to, not merely as the children of intermarried parents, but as the "victims" of intermarried parents, and as the "martyrs" of intermarried parents.

So, you can't reach the conclusion that this statute infringes a right under the Fourteenth Amendment without examining evidence on behalf of the state to show that the infringement is a reasonable one; just as reasonable, as far as we can determine—there's far more evidence of the reasonableness of a ban against interracial marriage than there is against polygamous, or incestuous marriage, so far as the scientific proposition is concerned. But I cannot conceive of this Court striking down a polygamy or incest statute on the basis of scientific evidence. And I submit that it would be no more appropriate for this Court to invalidate the miscegenetic statute on that basis.

Narrator: Chief Justice Warren was proud of his opinion in *Brown versus Board of Education*, striking down racial segregation in schools.

Warren: Mr. McIlwaine, didn't we, in the segregation cases, have also argued to us what was supposed to be "scientific evidence" to the effect that the whites would be injured by having to go to school with the Negroes?

McIlwaine: Your Honor, I . . .

Warren: Isn't that the same argument you're making here?

McIlwaine: Yes, sir, it is. But it is being made in a context in which the evidence in support of the proposition is existing evidence which is voluminous in its character, and which supports the view not of racial superiority or inferiority, but a simple matter of difference; that the difference is such that the progeny of the intermarried are harmed by it; and that the divorce rate arises from the difference, not from the "inferiority" or "superiority" of either race.

Narrator: Bernard Cohen spoke for the Lovings and their children. He put the Constitution in personal terms, and in their words.

Cohen: If the framers had the intent to exclude antimiscegenation statutes, it would have taken but a single phrase in the Fourteenth Amendment to say, "excluding antimiscegenation statutes." The language was broad. The language was sweeping. The language meant to include equal protection for Negroes. That was at the very heart of it, and that equal protection included the right to marry, as any other human being had the right to marry, subject to only the same limitations.

And that is the right of Richard and Mildred Loving to wake up in the morning, or to go to sleep at night, knowing that the sheriff will not be knocking on their door or shining a light in their face in the privacy of their bedroom, for "illicit cohabitation."

The Lovings have the right to go to sleep at night, knowing that should they not awake in the morning their children would have the right to inherit from them, under intestacy. They have the right to be secure in knowing that if they go to sleep and do not wake in the morning, that one of them, a survivor of them, has the right to Social Security benefits. All of these are denied to them.

The enormity of the injustices involved under this statute merely serves as indicia of how the civil liabilities amount to a denial of due process to the individuals involved. As I started to say before, no matter how we articulate this, no matter which theory of the due process clause, or which emphasis we attach to it, no one can articulate it better than Richard Loving, when he said to me: "Mr. Cohen, tell the Court I love my wife, and it is just unfair that I can't live with her in Virginia." I think this very simple layman has a concept of fundamental fairness, and ordered liberty, that he can articulate as a bricklayer, that we hope this Court has set out time and time again in its decisions on the due process clause.

Narrator: On June 2nd, 1967, Richard and Mildred Loving celebrated their ninth wedding anniversary. Ten days later, the Supreme Court added a present. The Lovings—and their kids—could sleep without any worries that Sheriff Brooks would drag them out of bed.

Like the *Brown* case, *Loving versus Virginia* was unanimous. And like *Brown*, Chief Justice Warren spoke for the Court. His opinion was short and blunt. Virginia's law against racially mixed marriages violated two provisions of the Fourteenth Amendment. The equal protection clause bans racial laws that do not serve a "permissible state objective." The state's only purpose, Warren said, was "to maintain White Supremacy." The law also violated the due process clause, which protects the right of liberty. That right includes the "fundamental freedom" to marry, without restriction on race.

The Lovings were thrilled with their anniversary present. "I feel free now," Mildred said. "It was a great burden." Rich was relieved. "It's hard to believe. Now I can put my arm around my wife in Virginia."

Racial attitudes change slowly, but they have changed with the law. Fifty years ago, nine out of ten Americans opposed mixed marriages. Recent polls show only one in four are still opposed, most of them older. There are now a million interracial couples in the United States, including Supreme Court justice Clarence Thomas and his wife.

Rich Loving died in 1975, but Mildred still lives in the white cinderblock house he built. She still meets some hostile people, but attitudes, she says, have really changed. "The Old South is going away." Sheriff Brooks is one person whose attitude hasn't changed. "I'm from the old school," he says, "I still think the law should be on the books." Rich Loving had this advice for his kids about who to marry: "I'd leave it up to them, let them decide for themselves." His daughter Peggy married a man of mixed race. She's proud of both her parents for the stand they took. Thanks to the Supreme Court, Peggy and her family don't have to worry about Sheriff Brooks any more.

EDITED SUPREME COURT OPINION
Loving v. Virginia, 1967

MR. CHIEF JUSTICE WARREN delivered the opinion of the Court.

This case presents a constitutional question never addressed by this Court: whether a statutory scheme adopted by the State of Virginia to prevent marriages between persons solely on the basis of racial classifications violates the equal protection and due process clauses of the Fourteenth Amendment. For reasons which seem to us to reflect the central meaning of those constitutional commands, we conclude that these statutes cannot stand consistently with the Fourteenth Amendment. . . .

Virginia is now one of sixteen States which prohibit and punish marriages on the basis of racial classifications. Penalties for miscegenation arose as an incident to slavery and have been common in Virginia since the colonial period. The present statutory scheme dates from the adoption of the Racial Integrity Act of 1924, passed during the period of extreme nativism which followed the end of the First World War. The central features of this Act, and current Virginia law, are the absolute prohibition of a "white person" marrying other than another "white person," a prohibition against issuing marriage licenses until the issuing official is satisfied that the applicants' statements as to their race are correct, certificates of "racial composition" to be kept by both local and state registrars, and the carrying forward of earlier prohibitions against racial intermarriage.

In upholding the constitutionality of these provisions in the decision below, the Supreme Court of Appeals of Virginia referred to its 1955 decision in *Naim* v. *Naim* . . . as stating the reasons supporting the validity of these laws. In *Naim,* the state court concluded that the State's legitimate purposes were "to preserve the racial integrity of its citizens," and to prevent "the corruption of blood," "a mongrel breed of citizens," and "the obliteration of racial pride," obviously an endorsement of the doctrine of White Supremacy.

. . . [T]he State argues that the meaning of the equal protection clause, as illuminated by the statements of the Framers, is only that state penal laws containing an interracial element as part of the definition of the offense must apply equally to whites and Negroes in the sense that members of each race are punished to the same degree. Thus, the State contends that, because its miscegenation statutes punish equally both the white and the Negro participants in an interracial marriage, these statutes, despite their reliance on racial classifications, do not constitute an invidious discrimination based upon race. The second argument advanced by the State assumes the validity of its equal application theory. The argument is that, if the equal protection clause does not outlaw miscegenation statutes because of their reliance on racial classifications, the question of constitutionality would thus become whether there was any rational basis for a State to treat interracial marriages differently from other marriages. On this question, the State argues, the scientific evidence is substantially in doubt and, consequently, this Court should defer to the wisdom of the state legislature in adopting its policy of discouraging interracial marriages.

Because we reject the notion that the mere "equal application" of a statute containing racial classifications is enough to remove the classifications from the Fourteenth Amendment's proscription of all invidious racial discriminations, we do not accept the State's contention that these statutes should be upheld if there is any possible basis for concluding that they serve a rational purpose. . . . [T]he fact of equal application does not immunize the statute from the very heavy burden of justification which the Fourteenth Amendment has traditionally required of state statutes drawn according to race.

The State argues that statements in the Thirty-ninth Congress about the time of the passage of the Fourteenth Amendment indicate that the Framers did not intend the Amendment to make unconstitutional state miscegenation laws. . . .[A]lthough these historical sources "cast some light" they are not sufficient to resolve the problem; "[a]t best, they are inconclusive. The most avid proponents of the post-War Amendments undoubtedly intended them to remove all legal distinctions among 'all persons born or naturalized in the United States.' Their opponents, just as certainly, were antagonistic to both the letter and the spirit of the Amendments and wished them to have the most limited effect." *Brown* v. *Board of Education*, 347 U. S. 483, 489 (1954). . . . We have rejected the proposition that the debates in the Thirty-ninth Congress or in the state legislatures which ratified the Fourteenth Amendment supported the theory advanced by the State, that the requirement of equal protection of the laws is satisfied by penal laws defining offenses based on racial classifications so long as white and Negro participants in the offense were similarly punished. . . . As we . . . demonstrated, the equal protection clause requires the consideration of whether the classifications drawn by any statute constitute an arbitrary and invidious discrimination. The clear and central purpose of the Fourteenth Amendment was to eliminate all official state sources of invidious racial discrimination in the States. . . .

There can be no question but that Virginia's miscegenation statutes rest solely upon distinctions drawn according to race. The statutes proscribe generally accepted conduct if engaged in by members of different races. Over the years, this Court has consistently repudiated "[d]istinctions between citizens solely because of their ancestry" as being "odious to a free people whose institutions are founded upon the doctrine of equality." *Hirabayashi* v. *United States*, 320 U. S. 81, 100 (1943). . . .

There is patently no legitimate overriding purpose independent of invidious racial discrimination which justifies this classification. The fact that Virginia prohibits only interracial marriages involving white persons demonstrates that the racial classifications must stand on their own justification, as measures designed to maintain White Supremacy. We have consistently denied the constitutionality of measures which restrict the rights of citizens on account of race. There can be no doubt that restricting the freedom to marry solely because of racial classifications violates the central meaning of the equal protection clause.

These statutes also deprive the Lovings of liberty without due process of law in violation of the due process clause of the Fourteenth Amendment. The freedom to marry has long been recognized as one of the vital personal rights essential to the orderly pursuit of happiness by free men.

Marriage is one of the "basic civil rights of man," fundamental to our very existence and survival. . . . To deny this fundamental freedom on so unsupportable a basis as the racial classifications embodied in these statutes, classifications so directly subversive of the principle of equality at the heart of the Fourteenth Amendment, is surely to deprive all the State's citizens of liberty without due process of law. The Fourteenth Amendment requires that the freedom of choice to marry not be restricted by invidious racial discriminations. Under our Constitution, the freedom to marry, or not marry, a person of another race resides with the individual and cannot be infringed by the State.

These convictions must be reversed.

It is so ordered.

BIBLIOGRAPHY

ALLEN, WILLIAM G. *The American Prejudice against Color.* Arno, 1969.

MYRDAL, GUNNAR. *An American Dilemma.* Harper, 1944.

PETTIGREW, THOMAS F. *A Profile of the American Negro.* Van Nostrand, 1964.

SCHUHMANN, GEORGE. "Miscegenation: An Example of Judicial Recidivism." *Journal of Family Law* 8, no. 1 (Spring 1968): 69.

SICKELS, ROBERT J. *Race, Marriage and the Law.* University of New Mexico Press, 1972.

WADLINGTON, WALTER. "The Loving Case: Virginia's Antimiscegenation Statute in Historical Perspective." *Virginia Law Review* 52, no. 7 (November 1966): 1189.

Palmer v. Thompson

403 U.S. 217 (1971)

In 1962, the city of Jackson, Mississippi, operated five public parks along with their recreational facilities on a racially segregated basis. Following a court decision invalidating segregation in these public accommodations, the city council opened them to all races, except for the swimming pools, which it voted to close. Black residents claimed that the city's action violated the equal protection clause of the Fourteenth Amendment and was motivated by racism. The Supreme Court ruled in 1971 that the city's racial motive was irrelevant and that it was not obligated to provide pools at all. "Nothing in the history or language of the Fourteenth Amendment," Justice Hugo Black wrote, "persuades us that the closing of the Jackson swimming pools to all its citizens constitutes a denial of the 'equal protection of the laws.' "

TRANSCRIPT OF EDITED AND NARRATED ARGUMENTS IN
Palmer v. *Thompson*, 403 U.S. 217 (1971)

Counsel for petitioner: Paul Rosen, Detroit, Michigan; William Kunstler, New
York, New York
Counsel for respondent: William Goodman, Jackson, Mississippi

Narrator: It's December 14th, 1970. Chief Justice Warren Burger has called the
case of *Palmer versus Thompson*. This is one of dozens of civil rights cases the
Court has considered since the justices outlawed school segregation in *Brown
versus Board of Education*. That historic decision in 1954 relied on the Constitution's Fourteenth Amendment, which guarantees to Americans, of all races, the
"equal protection of the laws." This is one of the Civil War amendments that
abolished slavery and protected former slaves from discrimination.

Today's argument comes from Mississippi. More than a century after the
Civil War, the Stars and Bars of the Confederate flag flew over the state capitol
in Jackson. During the civil rights struggle of the 1960s, Jackson remained a
stronghold of segregation. City police jailed hundreds of "Freedom Riders" who
tried to integrate the Greyhound bus station. Inspired by their example, Jackson's
black community asked city officials to integrate all public facilities, from parks
to libraries.

When the city refused, black citizens sued Mayor Allen Thompson in
federal court. The case came before Judge Sidney Mize, an avowed segregation-
ist. He called the city officials "high class gentlemen" and claimed that segregation served "the welfare of both races." Judge Mize accused the black plaintiffs
of "a deliberate attempt to create racial friction" in Jackson. But the judge could
not ignore Supreme Court precedent. He reluctantly granted all races a "right
to unsegregated use of public recreational facilities" in Jackson.

The city operated five public swimming pools. Only one was open to
blacks. Following the judicial decision, the city promptly closed all five pools.
Mayor Thompson announced that "we are not going to have any intermingling"
of the races in public pools.

Hazel Palmer and other Jackson residents sued Mayor Thompson to reopen
the swimming pools. Thirteen judges of the federal appeals court ruled on the
case. Seven agreed that Jackson officials were "racially motivated" in closing the
pools. But they accepted their claim that the pools were closed for "public safety"
and economic reasons. They also ruled that operating pools "is not an essential
public function" and that black citizens had "no constitutional right" to swim in
public pools. Six dissenting judges argued that the city wanted "to prevent blacks
and whites from swimming in the same water." Closing the pools, they said,
signified a "second-class citizenship" for Jackson's black citizens that violated the

Fourteenth Amendment. It also imposed a "badge of servitude" that was barred by the Thirteenth Amendment's ban on slavery.

The black plaintiffs appealed to the Supreme Court. The federal government supported them with a friend of the court brief. Two well-known civil rights lawyers, Paul Rosen of Detroit and William Kunstler of New York, will argue their case. Chief Justice Warren Burger welcomes Rosen.

Burger: Mr. Rosen, you may proceed whenever you're ready.

Rosen: If it please the Court, my name is Paul Rosen, and I, along with Mr. William Kunstler, will represent the petitioners in this oral argument. I intend to discuss the Fourteenth Amendment issues in this case; Mr. Kunstler will follow and discuss the Thirteenth Amendment issues.

This case represents but another attempt by the city of Jackson to nullify the Thirteenth and Fourteenth Amendments, to avoid the decision of *Brown versus Board of Education* and to deny black people their rights as guaranteed by the Civil War amendments. Until 1963, Jackson, Mississippi, operated its recreational facilities on a segregated basis—this is eight years after this Court in the *Dawson* case proclaimed that recreational facilities should no longer be operated on a segregated basis. But despite this, the city of Jackson maintained this policy.

Narrator: The case decided by Judge Mize was called *Clark versus Thompson.* Rosen discussed the reaction to his ruling.

Rosen: And what did the city of Jackson, Mississippi, do? Did they attempt to integrate the pools? Did they make any effort whatsoever in good faith? No, they did not. Indeed, the city of Jackson followed what the Fifth Circuit Court of Appeals called in 1963, and took judicial notice of, "an official, steel-hard, inflexible policy of official segregation." They closed the pools rather than integrate them. And so we have a new form of separation in Jackson, Mississippi: blacks and whites could not swim in the pools before *Clark versus Thompson;* blacks and whites do not swim in the pools after *Clark versus Thompson.*

Narrator: Rosen reminded the justices of their ruling in *Brown versus Board of Education.*

Rosen: When this Court said in *Brown* that the action of separating people created feelings of inferiority as to the status of black people in the community, that this action is no different. Black people know why the pools are closed! It's not to prevent white people from swimming with black people. Surely not the respondents would stand here and say that. It's to prevent black people from swimming with white people.

Narrator: Rosen dismissed the official reasons for closing the pools.

Rosen: The city maintains, and the court below found, that the, while the motivation for closing the pools was the integration order, that safety and economy would be affected if the pools were integrated. Now, there was no testimony as to any violence, there was no testimony as to economic loss. But it seems to me that all they are saying is that the manifestations of hatred and prejudice created by integration made it—in their minds—a problem to integrate the pools, to do what the Constitution requires.

Narrator: Justice Hugo Black's question about the city's motives led to a testy exchange.

Black: Have any of the cases we've had held anything from which it could be inferred that a state could not close up facilities that it did not want to operate, whatever their motive? (*Rosen:* I would say whatever the . . .) Whatever the motive? If it has power not to operate a certain kind of facilities. Have any of our cases held that the courts can compel them to open them up?

Rosen: The question of power, Your Honor, it seems to me, is that the state does not have the power to violate the Constitution.

Black: Of course not! Everybody knows that.

Narrator: Rosen moved to the difference between schools and pools. He cited the Court's nineteenth-century decision in *Plessy versus Ferguson*, upholding "separate but equal" facilities.

Rosen: The city argues that schools are essential and pools are not essential. It seems to me that that argument is the same argument that was made in *Plessy* between legal rights and political rights and social rights. It's the same kind of giving black people a little this, and a little that, doling out rights—any right that the white power structure determines is important for black people they will give them, and what they determine is not important they will not.

The essentialities argument would create probably the most horrendous problems and difficulties for black people. The black and a white child go to school together, and as they come home from school they go by a pool that's been closed because a federal court ordered it integrated. Does the black child have any doubt as to what his status in the community is? Does the black child have any doubt that he is inferior? And on the other hand, does the white child have any doubt that he is superior?

Narrator: William Kunstler followed Rosen. He claimed the Thirteenth Amendment did more than abolish slavery—it outlawed all vestiges of slavery.

Kunstler: If the amendment did abolish slavery, truly, and it did establish universal freedom, then our position is that it gives this Court the power, independent of any act of Congress, the power to abolish any incident of slavery. In other words, it authorized *all* branches of government—the executive, legislative, and judicial—to do everything, and I'll quote again from the *Civil Rights Cases,* "everything necessary and proper for abolishing all badges and incidents of slavery in the United States." And I guess the question, Your Honors, comes down to this: What is a badge and incident of slavery?

Narrator: Kunstler also cited the *Plessy* case, which dealt with segregated railroad coaches.

Kunstler: I think the general definition, that we would like to urge upon this Court, is that an incident of slavery is anything that makes a black man reasonably feel inferior to a white man. It's the opposite of what Mr. Justice Brown said in *Plessy.* He said, if the black race chooses to put that interpretation upon riding in segregated coaches, that's their look-out, not ours. But I submit that it is your look-out, our look-out, because this Court is really nothing more than an extension of the American personality, an extension of the American sociology.

And that is the heart of this case. That is why I think the Court must take a stand and say, yes, the closing of the pools violates the Thirteenth Amendment. That we as a Court have just as much responsibility as Congress, just as much responsibility as the executive, in wiping out these badges, because unless they are wiped out, no black person can feel secure in the United States, and every black person will begin eventually to build up a rage that is already sufficient enough, that will build up a rage inside that he knows that in white eyes he is an inferior person.

Narrator: William Goodman, Jr., argued for the Jackson officials. Chief Justice Burger.

Burger: Thank you, Mr. Kunstler. Mr. Goodman.

Goodman: Mr. Chief Justice, may it please the Court.

The district court in Jackson, Mississippi, declared that certain individual plaintiffs were entitled to the unsegregated use of all public recreational facilities. Now this included zoos, parks, auditoriums, libraries, golf courses—all public recreational facilities.

Now, what happened? From the way that case is cited in the briefs, I'm afraid you would draw the conclusion that the city appealed. The city accepted *Clark*. And from that day to this, every public facility in the city of Jackson, Mississippi, whether recreational or otherwise, which is open, is fully segregated [*sic*]. (Court: I think you mean . . .) Fully integrated; excuse me. I appreciate that, sir.

Narrator: Goodman turned a verbal error to his advantage.

Goodman: And while we are getting our words straight, if the Court please—and I am a little nervous—in fact, I'm scared—I would like to mention to the Court a few of the things that I think we can agree on between counsel, so that perhaps when some of my nervousness subsides, I can get down to the key things that we do not agree on. And we can agree on this: the decision in *Clark versus Thompson* was correct. It has never been questioned by the city of Jackson.

But if the Court please, here's where we get to the difference, and here's where we get to the heart of this lawsuit. The decision to close the swimming pools in Jackson, Mississippi, was not out of spite or hatred or any of the other insidious motives asserted in the briefs filed in this Court by the petitioners. While the decision to close the swimming pools came after the *Clark* case, it was not from a desire to crush black people or to reinstate badges of slavery, for goodness' sakes, or to discriminate against black people.

Narrator: Goodman claimed the trial record supported the city's actions.

Goodman: Here's what the record shows. The record shows, if the Court please, that the *Clark* decision brought new problems. Now here's the city council in the city of Jackson, Mississippi, in 1963. Right or wrong—and I contend in all deference it makes no difference—right or wrong, the city council of the city of Jackson honestly felt that the personal safety of some of its citizens and the maintenance of law and order could be endangered if swimming pools were integrated in that city at that time. Right or wrong. Right or wrong.

Narrator: Goodman was sidetracked by questions about which pools the city owned. Ten minutes later, he tried to get his argument back on track.

Goodman: Let me quickly, if the Court please, try to get on to the heart of the case. Now counsel, respectfully, they are searching to make this a constitutional case. And they throw out endless arguments in the hope that one of them will catch fire in the heart of this Court. They say, if the Court please, and they say this without authority, and they say it all the way through their briefs, that the city of Jackson, Mississippi, has the burden of proving that the closing of the pools was not for a discriminatory purpose.

What they're really saying is that whenever Jackson, Mississippi, is involved in a lawsuit—no matter what the proof is—this Court must assume that there was a discriminatory purpose. That's what they're saying. You see, the argument appeals to the past. The argument appeals to the popular criticism of the South in years gone by. I submit to the Court that the argument is an attempt to pin the badge of slavery that counsel discusses upon Jackson and cities of the Deep South, to ask you today—and I guess forever—to judicially assume, no matter what the proof is, that the motive of Jackson, Mississippi, was to discriminate.

Narrator: Goodman claimed that Jackson had moved beyond segregation.

Goodman: Now, I have no purpose before this honorable Court to attempt to justify any of the constitutional privileges that were denied blacks in the past, both in Jackson, Mississippi, and elsewhere throughout this country. But I say to the Court that Jackson, Mississippi, accepted the *Clark* decision. Jacksons's public facilities *are* integrated, totally. I think you're well aware that Jackson, Mississippi, has the most integrated school system in the United States. Jackson should not now or forever, unlike other litigants, have to prove itself not guilty; have to prove that it was not acting out of discrimination.

Narrator: Goodman shifted blame from city officials to violent "rednecks."

Goodman: The point that I'm trying to make, Your Honor, is that the decision was no more a reflection upon black people than it was a reflection upon a certain class of white people in Jackson, Mississippi. It was not a reflection on black people; it was unfortunately a reflection on the few rednecks, so to speak, among the white population of the city of Jackson.

Narrator: Goodman's argument on constitutional issues prompted a question from Chief Justice Burger.

Goodman: The Fifth Circuit put its finger on the answer in its opinion in this case, when it said the equal protection clause does not promise economic equality. If a badge of equality has been taken from anyone by the closing of a few swimming pools in Jackson, Mississippi, it has been taken from the poor people —the poor white people and the poor black people.

Burger: You would agree that that amendment promises equality of opportunity, though, doesn't it?

Goodman: Yes, sir. Yes, sir. It certainly does. But there is simply no way for a city, or a state, for that matter, to provide recreational opportunity of all sorts for all of its citizens, white or black. And when we step into the recreational area, if the Court please, this could be endless, because I could have my feelings hurt if a certain facility is not provided that's provided in some other city. And on and on.

Now, I submit in all deference that if the federal courts in this country get into the swimming pool business, I don't think it can stop with Jackson, Mississippi. Because, as I said a minute ago, these folks are not going to be satisfied with an order to reopen two, probably now, deteriorated pools in predominantly white neighborhoods. They're going to want other pools built; they're going to want them maintained; they're going to want tax monies levied if necessary; they're going to want them supervised; they're going to want people there; they're going to say there are not enough in the black neighborhoods, and on and on.

Narrator: A presidential commission warned that America was moving toward "two societies, one black, one white—separate and unequal." Paul Rosen appealed to that report in his closing argument.

Rosen: Our hope in this country is that if we can get white men to accept blacks as equal, that the threats that respondent talk about will soon leave us. This is what the Kerner Commission says; this is what this Court really said in *Brown*. We know that there are difficulties, but the solution is not repression; the solution is not closing facilities; the solution is to abide by the Constitution and to say once and for all that black men are free men, having the same rights that white men have.

Narrator: The Court decided the case on June 14th, 1971. Each year, that day honors the American flag. But the Confederate flag still waved above the capitol in Jackson. The justices ruled by one vote that Jackson could keep its swimming pools closed during the hot Mississippi summer.

Justice Hugo Black—from Mississippi's neighbor state, Alabama—wrote the majority opinion. He denied the city's action violated the Fourteenth Amendment, because whites and blacks were both denied access to the closed pools. Black admitted there was "some evidence" the pools were closed for racial reasons. But he found "substantial evidence" that safety and economic reasons were more important. The basic issue for Black was that Jackson had no "duty" to operate swimming pools. The city's motives—even "bad motives" based on racial antagonism—were irrelevant to Black. Jackson could close its pools, he wrote, "for any reason, sound or unsound."

The dissenting justices disagreed that racial motives were irrelevant. Justice William Douglas compared Mississippi to South Africa. He wrote that closing the pools smacked of "apartheid" in America. Justice Byron White, who enforced civil rights laws in the Kennedy administration, answered Justice Black in a lengthy opinion. He quoted Mayor Thompson's boast that "neither agitators nor President Kennedy will change the determination of Jackson to retain segregation." White claimed that city officials were "motivated by nothing but racial considerations." Closing the pools expressed, he said, an "official view that Negroes are so inferior that they are unfit" to swim with whites. These racial motives violated the Constitution's guarantee of "equal protection" to citizens of all races.

Mayor Thompson left office in 1969, boasting that "we have no trouble between the races" in Jackson. But the city's legal victory, two years later, angered the black community. Black voters began to register and challenge discriminatory election laws. When the Court ruled in 1971, the city council was all white. Ten years later, the first black joined the council. By 1992, three of seven members—and the council president—were black. Political power made a difference in Jackson. The five pools the city closed never reopened—they were crumbling monuments to segregation. But the city—half black, half white—has nine new public pools. Recreation has triumphed in Jackson over segregation.

EDITED SUPREME COURT OPINIONS
Palmer v. Thompson

MR. JUSTICE BLACK delivered the opinion of the Court.

In 1962 the city of Jackson, Mississippi, was maintaining five public parks along with swimming pools, golf links, and other facilities for use by the public on a racially segregated basis. Four of the swimming pools were used by whites only and one by Negroes only. Plaintiffs brought an action in the United States District Court seeking a declaratory judgment that this state-enforced segregation of the races was a violation of the Thirteenth and Fourteenth Amendments, and asking an injunction to forbid such practices. After hearings the District Court entered a judgment declaring that enforced segregation denied equal protection of the laws. . . .

. . . The city proceeded to desegregate its public parks, auditoriums, golf courses, and the city zoo. However, the city council decided not to try to operate the public swimming pools on a desegregated basis. Acting in its legislative capacity, the council surrendered its lease on one pool and closed four which the city owned. A number of Negro citizens of Jackson then filed this suit to force the city to reopen the pools and operate them on a desegregated basis. The District Court found that the closing was justified to preserve peace and order and because the pools could not be operated economically on an integrated basis. It held the city's action did not deny black citizens equal protection of the laws. . . .

Petitioners rely chiefly on the first section of the Fourteenth Amendment which forbids any State to "deny to any person within its jurisdiction the equal protection of the laws." There can be no doubt that a major purpose of this amendment was to safeguard Negroes against discriminatory state laws—state laws that fail to give Negroes protection equal to that afforded white people. . . . Here there has unquestionably been "state action" because the official local government legislature, the city council, has closed the public swimming pools of Jackson. The question, however, is whether this closing of the pools is state action that denies "the equal protection of the laws" to Negroes. It should be noted first that neither the Fourteenth Amendment nor any Act of Congress purports to impose an affirmative duty on a State to begin to operate or to continue to operate swimming pools. Furthermore, this is not a case where whites are permitted to use public facilities while blacks are denied access. It is not a case where a city is maintaining different sets of facilities for blacks and whites and forcing the races to remain separate in recreational or educational activities. . . .

Unless, therefore, as petitioners urge, certain past cases require us to hold that closing the pools to all denied equal protection to Negroes, we must agree with the courts below and affirm. . . .

Petitioners have also argued that respondents' action violates the equal protection clause because the decision to close the pools was motivated by a desire to avoid integration of the races. But no case in this Court has held that a legislative act may violate equal protection solely because of the motivations of the men who voted for it. . . .

First, it is extremely difficult for a court to ascertain the motivation, or collection of different motivations, that lie behind a legislative enactment. . . . Here, for example, petitioners have argued that the Jackson pools were closed because of ideological opposition to racial integration in swimming pools. Some evidence in the record appears to support this argument. On the other hand the courts below found that the pools were closed because the city council felt they could not be operated safely and economically on an integrated basis. There is substantial evidence in the record to support this conclusion. It is difficult or impossible for any court to determine the "sole" or "dominant" motivation behind the choices of a group of legislators. Furthermore, there is an element of futility in a judicial attempt to invalidate a law because of the bad motives of its supporters. If the law is struck down for this reason, rather than because of its facial content or effect, it would presumably be valid as soon as the legislature or relevant governing body repassed it for different reasons. . . .

Petitioners have argued strenuously that a city's possible motivations to ensure safety and save money cannot validate an otherwise impermissible state action. This proposition is, of course, true. Citizens may not be compelled to forgo their constitutional rights because officials fear public hostility or desire to save money. . . . But the issue here is whether black citizens in Jackson *are* being denied their constitutional rights when the city has closed the public pools to black and white alike. Nothing in the history or the language of the Fourteenth Amendment nor in any of our prior cases persuades us that the closing of the Jackson swimming pools to all its citizens constitutes a denial of "the equal protection of the laws."

Finally, some faint and unpersuasive argument has been made by petitioners that the closing of the pools violated the Thirteenth Amendment which freed the Negroes from slavery. . . . The denial of the right of Negroes to swim in pools with white people is said to be a "badge or incident" of slavery. Consequently, the argument seems to run, this Court should declare that the city's closing of the pools to keep the two races from swimming together violates the Thirteenth Amendment. To reach that result from the Thirteenth Amendment would severely stretch its short simple words and do violence to its history. . . .

MR. JUSTICE DOUGLAS, dissenting. . . .

May a State in order to avoid integration of the races abolish all of its public schools? That would dedicate the State to backwardness, ignorance, and existence in a new Dark Age. Yet is there anything in the Constitution that says that a State must have a public school system? Could a federal court enjoin the dismantling of a public school system? Could a federal court order a city to levy the taxes necessary to construct a public school system? Such supervision over municipal affairs by federal courts would be a vast undertaking, conceivably encompassing schools, parks, playgrounds, civic auditoriums, tennis courts, athletic fields, as well as swimming pools. . . .

In determining what municipal services may not be abolished the Court of Appeals drew the line between "an essential public function" and other public functions. Whether state constitutions draw that line is not our concern. Certainly there are no federal constitutional provisions which make that distinction.

Closing of the pools probably works a greater hardship on the poor than on the rich; and it may work greater hardship on poor Negroes than on poor whites, a matter on which we have no light. Closing of the pools was at least in part racially motivated. And, as stated by the dissenters in the Court of Appeals:

"The closing of the City's pools has done more than deprive a few thousand Negroes of the pleasures of swimming. It has taught Jackson's Negroes a lesson: In Jackson the price of protest is high. Negroes there now know that they risk losing even segregated public facilities if they dare to protest segregation. Negroes will now think twice before protesting segregated public parks, segregated public libraries, or other segregated facilities. They must first decide whether they wish to risk living without the facility altogether, and at the same time engendering further animosity from a white community which has lost its public facilities also through the Negroes' attempts to desegregate these facilities.

"The long-range effects are manifold and far-reaching. If the City's pools may be eliminated from the public domain, parks, athletic activities, and libraries also may be closed. No one can say how many other cities may also close their pools or other public facilities. The City's action tends to separate the races, encourage private discrimination, and raise substantial obstacles for Negroes asserting the rights of national citizenship created by the Wartime Amendments." 419 F. 2d 1222, 1236. . . .

I conclude that though a State may discontinue any of its municipal services —such as schools, parks, pools, athletic fields, and the like—it may not do so for the purpose of perpetuating or installing *apartheid* or because it finds life in a multi-racial community difficult or unpleasant. If that is its reason, then abolition of a designated public service becomes a device for perpetuating a segregated way of life. That a State may not do. . . .

MR. JUSTICE WHITE, with whom MR. JUSTICE BRENNAN and MR. JUSTICE MARSHALL join, dissenting.

I agree with the majority that the central purpose of the Fourteenth Amendment is to protect Negroes from invidious discrimination. Consistent with this view, I had thought official policies forbidding or discouraging joint use of public facilities by Negroes and whites were at war with the equal protection clause. Our cases make it unquestionably clear, as all of us agree, that a city or State may not enforce such a policy by maintaining officially separate facilities for the two races. It is also my view, but apparently not that of the majority, that a State may not have an official stance against desegregating public facilities and implement it by closing those facilities in response to a desegregation order. . . .

I am quite unpersuaded by the majority's assertion that it is impermissible to impeach the otherwise valid act of closing municipal swimming pools by resort to evidence of invidious purpose or motive. . . .

There is no dispute that the closing of the pools constituted state action. Similarly, there can be no disagreement that the desegregation ruling in *Clark* v. *Thompson* was the event that precipitated the city's decision to cease furnishing public swimming facilities to its citizens. . . .

The officials' sworn affidavits, accepted by the courts below, stated that loss of revenue and danger to the citizens would obviously result from operating the pools on an integrated basis. Desegregation, and desegregation alone, was the catalyst that would produce these undesirable consequences. Implicit in this official judgment were assumptions that the citizens of Jackson were of such a mind that they would no longer pay the ten- or twenty-cent fee imposed by the city if their swimming and wading had to be done with their neighbors of another race, that some citizens would direct violence against their neighbors for using pools previously closed to them, and that the anticipated violence would not be controllable by the authorities. Stated more simply, although the city officials knew what the Constitution required after *Clark* v. *Thompson* became final, their judgment was that compliance with that mandate, at least with respect to swimming pools, would be intolerable to Jackson's citizens. . . .

With all due respect, I am quite unable to agree with the majority's assertion . . . that there is "substantial evidence in the record" to support the conclusion of the lower courts that the pools could not be operated safely and economically on an integrated basis. Officials may take effective action to control violence or to prevent it when it is reasonably imminent. But the anticipation of violence in this case rested only on unsupported assertion, to which the *permanent* closing of swimming pools was a wholly unjustified response.

. . . In my view, the Fourteenth Amendment does not permit any official act—whether in the form of open refusal to desegregate facilities that continue to operate, decisions to delay complete desegregation, or closure of facilities—to be predicated on so weak a reed. Public officials sworn to uphold the Constitution may not avoid a constitutional duty by bowing to the hypothetical effects of private racial prejudice that they assume to be both widely and deeply held. Surely the promise of the Fourteenth Amendment demands more than nihilistic surrender. . . .

. . . Closing the pools without a colorable nondiscriminatory reason was every bit as much an official endorsement of the notion that Negroes are not equal to whites. . . . The city has only opposition to desegregation to offer as a justification for closing the pools, and this opposition operates both to demean the Negroes of Jackson and to deter them from exercising their constitutional and statutory rights. The record is clear that these public facilities had been maintained and would have been maintained but for one event: a court order to open them to all citizens without regard to race. I would reverse the judgment of the Court of Appeals and remand the cause for further proceedings. . . .

BIBLIOGRAPHY

CAKE, HELEN M. "Palmer v. Thompson: Everybody out of the
Pool." *Hastings Law Journal* 23, no. 1 (November 1971): 889.

MCADAM, DOUG. *Freedom Summer.* Oxford University Press, 1988.

MOODY, ANNE. *Coming of Age in Mississippi.* Dell, 1968.

"Palmer v. Thompson . . ." *Mississippi Law Journal* 43 (1972): 225.

SILVER, JAMES W. *Mississippi: The Closed Society.* Harcourt, Brace
and World, 1964.

"Swimming Pools: Black and White." *America*, June 26, 1971,
p. 645.

Regents of the University of California v. Bakke

438 U.S. 265 (1978)

$\mathbf{A}$llen Bakke was an aerospace engineer when he applied to the University of California medical school at Davis, which rejected him twice, in 1973 and 1974. After learning that the school reserved sixteen of one hundred places for "disadvantaged" members of racial minorities, Bakke sued the university, claiming that the school's racial quota violated his right to equal protection of the laws under the Fourteenth Amendment. In 1978, a divided Supreme Court declared the school's use of quotas unlawful and ordered Bakke's admission. But it also ruled that the Constitution allows "race-conscious" admissions programs designed to benefit minorities. "It is because of a legacy of unequal treatment," Justice Thurgood Marshall wrote, "that we now must permit the institutions of this society to give consideration to race in making decisions about who will hold the positions of influence, affluence, and prestige in America."

TRANSCRIPT OF EDITED AND NARRATED ARGUMENTS IN
Regents of the University of California v. *Bakke*, 438 U.S. 265 (1978)

Counsel for petitioner: Professor Archibald Cox, Harvard Law School, Cambridge, Massachusetts
Counsel for respondent: Reynold Colvin, San Francisco, California
Counsel for the United States as *amicus curiae:* Solicitor General Wade McCree, Washington, D.C.

Narrator: It's October 12th, 1977. Chief Justice Warren Burger has called a case that raises important issues of racial equality in American society. On trial today are programs their defenders call affirmative action and critics label as reverse discrimination.

Allen Bakke sits in the packed courtroom. He was born in Minnesota. His ancestors came from Norway. In 1962, he earned an engineering degree and then served four years as a Marine Corps officer, including seven months in Vietnam.

But he is more interested in medicine than space. In 1972, he applied to more than a dozen medical schools. Most told him he was too old at the age of 32. But he *almost* won admission to the University of California medical school at Davis. He was one of twenty-four hundred applicants. After his rejection, Bakke learned that sixteen of the school's one hundred places were reserved for "disadvantaged" members of racial minorities. The school rejected Bakke again in 1974. He sued the university, claiming that the school's racial quota violated his right to equal protection of the laws under the U.S. Constitution's Fourteenth Amendment. The California Supreme Court upheld Bakke's claim and ordered his admission to the Davis medical school.

Archibald Cox will argue the university's appeal. A noted Harvard Law School professor and former U.S. solicitor general, Cox became famous as the Watergate prosecutor fired by President Richard Nixon. Cox has argued dozens of cases before the Supreme Court. He is comfortable and confident at the lawyers' podium.

Chief Justice Burger: Mr. Cox, you may proceed whenever you're ready.

Cox: Mr. Chief Justice, may it please the Court.

This case, here on certiorari to the supreme court of California, presents a single vital question: whether a state university, which is forced by limited resources to select a relatively small number of students from a much larger number of well-qualified applicants, is free, voluntarily, to take into account the fact that a qualified applicant is black, Chicano, Asian, or Native American, in order to increase the number of qualified members of those minority groups trained for the educated professions and participating in them, professions from which minorities were long excluded because of generations of pervasive racial discrimination.

The answer which the Court gives will determine, perhaps for decades, whether members of those minorities are to have the kind of meaningful access to higher education in the professions which the universities have accorded them in recent years or are to be reduced to the trivial numbers which they were prior to the adoption of minority admissions programs.

Narrator: Racial minorities made up less than 2 percent of American medical students when the Davis campus opened in 1968. Cox explained the university's effort to increase those numbers.

Cox: There are three facts, realities, which dominated the situation that the medical school at Davis had before it, and which I think must control the decision of this Court. The first is that the number of qualified applicants for the nation's professional schools is vastly greater than the number of places available. That is a fact, and an inescapable fact.

The second fact, which there is no need for me to elaborate, but it is a fact: For generations, racial discrimination in the United States, much of it stimulated by unconstitutional state action, isolated certain minorities, condemned them to inferior education, and shut them out of the most important and satisfying aspects of American life, including higher education and the professions.

And then there is one third fact: There *is* no racially blind method of selection which will enroll today more than a trickle of minority students in the nation's colleges and professions. These are the realities which the University of California at Davis Medical School faced in 1968 and which, I say, I think the Court must face when it comes to its decision.

Narrator: Cox defended the school's minority admissions program against critics of racial quotas. Justice Potter Stewart asked a skeptical question.

Cox: I want to emphasize that the designation of sixteen places was not a quota, at least as I would use that word. Certainly it was not a quota in the older sense of an arbitrary limit put on the number of members of an unpopular group who would be admitted to an institution which was looking down its nose at them.

Stewart: It did put a limit on the number of white people, didn't it?

Cox: I think that it limited the number of nonminority, and therefore essentially white, yes. But there are two things to be said about that: one is that this was not pointing the finger at a group which had been marked as inferior in any sense; and it was undifferentiated, it operated against a wide variety of people. So I think it was not stigmatizing in the sense that the old quota against Jews was stigmatizing, in any way.

Narrator: Justice John Paul Stevens continued.

Stevens: The question is not whether the sixteen is a quota; the question is whether the eighty-four is a quota. And what is your answer to that?

Cox: I would say that neither is properly defined as a quota.

Stevens: And then, why not?

Cox: Because, in the first place—because of my understanding of the meaning of "quota." And I think the decisive things are the facts, and the operative facts are: This is not something imposed from outside, as the quotas are in employment, or the targets are in employment sometimes today. It was not a limit on the number of minority students. Other minority students were in fact accepted through the regular admissions program. It was not a guarantee of a minimum number of minority students, because all of them had to be, and the testimony is that all of them were, fully qualified.

Narrator: While Archibald Cox stressed the university's social goals, Justice Harry Blackmun tried to raise another question.

Cox: The decision of the university was that there are social purposes, purposes aimed in the end at eliminating racial injustice in this country and in bringing equality of opportunity; there will be purposes served by including minority students. Well, how important do you think it is? (Blackmun: Mr. Cox, is it the same . . .) We think it's this important. (Blackmun: Mr. Cox!) That's the significance of the number. (Blackmun: *Mr. Cox!*) And that's about the only significance.

Blackmun: Mr. Cox, is it the same thing as an athletic scholarship? (Cox: Well, I . . .) So many places reserved for athletic scholarships?

Cox: In the sense—I don't like to liken it to that in terms of its importance, but I think that there are a number of places that may be set aside for an institution's different aims, and the aim of some institutions does seem to be to have athletic prowess. So that in that sense this is a choice made to promote the school's, the faculty's, choice of educational, of social, and professional objectives. So I think there is a parallel, yes.

Blackmun: It's the aim of most institutions, isn't it, not just some?

Cox: Yes. But they have—of athletic?

Blackmun: Yes.

Cox: Well, I come from Harvard, sir. *(laughter)* I don't know whether it's our aim, but we don't do very well. *(laughter)*

Narrator: This inside joke between two Harvard Law graduates showed Cox's skill at deflecting hard questions. Once the laughter subsided, Justice William Rehnquist pressed the quota issue. What if the school raised the minority quota to *fifty* places in one hundred? Would this be *invidious* discrimination, designed to harm white applicants?

Cox: I would say that as the number goes up, the danger of invidiousness, or the danger that this is being done not for social purposes but to favor one group as against another group, the risk, if you will, of a finding of an invidious purpose to discriminate against is greater. And therefore, I think it's a harder case. But I would have to put the particular school in the context of all schools.

I'll be quite frank to say that I think one of the things which causes us all concern about these programs is the danger that they will give rise to some notion of group entitlement to numbers, regardless either of the ability of the individual or of—which is not always related to inability—ability in the narrow sense—or of their potential contribution to society. And I think that if the program were to begin to slide over in that direction, I would, first, as a faculty member, criticize and oppose it; as a constitutional lawyer, the farther it went, the more doubts I would have.

Narrator: Archibald Cox mentioned Allen Bakke only once.

Cox: While it is true that Mr. Bakke and some others, on the conventional standards for admission, would be ranked above the minority applicant, I want to emphasize that, in my judgment and I think in fact, that does not justify saying that the generally better-qualified people were excluded to make room for generally less qualified people.

It's quite clear that for some of the things that a medical school wishes to accomplish, and this medical school wished to accomplish, that the minority applicant may have qualities that are superior to those of his classmate who is not minority. He certainly will be more effective in bringing it home to the young Chicano that he too may become a doctor.

Narrator: Solicitor General Wade McCree spoke next. The second African-American in this post—Justice Thurgood Marshall was the first—McCree argued as *amicus curiae*—a friend of the Court.

McCree: Mr. Chief Justice, may it please the Court.

The interest of the United States of America as *amicus curiae* stems from the fact that the Congress and the executive branch have adopted many minority-sensitive programs that take race or minority status into account in order to achieve the goal of equal opportunity. The United States has also concluded that voluntary programs to increase the participation of minorities in activities throughout our society, activities previously closed to them, should be encouraged and supported.

This Court does not require a recital of the extent and duration of racial discrimination in America from the time it was enshrined in our very Constitution: in the three-fifths compromise, in the fugitive slave provision, and in the provision preventing the importation of such persons prior to 1808. And it continues until the present day, as the overburdened dockets of the lower federal courts, and indeed of this Court, will indicate, where there has been noncompliance with the decisions of this Court that have rediscovered and are still rediscovering the true genius of the Fourteenth Amendment.

Indeed, many children born in 1954, when *Brown* was decided, are today, twenty-three years later, the very persons knocking on the doors of professional schools, seeking admission, about the country. They are persons who, in many instances, have been denied the fulfillment of the promise of that decision, because of resistance to this Court's decision that was such a landmark when it was handed down.

Narrator: Wade McCree made an eloquent recital of America's troubled racial history. He reflected political divisions on this controversial issue by supporting race-conscious affirmative action programs, but he opposed strict racial quotas.

Now it was Allen Bakke's turn. His lawyer, Reynold Colvin, made his first argument before the Supreme Court. Unlike Archibald Cox, Colvin talked only of Allen Bakke and his rights.

Chief Justice Burger: Mr. Colvin.

Colvin: Mr. Chief Justice, and members of the Court.

It seems to me that the first thing that I ought to say to this honorable Court is that I am Allen Bakke's lawyer and Allen Bakke is my client. And I do not say that in any formal or perfunctory way. I say that because this is a lawsuit. It was a lawsuit brought by Allen Bakke up at Woodland in Yolo County, California, in which Allen Bakke, from the very beginning of this lawsuit, in the first paper we ever filed, stated the case. And he stated the case in terms of his individual right.

He stated the case in terms of the fact that he had twice applied for admission to the medical school at Davis and twice he had been refused, both in the years 1973 and in the year 1974. And he stated in that complaint what now, some three-and-a-half years later, proves to be the very heart of the thing that we're talking about at this juncture. He stated that he was excluded from that school because that school had adopted a racial quota which deprived him of the opportunity for admission into the school. And that's where the case started. It started with a suit against the university.

Narrator: Responding to Justice Lewis Powell, Colvin argued that Cox had evaded the issue of racial quotas.

Cox: Let me make a distinction on this quota question, if I may, Your Honor. There are many points in the university's brief where somehow, in order to take the sting out of the word "quota," the word "goal" is used. This is not a quota, they say, but it is a goal. We find that to be a real misuse of language.

Normally, if we have a goal, if we have a goal, if we are going to get a number of people in, we select a standard, and then above that standard we admit people in order to, in order to qualify. Precisely the opposite is true here. In this case, we have to follow what the factual situation is. Here, we have a quota where the number is first chosen, and then the number is filled regardless of the standard.

Narrator: Colvin claimed that Allen Bakke was *more* qualified than minority students admitted by the medical school.

Colvin: Look at the record in the case. In 1973, the average—not the range, but the average—of the people in the special admissions group was in the 35th percentile in science and in the 46th percentile in verbal. In 1974, the percentile in science—and this is an average and not a range—was 37, and in verbal 34. Allen Bakke, Allen Bakke took the test only once and his record is there. You'll find it on page 13 of our brief. He scored in the 97th percentile in science and in the 96th percentile in verbal.

The ultimate fact in this case, no matter how you turn it, is that Mr. Bakke was deprived of an opportunity to attend the school by reason of his race.

Narrator: Politely but firmly, Justice Powell asked Colvin to move on to the Constitution.

Powell: The university doesn't deny or dispute the basic facts. They are perfectly clear. We are here—at least I am here—primarily to hear a constitutional argument. You have devoted twenty minutes to laboring the facts, if I may say so. I would like help, I really would, on the constitutional issues.

Colvin: We have the deepest difficulty in dealing with this problem of quota, and many, many questions arise. For example, there is a question of numbers. What is the appropriate quota? What is the appropriate quota for a medical school? Sixteen, eight, thirty-two, sixty-four, one hundred? On what basis, on what basis is that quota determined?

Narrator: Justice William Rehnquist pressed the constitutional issue.

White: Well, what's your response to the assertion of the university that it was entitled to have a special program and take race into account, and that under the Fourteenth Amendment there was no barrier to its doing that, because of the interests that were involved? Now, what's your response to that?

Colvin: Our response to that is fundamentally, is fundamentally that race is an improper classification in this situation.

Narrator: Justice Thurgood Marshall asked whether Davis could reserve even *one* place for minorities. Colvin's negative answer provoked Marshall.

Marshall: So numbers are just unimportant?

Colvin: The numbers are unimportant. It is the principle of keeping a man out because of his race that is important.

Marshall: You're arguing about keeping somebody out, and the other side is arguing about getting somebody in.

Colvin: That's right.

Marshall: So it depends on which way you look at it, doesn't it?

Colvin: It depends on which way you look at it. The problem . . . (Marshall: It *does?*) The problem . . . (Marshall: It *does?*) If I may finish . . . (Marshall: It *does?*) The problem, the problem is . . .

Marshall: You're talking about your client's rights; don't these underprivileged people have some rights?

Colvin: They certainly have the rights to compete . . .

Marshall: To eat cake.

Narrator: Chief Justice Burger ended the heated argument.

Burger: Thank you, gentlemen; the case is submitted.

Narrator: It took the justices more than eight months to decide the *Bakke* case on June 28th, 1978. During their debate, two factions emerged on the Court. Four justices wanted to uphold the medical school's minority admissions program, including its quota plan. Another four wanted to strike down the plan and order Bakke's admission.

Debate ended when Justice Lewis Powell framed a compromise and joined two separate five-to-four majorities. Powell had personal experience with education and racial issues as former president of the Richmond, Virginia, school board. He joined one majority in holding that Congress had outlawed racial quotas in schools receiving federal funds. These justices ordered Davis medical school to admit Bakke.

They also said that schools could not consider race or ethnicity at all in choosing students. Powell disagreed. He felt that giving a "plus" to minority applicants would allow schools to achieve a better "mix" of students. The second majority ruled that the Constitution allowed "race-conscious" admissions programs designed to benefit minorities.

But the Court's compromise did not end debate on programs to overcome discrimination in education and employment. Since 1978, the Court has upheld some quota plans and struck down others, generally requiring strong evidence of past discrimination. In 1989, the Court ruled six-to-three that Richmond, Virginia, could not set aside 30 percent of public construction funds for minority businesses. They previously received less than one percent of these funds. The majority held that evidence only of past "societal discrimination" was not enough. Justice Marshall accused the majority of taking "a giant step backward" in American race relations.

And Allen Bakke? He graduated from the Davis medical school in 1982 and practices in Rochester, Minnesota. And by 1988, fifteen years after Bakke applied to Davis, the number of black doctors had increased from 2 percent to 3 percent.

EDITED SUPREME COURT OPINIONS
Regents of the University of California v. Bakke

MR. JUSTICE POWELL announced the judgment of the Court.

This case presents a challenge to the special admissions program of the petitioner, the Medical School of the University of California at Davis, which is designed to assure the admission of a specified number of students from certain minority groups. . . .

The Medical School of the University of California at Davis opened in 1968 with an entering class of fifty students. In 1971, the size of the entering class was increased to one hundred students, a level at which it remains. No admissions program for disadvantaged or minority students existed when the school opened, and the first class contained three Asians but no blacks, no Mexican-Americans, and no American Indians. Over the next two years, the faculty devised a special admissions program to increase the representation of "disadvantaged" students in each Medical School class. The special program consisted of a separate admissions system operating in coordination with the regular admissions process. . . .

Allan Bakke is a white male who applied to the Davis Medical School in both 1973 and 1974. In both years Bakke's application was considered under the general admissions program, and he received an interview. . . . In both years, applicants were admitted under the special program with grade point averages, MCAT scores, and benchmark scores significantly lower than Bakke's.

After the second rejection, Bakke filed the instant suit in the Superior Court of California. He sought mandatory, injunctive, and declaratory relief compelling his admission to the Medical School. He alleged that the Medical School's special admissions program operated to exclude him from the school on the basis of his race, in violation of his rights under the equal protection clause of the Fourteenth Amendment . . .

The guarantees of the Fourteenth Amendment extend to all persons. Its language is explicit: "No State shall . . . deny to any person within its jurisdiction the equal protection of the laws." . . . The guarantee of equal protection cannot mean one thing when applied to one individual and something else when applied to a person of another color. If both are not accorded the same protection, then it is not equal. . . . Racial and ethnic distinctions of any sort are inherently suspect and thus call for the most exacting judicial examination. . . .

We have held that in "order to justify the use of a suspect classification, a State must show that its purpose or interest is both constitutionally permissible and substantial, and that its use of the classification is 'necessary . . . to the accomplishment' of its purpose or the safeguarding of its interest." *In re Griffiths,* 413 U. S. 717, 721-722 (1973) . . . The special admissions program purports to serve the purposes of: (i) "reducing the historic deficit of traditionally disfavored minorities in medical schools and in the medical profession," Brief for Petitioner 32; (ii) countering the effects of societal discrimination; (iii) increasing the number of physicians who will practice in communities currently underserved; and (iv) obtaining the educational benefits that flow from an ethnically diverse student body. It is necessary to decide which, if any, of these purposes is substantial enough to support the use of a suspect classification.

If petitioner's purpose is to assure within its student body some specified percentage of a particular group merely because of its race or ethnic origin, such a preferential purpose must be rejected not as insubstantial but as facially invalid. Preferring members of any one group for no reason other than race or ethnic origin is discrimination for its own sake. This the Constitution forbids. . . .

We have never approved a classification that aids persons perceived as members of relatively victimized groups at the expense of other innocent individuals in the absence of judicial, legislative, or administrative findings of constitutional or statutory violations. . . .

Hence, the purpose of helping certain groups whom the faculty of the Davis Medical School perceived as victims of "societal discrimination" does not justify a classification that imposes disadvantages upon persons like respondent, who bear no responsibility for whatever harm the beneficiaries of the special admissions program are thought to have suffered. To hold otherwise would be to convert a remedy heretofore reserved for violations of legal rights into a privilege that all institutions throughout the Nation could grant at their pleasure to whatever groups are perceived as victims of societal discrimination. That is a step we have never approved. . . .

Physicians serve a heterogeneous population. An otherwise qualified medical student with a particular background—whether it be ethnic, geographic, culturally advantaged or disadvantaged—may bring to a professional school of medicine experiences, outlooks, and ideas that enrich the training of its student body and better equip its graduates to render with understanding their vital service to humanity.

Ethnic diversity, however, is only one element in a range of factors a university properly may consider in attaining the goal of a heterogeneous student body. Although a university must have wide discretion in making the sensitive judgments as to who should be admitted, constitutional limitations protecting individual rights may not be disregarded. . . .

It may be assumed that the reservation of a specified number of seats in each class for individuals from the preferred ethnic groups would contribute to the attainment of considerable ethnic diversity in the student body. But petitioner's argument that this is the only effective means of serving the interest of diversity is seriously flawed. In a most fundamental sense the argument misconceives the nature of the state interest that would justify consideration of race or ethnic background. It is not an interest in simple ethnic diversity, in which a specified percentage of the student body is in effect guaranteed to be members of selected ethnic groups, with the remaining percentage an undifferentiated aggregation of students. The diversity that furthers a compelling state interest encompasses a far broader array of qualifications and characteristics of which racial or ethnic origin is but a single though important element. Petitioner's special admissions program, focused *solely* on ethnic diversity, would hinder rather than further attainment of genuine diversity. . . .

The experience of other university admissions programs, which take race into account in achieving the educational diversity valued by the First Amendment, demonstrates that the assignment of a fixed number of places to a minority group is not a necessary means toward that end. . . .

In summary, it is evident that the Davis special admissions program involves the use of an explicit racial classification never before countenanced by this Court. It tells applicants who are not Negro, Asian, or Chicano that they are totally excluded from a specific percentage of the seats in an entering class. No matter how strong their qualifications, quantitative and extracurricular, including their own potential for contribution to educational diversity, they are never afforded the chance to compete with applicants from the preferred groups for the special admissions seats. At the same time, the preferred applicants have the opportunity to compete for every seat in the class.

The fatal flaw in petitioner's preferential program is its disregard of individual rights as guaranteed by the Fourteenth Amendment. . . . Such rights are not absolute. But when a State's distribution of benefits or imposition of burdens hinges on ancestry or the color of a person's skin, that individual is entitled to a demonstration that the challenged classification is necessary to promote a substantial state interest. Petitioner has failed to carry this burden. For this reason, that portion of the California court's judgment holding petitioner's special admissions program invalid under the Fourteenth Amendment must be affirmed. . . .

With respect to respondent's entitlement to an injunction directing his admission to the Medical School, petitioner has conceded that it could not carry its burden of proving that, but for the existence of its unlawful special admissions program, respondent still would not have been admitted. Hence, respondent is entitled to the injunction, and that portion of the judgment must be affirmed. . . .

Opinion of MR. JUSTICE BRENNAN, MR. JUSTICE WHITE, MR. JUSTICE MAR-
SHALL, and MR. JUSTICE BLACKMUN, concurring in the judgment in part and
dissenting in part.

The Court today, in reversing in part the judgment of the Supreme Court of
California, affirms the constitutional power of Federal and State Governments to
act affirmatively to achieve equal opportunity for all. The difficulty of the issue
presented—whether government may use race-conscious programs to redress the
continuing effects of past discrimination—and the mature consideration which
each of our Brethren has brought to it have resulted in many opinions, no single
one speaking for the Court. But this should not and must not mask the central
meaning of today's opinions: Government may take race into account when it acts
not to demean or insult any racial group, but to remedy disadvantages cast on
minorities by past racial prejudice, at least when appropriate findings have been
made by judicial, legislative, or administrative bodies with competence to act in
this area. . . .

Our Nation was founded on the principle that "all Men are created
equal." . . . The assertion of human equality is closely associated with the proposition that differences in color or creed, birth or status, are neither significant nor
relevant to the way in which persons should be treated. Nonetheless, the position
that such factors must be "constitutionally an irrelevance," . . . has never
been adopted by this Court as the proper meaning of the equal protection
clause. Indeed, we have expressly rejected this proposition on a number of
occasions. . . .

We conclude, therefore, that racial classifications are not *per se* invalid under
the Fourteenth Amendment. Accordingly, we turn to the problem of articulating what our role should be in reviewing state action that expressly classifies by
race. . . .

[B]ecause of the significant risk that racial classifications established for osten-
sibly benign purposes can be misused, causing effects not unlike those created by
invidious classifications, it is inappropriate to inquire only whether there is any
conceivable basis that might sustain such a classification. Instead, to justify
such a classification an important and articulated purpose for its use must be
shown. . . .

Davis' articulated purpose of remedying the effects of past societal discrimination is, under our cases, sufficiently important to justify the use of race-conscious admissions programs where there is a sound basis for concluding that
minority underrepresentation is substantial and chronic, and that the handi-
cap of past discrimination is impeding access of minorities to the Medical
School. . . .

Certainly, on the basis of the undisputed factual submissions before this
Court, Davis had a sound basis for believing that the problem of underrepresenta-

tion of minorities was substantial and chronic and that the problem was attributable to handicaps imposed on minority applicants by past and present racial discrimination. Until at least 1973, the practice of medicine in this country was, in fact, if not in law, largely the prerogative of whites. In 1950, for example, while Negroes constituted 10% of the total population, Negro physicians constituted only 2.2% of the total number of physicians. The overwhelming majority of these, moreover, were educated in two predominantly Negro medical schools, Howard and Meharry. By 1970, the gap between the proportion of Negroes in medicine and their proportion in the population had widened: The number of Negroes employed in medicine remained frozen at 2.2% while the Negro population had increased to 11.1%. The number of Negro admittees to predominantly white medical schools, moreover, had declined in absolute numbers during the years 1955 to 1964. . . .

Moreover, Davis had very good reason to believe that the national pattern of underrepresentation of minorities in medicine would be perpetuated if it retained a single admissions standard. For example, the entering classes in 1968 and 1969, the years in which such a standard was used, included only one Chicano and two Negroes out of the 50 admittees for each year. Nor is there any relief from this pattern of underrepresentation in the statistics for the regular admissions program in later years.

Davis clearly could conclude that the serious and persistent underrepresentation of minorities in medicine depicted by these statistics is the result of handicaps under which minority applicants labor as a consequence of a background of deliberate, purposeful discrimination against minorities in education and in society generally, as well as in the medical profession. From the inception of our national life, Negroes have been subjected to unique legal disabilities impairing access to equal educational opportunity. . . .

The second prong of our test—whether the Davis program stigmatizes any discrete group or individual and whether race is reasonably used in light of the program's objectives—is clearly satisfied by the Davis program.

It is not even claimed that Davis' program in any way operates to stigmatize or single out any discrete and insular, or even any identifiable, nonminority group. Nor will harm comparable to that imposed upon racial minorities by exclusion or separation on grounds of race be the likely result of the program. It does not, for example, establish an exclusive preserve for minority students apart from and exclusive of whites. Rather, its purpose is to overcome the effects of segregation by bringing the races together. True, whites are excluded from participation in the special admissions program, but this fact only operates to reduce the number of whites to be admitted in the regular admissions program in order to permit admission of a reasonable percentage—less than their proportion of the

California population—of otherwise underrepresented qualified minority appli-cants. . . .

We disagree with the lower courts' conclusion that the Davis program's use of race was unreasonable in light of its objectives. First, as petitioner argues, there are no practical means by which it could achieve its ends in the foreseeable future without the use of race-conscious measures. . . .

Second, the Davis admissions program does not simply equate minority status with disadvantage. Rather, Davis considers on an individual basis each applicant's personal history to determine whether he or she has likely been disad-vantaged by racial discrimination. The record makes clear that only minority applicants likely to have been isolated from the mainstream of American life are considered in the special program; other minority applicants are eligible only through the regular admissions program. . . .

Finally, Davis' special admissions program cannot be said to violate the Constitution simply because it has set aside a predetermined number of places for qualified minority applicants rather than using minority status as a positive factor to be considered in evaluating the applications of disadvantaged minority appli-cants. For purposes of constitutional adjudication, there is no difference between the two approaches. In any admissions program which accords special consider-ation to disadvantaged racial minorities, a determination of the degree of prefer-ence to be given is unavoidable, and any given preference that results in the exclusion of a white candidate is no more or less constitutionally acceptable than a program such as that as Davis. . . .

Accordingly, we would reverse the judgment of the Supreme Court of Cali-fornia holding the Medical School's special admissions program unconstitutional and directing respondent's admission, as well as that portion of the judgment enjoining the Medical School from according any consideration to race in the admissions process.

BIBLIOGRAPHY

ABERNATHY, CHARLES F. "Affirmative Action and the Rule of Bakke." *American Bar Association Journal* 64 (August 1978): 1234.

DREYFUS, JOEL, AND CHARLES LAWRENCE III. *The Bakke Case.* Harcourt, Brace, Jovanovich, 1979.

SCHWARTZ, BERNARD. *Beyond Bakke.* New York University Press, 1988.

"The Court's Affirmative Action." *New Republic.* July 8 & 15, 1978, p. 5.

TRIBE, LAWRENCE H. "Perspective on Bakke: Equal Protection, Procedural Fairness, or Structural Justice?" *Harvard Law Review* 92, 4 (February 1979): 864.

WHITE, DAVID M. "Pride, Prejudice and Prediction: From Brown to Bakke and Beyond." *Howard Law Journal* 22, 1 (1979): 375.

San Antonio v. Rodriguez

411 U.S. 1 (1973)

Demetrio Rodriguez is a Mexican-American parent whose three children attended public schools in the Edgewood district of San Antonio, Texas. Because state law based school financing primarily on property taxes, the largely Hispanic district could spend only $356 on each student in 1968. The affluent, mostly Anglo district of Alamo Heights spent almost twice as much on each student. Rodriguez claimed that this funding disparity deprived his kids of equal protection of the laws under the Fourteenth Amendment. A one-vote Supreme Court majority disagreed in 1973: "Education," Justice Lewis Powell wrote, "is not among the rights afforded explicit protection" by the Constitution. Fifteen years after this rebuff, Rodriguez won a ruling from the Texas supreme court that schools must equalize funding between poor kids and rich kids.

TRANSCRIPT OF EDITED AND NARRATED ARGUMENTS IN
San Antonio Independent School District v. *Rodriguez*, 411 U.S. 1 (1973)

Counsel for petitioner: Professor Charles Alan Wright, University of Texas Law School, Austin, Texas
Counsel for respondent: Arthur Gochman, San Antonio, Texas

Narrator: It's October 12th, 1972. Chief Justice Warren Burger will preside at today's arguments in *San Antonio Independent School District versus Rodriguez*. This case affects public schools, not only in San Antonio, but all of Texas, and other states as well. The legal issues and facts are complex, but they boil down to this: Does the Fourteenth Amendment's equal protection clause require states to provide equal funding for schools in rich and poor districts, measured by property values?

State and local control of education is rooted in American tradition and the principle of federalism. Schools are financed largely by property taxes. Districts with higher property values have more to spend on buildings, teachers, and facilities. The expansion of federal school aid in the 1960s channeled money into poor districts across the country. But it didn't challenge states' powers to base school funding on property taxes.

Today's case *does* challenge that state power in Texas. It began in San Antonio's Hispanic *barrio* in 1968, in the living room of Demetrio Rodriguez, a fourth-generation Texan, a Navy veteran, a sheet-metal mechanic for the Air Force. He has five kids. Three sons go to Edgewood Elementary School. The building is crumbling. Half the teachers are not certified. Ninety percent of the kids in the Edgewood district are Hispanic. Edgewood's voters taxed their small houses at the state's highest rate, but that only raised $26 per student in 1970. State and federal funds raised the total to $356, but that couldn't buy good schools or teachers.

The suburb of Alamo Heights looks down on Edgewood in more ways than geography. It's an Anglo area; doctors and lawyers live there. Its houses are worth eight times as much as Edgewood's. Even at the lowest tax rate, each student still got $333. State and federal funds made a total of $594, almost twice the Edgewood total. Alamo Heights can afford better teachers; 40 percent have master's degrees. The schools have tennis courts and pools.

Demetrio Rodriguez only got to the tenth grade. He wants his kids to go farther, to learn more. He tramped Edgewood's dusty streets, talked to other parents, and found a lawyer to help them, without charge. Arthur Gochman sued school officials and seven districts in BexarBay-areCounty. The Edgewood parents won a victory in 1971. Federal judges ruled that property-tax funding hurt kids in poor districts and violated the Constitution's equal protection clause. State and local officials appealed to the Supreme Court.

There's an irony in today's argument. The San Antonio school district has switched sides and now supports the Edgewood parents, along with civil rights and teachers groups. But thirty states have lined up with Texas, to support the property-tax system. Arguing for Texas is Charles Alan Wright, a noted constitutional lawyer at the University of Texas. He begins by quoting an influential study of school funding.

Wright: Mr. Chief Justice, and may it please the Court.

I would like to take as the text for my argument this morning a sentence from an article that Professor Coons and his collaborators, Messrs. Sugerman and Clune, wrote last year. It's quoted and cited at page 44 of my initial brief. They said: "Of all public functions, education in its goals and methods is least understood and most in need of local variety, experimentation, and independence."

That, I think, is wise counsel. I believe that is the argument for reversal in this case. In our view the Texas system of school finance—imperfect as it is, and we conceded its imperfections in our brief—the Texas system does allow for local variety, experimentation, and independence; not as much as I would like it to, but that is its goal, that is its rationale. And, for that reason, there is a rational basis to it, and I will undertake to develop, of course, in a moment, our view that the rational basis test is the appropriate test.

Narrator: The study that Wright quoted stated as "Proposition One" that school districts should equally share the state's wealth. The lower court agreed, but Wright differed.

Wright: The view adopted by the district court, that there is a rigid constitutional mandate that the quality of education may not be a function of wealth, except the wealth of the state as a whole, in my submission is based on educational assumptions about matters that are today not understood and which educators are not ready to form firm judgments; and it would seriously inhibit, if it would not destroy altogether, the possibilities for local variety, experimentation, and independence of which Messrs. Coons, et al., quite properly speak so warmly.

Proposition One, the proposition adopted by the district court in this case, would impose a constitutional straitjacket on the public schools of fifty states. It would mean that hereafter and permanently—or at least until a new book is written and the Constitution changes again—that all measurements in terms of education, the public schools, must be in terms of per-capita or per-pupil student expenditures, even though there may be many other things that we ought to be worrying about in an effort to cure the problems of public education.

Narrator: Almost half the school money in Texas comes from the state's Minimum Foundation School Program. Justice Byron White had tough questions about the program.

White: Would you say it would violate the equal protection clause if in some way a court did decide what was a minimum level of education? If it was found that many districts in Texas did not come up to that level, and couldn't really, under the formula because the property in this particular district is just too limited and the state foundation program just doesn't bring it up to a minimum level?

Wright: I think that would be a much harder constitutional case for me to defend, yes. I don't want to concede that I would necessarily lose it, because it's not my case.

White: Apparently then we must decide then whether it would be—to sustain you, we must agree with you that the foundation program brings it up to a minimum level?

Wright: No, I think that is simply not an issue here. There is hardly so much as an allegation . . .

White: If there is a violation if it didn't, don't we have to decide that it does?

Wright: I don't think you have to decide that. I am prepared for purposes of the present argument, Justice White—without foreclosing what I may say the next time I am up before you in a different case—to concede that there is a constitutional minimum that could be required.

Narrator: Chief Justice Burger followed up.

Burger: Is there a question, however, that once the state undertakes to furnish education, then it must furnish a certain minimal adequate education for everybody? Once they start to go down that row they must follow through?

Wright: We certainly must do it for everybody, yes. If we are going to do it for any, then we must do it for every young person in the state.

Narrator: Justice William O. Douglas raised another issue.

Douglas: As I read this record, Mr. Wright, it seemed to me that the testimony —I'm not sure about the findings—pretty clearly demonstrate that there is unequal treatment of these respondents who are Americans of Spanish ancestry at educational levels. Is that any part of this litigation?

Wright: The racial issue is in this litigation, yes, Justice Douglas. It is a major portion of the plaintiffs' complaint. The trial court did not rely on it in its opinion. It put its holding squarely on the dollar inequality, without regard to whether the particular plaintiffs were of Spanish ancestry, or Anglo, or black. But the issue is certainly there.

We think that the issue is one that is fairly readily answered: that although it is of course quite true that in the Edgewood School District in Bexar County, Texas, the great majority of the students are of Spanish origin, and not as much money is spent there as in other school districts, but we doubt that this would be found to be true as a general matter; that the poor school districts are not that congruent with racial distributions; that it is, in other words, a happenstance. We have a case in which we have particular plaintiffs who are Mexican-American and who live in a district with low taxable resources.

Narrator: Under Supreme Court precedent, the justices must decide this basic question: Is education a fundamental right under the Constitution? If it is, Texas must show a *compelling* reason for its property tax system. If not, it only has to show a rational basis for the system, an easier standard to meet. Wright tackled the question.

Wright: We contend, of course, that if we are subject only to the rational basis test, this is not one of those cases in which we must demonstrate a compelling state interest in order to justify the results for which we argue and justify the state plan. And we think that there are quite a number of very recent cases from this Court—some of them ignored by the lower court and some of them still more recent—that show exactly that, and show that this Court is not going to impose a constitutional straitjacket on the states in difficult, intractable questions of social reform, welfare, economics.

The appellees undertake to distinguish these and to suggest that in some way the educational needs of the poor are fundamental, while their needs for food, and for housing, are not. And, with respect, this is a distinction that I think simply is not a tenable one; that it is hard to say that a higher salaried school teacher is more fundamental to a poor child than food or a sound roof over his head.

Narrator: Arthur Gochman argued for the children of the San Antonio *barrio* and other poor districts in Texas.

Gochman: Mr. Chief Justice, and may it please the Court.

The court below held the Texas system unconstitutional because it distributes educational benefits on the basis of district wealth. The court said, as might be expected: "Those districts most rich in property also have the highest median family income, and the lowest percentage of minority pupils; while the poorer districts are poorer in income, and predominantly minority in composition."

The court further found that there was no rational *or* compelling reason that could be offered for this invidious discrimination. This Court is to decide whether or not to reverse the lower court and approve district wealth as a proper basis for distributing public school education.

The defendants admit that there is a perfect correlation between the property tax base per student and the amount of dollars each child gets for his education.

Narrator: Gochman faced a skeptical question.

Blackmun: Let me be sure I understand you. Do you say that there is an inevitable correlation between district wealth and income of families?

Gochman: That is not what I just said a moment ago, but there is. The record shows it, to this extent, that as to the poorest districts—as to the poorest districts and the richest districts, the poorest people live in the poorest districts and the richest people live in the richest districts. And in Bexar County, it perfectly correlates.

Blackmun: My question is whether this is a necessary correlation?

Gochman: No, Your Honor, it's not. But we probably wouldn't have a lawsuit if it wasn't that way, because this kind of discrimination falls most heavily on the poor. The poor have nowhere to go.

Narrator: Gochman raised the racial issue that Wright had dismissed. Justice William Rehnquist had doubts.

Gochman: We say the discrimination is based upon the wealth of the districts; but we say that that discrimination falls most heavily upon the poor and the minorities. And, in that regard and with regard to the racial discrimination, this is not segregation where you have to prove that the segregation discriminates.

The discrimination is there on its face that the minorities get less, both in Bexar County and statewide.

Rehnquist: You don't contend, do you, that Texas set up this system of district school financing with the purpose of discriminating against minorities, do you?

Gochman: I contend that, objectively, Texas did what it did—and it could have done something else—and what it did discriminates against minorities.

Narrator: Some justices worried about the Supreme Court becoming a national school board. They pressed Gochman about the limits of his argument. Chief Justice Burger pushed the hardest.

Blackmun: Would you carry your general theory across the state line?

Gochman: No, Your Honor. I carry the equal protection clause to be "no state shall," and it's the state's obligation. The state has set up this school system.

Burger: The logic of it—laying aside the Fourteenth Amendment emphasis on state—the logic of it, however, would apply across state lines, wouldn't it?

Gochman: No, Your Honor, I think . . .

Burger: The logic of the egalitarian concept that you're arguing. (Gochman: No, I think we're talking about . . .) Why should people in Texas, for example, have better schools than the people in Rhode Island—if they are better, and I don't know whether they are or not.

Gochman: As a moral proposition, maybe so. But this is a state—it's now a state function, not a federal function.

Burger: I said, laying aside that limitation, the logic of your argument would apply with equal force, whether you call it "moral grounds" or "egalitarian philosophy" or whatever.

Narrator: Chief Justice Burger returned to the basic question: Is education a fundamental right under the Constitution?

Burger: How would you rate such items as the need for police protection, fire protection, public health facilities? Where would you grade them, with respect to public education? Higher? Lower? Or on the same level as the functions of state government?

Gochman: I think what's important is the constitutional importance of education. That is, education affects matters guaranteed by the Bill of Rights. It's preservative of other rights, unlike some of these other services. It's related to every important right we have. It's related to the right to vote, speech, jury service—on a federal jury you can't serve if you can't read, write, understand, and speak the English language. It's education this Court has used as the high-water mark for measuring the importance of other rights.

Burger: How about public health to education, public health facilities?

Gochman: Public health, food, lodging—those things are of great economic importance. But they are not matters that are related to those things guaranteed by the Bill of Rights. And in importance, education lies at the apex, up and down the ladder. It's important to the free enterprise system, to the individual, not to be poor. It's important to fulfill individual potential. It's universally relevant. And it's the only thing the state provides that it compels you to utilize for this period of time. In fact, I don't know of anything it compels you to utilize for any length of time. But a child has to go to school for ten years. That's the importance the state puts on it. It molds the character and the personality of the individual. And it's vital for the United States to compete in the world.

Narrator: Gochman turned from constitutional issues to dollars and cents. The property tax system, he argued, kept poor kids in poor schools.

Gochman: But, they seek to rationalize this and say it's all right, on the basis of local control, on the basis of diversity, variety, independence—the one thing the Texas system does *not* have—because those that tax at the highest rates, as I said a moment ago, have the lowest expenditures per pupil; and those that tax at the lowest rate have the highest expenditures per pupil. There is just the reverse of local control.

In San Antonio, Edgewood taxes at a rate 20 percent higher than Alamo Heights. But they raise thirty-some-odd dollars a pupil. Alamo Heights raises over $400 a pupil. It is the property tax base that determines how much you have for a child's education. And who set that base? And who set that standard? The state. And they agree that this is a state system of public school education and these school districts were set up by the state for the convenience of the state in affording public school education. They also agree that these district boundaries serve no educational function and they have no rational basis.

Narrator: Gochman didn't conceal his scorn for Wright's argument about the state's Minimum Foundation Program.

Brennan: What is your answer to Mr. Wright's suggestion that the state foundation contribution is sufficient to provide an adequate education?

Gochman: We show that it really doesn't provide any minimum. The minimum is what the school at the bottom gets. But in addition to that, what is a "minimum"? What kind of a morass is Mr. Wright asking you to get into? What is a minimum? Is a minimum giving him the second grade, or giving him twelve years, when he comes out at the end equal to an Alamo Heights second grade? Are we going to have two classes of citizens—minimum-opportunity citizens, and first-class citizens?

Narrator: Wright returned to the podium for a brief rebuttal. He had diplomatic words for Demetrio Rodriguez and the Edgewood parents.

Wright: These people have opened the eyes of the whole country to a very serious problem. I think that everyone in this courtroom would agree that what we want is better education for all children and especially for poor children; that the real differences between us are whether a new system should be adopted because this Court finds that the Constitution requires it or whether we look to legislatures to provide remedies; and the difference about whether the proposals they make would indeed lead to better education, or only more expensive education; whether they would relieve poor children or only children who happen to live in poor school districts.

Narrator: Chief Justice Burger.

Burger: Thank you, Mr. Wright; thank you, Mr. Gochman. The case is submitted.

Narrator: Five months later, on March 21st, 1973, the Court upheld the property-tax basis of school funding in Texas. The hard questions posed by the *Rodriguez* case are reflected by the five-to-four vote and written opinions on both sides that cover 137 pages. The close vote exposed deep divisions over the Court's role in providing remedies for social and economic inequality in America.

Justice Lewis Powell wrote the majority opinion. Powell was a former school board member in Richmond, Virginia. He generally sided with state and local governments, but he also knew the reality of poor schools in poor districts.

His opinion raised two basic questions. First, does the constitution protect poor people against discrimination, like racial and religious minorities? Second, is education a fundamental right under the Constitution?

Powell answered "no" to both questions. The Texas school funding system, he wrote, did not discriminate against "any definable category of 'poor' people." Students in Edgewood just happened to live in a poor district. In Powell's view, the equal protection clause does not require "absolute equality" between schools, provided all students get an "adequate" education. Powell admitted "the vital role of education" in producing good citizens and informed voters. But education, he wrote, "is not among the rights afforded explicit protection" by the Constitution. Better schools for poor kids should not come from the Court, Powell said, but from Texas lawmakers.

Justice Thurgood Marshall spoke for the kids of Edgewood. He answered "yes" to both of Powell's questions. The schoolchildren of property-poor districts in Texas *were* a definable group that deserved judicial protection. And education, Marshall said, *is* a fundamental right that "directly affects the ability of a child" to become a good citizen and informed voter. Unlike Powell, Marshall had little faith in Texas lawmakers. Holding out "the hope of an ultimate 'political' solution sometime in the indefinite future," he wrote, means that "countless children unjustifiably receive inferior educations."

As Justice Marshall predicted, Texas lawmakers ignored the school problem year after year. In 1985, Rodriguez joined another lawsuit, this time in state court. This case ended with a victory. The Texas Supreme Court ruled in 1989 that the property tax system violated the state constitution. But lawmakers did not finally reform the system until 1991.

Demetrio Rodriguez waited twenty-three years for better schools in Edgewood. His kids have all graduated. But his grandchildren can get a decent education. "That's the only thing you can give a poor people," Rodriguez says. "Give them an education and they'll be better citizens."

EDITED SUPREME COURT OPINIONS
San Antonio v. Rodriguez

MR. JUSTICE POWELL delivered the opinion of the Court.

This suit attacking the Texas system of financing public education was initiated by Mexican-American parents whose children attend the elementary and secondary schools in the Edgewood Independent School District, an urban school district in San Antonio, Texas. They brought a class action on behalf of schoolchildren throughout the State who are members of minority groups or who are poor and reside in school districts having a low property tax base. Named as defendants were the State Board of Education, the Commissioner of Education, the State Attorney General, and the Bexar County (San Antonio) Board of Trustees. The complaint was filed in the summer of 1968 and a three-judge court was impaneled in January 1969. In December 1971 the panel rendered its judgment in a *per curiam* opinion holding the Texas school finance system unconstitutional under the equal protection clause of the Fourteenth Amendment. The State appealed, and we noted probable jurisdiction to consider the far-reaching constitutional questions presented. . . . For the reasons stated in this opinion, we reverse the decision of the District Court.

The first Texas State Constitution, promulgated upon Texas' entry into the Union in 1845, provided for the establishment of a system of free schools. Early in its history, Texas adopted a dual approach to the financing of its schools, relying on mutual participation by the local school districts and the State. . . .

Until recent times, Texas was a predominantly rural State and its population and property wealth were spread relatively evenly across the State. Sizable differences in the value of assessable property between local school districts became increasingly evident as the State became more industrialized and as rural-to-urban population shifts became more pronounced. The location of commercial and industrial property began to play a significant role in determining the amount of tax resources available to each school district. These growing disparities in population and taxable property between districts were responsible in part for increasingly notable differences in levels of local expenditure for education.

. . . The District Court held that the Texas system discriminates on the basis of wealth in the manner in which education is provided for its people. . . . Finding that wealth is a "suspect" classification and that education is a "fundamental" interest, the District Court held that the Texas system could be sustained only if the State could show that it was premised upon some compelling state interest. . . . On this issue the court concluded that "[n]ot only are defendants unable to demonstrate compelling state interests . . . they fail even to establish a reasonable basis for these classifications."

Texas virtually concedes that its historically rooted dual system of financing education could not withstand the strict judicial scrutiny that this Court has found appropriate in reviewing legislative judgments that interfere with fundamental constitutional rights or that involve suspect classifications. . . .

This, then, establishes the framework for our analysis. We must decide whether the Texas system of financing public education operates to the disadvantage of some suspect class or impinges upon a fundamental right explicitly or implicitly protected by the Constitution, thereby requiring strict judicial scrutiny. . . .

We are unable to agree that this case, which in significant aspects is *sui generis*, may be so neatly fitted into the conventional mosaic of constitutional analysis under the Equal Protection Clause. Indeed, for the several reasons that follow, we find neither the suspect-classification nor the fundamental-interest analysis persuasive. . . .

The case comes to us with no definitive description of the classifying facts or delineation of the disfavored class. . . . The precedents of this Court provide the proper starting point. The individuals, or groups of individuals, who constituted the class discriminated against in our prior cases shared two distinguishing characteristics: because of their impecunity they were completely unable to pay for some desired benefit, and as a consequence, they sustained an absolute deprivation of a meaningful opportunity to enjoy that benefit. . . .

Only appellees' first possible basis for describing the class disadvantaged by the Texas school-financing system—discrimination against a class of definably "poor" persons—might arguably meet the criteria established in . . . prior cases. Even a cursory examination, however, demonstrates that neither of the two distinguishing characteristics of wealth classifications can be found here. First, in support of their charge that the system discriminates against the "poor," appellees have made no effort to demonstrate that it operates to the peculiar disadvantage of any class fairly definable as indigent, or as composed of persons whose incomes are beneath any designated poverty level. Indeed, there is reason to believe that the poorest families are not necessarily clustered in the poorest property districts. . . .

Second, neither appellees nor the District Court addressed the fact that, unlike each of the foregoing cases, lack of personal resources has not occasioned an absolute deprivation of the desired benefit. The argument here is not that the children in districts having relatively low assessable property values are receiving no public education; rather, it is that they are receiving a poorer quality education than that available to children in districts having more assessable wealth. Apart from the unsettled and disputed question whether the quality of education may be determined by the amount of money expended for it, a sufficient answer to appellees' argument is that, at least where wealth is involved, the equal protection clause does not require absolute equality or precisely equal advantages. . . .

We thus conclude that the Texas system does not operate to the peculiar disadvantage of any suspect class. But in recognition of the fact that this Court has never heretofore held that wealth discrimination alone provides an adequate basis for invoking strict scrutiny, appellees have not relied solely on this contention. They also assert that the State's system impermissibly interferes with the exercise of a "fundamental" right and that accordingly the prior decisions of this Court require the application of the strict standard of judicial review. . . . It is this question—whether education is a fundamental right, in the sense that it is among the rights and liberties protected by the Constitution—which has so consumed the attention of courts and commentators in recent years.

In *Brown* v. *Board of Education*, 347 U.S. 483 (1954), a unanimous Court recognized that "education is perhaps the most important function of state and local governments." . . .

Nothing this Court holds today in any way detracts from our historic dedication to public education. We are in complete agreement with the conclusion of the three-judge panel below that "the grave significance of education both to the individual and to our society" cannot be doubted. But the importance of a service performed by the State does not determine whether it must be regarded as fundamental for purposes of examination under the equal protection clause. . . .

. . . It is not the province of this Court to create substantive constitutional rights in the name of guaranteeing equal protection of the laws. Thus, the key to discovering whether education is "fundamental" is not to be found in comparisons of the relative societal significance of education as opposed to subsistence or housing. Nor is it to be found by weighing whether education is as important as the right to travel. Rather the answer lies in assessing whether there is a right to education explicitly or implicitly guaranteed by the Constitution. . . .

Education, of course, is not among the rights afforded explicit protection under our Federal Constitution. Nor do we find any basis for saying it is implicitly so protected. . . . It is appellees' contention, however, that education is distinguishable from other services and benefits provided by the State because it bears a peculiarly close relationship to other rights and liberties accorded protection under the constitution. Specifically, they insist that education is itself a fundamental personal right because it is essential to the effective exercise of First Amendment freedoms and to intelligent utilization of the right to vote. In asserting a nexus between speech and education, appellees urge that the right to speak is meaningless unless the speaker is capable of articulating his thoughts intelligently and persuasively. The "marketplace of ideas" is an empty forum for those lacking basic communicative tools. Likewise, they argue that the corollary right to receive information becomes little more than a hollow privilege when the recipient has not been taught to read, assimilate, and utilize available knowledge.

A similar line of reasoning is pursued with respect to the right to vote. Exercise of the franchise, it is contended, cannot be divorced from the educational foundation of the voter. The electoral process, if reality is to conform to the democratic ideal, depends on an informed electorate: a voter cannot cast his ballot intelligently unless his reading skills and thought processes have been adequately developed.

We need not dispute any of these propositions. The Court has long afforded zealous protection against unjustifiable governmental interference with the individual's rights to speak and to vote. Yet we have never presumed to possess either the ability or the authority to guarantee to the citizenry the most *effective* speech or the most *informed* electoral choice. That these may be desirable goals of a system of freedom of expression and of a representative form of government is not to be doubted. These are indeed goals to be pursued by a people whose thoughts and beliefs are freed from governmental interference. But they are not values to be implemented by judicial intrusion into otherwise legitimate state activities.

Even if it were conceded that some identifiable quantum of education is a constitutionally protected prerequisite to the meaningful exercise of either right, we have no indication that the present levels of educational expenditures in Texas provide an education that falls short.

. . . Furthermore, the logical limitations on appellees' nexus theory are difficult to perceive. How, for instance, is education to be distinguished from the significant personal interests in the basics of decent food and shelter? Empirical examination might well buttress an assumption that the ill-fed, ill-clothed, and ill-housed are among the most ineffective participants in the political process.

. . . We have carefully considered each of the arguments supportive of the District Court's finding that education is a fundamental right or liberty and have found those arguments unpersuasive. . . .

The consideration and initiation of fundamental reforms with respect to state taxation and education are matters reserved for the legislative processes of the various States and we do no violence to the values of federalism and separation of powers by staying our hand. We hardly need add that this Court's action today is not to be viewed as placing its judicial imprimatur on the status quo. The need is apparent for reform in tax systems which may well have relied too long and too heavily on the local property tax. And certainly innovative thinking as to public education, its methods and its funding is necessary to assure both a higher level of quality and greater uniformity of opportunity. These matters merit the continued attention of the scholars who already have contributed much to their challenges. But the ultimate solutions must come from the lawmakers and from the democratic pressures of those who elect them.

Reversed.

MR. JUSTICE MARSHALL, with whom MR. JUSTICE DOUGLAS concurs, dissenting.

The Court today decides, in effect, that a State may constitutionally vary the quality of education which it offers its children in accordance with the amount of taxable wealth located in the school districts within which they reside. . . . More unfortunately . . . the majority's holding can only be seen as a retreat from our historic commitment to equality of educational opportunity and as unsupportable acquiescence in a system which deprives children in their earliest years of the chance to reach their full potential as citizens. . . .

In my judgment, the right of every American to an equal start in life, so far as the provision of a state service as important as education is concerned, is far too vital to permit state discrimination on grounds as tenuous as those presented by this record. Nor can I accept the notion that it is sufficient to remit these appellees to the vagaries of the political process which, contrary to the majority's suggestion, has proved singularly unsuited to the task of providing a remedy for this discrimination. I, for one, am unsatisfied with the hope of an ultimate "political" solution sometime in the indefinite future while, in the meantime, countless children unjustifiably receive inferior educations that "may affect their hearts and minds in a way unlikely ever to be undone." *Brown* v. *Board of Education*, 347 U.S. 483, 494 (1954). I must therefore respectfully dissent. . . .

The appellants do not deny the disparities in educational funding caused by variations in taxable district property wealth. They do contend, however, that whatever the differences in per-pupil spending among Texas districts, there are no discriminatory consequences for the children of the disadvantaged districts. . . . In their view, there is simply no denial of equal educational opportunity to any Texas schoolchildren as a result of the widely varying per-pupil spending . . .

. . . We sit, however, not to resolve disputes over educational theory but to enforce our Constitution. It is an inescapable fact that if one district has more funds available per pupil than another district, the former will have greater choice in educational planning than will the latter. In this regard, I believe the question of discrimination in educational quality must be deemed to be an objective one that looks to what the State provides its children, not to what the children are able to do with what they receive. . . . Indeed, who can ever measure for a child the opportunities lost and the talents wasted for want of a broader, more enriched education? Discrimination in the opportunity to learn that is afforded a child must be our standard. . . .

In my view, then, it is inequality—not some notion of gross inadequacy—of educational opportunity that raises a question of denial of equal protection of the laws. I find any other approach to the issue unintelligible and without directing principle. Here, appellees have made a substantial showing of wide variations in educational funding and the resulting educational opportunity afforded to the schoolchildren of Texas. This discrimination is, in large measure, attributable to significant disparities in the taxable wealth of local Texas school districts. This is a sufficient showing to raise a substantial question of discriminatory state action in violation of the equal protection clause. . . . Texas has chosen to provide free public education for all its citizens, and it has embodied that decision in its constitution. Yet, having established public education for its citizens, the State, as a direct consequence of the variations in local property wealth endemic to Texas' financing scheme, has provided some Texas schoolchildren with substantially less resources for their education than others. Thus, while on its face the

Texas scheme may merely discriminate between local districts, the impact of that discrimination falls directly upon the children whose educational opportunity is dependent upon where they happen to live. Consequently, the District Court correctly concluded that the Texas financing scheme discriminates from a constitutional perspective, between schoolchildren on the basis of the amount of taxable property located within their local districts. . . .

The Court seeks solace for its action today in the possibility of legislative reform. The Court's suggestions of legislative redress and experimentation will doubtless be of great comfort to the schoolchildren of Texas' disadvantaged districts, but considering the vested interests of wealthy school districts in the preservation of the status quo, they are worth little more. The possibility of legislative action is, in all events, no answer to this Court's duty under the Constitution to eliminate unjustified state discrimination. In this case we have been presented with an instance of such discrimination, in a particularly invidious form, against an individual interest of large constitutional and practical importance. To support the demonstrated discrimination in the provision of educational opportunity the State has offered a justification which, on analysis, takes on at best an ephemeral character. Thus, I believe that the wide disparities in taxable district property wealth inherent in the local property tax element of the Texas financing scheme render that scheme violative of the Equal Protection Clause.

I would therefore affirm the judgment of the District Court.

BIBLIOGRAPHY

COON, J. E."In a Manner Restrained . . . " Nation, April 30, 1973, p. 27.

COOPER, JOSEPH H. "The Dollars and Sense of Public Education." Urban Lawyer 6, no. 1 (Winter 1974): 138.

EISEN, CHERYL R."Equal Protection of the Laws: Education is not a Fundamental Right." University of Florida Law Review 26 (1973–74): 155.

IRONS, PETER. The Courage of their Convictions, ch. 12. Penguin, 1990.

MANNIX, MARY R. "San Antonio Independent School District

v. Rodriguez: The Court Places Limits on the New Equal Protection." *Columbia Human Rights Law Review* 6, no. 1 (Spring 1974): 195.

YOUNG, ROWLAND L. "Supreme Court Report," *American Bar Association Journal* 59, (June 1973): 647.

PART FIVE:

"A Right of Personal Privacy"

AMERICANS HAVE ALMOST a split personality on the issue of personal privacy. Many people condemn tabloid newspapers and television shows that expose the private lives of celebrities and politicians. But millions buy these papers and watch a top-rated program that shows videos of embarrassing moments in people's lives. Most of us feel strongly that, when we close our doors, particularly our bedroom doors, prying eyes and ears should stay out. We believe that sex is a matter for personal choice and decision. But there is an eager audience for talk shows that deal in sexual intimacy and fantasy. Privacy has become hard to protect in a society that is full of cameras and curious neighbors.

Believing in a "right of privacy" is much easier than drawing the legal boundaries of that right. Judges and scholars have debated the issue for more than a century, since the *Harvard Law Review* published an article in 1890 entitled "The Right to Privacy." Even during the Victorian era of prudery and censorship, the "yellow press" offered sex and sensation to its many readers. Two Boston lawyers, Louis Brandeis and Samuel Warren, expressed concern that "instantaneous photographs and newspaper enterprise have invaded the sacred precincts of private and domestic life." Brandeis and Warren argued that the law should give each person the right "to be let alone" in an increasingly intrusive society.

Almost forty years later, Brandeis put his law review article—almost verbatim —into a Supreme Court opinion as a justice. He dissented in a 1928 case that upheld the government's right to place wiretaps on telephones without judicial warrants. Brandeis wrote that the Constitution gave Americans "the right to be let alone," which he called "the right most valued by civilized men." He denounced "every unjustifiable intrusion by the Government upon the privacy of the individual."

Brandeis said nothing in his article or judicial opinion about extending the "right of privacy" to decisions about sex, procreation, contraception, abortion, or homosexuality. He did not link the privacy right he defended to the "liberty" right that is protected by the Constitution's due process clauses against official restriction. In fact, Brandeis joined a 1927 opinion that upheld the forced sterilization of Carrie Buck, who was committed to a Virginia hospital for the "feebleminded." Carrie's real crime was "moral delinquency" for having an illegitimate child. Justice Oliver Wendell Holmes wrote for the Supreme Court that sterilizing Carrie would protect society from further "socially inadequate offspring" and that her "liberty" interest did not limit the state's power to "prevent those who are manifestly unfit from continuing their kind."

Fifteen years later, the Supreme Court drew the line at an Oklahoma law that provided for sterilization of "habitual criminals" who were convicted of three felonies. Jack Skinner was ordered to be "rendered sexually sterile" for crimes that included chicken theft. Writing for the Court in 1942, Justice William O. Douglas said the Oklahoma law "involves one of the basic civil rights of man. Marriage and procreation are fundamental to the very existence and survival of the race." Chicken theft was not a crime for which Skinner could be "forever deprived of a basic liberty," his right to have children.

The first justice to connect decisions about sex with the "right to privacy" was John Marshall Harlan, noted as a judicial conservative. He dissented from a 1961 decision to dismiss a challenge to a Connecticut law that prevented doctors from giving contraceptives to patients. Harlan cited the *Skinner* case in writing that the due process clause protected "the privacy of the home" and prevented the state from "enforcing its moral judgment by intruding upon the most intimate details of the marital relation with the full power of the criminal law."

Four years later, the Court accepted another challenge to the same Connecticut birth-control law, brought by the same doctor. During these exciting years— the "New Frontier" of President John Kennedy and the "Great Society" of Lyndon Johnson—the country changed more than the Court. Publication in 1963 of Betty Friedan's *The Feminine Mystique* galvanized a growing women's movement. The Court responded to demands that decisions about childbearing be removed from Victorian restraints. Justice Douglas, who wrote the *Skinner* opinion in 1942, wrote in the *Griswold* case in 1965 that states could not invade "the zone of privacy" that protected couples from police searches of "marital bedrooms for telltale signs of the use of contraceptives." Douglas defended in his two opinions the rights both to have children and not to have children.

In 1973, the Court extended the "privacy" right from contraception to abortion in *Roe* v. *Wade*. The lawyers who argued this case differed on virtually every question. Their most fundamental disagreement related to whether an unborn fetus was a "person" under the Constitution and was protected against deprivation of life by the due process clause. They also debated whether the same clause protected the "liberty" of a woman to terminate her pregnancy. Justice Harry Blackmun's majority decision struck a compromise on these questions. He ruled that women had "a right of personal privacy" that included abortion. States could not interfere with that right during the first trimester of pregnancy. But states could "regulate the abortion procedure" during the second trimester to protect maternal health. And Blackmun agreed that states can protect the "potential human life" of the fetus by prohibiting abortion during the last trimester of pregnancy.

The *Roe* case has sparked more controversy than any other social issue in the past three decades. Arguments over abortion reveal that Americans are deeply split by religious, political, and cultural disputes. These divisions go beyond abortion to a wider range of personal behavior and belief. One side in this debate argues for "traditional" values and for legal restraints on "immoral" acts like pornography and homosexuality. Those on the other side emphasize values of "autonomy" and personal choice. This is not a new debate. Its roots are deep in Puritan days, in conflicts between those who place community first and those who stress individual rights. But some of the questions are new. Can the federal government ban the importation of RU-486, a French drug that induces abortions without surgery? Should the military services be allowed to dismiss gay and lesbian soldiers who have served with distinction?

There are no easy answers to these hard questions. Some people argue that the Constitution does not contain the words "abortion" or "privacy." Unless they are named, these rights cannot be protected against governmental restriction. But the Constitution also does not contain the words "telephone" or "automobile." The Supreme Court has left no doubt that Americans are protected against unlawful searches of any kind, from telephone booths to car trunks. But the Constitution includes many unanswered questions. Are the rights of pregnant women affected by those of "potential human lives" in their wombs? Does the "liberty" clause stretch from the "marital bedroom" to the bedrooms of gays and lesbians?

The general phrases of the Constitution cannot answer these questions without reference to public opinion and judicial values. And the answers depend as much on persons as on principles. Asking Justice Blackmun about abortion, or homosexual rights, or any "privacy" issue, will provide an entirely different answer than asking Chief Justice Rehnquist. Their differences on these questions, like those of many Americans, are rooted in Puritan days and debates. Some questions have no easy answers.

Roe v. Wade

410 U.S. 113 (1973)

Some controversial issues in American society do not get resolved by a judicial decision, as the continuing debate over abortion illustrates. In 1970, an unmarried woman in Dallas, Texas, learned that she was pregnant. She immediately sought an abortion, which was denied under an 1854 Texas law prohibiting any abortion unless the woman's life was endangered. Using the pseudonym of "Jane Roe," she challenged the law, claiming that it violated her right of privacy under the Constitution. In 1973, the Supreme Court struck down state laws against abortion; the Fourteenth Amendment's protection of liberty, Justice Harry Blackmun wrote, is "broad enough to encompass a woman's decision" whether or not to terminate her pregnancy. But the Court recognized the state's interest in protecting the "potentiality of human life" after the first trimester of pregnancy, allowing restrictions on abortion.

TRANSCRIPT OF EDITED AND NARRATED ARGUMENTS IN
Roe v. *Wade*, 410 U.S. 113 (1973)

Counsel for petitioner: Sarah Weddington, Dallas, Texas
Counsel for respondents: Jay Floyd and Robert Flowers, Austin, Texas

Chief Justice Burger: We'll hear arguments in Number 18, *Roe* against *Wade*.

Narrator: It's December 13th, 1971. Chief Justice Warren Burger has called a case that raises an unsettled and unsettling issue in American society, abortion. Only seven justices sit behind the bench. Two longtime justices, Hugo Black and John Harlan, died recently and have not yet been replaced. Lawyers, reporters, spectators pack the courtroom. Sarah Weddington argues for Jane Roe.

Chief Justice Burger: Mrs. Weddington, you may proceed whenever you're ready.

Sarah Weddington: Mr. Chief Justice, and may it please the court.

Certainly Jane Roe brought her suit as soon as she knew she was pregnant. As soon as she had sought an abortion and been denied, she came to federal court. She came on behalf of a class of women, and I don't think there's any question but that women in Texas continue to desire abortions and to seek them out, outside our state.

Narrator: In 1970, an unmarried pregnant woman, using the pseudonym Jane Roe, sued Henry Wade, the Dallas, Texas, district attorney. Two young lawyers, Sarah Weddington and Linda Coffee, asked the federal court to declare unconstitutional the Texas criminal law prohibiting any abortion not intended to save the mother's life. They also sought to bar the district attorney from enforcing the law.

The federal judges ruled that the Texas law violated the Ninth Amendment to the U.S. Constitution, which reserves to the people those rights not granted to the states. But the judges declined to block enforcement of the law. Both sides appealed to the Supreme Court. Sarah Weddington is making her first argument to the Court.

Weddington: In Texas, the woman is the victim. The state cannot deny the effects that this law has on the women of Texas. Certainly there are problems regarding even the use of contraception. Abortion now for a woman is safer than childbirth. In the absence of abortion, or legal, medically safe abortions, women often result to the illegal abortion, which certainly carry risks of death, all the side effects such as severe infection, permanent sterility, all the complications that result. And in fact, if the woman is unable to get either a legal abortion or an illegal abortion in our state, she can do a self-abortion, which is certainly, perhaps, by far the most dangerous. And that is no crime.

Narrator: Weddington said that Texas allowed no abortions, if pregnancy did not endanger a woman's life.

Weddington: If the pregnancy would result in the birth of a deformed or defective child, she has no relief. Regardless of the circumstances of conception, whether it was because of rape, incest, whether she is extremely immature, she has no relief.

Narrator: She moved on to the law's impact on women.

Weddington: I think it's without question that pregnancy to a woman can completely disrupt her life. It disrupts her body, it disrupts her education, it disrupts her employment, and it often disrupts her entire family life. And we feel that because of the impact on the woman, this certainly, inasfar as there are any rights which are fundamental, is a matter which is of such fundamental and basic concern to the woman involved that she should be allowed to make the choice as to whether to continue or to terminate her pregnancy.

Narrator: Justice Potter Stewart shifted the discussion to constitutional issues.

Stewart: Mrs. Weddington, so far on the merits you've told us about the important impact of this law and made a very eloquent policy argument against it. I trust you are going to get to what provisions of the Constitution you rely on. Because, of course, we'd like to sometimes, but we cannot here be involved simply with matters of policy, as you know.

Weddington: Your honor, in the lower court, as I'm sure you're aware, the court held that the right to determine whether or not to continue a pregnancy rested upon the Ninth Amendment, which of course reserves those rights not specifically enumerated to the government, to the people. I do feel that it is, that the Ninth Amendment is an appropriate place for the freedom to rest. I think the Fourteenth Amendment is equally an appropriate place, under the rights of persons to life, liberty, and the pursuit of happiness. I think inasfar as liberty is meaningful, that liberty to these women would mean liberty from being forced to continue the unwanted pregnancy.

Stewart: You're relying in this branch of your argument simply on the due process clause of the Fourteenth Amendment?

Weddington: We had originally brought the suit alleging both the due process clause, equal protection clause, the Ninth Amendment, and a variety of others.

Stewart: And anything else that might obtain? *(laughter)*

Weddington: Yeah, right.

Narrator: Sarah Weddington responded with this concise statement.

Weddington: One of the purposes of the Constitution was to guarantee to the individual the right to determine the course of their own lives.

Narrator: Justice Byron White pressed the troubling question of how far the right to an abortion would go.

White: Will that take you right up to the time of birth?

Weddington: It is our position that the freedom involved is that of a woman to determine whether or not to continue a pregnancy. Obviously, I have a much more difficult time saying that the state has no interest in late pregnancy.

White: Why? Why is that?

Weddington: I think it's more the emotional response to a late pregnancy, rather than it is any constitutional . . .

White: Emotional response by whom?

Weddington: I guess by persons considering the issue outside the legal context. The Constitution, as I see it, gives protections to people *after* birth.

Narrator: Sarah Weddington sat down at the counsel table with Linda Coffee. Texas assistant attorney general Jay Floyd began with an attempt at humor.

Floyd: Mr. Chief Justice, may it please the Court. It's an old joke, but when a man argues against two beautiful ladies like this, they're going to have the last word.

Narrator: No one laughed. Chief Justice Burger looked annoyed. After an embarrassed silence, Jay Floyd argued that the case was moot because Jane Roe was no longer pregnant. One of the justices pushed Floyd.

Stewart: What procedure would you suggest for *any* pregnant female in the state of Texas ever to get any judicial consideration of this constitutional claim?

Floyd: Your Honor, let me answer your question with a statement, if I may. I do not believe it can be done. There are situations in which, of course, as the Court knows, no remedy is provided. Now I think she makes her choice prior to the time she becomes pregnant. That is the time of the choice. It's like, more or less, the first three or four years of our life we don't remember anything. But once a child is born, a woman no longer has a choice, and I think pregnancy may terminate that choice. That's when.

Stewart: Maybe she makes her choice when she decides to live in Texas. (*laughter*)

Narrator: Floyd's claim that *no* woman could challenge the Texas law prompted more questions.

Stewart: In a constitutional case of this kind, it becomes quite vital sometimes to rather precisely identify what the asserted interest of the state is.

Floyd: The protection of the mother, at one time, may still be the primary. But the policy considerations, Mr. Justice, would seem to me to be for the state legislature to make a decision.

Stewart: Certainly that's true. Policy questions are for legislative and executive bodies, both the state and federal governments. But we have here a constitutional question, and in deciding it, assessing it, it's important to know what the asserted interest of the state is in the enactment of this legislation.

Floyd: I am, and this is just from my . . . I speak personally, if I may. I would think that even when this statute was first passed, there was some concern for the unborn fetus.

Stewart: When was it enacted?

Floyd: I believe it was 1859 was the original statute. This, I believe, was around 1900, 1907.

Narrator: Justice Thurgood Marshall and Jay Floyd debated the question of when life begins.

Floyd: We say there is life from the moment of impregnation.

Marshall: And do you have any scientific data to support that?

Floyd: Well, we begin, Mr. Justice, in our brief, with the development of the human embryo, carrying it through to the development of the fetus from about seven to nine days after conception.

Marshall: Well, what about six days?

Floyd: We don't know.

Marshall: Well, this statute goes all the way back to one hour.

Floyd: I don't . . . Mr. Justice, there are unanswerable questions in this field. *(laughter)*

Marshall: I appreciate it.

Floyd: This is an artless statement on my part.

Marshall: I withdraw the question.

Floyd: Thank you. Or when does the soul come into the unborn, if a person believes in a soul? I don't know.

Narrator: Jay Floyd argued that the justices had nothing to decide.

Floyd: There is nothing in the United States Constitution concerning birth, contraception, or abortion. We think these matters are matters of policy, which should be properly addressed by the state legislature.

Narrator: After oral argument, the justices discuss and vote on cases behind the closed doors of the Court's conference room. On rare occasions, the Court does not decide a case and schedules further argument. *Roe versus Wade* was one of these cases. The Court does not disclose its reasons. Perhaps the justices felt that such an important and controversial issue as abortion deserved a vote by the full Court of nine justices.

On October 11th, 1972, when the argument resumed, Lewis Powell and William Rehnquist had joined the Court. Sarah Weddington returned for Jane Roe. She had stumbled in her first argument on the constitutional basis for abortion rights. She tried now to repair the damage.

Weddington: In our original brief, we alleged a number of constitutional grounds. The main ones that we are relying on before this Court are the Fifth, the Ninth, and the Fourteenth Amendments. There is a great body of precedent. Certainly we cannot say that there is in the Constitution, so stated, the right to an abortion. But neither is there stated the right to travel or some of the other very basic rights that this Court have held are under the United States Constitution.

The Court has in the past, for example, held that it is the right of the parents, and of the individual, to determine whether or not they will send their child to private school; whether or not their children will be taught foreign languages; whether or not they will have offspring—the *Skinner* case; whether, the right to determine for themselves whom they will marry—*the Loving* case.

Griswold, of course, is the primary case, holding that the state could not interfere in the question of whether or not a married couple would use birth control. And since then this Court, of course, has held that the individual has the right to determine—whether they are married or single—whether they will use birth control. So there is a great body of cases, decided in the past by this Court, in the areas of marriage, sex, contraception, procreation, childbearing, and education of children, which says that there are certain things that are so much a part of the individual concern that they should be left to the determination of the individual.

Narrator: Weddington pointed to New York State, which repealed its law against abortion in 1971.

Weddington: There have been something like sixteen hundred Texas women who have gone to New York City alone for abortions in the first nine months of 1971. The overall maternal death rate from legal abortion in New York dropped to 3.7 per one hundred thousand abortions in the last half of 1971, and that, in fact, is less than half the death rate associated with live delivery for women. That in fact the maternal mortality rate has decreased by about two-thirds, to a record low in New York in 1971.

Narrator: These facts did not satisfy Justice Byron White. He asked if it were critical to the case that the Fourteenth Amendment did *not* protect a fetus.

Weddington: If a state could show that the fetus was a person under the Fourteenth Amendment, or under some other amendment or part of the Constitution, then you would have the situation of trying . . . you would have a state compelling interest, which in some instances can outweigh a fundamental right.

Narrator: Justice White exploited her concession on this crucial point.

Court: Well, do I get from this then that your case depends primarily on the proposition that the fetus has no constitutional rights?

Weddington: It depends on saying that the woman has a fundamental constitutional right and that the state has not proved any compelling interest for regulation in the area. Even if the Court at some point determined the fetus to be entitled to constitutional protection, you would still get back into the weighing of one life against another.

White: And that's what's involved in this case—weighing one life against another?

Weddington: No, Your Honor. I said that would be what would be involved *if* the facts were different and the state could prove that there was a person with a constitutional right.

Stewart: If it were established that an unborn fetus is a person, within the protection of the Fourteenth Amendment, you would have almost an impossible case here, would you not?

Weddington: I would have a *very* difficult case.

Stewart: You certainly would.

Narrator: Assistant Attorney General Robert Flowers replaced Jay Floyd at the podium. Flowers jumped on Weddington's concession about fetal rights but encountered a quizzical justice, Harry Blackmun.

Flowers: It is impossible for me to trace, within my allocated time, the development of the fetus from the date of conception to the date of its birth. But it is the position of the state of Texas that upon conception we have a human being, a person within the concept of the Constitution of the United States and that of Texas also.

Stewart: Now how should that question be decided? Is it a legal question, a constitutional question, a medical question, a philosophical question, a religious question, or what is it?

Flowers: Your Honor, we feel that it could be best decided by a legislature, in view of the fact that they can bring before it the medical testimony, the actual people who do the research. But we do have . . .

Stewart: You think then it's basically a medical question?

Flowers: From a constitutional standpoint, no sir. I think it's fairly and squarely before this Court. We don't envy the Court for having to make this decision.

Narrator: Flowers faced the same question Justice White posed to Weddington of balancing lives.

White: If you're correct that the fetus is a person, then I don't suppose you'd have . . . the state would have great trouble permitting an abortion (Flowers: Yes, sir) in any circumstance? (Flowers: It would, yes, sir) To save the life of the mother, or her health, or anything else?

Flowers: Well, there would be the balancing of the two lives. And I think that . . .

White: What would you choose? Would you choose to kill the innocent one, or what?

Flowers: Well, in our statute the state did choose that way, Your Honor, in protection of the mother.

Narrator: Flowers pressed ahead, but encountered sharp questions.

Flowers: Gentlemen, we feel that the concept of a fetus being within the concept of a person, within the framework of the United States Constitution and the Texas constitution, is an extremely fundamental thing.

Stewart: Of course, if you're right about that, you can sit down. You've won your case, except insofar as maybe the Texas abortion law presently goes too far in allowing abortions.

Flowers: Yes, sir. That's exactly right. We feel that this is the only question really that this Court has to answer. We have a . . .

White: You think the case is over for you? You've lost your case if the fetus or the embryo is not a person, is that it?

Flowers: Yes, sir, I would say so.

White: You mean, you mean the state has no interest of its own that it can assert?

Flowers: Oh, we have other interests, Your Honor. Preventing promiscity*sic*, say.

Narrator: Justice Marshall pushed Flowers harder.

Marshall: I want you to give me a medical, recognizable medical writing of any kind that says that at the time of conception that the fetus is a person.

Flowers: I do not believe that I could give that to you without researching through the briefs that have been filed in this case, Your Honor.

Narrator: Flowers's arguments that the fetus was a person under the Constitution and that abortion was a legislative, not a judicial issue, provoked another round of questions.

Stewart: If you're right that an unborn fetus is a person, then you can't leave it to the legislature to play fast and loose in dealing with that person. In other words, if you're correct in your basic submission that an unborn fetus is a person, then aoortion laws such as that which New York has is grossly unconstitutional, isn't it?

Flowers: That's right.

Stewart: Allowing the killing of people, of persons.

Flowers: Your honor, Massachusetts, I might point out . . .

Stewart: You can't leave this up to the legislature. This is a constitutional problem, isn't it?

Flowers: Well, if there would be any exceptions within this . . .

Stewart: And the basic constitutional question, initially, is whether or not an unborn fetus is a person, isn't it?

Flowers: Yes, and entitled to the constitutional protections.

Stewart: That's critical to this case, is it not?

Flowers: Yes, sir, it is.

Narrator: Flowers ended with these words.

Flowers: I think that here is exactly what we're facing in this case: Is the life of this unborn fetus paramount over the woman's right to determine whether or not she shall bear a child? This Court has been diligent in protecting the rights of the minorities, and, gentlemen, we say that this *is* a minority, a silent minority, the true silent minority. Who is speaking for these children? Where is the counsel for these unborn children, whose life is being taken? Where is the safeguard of the right to trial by jury? Are we to place this power in the hands of a mother, in a doctor? All of the constitutional rights, if this person has the person concept. What would keep a legislature, under this grounds, from deciding who else might or might not be a human being, or might not be a person?

Narrator: In her rebuttal, Weddington stressed the significance of the decisions that faced both pregnant women and the nine men on the Supreme Court bench.

Weddington: No one is more keenly aware of the gravity of the issues or the moral implications of this case. But it *is* a case that must be decided on the Constitution. We do not disagree that there is a progression of fetal development. It is the conclusion to be drawn from that upon which we disagree. We are not here to advocate abortion. We do not ask this Court to rule that abortion is good or desirable in any particular situation. We *are* here to advocate that the decision as to whether or not a particular woman will continue to carry or will terminate a pregnancy is a decision that should be made by that individual. That in fact she has a constitutional right to make that decision for herself, and that the state has shown no interest in interfering with that decision.

Narrator: Chief Justice Burger.

Burger: Thank you, Mrs. Weddington; thank you, Mr. Flowers. The case is submitted.

Narrator: Three months later, the Supreme Court decided *Roe versus Wade.* On January 22d, 1973, by a vote of seven-to-two, the justices struck down the Texas law and upheld a constitutional right to abortion. Justice Harry Blackmun, who once considered becoming a doctor, wrote the majority opinion.

Blackmun acknowledged the "emotional nature" of the abortion controversy, but the Court's task, he said, was to "resolve the issue by constitutional measurement," free of emotion. He found that yardstick in the Fourteenth Amendment's concept of personal liberty, which included a right to privacy, he said, "broad enough to encompass a woman's decision" whether or not to terminate her pregnancy.

The central issue in the arguments, and the Court's opinion, focused on whether the fetus was a person and thus protected by the Constitution against deprivation of life. "If this suggestion of personhood is established," Blackmun said, Jane Roe's case collapses. Sarah Weddington conceded as much on reargument, he noted. On the other hand, Robert Flowers could cite no case holding that a fetus *was* a person. Consequently, the Court would only consider the rights of pregnant women to an abortion. But this right was not absolute. As the fetus grew toward viability, able to live outside the womb, the state had a legitimate interest in protecting it. Blackmun divided pregnancy into trimesters, or three-month periods. During the first, states could not interfere with the abortion decision. States *could* regulate abortion procedures during the second trimester. And abortion could be prohibited entirely during the last three months of pregnancy.

Justices Byron White and William Rehnquist dissented in *Roe versus Wade.* Rehnquist denied that the Constitution contained a privacy right. Abortion laws, he wrote, are the kind of social and economic legislation that elected lawmakers should vote on. White argued for fetal personhood and accused the majority of an exercise of "raw judicial power."

Since 1973, political battles over *Roe versus Wade* have prompted dozens of state efforts to restrict abortions. Ruling in cases from Missouri and Pennsylvania, the Court in 1989 and 1992 upheld laws that restricted access to abortion. The justices now face state laws that ban almost all abortions. This will force a decision on whether to overrule *Roe versus Wade* entirely.

Sarah Weddington and the state's lawyers spoke to the Supreme Court for two hours about abortion. Since then, Americans have spent thousands of hours in passionate argument on this issue. The arguments we heard only began a process of decision the Court, and the country, have not yet concluded.

EDITED SUPREME COURT OPINIONS
Roe v. Wade

MR. JUSTICE BLACKMUN delivered the opinion of the Court . . .

We forthwith acknowledge our awareness of the sensitive and emotional nature of the abortion controversy, of the vigorous opposing views, even among physicians and of the deep and seemingly absolute convictions that the subject inspires. One's philosophy, one's experiences, one's exposure to the raw edges of human existence, one's religious training, one's attitudes toward life and family and their values, and the moral standards one establishes and seeks to observe, are all likely to influence and to color one's thinking and conclusions about abortion.

In addition, population growth, pollution, poverty, and racial overtones tend to complicate and not to simplify the problem.

Our task, of course, is to resolve the issue by constitutional measurement, free of emotion and of predilection. We seek earnestly to do this, and, because we do, we have inquired into, and in this opinion place some emphasis upon, medical and medical-legal history and what that history reveals about man's attitudes toward the abortion procedure over the centuries. We bear in mind, too, Mr. Justice Holmes' admonition in his now-vindicated dissent in *Lochner* v. *New York*, 198 U.S. 45, 76 (1905):

> "[The Constitutionis made for people of fundamentally differing views, and the accident of our finding certain opinions natural and familiar or novel and even shocking ought not to conclude our judgment upon the question whether statutes embodying them conflict with the Constitution of the United States." . . .

The principal thrust of appellant's attack on the Texas statutes is that they improperly invade a right, said to be possessed by the pregnant woman, to choose to terminate her pregnancy. Appellant would discover this right in the concept of personal "liberty" embodied in the Fourteenth Amendment's due process clause; or in personal, marital, familial, and sexual privacy said to be protected by the Bill of Rights or its penumbras . . .

Three reasons have been advanced to explain historically the enactment of criminal abortion laws in the nineteenth century and to justify their continued existence. . . . It has been argued occasionally that these laws were the product of a Victorian social concern to discourage illicit sexual conduct. Texas, however, does not advance this justification in the present case, and it appears that no court or commentator has taken the argument seriously. . . .

A second reason is concerned with abortion as a medical procedure. When most criminal abortion laws were first enacted, the procedure was a hazardous one for the woman. . . . Modern medical techniques have altered this situation. Appellants and various *amici* refer to medical data indicating that abortion in early pregnancy, that is, prior to the end of the first trimester, although not without its risk, is now relatively safe. Mortality rates for women undergoing early abortions, where the procedure is legal, appear to be as low as or lower than the rates for normal childbirth.

The State has a legitimate interest in seeing to it that abortion, like any other medical procedure, is performed under circumstances that insure maximum safety for the patient. This interest obviously extends at least to the performing physician and his staff, to the facilities involved, to the availability of after-care, and to adequate provision for any complication or emergency that might arise. The prevalence of high mortality rates at illegal "abortion mills" strengthens, rather than weakens, the State's interest in regulating the conditions under which abortions are performed. Moreover, the risk to the woman increases as her pregnancy continues. Thus, the State retains a definite interest in protecting the woman's own health and safety when an abortion is proposed at a late stage of pregnancy.

The third reason is the State's interest—some phrase it in terms of duty—in protecting prenatal life. Some of the argument for this justification rests on the theory that a new human life is present from the moment of conception. The State's interest and general obligation to protect life then extends, it is argued, to prenatal life. Only when the life of the pregnant mother herself is at stake, balanced against the life she carries within her, should the interest of the embryo or fetus not prevail. Logically, of course, a legitimate state interest in this area need not stand or fall on acceptance of the belief that life begins at conception or at some other point prior to live birth. In assessing the State's interest, recognition may be given to the less rigid claim that as long as at least *potential* life is involved, the State may assert interests beyond the protection of the pregnant woman alone. . . .

It is with these interests, and the weight to be attached to them, that this case is concerned.

The Constitution does not explicitly mention any right of privacy. In a line of decisions, however, . . . the Court has recognized that a right of personal privacy, or a guarantee of certain areas or zones of privacy, does exist under the Constitution. . . . These decisions make it clear that only personal rights that can be deemed "fundamental" or "implicit in the concept of ordered liberty," *Palko* v. *Connecticut*, 302 U. S. 319, 325 (1937), are included in this guarantee of personal privacy. They also make it clear that the right has some extension to activities relating to marriage, . . . procreation, . . . contraception, . . . family relationships, . . . and child rearing and education . . .

This right of privacy, whether it be founded in the Fourteenth Amendment's concept of personal liberty and restrictions upon state action, as we feel it is, or, as the District Court determined, in the Ninth Amendment's reservation of rights to the people, is broad enough to encompass a woman's decision whether or not to terminate her pregnancy. The detriment that the State would impose upon the pregnant woman by denying this choice altogether is apparent. Specific and direct harm medically diagnosable even in early pregnancy may be involved. Maternity, or additional offspring, may force upon the woman a distressful life and future. Psychological harm may be imminent. Mental and physical health may be taxed by child care. There is also the distress, for all concerned, associated with the unwanted child, and there is the problem of bringing a child into a family already unable, psychologically and otherwise, to care for it. In other cases, as in this one, the additional difficulties and continuing stigma of unwed motherhood may be involved. All these are factors the woman and her responsible physician necessarily will consider in consultation.

On the basis of elements such as these, appellant and some *amici* argue that the woman's right is absolute and that she is entitled to terminate her pregnancy at whatever time, in whatever way, and for whatever reason she alone chooses. With this we do not agree. Appellant's arguments that Texas either has no valid interest at all in regulating the abortion decision, or no interest strong enough to support any limitation upon the woman's sole determination, are unpersuasive. The Court's decisions recognizing a right of privacy also acknowledge that some state regulation in areas protected by that right is appropriate. As noted above, a State may properly assert important interests in safeguarding health, in maintaining medical standards, and in protecting potential life. At some point in pregnancy, these respective interests become sufficiently compelling to sustain regulation of the factors that govern the abortion decision. The privacy right involved, therefore cannot be said to be absolute. In fact, it is not clear to us that the claim asserted by some *amici* that one has an unlimited right to do with one's body as one pleases bears a close relationship to the right of privacy previously articulated in the Court's decisions. The Court has refused to recognize an unlimited right of this kind in the past. . . .

We, therefore, conclude that the right of personal privacy includes the abortion decision, but that this right is not unqualified and must be considered against important state interests in regulation. . . .

. . . Appellant, as has been indicated, claims an absolute right that bars any state imposition of criminal penalties in the area. Appellee argues that the State's determination to recognize and protect prenatal life from and after conception constitutes a compelling state interest. As noted above, we do not agree fully with either formulation.

The appellee and certain *amici* argue that the fetus is a "person" within the language and meaning of the Fourteenth Amendment. In support of this, they outline at length and in detail the well-known facts of fetal development. If this suggestion of personhood is established, the appellant's case, of course, collapses, for the fetus' right to life would then be guaranteed specifically by the Amendment. . . .

The Constitution does not define "person" in so many words. Section 1 of the Fourteenth Amendment contains three references to "person." . . . [But] the use of the word is such that it has application only postnatally. None indicates, with any assurance, that it has any possible pre-natal application. . . . In short, the unborn have never been recognized in the law as persons in the whole sense.

In view of all this, we do not agree that, by adopting one theory of life, Texas may override the rights of the pregnant woman that are at stake. We repeat, however, that the State does have an important and legitimate interest in preserving and protecting the health of the pregnant woman, whether she be a resident of the State or a nonresident who seeks medical consultation and treatment there, and that it has still another important and legitimate interest in protecting the potentiality of human life. These interests are separate and distinct. Each grows in substantiality as the woman approaches term and, at a point during pregnancy, each becomes "compelling."

With respect to the State's important and legitimate interest in the health of the mother, the "compelling" point, in the light of present medical knowledge, is at approximately the end of the first trimester. . . .

This means, on the other hand, that, for the period of pregnancy prior to this "compelling" point, the attending physician, in consultation with his patient, is free to determine, without regulation by the State, that in his medical judgment, the patient's pregnancy should be terminated. If that decision is reached, the judgment may be effectuated by an abortion free of interference by the State. . . .

With respect to the State's important and legitimate interest in potential life, the "compelling" point is at viability. This is so because the fetus then presumably has the capability of meaningful life outside the mother's womb. State regulation protective of fetal life after viability thus has both logical and biological justifications. If the State is interested in protecting fetal life after viability, it may go so far as to proscribe abortion during that period, except when it is necessary to preserve the life or health of the mother. . . .

Measured against these standards, Art. 1196 of the Texas Penal Code, in restricting legal abortions to those "procured or attempted by medical advice for the purpose of saving the life of the mother," sweeps too broadly. The statute makes no distinction between abortions performed early in pregnancy and thos ' performed later, and it limits to a single reason, "saving" the mother's life, the legal justification for the procedure. The statute, therefore, cannot survive the constitutional attack made upon it here. . . .

To summarize and to repeat:

1. A state criminal abortion statute of the current Texas type, that excepts

from criminality only a *life-saving* procedure on behalf of the mother, without regard to pregnancy stage and without recognition of the other interests involved, is violative of the due process clause of the Fourteenth Amendment.

(a) For the stage prior to approximately the end of the first trimester, the abortion decision and its effectuation must be left to the medical judgment of the pregnant woman's attending physician.

(b) For the stage subsequent to approximately the end of the first trimester, the State, in promoting its interest in the health of the mother, may, if it chooses, regulate the abortion procedure in ways that are reasonably related to maternal health.

(c) For the stage subsequent to viability, the State in promoting its interest in the potentiality of human life may, if it chooses, regulate, and even proscribe, abortion except where it is necessary, in appropriate medical judgment, for the preservation of the life or health of the mother. . . .

MR. JUSTICE REHNQUIST, dissenting.

The Court's opinion brings to the decision of this troubling question both extensive historical fact and a wealth of legal scholarship. While the opinion thus commands my respect, I find myself nonetheless in fundamental disagreement with those parts of it that invalidate the Texas statute in question, and therefore dissent. . . .

. . . I have difficulty in concluding, as the Court does, that the right of "privacy" is involved in this case. Texas, by the statute here challenged, bars the performance of a medical abortion by a licensed physician on a plaintiff such as Roe. A transaction resulting in an operation such as this is not "private" in the ordinary usage of that word. Nor is the "privacy" that the Court finds here even a distant relative of the freedom from searches and seizures protected by the Fourth Amendment to the Constitution, which the court has referred to as embodying a right to privacy. . . .

. . . I agree with the statement of Mr. Justice Stewart in his concurring opinion that the "liberty," against deprivation of which without due process the Fourteenth Amendment protects, embraces more than the rights found in the Bill of Rights. But that liberty is not guaranteed absolutely against deprivation, only against deprivation without due process of law. . . . But the Court's sweeping invalidation of any restrictions on abortion during the first trimester is impossible to justify under that standard, and the conscious weighing of competing factors that the Court's opinion apparently substitutes for the established test is far more appropriate to a legislative judgment than to a judicial one. . . .

[T]he adoption of the compelling state interest standard will inevitably require this Court to examine the legislative policies and pass on the wisdom of these policies in the very process of deciding whether a particular state interest put forward may or may not be "compelling." The decision here to break pregnancy into three distinct terms and to outline the permissible restrictions the State may impose in each one, for example, partakes more of judicial legislation than it does of a determination of the intent of the drafters of the Fourteenth Amendment.

The fact that a majority of the States reflecting, after all, the majority sentiment in those States, have had restrictions on abortions for at least a century is a strong indication, it seems to me, that the asserted right to an abortion is not "so rooted in the traditions and conscience of our people as to be ranked as fundamental," *Snyder* v. *Massachusetts*, 291 U.S. 97, 105 (1934). Even today, when society's views on abortion are changing, the very existence of the debate is evidence that the "right" to an abortion is not so universally accepted as the appellant would have us believe.

To reach its result, the Court necessarily has had to find within the scope of the Fourteenth Amendment a right that was apparently completely unknown to the drafters of the Amendment. . . .

BIBLIOGRAPHY

ELY, JOHN HART. "The Wages of Crying Wolf: A Comment on Roe v. Wade." *Yale Law Journal* 82, no. 5 (April 1973): 920.

FAUX, MARIAN. *Roe v. Wade*. Macmillan, 1988.

LUKER, KRISTIN. *Abortion and the Politics of Motherhood*. University of California Press, 1984.

PATTON, DOROTHY E. "Roe v. Wade: Its Impact on Rights of Choice in Human Reproduction." *Columbia Human Rights Law Review* 5, no. 1 (Spring 1973): 497.

PATTON, DOROTHY E., AND HARRIET F. PILPEL. "Abortion, Conscience and the Constitution . . . " *Columbia Human Rights Law Review* 6, no. 1 (Spring 1974): 279.

STENGEL, ELIZABETH BELL. "Abortion: The Battle Is Not Over." *Ms.*, February, 1975, p. 98.

Bowers v. Hardwick

478 U.S. 186 (1986)

The gay rights movement, which emerged from the political closet in the 1970s, gave voice to a community whose demands raised unprecedented legal questions. In 1982, Michael Hardwick was arrested in Atlanta, Georgia, while he was having sex with another adult male in his bedroom. He was charged with sodomy, which carried a possible twenty-year sentence under Georgia law. Although charges were later dropped, Hardwick filed suit against Georgia's attorney general, claiming the law violated his right to privacy under the Constitution. The law, he contended, simply endorsed the majority's belief that sodomy is immoral. By one vote, the Supreme Court rejected his challenge in 1986, ruling that laws cannot be invalidated only because they represent "essentially moral" choices, and that nothing in the Constitution "would extend a fundamental right to homosexuals to engage in acts of consensual sodomy."

TRANSCRIPT OF EDITED AND NARRATED ARGUMENTS IN
Bowers v. *Hardwick*, 478 U.S. 186 (1986)

Counsel for petitioner: Michael Hobbs, Atlanta, Georgia
Counsel for respondent: Professor Laurence Tribe, Harvard Law School, Cambridge, Massachusetts

Chief Justice Burger: The Court will hear arguments first this morning in *Bowers* against *Hardwick.*

Narrator: It's March 31st, 1986. Chief Justice Warren Burger has called a case that deals with a sensitive topic: the sexual practice known as sodomy. This case challenges a Georgia law, passed in 1816, which reads: "A person commits the offense of sodomy when he performs or submits to any sexual act involving the sex organs of one person and the mouth or anus of another."

Sex is a taboo subject for some people, and sodomy is a practice that few will discuss in public. But it's as old as the human race. Recent studies show that 80 to 90 percent of all married couples engage in oral sex. About the same number of homosexual couples also do. One medical study showed that four out of five people consider oral sex to be normal behavior.

But public tolerance of sodomy—and widespread practice—are not matched by legal tolerance. Many persons consider it immoral or sinful. Sodomy has been condemned on Biblical grounds. Others see it as perversion, a symptom of sick minds. All the original American colonies adopted English law that made sodomy a crime. All fifty states agreed until 1960. But attitudes toward sex have changed, and laws began changing. By 1986, twenty-six states had dropped laws against sodomy.

But in Georgia, the maximum penalty for sodomy is twenty years in prison. The law applies to any person, married or single, heterosexual or homosexual. This case began in Atlanta, where Michael Hardwick worked in a gay bar. A police officer ticketed him for drinking beer outside the bar. He paid the fine, but there was a mixup and the officer obtained an arrest warrant. He entered Hardwick's house, opened the bedroom door, and saw him having oral sex with a male friend.

The officer arrested the two men for sodomy, handcuffed them, and tossed them in the drunk tank. The district attorney dropped the charges, but Hardwick did not drop the case. Aided by the American Civil Liberties Union, he sued the state's attorney general, Michael Bowers. A married couple, known as John and Mary Doe, joined the suit. A federal appellate court ruled that "private consensual sexual behavior among adults" was a "fundamental right," protected by the Constitution.

The judges cited two Supreme Court decisions—*Griswold* versus *Connecticut* and *Roe* versus *Wade*—that established a right to privacy in matters of procreation and pregnancy. An assistant attorney general, Michael Hobbs, argues for the state. He limits his argument to Michael Hardwick's case.

Hobbs: Mr. Chief Justice, and may it please the Court.

This case presents the question of whether or not there is a fundamental right under the Constitution of the United States to engage in consensual private homosexual sodomy.

It is our position that there is no fundamental right to engage in this conduct and that the state of Georgia should not be required to show a compelling state interest to prohibit this conduct. There is certainly no textual support for this proposition. And, contrary to the views expressed by the Eleventh Circuit Court of Appeals and the respondent, it is suggested that there is no precedential support in the decisions of this Court for the proposition that there is a fundamental right to engage in sexual relationships outside of the bonds of marriage.

Many of this Court's decisions have followed the history and traditions of our nation in making its determination as to whether or not a particular activity is entitled to constitutional protection as a fundamental right. Thus far this Court has concluded that the right of privacy includes matters which involve marriage, the family, procreation, abortion, childrearing, and child education. It has never concluded, and I would suggest to the Court that there is no constitutional warrant to conclude, that there should be a fundamental right to engage in homosexual sodomy or any other type of extramarital sexual relationships.

Narrator: Stevens asked about John and Mary Doe.

Stevens: Do you think it would be constitutional or unconstitutional to apply it to a married couple?

Hobbs: I believe that it would be unconstitutional.

Stevens: You think it would be unconstitutional?

Hobbs: Yes, sir.

Stevens: Well, what is the right that would be protected of the married person in that situation, in your view?

Hobbs: The right of marital privacy as identified by the Court in *Griswold.*

Stevens: And this conduct, though it is traditionally frowned upon, as I understand your brief, you say would nevertheless be constitutionally protected in the marital setting?

Hobbs: Yes, your honor, based upon this Court's findings in *Griswold* versus *Connecticut,* in which Justice Douglas stated the right of marital intimacy is older than our Bill of Rights. It harkens back to the heritage of . . .

Stevens: He didn't say anything about this kind of conduct.

Hobbs: That is correct, Your Honor.

Narrator: Hobbs tried to limit the reach of fundamental rights.

Hobbs: The Court has previously described fundamental rights, whether they be under the general heading of a right of privacy or other fundamental rights, as those which are so rooted in the conscience of our people as to be truly fundamental. Principles of liberty and justice which lie at the base of our civil and political institutions, privileges which have long been recognized, a common law as essential to the orderly pursuit of happiness by free men.

Concededly there are certain kinds of highly personal relationships which are entitled to heightened sanctuary from the state and intrusion. The respondents would urge, and the Eleventh Circuit has concluded, that the relationship involved in this case is entitled to constitutional protection as a fundamental right under the right of intimate association. Only a limited number of associations and relationships have been found by this Court to be entitled to constitutional protection: those that attend marriage, the family, raising children, and cohabitation with one's relatives. This Court has described those relationships as personal bonds which have played a critical role in the culture and traditions of the nation by cultivating and transmitting shared ideals and beliefs.

As this Court indicated in *Roe* versus *Wade,* the right of privacy is not limited. It is not absolute, pardon me. There must be limits, and it is submitted in finding these limits we must be wary of creating a regime in the name of a constitutional right which is little more than one of self-gratification and indulgence. The Constitution must remain a charter of tolerance for individual liberty. We have no quarrel with that. But it must not become an instrument for a change in the social order.

Narrator: Hobbs asked the Court to close the door on sodomy.

Hobbs: The respondents have made a crack-in-the-door argument that if the Eleventh Circuit's decision is affirmed in this case it will not go beyond consensual private homosexual sodomy. But it is submitted that this crack-in-the-door argument is truly a Pandora's box, for I believe that if the Eleventh Circuit's decision is affirmed that this Court will quite soon be confronted with questions concerning the legitimacy of statutes which prohibit polygamy; homosexual, same-sex marriage; consensual incest; prostitution; fornication; adultery; and possibly even personal possession in private of illegal drugs.

Narrator: Hobbs appealed to morality.

Hobbs: Moral issues and social issues, it is submitted to the Court, should be decided by the people of this nation. And laws which are written concerning those issues or rescinded concerning those issues should be made by the representatives of those people. Otherwise, the natural order of the public debate and the formulation of consensus concerning these issues, it is submitted, would be interrupted and misshapen.

It is a right of the nation and of the states to maintain a decent society, representing the collective moral aspirations of the people. The Eleventh Circuit and the respondents in this case, by failing to adhere to the traditions, the history, of this nation and the collective conscience of our people, would remove from this area of legitimate state concern a most important function of government and possibly make each individual a law unto himself. It is submitted to this Court that this is not the balance that our forefathers intended between individual liberties and legitimate state legislative prerogatives.

Thank you very much, Your Honors.

Narrator: Chief Justice Burger welcomes Michael Hardwick's lawyer. Laurence Tribe is a Harvard law professor and constitutional scholar.

Burger: Mr. Tribe.

Tribe: Mr. Chief Justice, and may it please the Court.

This case is about the limits of governmental power. The power that the state of Georgia invoked to arrest Michael Hardwick in the bedroom of his own home is not a power to preserve public decorum. It is not a power to protect children in public or in private. It is not a power to control commerce or to outlaw the infliction of physical harm or to forbid a breach in a state-sanctioned relationship such as marriage or, indeed, to regulate the terms of a state-sanctioned relationship through laws against polygamy or bigamy or incest.

The power invoked here, and I think we must be clear about it, is the power to dictate in the most intimate and, indeed, I must say, embarrassing detail how every adult, married or unmarried, in every bedroom in Georgia will behave in the closest and most intimate personal association with another adult. I think it includes all physical, sexual intimacies of a kind that are not demonstrably physically harmful, that are consensual and noncommercial in the privacy of the home.

Narrator: Tribe asked the Court to close the door to police.

Tribe: Indeed, Mr. Hobbs said that under his theory the states should be able, without providing a compelling justification, to punish—his words were "irresponsible liaisons" outside the bonds of marriage. So, imagine for a moment an ordinance or a statute that says unmarried couples may hold hands and they may perhaps embrace lightly, but extended caresses or kissing with the mouth is forbidden.

Now, in their theory, even if this occurs in the home, under their theory as long as the state says a majority of our legislators disapprove of this conduct and, indeed, there is a long history of disapproving things that might lead to greater intimacies among unmarried people, we can outlaw it; not just outlaw it, but we can resist a request for a more particularized explanation of why.

What we suggest is that when the state asserts the power to dictate the details of intimacies in what they call irresponsible liaison, even in the privacy of the home, that it has a burden to justify its law through some form of heightened scrutiny.

Narrator: The Court applies "heightened scrutiny" to cases that affect "fundamental rights." Justice Sandra O'Connor asked Tribe to explain.

O'Connor: Well, Mr. Tribe, how do you propose that these other situations be analyzed—by some sort of heightened scrutiny as well? And are you suggesting that there is a compelling state interest, or what is it you are saying?

Tribe: I think, Justice O'Connor, there are two approaches, either of which would lead to the same result. One is that the recognized power of the state to protect children and to protect relationships and to prevent harmful conduct is such that it would be pointless to require heightened scrutiny any more than this Court does of the minimum wage laws or other laws regulating special relationships. And that, therefore, minimum rationality would suffice. The other approach would be to say that, if it is in the privacy of the home, scrutiny should be somewhat heightened, but it seems to me that it would be very easy for the state to show compelling justification and a compelling interest.

Narrator: Justice Lewis Powell restated an earlier question.

Powell: Professor Tribe, let's come back to the privacy of the home and part of the question I asked you, that I don't think I gave you an opportunity to answer. Would you distinguish the home between the back of an automobile?

Tribe: Certainly, Justice Powell.

Powell: And a public toilet, of course.

Tribe: Certainly. We would say that in . . .

Powell: What about a hotel room overnight?

Tribe: We think that a hotel room overnight is not entitled to the same degree of protection; but frankly, I do not know precisely where the line would be drawn.

Narrator: Tribe argued the Constitution should reflect evolving views on sex. Justice William Rehnquist had a question.

Rehnquist: Mr. Tribe, if this evolution is taking place, as you suggest, and you may well be right, why isn't it more proper for this Court to let it be reflected in the majority rule where, you know, states have repealed these statutes?

Tribe: Justice Rehnquist, we do think that that trend is at least relevant for the question of whether this is self-evidently evil. But, this Court has never before held that when a personal right is protected by the Constitution, just because those persons might be able to obtain political redress, the right no longer deserves judicial protection.

Narrator: Justice Byron White joined the debate.

White: How do you articulate this right or this process of declaring a—you say it is a fundamental right or is it a—how should we go about identifying some new right that should give protection?

Tribe: Well, Justice White, I think the method that this Court used in both *Griswold* and in *Roe* of looking to tradition in terms of the protection of the place where an act occurs and of looking to a tradition in terms of recognizing autonomous personal control over intimacy is an appropriate process to employ.

White: Professor, what provision of the Constitution do you rely on, or that we should rely on, to strike down this statute?

Tribe: The liberty clause of the Fourteenth Amendment, Justice White, as given further meaning and content by a course of decisions over half a century.

Narrator: Tribe appealed to liberty.

Tribe: Now, if liberty means anything in our Constitution, especially given the Ninth Amendment's proposition that it is not all expressly enumerated, if liberty means anything it means that the power of government is limited in a way that requires an articulated rationale by government for an intrusion on freedom as personal as this. It is not a characteristic of governments devoted to liberty that they proclaim the unquestioned authority of Big Brother to dictate every detail of intimate life in the home.

We are saying that there is a fundamental right to restrict government's intimate regulation of the privacies of association like in the home. The principle that we champion is a principle of limited government; it is not a principle of a special catalogue of rights.

Robert Frost once said that home is the place where, when you go there, they have to take you in. I think constitutionally home is the place where, when the government would tell you in intimate detail what you must do there and how to behave there, they have to give you a better reason why than simply an invocation of the majority's morality, which tautalogically would vindicate without any scrutiny by this Court literally every intimate regulation of everything one can do in the home.

It doesn't denigrate the special place of family and parenthood and marriage in our society to recognize the principle of limited government. On the contrary, if there is something special and unique about parental authority it is that we do not cede to Big Brother the same unquestioned deference that children are perhaps supposed to give to their parents.

Narrator: The Court decided Michael Hardwick's case on June 30th, 1986. The justices were closely divided, five-to-four. They were far apart on constitutional issues. The two lawyers gave the justices different grounds for ruling. Michael Hobbs stressed morality. Laurence Tribe appealed to liberty. Justice Byron White wrote for the majority. His opinion made a clear choice. "The law," he wrote, "is constantly based on notions of morality." White added that Georgia's law reflected beliefs "that homosexual sodomy is immoral and unacceptable."

White denied that the Constitution's liberty clauses "extend a fundamental right to homosexuals to engage in acts of consensual sodomy." The Constitution only protects rights "deeply rooted" in history and tradition. Relations of family, marriage, and procreation meet this test, White said, but homosexual relations do not. Chief Justice Burger used stronger language. His concurring opinion called laws against sodomy "firmly rooted in Judeo-Christian moral and ethical standards." The Court should not, he said, "cast aside millenia of moral teaching."

Justice Harry Blackmun wrote for the dissenters. He read the Constitution as "protecting the individual's liberty interest in decisions concerning sexual relations." Blackmun would give all persons "the right to choose for themselves how to conduct their intimate relationships." He criticized the majority for relying on Judeo-Christian morality. Laws must have more justification than "conformity to religious doctrine."

Blackmun also chided the majority for its "obsessive focus on homosexual activity." Heterosexuals are equally subject to punishment under Georgia law. Blackmun noted that elected prosecutors "seem not to have any desire" to charge straight people with sodomy. Michael Hardwick's "right of intimate association," Blackmun said, "does not depend in any way on his sexual orientation."

There is an important footnote to this case. It illustrates the human factor in judging. Justice Lewis Powell added a reluctant concurrence to the majority opinion. He was troubled by the twenty-year prison term for sodomy. Powell retired from the Court in 1987. Three years later, he revealed that he initially voted against the Georgia law, but changed his vote before the decision. "I probably made a mistake," Powell confessed. But the Court's decision remains on the books.

EDITED SUPREME COURT OPINIONS
Bowers v. Hardwick

JUSTICE WHITE delivered the opinion of the Court.

In August 1982, respondent Hardwick (hereafter respondent) was charged with violating the Georgia statute criminalizing sodomy by committing that act with another adult male in the bedroom of respondent's home. After a preliminary hearing, the District Attorney decided not to present the matter to the grand jury unless further evidence developed.

Respondent then brought suit in the Federal District Court, challenging the constitutionality of the statute insofar as it criminalized consensual sodomy. He asserted that he was a practicing homosexual, that the Georgia sodomy statute, as administered by the defendants, placed him in imminent danger of arrest, and that the statute for several reasons violates the Federal Constitution. The District Court granted the defendants' motion to dismiss for failure to state a claim. . . .

A divided panel of the Court of Appeals for the Eleventh Circuit reversed. . . . Relying on our decisions, . . . the court . . . [held] that the Georgia statute violated respondent's fundamental rights because his homosexual activity is a private and intimate association that is beyond the reach of state regulation by reason of the Ninth Amendment and the due process clause of the Fourteenth Amendment. . . . [W]e granted the Attorney General's petition for certiorari questioning the holding that the sodomy statute violates the fundamental rights of homosexuals. We agree with petitioner that the Court of Appeals erred, and hence reverse its judgment.

This case does not require a judgment on whether laws against sodomy between consenting adults in general, or between homosexuals in particular, are wise or desirable. It raises no question about the right or propriety of state legislative decisions to repeal their laws that criminalize homosexual sodomy, or of state-court decisions invalidating those laws on state constitutional grounds. The issue presented is whether the Federal Constitution confers a fundamental right upon homosexuals to engage in sodomy and hence invalidates the laws of the many States that still make such conduct illegal and have done so for a very long time. The case also calls for some judgment about the limits of the Court's role in carrying out its constitutional mandate.

We first register our disagreement with the Court of Appeals and with respondent that the Court's prior cases have construed the Constitution to confer a right of privacy that extends to homosexual sodomy and for all intents and purposes have decided this case. The reach of this line of cases was sketched in . . . *Skinner* v. *Oklahoma ex rel. Williamson*, . . . with procreation; *Loving* v. *Virginia*, . . . with marriage; *Griswold* v. *Connecticut*, . . . and *Eisenstadt* v. *Baird* . . . with contraception; and *Roe* v. *Wade*, . . . with abortion. The latter three cases were interpreted as construing the due process clause of the Fourteenth Amendment to confer a fundamental individual right to decide whether or not to beget or bear a child. . . .

Accepting the decisions in these cases and the above description of them, we think it evident that none of the rights announced in those cases bears any resemblance to the claimed constitutional right of homosexuals to engage in acts of sodomy that is asserted in this case. No connection between family, marriage, or procreation on the one hand and homosexual activity on the other has been demonstrated, either by the Court of Appeals or by respondent. Moreover, any claim that these cases nevertheless stand for the proposition that any kind of private sexual conduct between consenting adults is constitutionally insulated from state proscription is unsupportable. . . .

Precedent aside, however, respondent would have us announce, as the Court of Appeals did, a fundamental right to engage in homosexual sodomy. This we are quite unwilling to do. It is true that despite the language of the due process clauses of the Fifth and Fourteenth Amendments, which appears to focus only on the processes by which life, liberty, or property is taken, the cases are legion in which those clauses have been interpreted to have substantive content, subsuming rights that to a great extent are immune from federal or state regulation or proscription. . . .

Striving to assure itself and the public that announcing rights not readily identifiable in the Constitution's text involves much more than the imposition of the Justices' own choice of values on the States and the Federal Government, the Court has sought to identify the nature of the rights qualifying for heightened judicial protection. In *Palko* v. *Connecticut*, 302 U. S. 319, 325, 326 (1937), it was said that this category includes those fundamental liberties that are "implicit in the concept of ordered liberty," such that "neither liberty nor justice would exist if [they] were sacrificed." A different description of fundamental liberties appeared in *Moore* v. *East Cleveland* (1977) . . . where they are characterized as those liberties that are "deeply rooted in this Nation's history and tradition." . . .

It is obvious to us that neither of these formulations would extend a fundamental right to homosexuals to engage in acts of consensual sodomy. Proscriptions against that conduct have ancient roots. . . . Sodomy was a criminal offense at common law and was forbidden by the laws of the original thirteen States when they ratified the Bill of Rights. In 1868, when the Fourteenth Amendment was ratified, all but five of the thirty-seven States in the Union had criminal sodomy laws. In fact, until 1961, all fifty States outlawed sodomy, and today, twenty-four States and the District of Columbia continue to provide criminal penalties for sodomy performed in private and between consenting adults. . . . Against this background, to claim that a right to engage in such conduct is "deeply rooted in this Nation's history and tradition" or "implicit in the concept of ordered liberty" is, at best, facetious.

Nor are we inclined to take a more expansive view of our authority to discover new fundamental rights imbedded in the due process clause. The Court is most vulnerable and comes nearest to illegitimacy when it deals with judge-made constitutional law having little or no cognizable roots in the language or design of the Constitution. . . . There should be, therefore, great resistance to expand the substantive reach of those clauses, particularly if it requires redefining the category of rights deemed to be fundamental. Otherwise, the Judiciary necessarily takes to itself further authority to govern the country without express constitutional authority. The claimed right pressed on us today falls far short of overcoming this resistance. . . .

. . . The right pressed upon us here has no similar support in the text of the constitution, and it does not qualify for recognition under the prevailing principles for construing the Fourteenth Amendment. Its limits are also difficult to discern. Plainly enough, otherwise illegal conduct is not always immunized whenever it occurs in the home. Victimless crimes, such as the possession and use of illegal drugs, do not escape the law where they are committed at home. . . . And if respondent's submission is limited to the voluntary sexual conduct between consenting adults, it would be difficult, except by fiat, to limit the claimed right to homosexual conduct while leaving exposed to prosecution adultery, incest, and other sexual crimes even though they are committed in the home. We are unwilling to start down that road.

Even if the conduct at issue here is not a fundamental right, respondent asserts that there must be a rational basis for the law and that there is none in this case other than the presumed belief of a majority of the electorate in Georgia that homosexual sodomy is immoral and unacceptable. This is said to be an inadequate rationale to support the law. The law, however, is constantly based on notions of morality, and if all laws representing essentially moral choices are to be invalidated under the due process clause, the courts will be very busy indeed. Even respondent makes no such claim, but insists that majority sentiments about the morality of homosexuality should be declared inadequate. We do not agree, and are unpersuaded that the sodomy laws of some twenty-five States should be invalidated on this basis.

Accordingly, the judgment of the Court of Appeals is

Reversed.

JUSTICE BLACKMUN, with whom JUSTICE BRENNAN, JUSTICE MARSHALL, and JUSTICE STEVENS join, dissenting.

This case is no more about "a fundamental right to engage in homosexual sodomy," as the Court purports to declare, . . . than *Stanley v. Georgia*, 394 U. S. 557)1969, was about a fundamental right to watch obscene movies. . . . Rather, this case is about "the most comprehensive of rights and the right most valued by civilized men," namely "the right to be let alone." *Olmstead v. United States*, . . . (1928) (Brandeis, J., dissenting). . . .

. . . I believe we must analyze respondent Hardwick's claim in the light of the values that underlie the constitutional right to privacy. If that right means anything, it means that, before Georgia can prosecute its citizens for making choices about the most intimate aspects of their lives, it must do more than assert that the choice they have made is an " 'abominable crime not fit to be named among Christians.' " . . .

[T]he Court's almost obsessive focus on homosexual activity is particularly hard to justify in light of the broad language Georgia has used. Unlike the Court, the Georgia Legislature has not proceeded on the assumption that homosexuals are so different from other citizens that their lives may be controlled in a way that would not be tolerated if it limited the choices of those other citizens. . . . Rather,

Georgia has provided that "[a] person commits the offense of sodomy when he performs or submits to any sexual act involving the sex organs of one person and the mouth or anus of another." Ga. Code Ann. §16-6-2(a) (1984). The sex or status of the persons who engage in the act is irrelevant as a matter of state law. . . . I therefore see no basis for the Court's decision to treat this case as an "as applied" challenge to §16-6-2. . . . or for Georgia's attempt both in its brief and at oral argument, to defend §16-6-2 solely on the grounds that it prohibits homosexual activity. Michael Hardwick's standing may rest in significant part on Georgia's apparent willingness to enforce against homosexuals a law it seems not to have any desire to enforce against heterosexuals. . . . But his claim that §16-6-2 involves an unconstitutional intrusion into his privacy and his right of intimate association does not depend in any way on his sexual orientation. . . .

"Our cases long have recognized that the Constitution embodies a promise that a certain private sphere of individual liberty will be kept largely beyond the reach of government." *Thornburgh* v. *American College of Obstetricians & Gynecologists*. . . . In construing the right to privacy, the court has proceeded along two somewhat distinct, albeit complementary, lines. First, it has recognized a privacy interest with reference to certain *decisions* that are properly for the individual to make. . . . Second, it has recognized a privacy interest with reference to certain *places* without regard for the particular activities in which the individuals who occupy them are engaged. . . .

The Court concludes today that none of our prior cases dealing with various decisions that individuals are entitled to make free of governmental interference "bears any resemblance to the claimed constitutional right of homosexuals to engage in acts of sodomy that is asserted in this case." . . . While it is true that these cases may be characterized by their connection to protection of the family, . . . the Court's conclusion that they extend no further than this boundary ignores the warning (in *Moore* v. *East Cleveland*) . . . against "closing our eyes to the basic reasons why certain rights associated with the family have been accorded shelter under the Fourteenth Amendment's due process clause." We protect those rights not because they contribute, in some direct and material way, to the general public welfare, but because they form so central a part of an individual's life. "[T]he concept of privacy embodies the 'moral fact that a person belongs to himself and not others nor to society as a whole" *Thornburgh* v. *American College of Obstetricians & Gynecologists*, . . . We protect the decision whether to have a child because parenthood alters so dramatically an individual's self-definition, not because of demographic considerations or the bible's command to be fruitful and multiply. . . . And we protect the family because it contributes so powerfully to the happiness of individuals, not because of a preference for stereotypical households. . . .

Only the most willful blindness could obscure the fact that sexual intimacy is "a sensitive, key relationship of human existence, central to family life, community welfare, and the development of human personality," *Paris Adult Theatre I v. Slaton*. . . . The fact that individuals define themselves in a significant way through their intimate sexual relationships with others suggests, in a Nation as diverse as ours, that there may be many "right" ways of conducting those relationships, and that much of the richness of a relationship will come from the freedom an individual has to *choose* the form and nature of these intensely personal bonds. . . .

In a variety of circumstances we have recognized that a necessary corollary of giving individuals freedom to choose how to conduct their lives is acceptance of the fact that different individuals will make different choices. . . . The Court claims that its decision today merely refuses to recognize a fundamental right to engage in homosexual sodomy; what the Court really has refused to recognize is the fundamental interest all individuals have in controlling the nature of their intimate associations with others. . . .

The behavior for which Hardwick faces prosecution occurred in his own home, a place to which the Fourth Amendment attaches special significance. The Court's treatment of this aspect of the case is symptomatic of its overall refusal to consider the broad principles that have informed our treatment of privacy in specific cases. Just as the right to privacy is more than the mere aggregation of a number of entitlements to engage in specific behavior, so too, protecting the physical integrity of the home is more than merely a means of protecting specific activities that often take place there. Even when our understanding of the contours of the right to privacy depends on "reference to a 'place,' " *Katz v. United States*, . . . "the essence of a Fourth Amendment violation is 'not the breaking of [a person's] doors, and the rummaging of his drawers,' but rather is "the invasion of his indefeasable right of personal security, personal liberty and private property.' "

. . . "The right of the people to be secure in their . . . houses," expressly guaranteed by the Fourth Amendment, is perhaps the most "textual" of the various constitutional provisions that inform our understanding of the right to privacy. . . . Indeed, the right of an individual to conduct intimate relationships in the intimacy of his or her own home seems to me to be the heart of the Constitution's protection of privacy. . . .

The core of petitioner's defense of §16-6-2, however, is that respondent and others who engage in the conduct prohibited by §16-6-2 interfere with Georgia's exercise of the " 'right of the Nation and of the States to maintain a decent society,' " . . . It is precisely because the issue raised by this case touches the heart of what makes individuals what they are that we should be especially sensitive to the rights of those whose choices upset the majority. . . .

The assertion that "traditional Judeo-Christian values proscribe" the conduct involved . . . cannot provide an adequate justification for §16-6-2. That certain, but by no means all, religious groups condemn the behavior at issue gives the State no license to impose their judgments on the entire citizenry. The legitimacy of secular legislation depends instead on whether the State can advance some justification for its law beyond its conformity to religious doctrine. . . .

"The Constitution cannot control such prejudices, but neither can it tolerate them. Private biases may be outside the reach of the law, but the law cannot, directly or indirectly, give them effect." *Palmore* v. *Sidoti* . . . Petitioner and the Court fail to see the difference between laws that protect public sensibilities and those that enforce private morality. Statutes banning public sexual activity are entirely consistent with protecting the individual's liberty interest in decisions concerning sexual relations: the same recognition that those decisions are intensely private which justifies protecting them from governmental interference can justify protecting individuals from unwilling exposure to the sexual activities of others. But the mere fact that intimate behavior may be punished when it takes place in public cannot dictate how States can regulate intimate behavior that occurs in intimate places. . . .

The case involves no real interference with the rights of others, for the mere knowledge that other individuals do not adhere to one's value system cannot be . . . an interest that can justify invading the houses, hearts, and minds of citizens who choose to live their lives differently. . . . I can only hope that here, . . . the court soon will reconsider its analysis and conclude that depriving individuals of the right to choose for themselves how to conduct their intimate relationships poses a far greater threat to the values most deeply rooted in our Nation's history than tolerance of nonconformity could ever do. Because I think the Court today betrays those values, I dissent.

BIBLIOGRAPHY

CARLIN, DAVID R., JR. "The Court and the Right of Privacy," *Commonweal* 113, no. 15 (September 12, 1986) 456.

IRONS, PETER. *The Courage of Their Convictions*, p. 379. Penguin, 1990.

KOHLER, MARK F. "History, Homosexuals, and Homophobia: The Judicial Intolerance of Bowers v. Hardwick." *Connecticut Law Review* 19, no. 3 (Spring 1987): 129.

MARCUS, ERIC. *Making History: The Struggle for Gay and Lesbian Equal Rights*. HarperCollins, 1992.

ROBINSON, DAVID, JR. "Sodomy and the Supreme Court." *Commentary* 82, no. 4 (October 1986): 57.

VIEIRA, NORMAN. "Hardwick and the Right of Privacy." *University of Chicago Law Review* 55, no. 4 (Fall 1988): 1181.

Listed below are all the justices who sat on the Supreme Court between 1955 and 1989, during the arguments of cases in *May It Please the Court*. They are listed by the president who nominated them, with dates of service in parentheses.

Nominated by President Franklin D. Roosevelt
Hugo L. Black (1937–1971)
Stanley F. Reed (1938–1957)
Felix Frankfurter (1939–1962)
William O. Douglas (1939–1975)

Nominated by President Harry Truman
Harold H. Burton (1945–1958)
Tom C. Clark (1949–1967)
Sherman Minton (1949–1956)

Nominated by President Dwight D. Eisenhower
Earl Warren (Chief Justice, 1953–1969)
John Marshall Harlan (1955–1971)
William J. Brennan, Jr. (1956–1990)
Charles E. Whittaker (1957–1962)
Potter Stewart (1958–1981)

Nominated by President John F. Kennedy
Byron R. White (1962–1993)
Arthur J. Goldberg (1962–1965)

Nominated by President Lyndon B. Johnson
Abe Fortas (1965–1969)
Thurgood Marshall (1967–1991)

Nominated by President Richard M. Nixon
Warren E. Burger (Chief Justice, 1969–1986)
Harry A. Blackmun (1970–   )
Lewis F. Powell, Jr. (1972–1987)
William H. Rehnquist (1972, Chief Justice, 1986–   )

Nominated by President Gerald Ford
John Paul Stevens (1975–   )

Nominated by President Ronald Reagan
Sandra Day O'Connor (1981–   )
Antonin Scalia (1986–   )
Anthony M. Kennedy (1988–   )